MW01105001

Paul Smith & Louise Callan

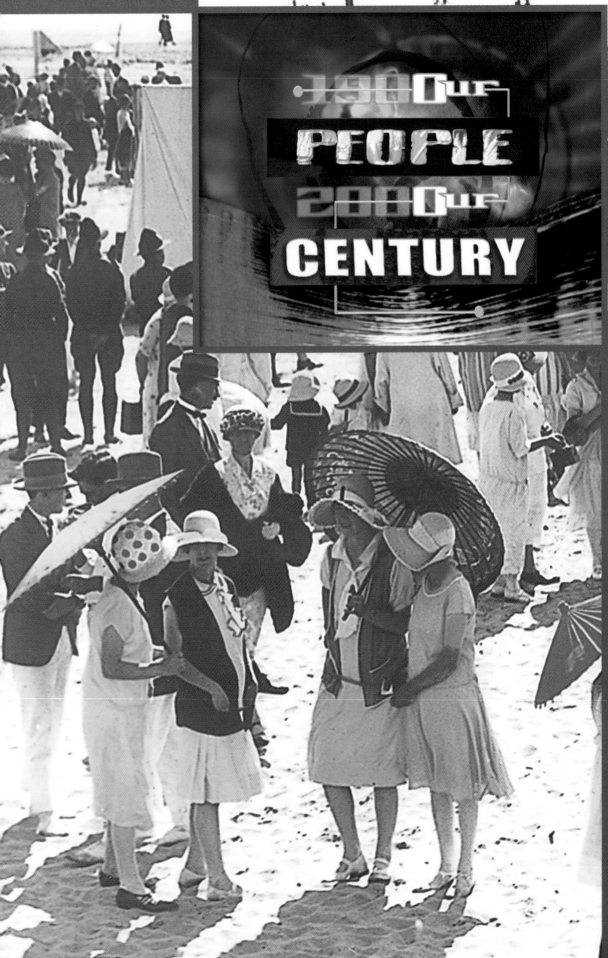

Our PEOPLE Our CENTURY

ONe

NZ ON AIR
Irirangi TE MOTU

Hodder Moa Beckett

Editor's Note

A book of this scope would not be possible without the commitment and enthusiasm of a large number of people. I would like to thank the authors, Louise Callan and Paul Smith, for their passion and fortitude throughout the duration of the project. They have independently researched and written a fascinating and detailed text that draws on a comprehensive range of sources. The decision was made early on to adopt a lively narrative approach and in this they have succeeded, as well as providing a chronological overview of the century which places the family stories from the television series in context.

The Historic Branch of the Department of Internal Affairs, headed by Dr Claudia Orange, provided invaluable comments on all material. I would also like to acknowledge Ninox Films Ltd, in particular David Baldock, David Filer and the reseachers, who gave us every assistance in compiling the material so that it reflects the themes and scope of the television series.

Special thanks also to Nick Turzynski for the superb design and Sally Fullam, design assistant, for their work in putting the book together.

The photographic research took us to many libraries and people, whose assistance was invaluable. I would like to thank all the photo researchers involved, especially Ann Andrews, who came on board at short notice, and Maria McGivern and Craig Wishnowsky from Hodder Moa Beckett.

Janette Howe
Managing Editor

ISBN 1-86958-716–2

© 1999 – Original text Television New Zealand and Ninox Films Limited
The moral rights of the authors have been asserted

© 1999 Design and format – Hodder Moa Beckett Publishers Limited

Published in 1999 by Hodder Moa Beckett Publishers Limited,
[a member of the Hodder Headline Group]
4 Whetu Place, Mairangi Bay, Auckland, New Zealand

Produced and designed by Hodder Moa Beckett Publishers Ltd

Film by Microdot, Auckland
Printed by Toppan Printing Co, Hong Kong

Acknowledgements

The authors would like to thank the following for their help, support and guidance: Melita Smith; Tony Reid; Sherrill Tapsell; Max Cryer; librarians at the Auckland City Council's Central Library, especially those in the Auckland Research Centre and Special Collections who, although busy, always found time to help; the Auckland War Memorial Museum Library; the *New Zealand Herald*; News Media Library, Auckland; Seddon Hill; Merv Smith; Al Morrison; Allan Martin; Ian Shirley; Tom Newnham; Dick Scott; John Callan at the Institute of Geological and Nuclear Sciences; Ross Ferguson at HortResearch, Auckland; Claudia Orange and the staff of the Historical Branch, Internal Affairs; production reseachers Kay Seatter-Dunbar, Carolyn Avery, Libby Hakaraia, Buddy Mikaere, Hannah Belcher and photographic researcher Ann Andrews; Angela Griffen.

A special thank you also goes to: Joan McCracken and her staff at the Alexander Turnbull Library Picture Collection of The National Library of New Zealand Te Puna Matauranga o Aotearoa; Ron Fox at the *Evening Post*; John Lees at the Royal New Zealand Navy Museum; Carolyn Cameron at the Newsmedia Picture Library; Carolyn Stringer at Auckland City Libraries; Gordon Maitland at Auckland Museum; Suzanne Knight at the Museum of New Zealand Te Papa Tongarewa; Fiona Kingston of the New Zealand Magazines Archive; Nelson Provincial Museum; The Kippenberger Military Archive and Research Library, Queen Elizabeth II Army Memorial Museum, Waiouru; The New Zealand Film Archive; Hawke's Bay Cultural Trust – Hawke's Bay Museum; Canterbury Museum; Whakatane District Museum and Gallery; Waihi Arts Centre & Museum; Auckland City Art Gallery; National Archives; *Metro* magazine; The New Zealand AIDS Foundation; Photosport; Tranz Picture Library; Fotopress; Phil Warren; Linda Bryder; Allan Wild; Marti Friedlander; Gil Hanly; Ans Westra; Bruce Jarvis; Bob Brockie; Peter Bromhead; and all those who gave permission for extracts and photos to be included.

Foreword
by Sir Paul Reeves

The first picture in Chapter One of this book shows Newtown, the sprawling Wellington suburb where I grew up and where my mother lived for nearly fifty years. Our house was on an eighth of an acre section and we shared the outside lavatory with the neighbours. In fact the dividing wall between the two properties went through this "double seater dunny" as we called it. The images and memories are still vivid: warming up the wireless before turning up the volume, men on the dole walking past the house on their way to Melrose, the same men marching away to war, my mother cleaning pro-Japanese slogans off the tram sheds wall, the lions roaring at the zoo.

Poverty is a matter of the mind as well as the pocket. I did not feel poor but I know that an absence of money made my parents feel powerless. They used to argue about buying me a pair of shoes. My father's ambition was security not promotion. He chose my brother's first job on the basis of the pension he would get on retirement.

They say that every age is different but the century we are leaving has some recurring themes. We have been bruised by economic systems that seem to value acquisition and competition over cooperation and self sufficiency. My parents were always short of money and it did not help that my father had chronic respiratory problems. The economic system we lived under then – and I do not think it has changed very much – had a very distorted view of human nature. It did not recognise that the unpaid economy of raising and protecting the children, maintaining the household as best you can, growing food on the allotment, renting a house – is in fact the fundamental economic system of every age.

Basically that is what my mother did. But economics are totally patriarchal. Her work was like that of a volunteer or a slave, it was deemed to be unproductive and uneconomic. Each Saturday morning she would light up the copper. We would have our weekly baths and she would do the washing. It was never easy but there were things that sustained us and even made life pleasurable. I had a favourite aunt and uncle who had no children of their own, the local church spoke of values, which were within but also beyond our immediate situation, and school was a place where sitting up straight and learning the tables never got in the way of the serious business of playing and acting out the primal patterns of our imaginations. "Who wants to play goodies and baddies?" we would call out.

Today there are people who believe that the best way of managing an economy is not to manage it at all but to leave it to an invisible hand. But human nature is better than this or any other economic system allows it to be. I marvel at the ability of New Zealanders, Maori and Pakeha, to laugh and to survive. Sometimes we do more than that. There are moments when we invent, stand our ground or even love one another. It has not been an easy century but we are stronger for it. I look forward to what lies ahead.

Contents

No Millionaires or Paupers, Please

Disease & Strife

Introduction
by David Harry Baldock

O ur People, Our Century was originally conceived as a television series with a book attached. Combined, the series and the book give us as New Zealanders a true understanding of our lives and the lives of our forebears through the last hundred years. In doing so, it also gives meaning and understanding to our culture and identity in much the same way as Jamie Belich increased our understanding of the history of the Land Wars. This book and the accompanying television series have standing because they are told by the people – for the people.

Many attempts in the past have been made to integrate television series and books of the same subject with varying degrees of success. One usually leads with the other seeming just a reproduction in another medium. In this instance both the television series and the book work together to enhance and enrich the other. To understand how this evolved, I need to take you back to when the project started.

In 1995, television journalist and researcher David Filer approached me with the concept of developing a series for the turn of the century. There were already several of my colleagues looking for the right formula but none had yet been commissioned. We knew we needed to chronicle the significant events of the century and we also knew we had to stick rigidly to the New Zealand context. Several other productions throughout the world were already under way (BBC, Discovery, CNN) which were looking at the global picture, but no one else would even touch on New Zealand.

This was to be our focus. But we needed an edge. That was to eventuate with the decision to drive the history from the perspective of ordinary New Zealanders – how their own families had grown and weathered the economic, personal and natural storms of the century. History for me had always been driven by events and their subsequent effects on people. Our approach was to follow the families, tracing their highs and lows, and then to look at the broader picture to see what events had caused them to react the way they did. So through the very specific individual experiences of our families we would understand the events that contributed to make us all the New Zealanders we are today.

I asked Ray Waru from Te Reo Television to join the project as co-producer. As we were to tell the bi-cultural and multicultural story of New Zealand then our production approach and team needed to reflect this. Besides, it was to be a huge undertaking and we needed the best team possible.

We divided the century into manageable blocks and started the search for families that could take us through the century. They needed to fit certain constraints: they needed to know their own history, have visual records of it, be strong storytellers and have an understanding of where they fitted into the whole as New Zealanders.

TV ONE committed to the series for development in late 1995 with NZ On Air approving the largest budget for a documentary series in its history early in 1996. We were joined by the Historical Branch of Internal Affairs under Jock Phillips for factual research and Claudia Orange and the Dictionary of New Zealand assisted greatly with finding the families.

It took another year before finance was confirmed, and in the meantime the structure had changed. To better fit the television model, each episode was to be theme-based and the stories of the accompanying families would span the entire century within that episode. This had a major impact on the series, the number of families grew to over 25 and, because of its structure, the television series could only deal with events through the century when the families were actually involved.

During production I was introduced to Kevin Chapman and Janette Howe who were to publish this book. They instantly understood our approach and the complementary strengths of the book and the series. The decision was made to allow the book to develop along the lines of the original concept. It would be a sequential look at the century and be driven by events with family stories supporting where appropriate. Along with the appointment of Paul Smith and Louise Callan as researchers and writers, these were decisions which laid the foundation for a truly integrated book and television series; each supporting the other and giving depth and breadth where the other could not.

I am extremely proud of this book and series, especially for my children, Harry, James and Megan. It gives us all as New Zealanders a context from which to understand our history, to know our present and to prepare us for our future.

David Harry Baldock
Producer, Ninox Films Ltd.

1900

1910

Chapter 1

No Millionaires or Paupers, Please

Every story begins before the beginning. And before the story of the 20th century opened, some of the worst features of the Old World had already blighted the New. In towns, thousands lived in slum conditions. In the country, new settlers eager for land and opportunities were often locked out of property ownership. At work, many were exploited by their employers, and newspaper investigations in the 1880s revealed how some employers abused staff through "sweated labour". The 1890 Royal Commission found child labour, unsanitary factories, long hours and low pay. Girl apprentices worked for 12 months without pay only to be dismissed out of hand at the end of this period; one baker had to work for 108 to 112 hours a week; seven women were found working in a cellar four metres by two and a half metres.

The late Mr. Seddon wheeling a barrow of clay at the turning of the first sod of the Lawrence-Roxburgh Railway Works.
GUY, PHOTO.

God's Own Country and proud of it – Premier Richard Seddon at the turning of the first sod of the Lawrence-Roxburgh railway works.

The Commission's findings caused widespread public concern and added to growing pressure for social change which was met by the new Liberal Government after it came to power in 1891. One of its first challenges was to break up sprawling country estates and so allow them to be farmed by more people. In 1890, some 422 families and companies, fewer than 1 per cent of all landowners, controlled an estimated 64 per cent of the freehold estate.[1] Concerns over access to land for small farmers had been a constant theme since European settlement began. Public feeling against concentration of land ownership ran high, and at the highest level.

When the Liberals took office, the country was nearing the end of "the Long Depression" which some historians believe lasted 30 years from 1865. A fall in wool prices was a key factor triggering widespread poverty and unemployment. It also resulted in the mass departure of former immigrants in what became known as the "Exodus". Between 1862 and 1870, an estimated 75,000 people left the country; between 1885 and 1892, a further 125,000 sailed away.

At first it was depressing. Then it became alarming…. The intercolonial vessels took passengers from New Zealand's shores at the rate of 1,400 a month…. The holds of the vessels were fitted up with temporary berths, and the rush of passengers was so great that sometimes cargo was refused.[2]

Many immigrants had come to New Zealand with the hope that they would own their own land. But they arrived in a society in which laissez-faire, the unregulated freedom of action for owners of capital, dominated. For the Government, the interests of this oligarchy came first.

In Wellington's Newtown in the first years of the century, there was little choice but to know your neighbour intimately because houses were so closely crammed together.

ATL G-19663-1/1

Watched by fellow politicians, Premier "King Dick" Seddon in full flight at a public meeting.

Whatever names the groups in the House of Representatives gave themselves, they remained the representatives of property, scrambling for public money to be spent in their districts.[3]

The harshness of the Long Depression spurred the need for social change. Trade unionists increased their agitation for better working conditions while others campaigned on other issues, including votes for women. In the late 1880s, the economy slowly began to recover and allowed a new, reform-minded Liberal Government to implement its policies.

In the area of land reform, Liberal Premier John Ballance clearly signalled that, for privilege and the gentry, time was up. He told Parliament in a flourish of rhetoric:

I care not if dozens of large landowners leave the country. For the prosperity of this country does not depend on this class. It depends upon ourselves, upon the rise of our industries, and upon markets being secured in other countries, and not upon such fictitious things as whether the large capitalists remain or leave the colony.[4]

Labour Minister William Pember Reeves described the large estates as "social pests". The Liberals did not quite exterminate them; but, using a mixture of repurchase, freehold and leasehold, they successfully broke up the big estates to allow closer settlement.

Between 1892 and 1912, the Government bought over 200 estates covering 1.3 million acres and settled 7,000 new farmers and their families.[5] When the Victorian Minister of Lands visited the 84,755-acre North Canterbury Cheviot Estate in 1899 after the Government had taken it over, he reported:

We thus completed our inspection of an estate which six years ago was nothing short of a great sheep walk owned by one man, who at most employed but the ordinary station hands, but which now, studded with comfortable homesteads, townships, schools, well-fenced and well-cultivated farms, supports a population of upward of 1,200 persons.[6]

This attack on privilege was a revolution – but one marked by moderation and practicality.

Land reform was one of numerous Liberal measures which transformed New Zealand and won international admiration. Reeves' enthusiasm for social justice led to workplace legislation which resulted in the most enlightened labour environment in the world. He regulated hours of work and factory conditions and in 1894 introduced the world's first system of compulsory arbitration. His Industrial Conciliation and Arbitration Act pioneered the way towards more harmonious labour relations and its key features endured for 90 years.

The Act's purpose was clear from its title: "An Act to encourage the formation of Industrial Unions and to facilitate the settlement of industrial disputes by conciliation and arbitration." While unions and employers were involved in conciliation or arbitration, they could not strike or lock out.

In the 1900 Yearbook, the Secretary of Labour reviewed our labour legislation:

The general tendency of these laws is to ameliorate the position of the worker by preventing social oppression through undue influences, or through unsatisfactory conditions of sanitation.[7]

He added that the laws had already done much to improve the lives of workers.

After Ballance died in 1893, the year New Zealand women won the right to vote, his successor, Richard "King Dick" Seddon, continued the momentum of radical social reform. In 1898, he introduced New Zealand's first social welfare measure – the Old Age Pensions Act. The pension, among the first in the world, was means-tested, and provided a maximum of £18 a year in monthly instalments.

ATL F-52516-1/2

NOTICE
——— TO ———
EPICENE WOMEN.

ELECTIONEERING WOMEN

ARE REQUESTED NOT TO CALL HERE.

They are recommended to go home, to look after their children, cook their husband's dinners, empty the slops, and generally attend to the domestic affairs for which Nature designed them.

By taking this advice they will gain the respect of all right-minded people—an end not to be attained by unsexing themselves and meddling in masculine concerns of which they are profoundly ignorant.

HENRY WRIGHT.

103, Mein Street.
Wellington.

Women being put in their 'right' place – the domestic sphere.

Just paid – pensioners pick up their benefits.

ATL F29948-1/2 (National Archives: Pegler Collection)

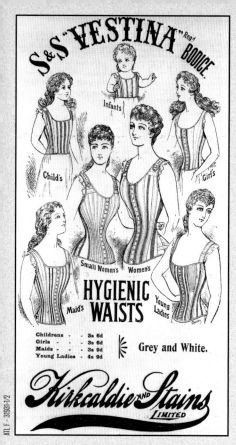

Wellington's Kirkcaldie and Stains try a new beauty angle – hygienic waists (1900).

However, it came with numerous qualifications. Recipients had to be 65 years or over, resident in New Zealand for the past 25 years, and of good character. They also had to be British subjects – Chinese and other Asians did not get the pension.

Refrigeration contributed to land reform by helping to make small farming more viable. In 1882, the first shipment of refrigerated meat was shipped from New Zealand to London and stimulated the growth of the meat and dairy industries. As the old century closed and the new one beckoned, New Zealand moved from depression, and in some cases oppression, to prosperity.

In its first editorial of the century, on January 1 1900, the *New Zealand Herald* noted the trend with satisfaction:

> *The past year has been one of great prosperity over nearly the whole world. Observers in England have been struck with the marked improvement in almost all branches of trade and industry.... The same remarks apply to the United States... and the Continent of Europe.... We in New Zealand have had our full share of this wondrous prosperity. The colony was never in a more healthy condition than it is at present. There is an increasing demand for its principal products, and prices have, in some lines like that of wool, greatly advanced, and in others been well maintained. And so far as can be seen this satisfactory condition is likely to continue....*

From 1895 until the First World War, exports increased sharply and almost continuously, trebling in value in 20 years.[8]

Everything pointed to a thriving, active young country. The area of occupied land rose by one quarter from under 32 million acres in 1891 to just over 40 million acres in 1911. More significantly, the area of sown grasses, on which the bulk of pastoral production took place, doubled from less than seven million acres in 1891 to just over 14 million acres in 1911. The number of sheep rose by more than a quarter, the number of cattle more than doubled, and the output of coal trebled.

Prosperity and social legislation led to New Zealand being described admiringly as a "social laboratory" and many writers, radicals and philosophers journeyed south to see the experiment first hand. One of them was Henry Demarest Lloyd, a journalist and author. He saw us not as radicals but as plain people intent on providing a fair living for all. He also found us:

> *... the most homogeneous Anglo-Saxon blend, the most harmonious constituency of our race there is anywhere – English predominant, Scotch next, Irish third. There is practically no other blood; the foreigners and Maoris are too few to colour the strain.*

Lloyd found parallels between the temperate climate and the moderate nature of the people and their politics. "The purpose one hears them most often avow is that they mean to have no millionaires or paupers...."

The Old World leash had been slipped and he noted: "These English people found themselves in a place and in a time in which the English tendencies could run instead of crawl, and they ran." Lloyd found no Utopia, no paradise in the country he dubbed "Newest England".

TABLE XIII.- Causes of Insanity.

Causes	Auckland			Christchurch			Dunedin (Seacliff)			Hokitika			Nelson			Porirua			Wellington			Ashburn Hall (Private Asylum)			Total		
	M	F	T	M	F	T	M	F	T	M	F	T	M	F	T	M	F	T	M	F	T	M	F	T	M	F	T
Adolescence							1	1	2																1	1	2
Adverse circumstances	1	0	1				3	1	4																4	1	5
Amenorrhoea				0	1	1																			0	1	1
Apoplexy							0	1	1																0	1	1
Appendicitis																						1	0	1	1	0	1
Business Worry																						1	0	1	1	0	1
Cerebral tumours							1	0	1																1	0	1
Child-bearing and puerperal	0	2	2				0	1	1							0	2	2	0	9	9				0	14	14
Climacteric	0	2	2										0	1	1	0	1	1				0	1	1	0	5	5
Congenital and hereditary	18	12	30	12	5	17	7	13	20	1	2	3	1	0	1	1	4	5	6	9	15	1	1	2	47	46	98
Deafness	0	1	1																						0	1	1
Disappointment																0	1	1							0	1	1
Dissolute life	1	4	5																						1	4	5
Domestic trouble and anxiety				0	2	2	0	9	9																0	11	11
Drink	11	1	12	9	0	9	14	2	16	2	0	2	3	0	3	1	1	2	6	3	9	1	1	2	47	5	55
Ear disease							0	1	1																0	1	1
Epilepsy	2	2	4	4	1	5	2	3	5	0	2	2							4	2	6	0	1	1	12	11	23
Financial troubles	2	0	2										1	0	1										3	0	3
Fright																0	1	1							0	1	1
General paralysis													1	0	1										1	0	1
Gonorrhoea							1	0	1																1	0	1
Grief																0	2	2	0	2	2				0	4	4
Hysteria																			0	1	1				0	1	1
Ill health				0	4	4													0	3	3				0	7	7
Influenza	3	0	3													1	0	1	1	0	1	0	1	1	5	1	6
Injury	1	0	1				1	0	1				2	0	2				1	0	1				5	0	5
Love							1	1	2							0	1	1							1	2	3
Masturbation	3	0	3	3	0	3	9	1	10							1	0	1	8	2	10				24	3	27
Opium																0	1	1							0	1	1
Organic				5	0	5																			5	0	5
Organic cerebral disease							0	1	1																0	1	1
Overwork							0	1	1										1	0	1				1	1	2
Phthisis																			1	0	1				1	0	1
Privation	1	0	1	2	0	2																			3	0	3
Previous attack				1	6	7																0	2	2	1	8	9
Religion				2	0	2							1	1	2	3	4	7							6	7	13
Remorse																0	1	1							0	1	1
Seduction				0	1	1																			0	1	1
Senile decay	4	2	6	3	2	5	4	0	4	5	0	5	1	0	1										17	4	21
Sexual																0	1	1							0	1	1
Shock							2	1	3										0	1	1				2	2	4
Solitude	2	0	2				3	1	4				0	1	1	0	1	1	3	0	3				8	3	11
Sunstroke	1	0	1													0	1	1	0	1	1				1	2	3
Syphilis	2	0	2							1	0	1													3	0	3
Tuberculosis																0	1	1							0	1	1
Typhoid																0	1	1							0	1	1
Uterine trouble							0	1	1				0	1	1				0	4	4				0	6	6
Worry	2	6	8													0	1	1	4	2	6				6	9	15
Unknown	7	4	11	8	8	16	13	13	26	4	4	8	2	4	6	1	21	22	20	19	39				55	73	128
Totals	61	36	97	49	30	79	62	52	114	13	8	21	13	8	21	4	44	48	58	62	120	4	7	11	264	247	511

Anything from deafness to disappointment, adolescence and even influenza were listed as causes of insanity, as this 1901 official report to the House of Representatives shows.

New Zealand has reached no final "social solutions", and no New Zealander, citizen or official, can be found who would pretend that it had. All that they claim is that they have tried to find solutions, and they believe that the fair-minded observer will declare that they are entitled to "report progress" to the rest of us. They certainly are experimental. They know it and are proud of it....

Lloyd believed the state had acted as a silent partner to the enterprise of the individual and suggested that this again was plain pragmatism.

The New Zealand idea is the opposite of that of some theoretical creators of society, that the rich are to become richer and the poor poorer, until the whole population has been sifted into brutes of money and brutes of misery, who will then fight out the social question to the death.[9]

Even so, the New Zealand Lloyd examined was far from perfect. Seddon may have called it God's Own Country, but some sections of it desperately needed

Automatic Stamp Vending Machine

Kiwi ingenuity invented – then almost defeated – one of the first New Zealand innovations of the 20th century. On June 15, 1905, the world's first automatic stamp vending machine went on public trial at the Chief Post Office in Wellington.

It sold nearly 4,000 stamps but then one wily customer figured that the machine could not tell the difference between a penny and a lead disc. He was right, and the machine, made by R. J. Dickie, foreign mail clerk at the Chief Post Office and Wellington photographer J. H. Brown, returned from its trial for improvements. In July that year they produced the second version, followed in 1906 by yet another improved version for public trial.

Their invention proved to be a success internationally and in 1909 won a gold medal at the Seattle Exhibition. It was subsequently produced by a British company and in 1913 New Zealand's cautious Post Office, which had pioneered the device, finally ordered 100 from the United Kingdom. Five years later the Government bought the patent and began production at the Post and Telegraph workshops.

Source: Hamish Keith, *New Zealand Yesterdays: A Look at Our Recent Past*, Reader's Digest Services, Sydney NSW, 1984, p. 132.

Chinese running a lottery shop
showing books of tickets.

practical rather than divine prescriptions. Parts of Dunedin were characterised by ugly slums, which the *Otago Daily Times* crusaded against. In Auckland, the situation was just as bad. In its slums, wind and rain poured through the broken windows and damaged roofs of wooden houses. Damp and unsanitary, they were breeding grounds for disease. Water supply was for those who could pay – others collected it from wells or rainwater tanks. Toilets were backyard affairs, literally back-to-back privies.

In Auckland, the poor clustered in the hollows of the land in places like Freeman's Bay, while the wealthy literally took the high ground. On the city's ridges, which were served by horse-drawn trams, they built houses with often as many as 15 rooms, employed servants and had the luxury of a water closet. Electricity slowly supplanted gas lighting in the cities, but its reliability and safety were often questioned at the time. Gas remained to light homes and some city streets until after the First World War.

As local authorities developed drainage and sewerage systems, the quaintly titled "night soil man" plied his trade. His unenviable job was to collect excrement from the houses, and he remained a familiar presence, clattering through the dark streets with his malodorous cargo.

So insensitive was this society to the needs of the psychiatrically ill, Auckland City night soil was dumped near the Auckland asylum. "It has been going on for a considerable period within a comparatively short radius of the Asylum," complained the medical superintendent, R. M. Beattie.

And the band played on... Saturday
in the park in Hastings.

… I am bound to affirm that sickness has occurred in the Asylum for which I can assign no other cause. It seems to me most unfortunate, and most extraordinary that the city should permit a nuisance, whether dangerous or otherwise, in such close proximity to a building where they house nearly 500 of their most helpless and most wretched people.[10]

One case of bubonic plague was reported in Auckland in 1900 and the Government introduced special measures to prevent its spread. This outbreak contributed to the establishment of the Department of Public Health; however, eight more people were to die from the disease during the decade.

If slums and their associated health problems challenged Pakeha, the conditions for Maori were far worse. It was an era when it was widely accepted that Maori would simply die out. In 1896, they were at their lowest ebb with only 42,000 but by the 1901 census showed a slight increase. Maori had been hit by war, disease, and punitive land confiscations but they were beginning to adapt, and in 1900 had a representative in Cabinet in the form of James Carroll. Later other Maori leaders – Apirana Ngata (1905), Peter Buck (1909), and Dr Maui Pomare (1911) – also entered Parliament to win a better future for their race.

Yet when Dr Pomare, then a Maori health officer, took the pulse of his people in 1906, he found it faint. He reported that bad housing, feeding, clothing, unventilated rooms and unwholesome pas "all opposed the perpetuation of the race". In his official report he added:

… but a deeper knowledge of the Maori reveals to us the fact that these are not the only potent factors in the causation of his decay. Like an imprisoned bird of the forest, he pines for the liberty and freedom of his alpine woods. This was a warrior race, used to fighting for liberty or to death. All this has gone. Fighting is no more. There is no alternative but to become a Pakeha. Was not this saying uttered by the mouth of a dying chief many generations ago: Kei muri i te awa kapara he tangata ke, mana te ao, he ma. (Shadowed behind the tattooed face, a stranger stands, he who owns the earth and he is white.)[11]

If Maori still suffered discrimination at the hands of a heavily Anglo-Saxon community, it was nothing compared to the distaste for Chinese. In 1900 New Zealand's population was 810,536 and the number of Chinese was 3,077 – of whom just 34 were women. However, ever since a handful of Chinese had entered the country during the Central Otago goldrush in the 1860s, politicians, the press and public disquiet combined to create a series of moral panics.

Variously at stake was the future of the white race, employment and the society's moral well-being. Earlier legislation approved of by Seddon had imposed a poll tax of £100 on every Chinese. In 1907, they faced a compulsory reading test in English and a year later were forced to give a thumbprint when entering the country.

In the worst racial incident, an elderly Chinese, Joe Kum Yung, was shot in the head as he walked along Haining Street in Wellington. The only witness gave a vague description of the killer, but the next morning a young man, Edward Lionel Terry, walked into a Wellington Police Station, handed the duty constable a revolver and admitted to the murder. "I take an interest in alien immigration and I took this means of bringing it under public notice," he said.

Sir Apirana Ngata, member for Eastern Maori and one of the most influential of Maori leaders.

Doctor, later Sir Maui Pomare, MP for Western Maori.

Sir Peter Buck, a doctor, who like Pomare, entered politics with the aim of improving conditions for Maori.

The Big Game, Small Ball — and a Missing Dog

Cartoonist Trevor Lloyd's celebration of the 1905 All Blacks beating England.

Rugby was sometimes played in humble and occasionally comic circumstances, as country editor J.H. Claridge, with his eye for rustic eccentricities, noted:

The locality is a settlement in the King Country, main trunk line. A sawmill team who called themselves The Botflies had arranged to play another team rejoicing in the title of The Savages... both teams possessed representative players. The game had been announced by a half column advt. in the local paper, and a brass band engaged; also a booth erected for hop beer (3 per cent only alcohol allowed by law in a prohibited district; an outside brewer was fined £50 for sending a consignment overproof). A fine day, and a large crowd of surrounding residents — saw-mill hands, bush fellers, navvies, Maoris and land-investigators.

The football ground was situated next to a raupo swamp. A Savage player known as "Curly" Re'dair — his hair was black and straight as a Red Indian's — by a superhuman effort in the second spell, kicked the ball into the middle of the swamp; it was unsafe for a human to venture in. The game was held up until a spectator offered to go home for his retriever dog. The offer was gladly accepted, as no other match ball was known to exist in the village, and the spectator left on his errand of charity. After an hour's wait for the dog, the band played On the Ball *and* We Won't Go Home Till Morning.

Somebody mentioned that the local stationer sold footballs. The referee sent a boy for one. "Bring the largest you can get and charge it to the Savages," he said. The boy returned with a diminutive school ball, and most ridiculous play followed, the crowd laughing and jeering at the players and antics of the small ball, because no one knew in what direction it intended to go. The game ended in darkness — Savages 15, Bots 14.

What became of the owner of the dog? While on his way home for the dog he was called into a house and invited to take a glass of whisky. Then the dog was forgotten. Half a dozen men were there – a "syndicate" – who had, as was often the custom, bought a case (2 doz bottles) of spirit.[i]

---

[i] James Henry Claridge, *75 Years in New Zealand: Midst Pakeha and Maori*, J H Claridge, Auckland, c. 1938, p. 74.

At his trial, the jury retired briefly before finding him guilty and making a strong recommendation for mercy on the grounds that the prisoner was not responsible for his action, "as he was suffering from a craze caused by his intense hatred towards the mixing of British and alien races".[12] His death sentence was commuted to life imprisonment and he spent the rest of his life in mental hospitals.

The nation's often hysterical ethnic animosities touched Dalmatians and "Hindoos" as well, but there was little doubt as the century began that this was indeed a lucky country for many: trade was burgeoning and the general optimism was reflected in the birth rates, which had been in decline for years.

The number of births registered in 1900 was 19,546, or 25.60 in every thousand people. In 1910, the figure had risen to 25,984 (26.17). More people married – and divorced. The mean age for partners was 29 years for men and between 25 and 26 years for women throughout the decade.[13]

As the society matured, its population became increasingly urbanised – by 1911, just over 50 per cent lived in cities or boroughs, a trend which was to intensify throughout the century.

New Zealand had energy and optimism to burn but, mimicking Mother England, showed it in a very mannered way. On New Year's Eve 1899, a large crowd gathered on the Queen Street wharf in Auckland to cheer in the new century, and the *New Zealand Herald* reported:

As the clock struck the midnight hour, the bells of all the vessels in harbour were set ringing and kept going for some time, but beyond that there was no demonstration. The ferry steamer Eagle made two excursion trips around the harbour last night being crowded with passengers on both occasions.

It had been a busy New Year's Eve. At the Auckland Domain, the Sunday School Union held a children's festival. In keeping with the marine tradition of the North Shore, the Devonport Wesleyan Sunday School held a "water excursion" to Motutapu Island and provided amusements, food and a huge range of sporting activities for the children. That evening, the Auckland Opera House was also full for the melodrama *Woman and Wine*.

New Year's celebrations were, however, overshadowed by the South African (Boer) War which, with horse racing a close second, dominated the pages of the dailies. As the new century opened, hints of what lay ahead were already clear.

1900 was marked by war, plague, the "yellow peril", a Maori renaissance, and increasing urbanisation. Just as obvious were the components of the Kiwi character. They included fair play, a passion by both sexes for sports, racing – and rugby. We also had a fatal predilection for going to war – New Zealanders responded to both rugby and war with enthusiasm, sending more troops to South Africa in 1899 than any other colony and priding themselves on the record of the

The Mutual Fund Building

The Mutual Fund Building in Bond Street Dunedin was built in 1909 and is considered New Zealand's first skyscraper. The design and construction methods have their origins in the early Chicago skyscrapers. It was originally the head office of the New Zealand Express Company.

Estate of Robin Morrison, Auckland Museum

The cinema begins to exert its appeal, courtesy of Buckingham's.

A sticky wicket for young backblocks cricketers.

Dance, vaudeville, opera and theatre were all brought to Kiwis by numerous touring companies.

1905 All Blacks who thrashed the English. Touring the British Isles, the team lost only one of their 32 games – controversially – and scored 830 points, conceding only 39.

Author Paul Gooding wrote at the turn of the century:

> *New Zealanders are a busy, independent and pleasure-loving people. Their popular sports are horse-racing, football, cricket, tennis, golf, swimming and yachting. In every part of the country there is a weekly half holiday [Saturday afternoons] for factories, shops, offices, the building trades, etc., and in addition, there are from six to seven full holidays each year. Proof that New Zealanders enjoy themselves may be seen on any clement Saturday night when, in the cities, thousands leisurely stroll the streets, crowding the footpaths and filling the roadways from kerb to kerb.*[14]

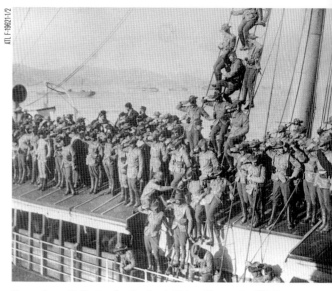

Troops leave Wellington for the South African War on the "SS Waiwera".

Photographs of the time show bustling city centres, although by 1902, one year after Queen Victoria's death, the only asphalted road was Queen Street in Auckland. City streets sprang to life every day as office and shop workers alighted from horse-drawn trams, and hawkers set up their wares for street sales.

At night, the era's rich cultural life showed that New Zealanders in this Edwardian era cared for more than just sport and the outdoors. They flocked to see opera and vaudeville, musical comedy and Shakespeare performed by numerous troupes who visited the country. Among the stars who toured were Dame Clara Butt, and Ignace Paderewski. Dame Nellie Melba visited twice, and was so popular that crowds gathered outside hotels to catch a glimpse of her. At the time, opera was not regarded as elite entertainment, as musicologist and author Adrienne Simpson noted:

> *Opera was family fare, played in theatres that were used for many different types of entertainment. Although an element of social or intellectual snobbery may have motivated some patrons in the boxes or dress circle, large areas of cheap seating ensured that audiences had a wide social spread. Opera airs were "popular" music, as likely to be heard on a barrel organ as in the theatre.*[15]

Edwardians enthusiastically welcomed The New – everything from electricity to bicycles. On the streets, horse-drawn transport gradually gave way to electric trams. Auckland had them by 1902, and Dunedin and Wellington followed in the next two years. By 1905, Christchurch too had trams – but the plains city was more interested in the new-fangled bicycles.

Equally new, but barely tolerated, was the motor car – an innovation which scared horses and upset authorities. They roared noisily into the era, their speed provoking both admiration and censure. Speed limits were imposed partly to protect the horses, and so the horseless carriages which transformed cities crawled along at city speed limits as low as 4 miles per hour in Christchurch.

Throughout the Edwardian decade, a love of and loyalty to all things British shone through. But even at this early stage, some New Zealanders also shared the Maori culture.

In 1905, when she was 14, Florence Woodhead (later Florence Harsant) travelled with her family from Taranaki by ship, train, coach, and finally steamer to the village of Waitahanui on the shores of Lake Taupo. Her father had taken up a position as teacher of the Maori school there, though he could speak no Maori and the local Maori could speak no English. Florence helped her father at the school, became a fluent Maori speaker and observed the customs and homes of the local people.

The first New Zealand-made car.

In the centre of the village was a large raupo building which we learned was the "wharepuni" or main meeting house. All the houses were of raupo, consisting of one room, one door and window, an earthen floor, which was covered with "whariki", flax mats, except for a hollowed out place in the middle of the room. In this, on cold nights would be placed red embers of manuka.

Trams everywhere in turn-of-the-century Courtenay Place, Wellington.

She described her father's first attempts at teaching, and the way the whole Maori community involved itself – with parents learning multiplication alongside their children. She watched mundane rituals, like women washing their clothes on flat boards or stones in the lake water, and spreading them on bushes to dry, and described their diet: trout, mutton birds, duck, pukeko, wild pigs and fresh crayfish, eaten (to her horror) alive. This was supplemented by potatoes, kumara and sweet corn grown in local gardens; for greens, they used watercress and puha. The women also made leavened bread in camp ovens. The only work the men did was during the shearing season when they would go to the Rangitaiki Plains to big sheep stations.

Florence used to take gruel regularly to a very old chieftainess, who was tattooed not only on her chin and eyes, but on her arms and legs.

Packed steam tram with trailers, Christchurch.

She did not like the Pakeha. She said before the Pakeha came, the men were strong and active. They would hunt and fish, help till the soil, become skilled in the art of warfare, but now – and she would spit on the ground – they are lazy, they drink the waipiro and let the women work. "Our men were strong and straight like trees, now they are fat and big in the stomach! Aue! Aue!" and she would bow her head and weep for the past.

ATL F-21075-1/2

Showtime! Maori children performing an action song.

Preparing kai at Ohinemutu, 1907.

Florence agreed:

> *... their physical condition had deteriorated, Consumption and other diseases were rife amongst them. They no longer lived close to nature but were divided between two separate modes of life.* [16]

And Maori were still losing their land – between 1891 and 1911 nearly four million acres passed out of their hands. It was ironic that one of the "great estates" that the Liberals succeeded in breaking up for settlement by small farmers was Maori-owned land. It was considered unproductive, and Minister of Lands John McKenzie saw Maori communal ownership as a serious block to progress. Under the Liberals, 2,729,000 acres of Maori land were bought by the Government between 1892 and 1900. It was acquired for a price of 4 to 6 shillings an acre and sold for six times as much. McKenzie, a Scot who never forgot the harsh treatment meted out to tenants by landlords in his homeland, believed the state would be a more benevolent purchaser than the land speculators of Auckland.

> *He held a poor view of Maori farming ability and seemed unaware that some tribes had engaged in successful sheepfarming. No compensation was made to Maori settlers whereas the big estate owners were generously compensated and allowed to keep large areas for themselves.* [17]

ATL C-2497 (Hislop Album)

The MacGibbons
The Demon Drink

At the turn of the century and for the first two decades, the temperance movement was a potent political and moral force in New Zealand. It was particularly strong in the south of the South Island amongst Scottish Presbyterians and their descendants. Large areas of Southland were technically dry, but despite that alcohol was still available. The Presbyterians' rigid puritanism could be distinctly flexible where drink was concerned, as Bruce MacGibbon remembers. He was about eight when he followed family tradition and signed on to the Band of Hope, taking the pledge not to drink alcohol.

There was strict prohibition but the dry districts were misnomers because in our view the drink in the dry districts was greater than in the ones where they'd got a licence.

He remembers seeing barrels from the brewery across the street from the high school in Gore disappearing down the road to be secreted in the guard's van of trains travelling south to Invercargill. A few kegs would be smuggled off at various stops along the way. Those waiting thirstily knew they would be in trouble with the law if they were discovered. They usually solved the problem by drinking the lot on arrival, "sometimes with dire results". His nephew John MacGibbon says that despite signing the pledge some early MacGibbons did drink.

There seemed to be a distinction among the Scots between medicinal uses of Scotch in particular and over-indulgence. The earliest MacGibbon, old John senior, sold brandy in Dunedin. And when he was running an accommodation house in Mataura in the 1860s, every Sunday night when he had Bible reading with the family, if he heard the bell that indicated someone wanted to be ferried across the river to buy grog, he'd drop the Bible and attend to business.

However, there were some who did not drink, despite others' best efforts. Bruce was told stories of how Scottish farmers from the district used to come into Mataura where his uncle was the bank manager and take him to the pub across the road to ply him with whisky. What they didn't know was that his uncle had an arrangement with the publican.

He had "special whisky", coloured like whisky but I think it was cold tea or something like that. And he used to drink these. The old Scots were plying him with whisky, shouting him. They'd get as high as anything; and he was still sober. They could never understand it.

John MacGibbon (second from left) and neighboyrs relax with a lemonade. John was a noted abstainer.

There was also a healthy business in illicit, locally made whisky – Hokonui. Owners of whisky stills in the Hokonui Hills took great care to ensure they wouldn't be found. Bruce MacGibbon still remembers the time his father took him shooting rabbits on a local farmer's property; but not before they had received explicit instructions on where to go… and not to go.

There were rabbits for miles in those days, too. But the farmer said, "When you look at the house, go up the left hand side, there's rabbits there. But on the right hand side – no rabbits." Don't forget, these farms had great big snow tussock about as tall as me. Dad shot with a shotgun and he went up one valley, and I had the rifle and went up another. I didn't see a rabbit, so I came back. Dad, he didn't see a rabbit. But he came back down the right hand side where he was told not to go. And down amongst these snow tussock there was three stills bubbling away: Hokonui. It was quite an industry there, no doubt about it. And, of course, Hokonui also used to go into the pubs to dilute the Scotch whisky that came from overseas.

Source: Edited Ninox transcripts from *Our People, Our Century*, 1999.

Shrinking Distance

By 1908, railways, cars and, increasingly, telephones began to bring the country closer together. Horses and bullocks still supplied its needs on back country mud tracks masquerading as roads. Many, however, were impassable except for bullock carts and the motor car was still regarded as an expensive oddity. The first two arrived in Wellington in 1898 and by 1905 there were 500. Five years later there were 3,500.

Turn-of-the-century freight ways – bullocks hauling their loads through the Stratford District.

In other ways too, we came together. The first telephone exchanges opened in 1881 though, partly because of cost, the subscription base remained relatively low. By 1904, the number of telephones was only 12,000. Six years later, there were 29,681 telephones, many of them in the popular "candlestick" shape with separate, tulip-shaped mouth and ear pieces. In the next decade, however, the take-up rate of both telephones and cars soared as New Zealanders modernised.

The pleasures of a picnic – with service – in Auckland, 1900.

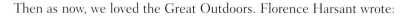

Not so much a beach as a promenade – Takapuna at the turn of the century.

Then as now, we loved the Great Outdoors. Florence Harsant wrote:

It was a free life…. Time never dragged. My brother and I would go with the boys and girls, exploring all over the great flat, follow the crystal clear river up to its source in the hills, watching the trout making their way up there to spawn.[18]

On New Year's Day 1907, the lure of the land drew some to the beach – and others to the bush, where writer I. V. Hughes captured the bucolic pleasures of a picnic:

[Men, women and children] hang over the sides of wagons or sit more sedately on the seats of brakes and gigs, indifferent to the clouds of dust churned up by horses' hooves and iron-shod wheels… Bushwackers from the mill, cow cockies and their families, the few "gentry" such as the mill manager, some station holders and the local minister are all there. There are Maoris from the flax-mill further down the river, bullockies, drovers, and a sprinkling of townie visitors conspicuous in their fal-de-rals….

There is an aromatic tang in the air from the tea-tree fire kindled under the huge copper [vat] which is to supply water for the tea. Ah, the incense of burning tea-tree! As the smoke rises in a blue, tenuous column children dismount from ponies, spill out of traps and buggies, and soon there comes the thud of small booted feet as the young folk run and shout and play in the manner of children of any time and race. Family groups settle under the shade of giant kahikateas and picnic baskets are unpacked. Then Bill, the blacksmith, unfamiliar in white shirt and his best moleskins and minus his leather apron, begins on his job as Master of Ceremonies.[19]

The land Kiwis loved so much was also being tamed and its distances shrunk. The 1870s had seen the beginnings of an ambitious programme of building railways. With an eye always on development, the State financed and planned the system and in 1908 the North Island Main Trunk – the crowning achievement of New Zealand's railway age – was completed. The Central North Island section had taken 23 years to build and included incredible engineering feats such as the Raurimu Spiral with its two tunnels, three horseshoe curves and a complete circle, to enable a climb of 550 metres in 25 kilometres.[20] A year after its completion, the first regular passenger express trains began running between Auckland and Wellington, covering 685 kilometres in nearly 20 hours.

When he visited the country, Henry Demarest Lloyd praised the country's public ownership of its roads and railway and the accountability that offered:

> *There is no Vanderbilt to say "the public be damned".… Every detail of policy regarding the extension, operation and manning of the highways is public business, universally acknowledged to be such by the people, press, Parliament and ministry and business interests.*[21]

But by the end of the decade, the first signs of increased factionalism were growing as labour and political conservatives mobilised.

ATL F-154973-1/2 (Burton Bros Collection)

Sail versus steam in the Auckland harbour.

Black smoke against white mountains as an engine struggles up the Raurimu Spiral.

ATL F-61100-1/2

Alice Evans

The Frontiers of Memory

I n 1915, four-year-old Alice Wagener went North with her parents, leaving her doting maternal grandparents and the familiarity of Auckland. Alice (later Evans) had begun a journey which was to shape her life and eventually make her both a teacher and author whose stories bring to life the frontier of the Far North. But all she felt when she boarded the steamer taking them North was fear and confusion. Soon after embarking, she was all at sea in more ways than one:

I was horribly seasick for the twenty-four hours that it took to get here. I was the eldest and I had a little sister and a brother and my mother was too busy looking after them to be worrying a great deal about what was happening to me. So I had a most miserable trip up in this thing... the water seemed to be coming in through the portholes any minute. I thought I was going to be drowned....

The vessel stopped just outside the Houhora Harbour and Alice's first memory of landing was being let down the side of the steamer in a large mail hamper:

I wondered what on earth was going to happen to me, coming down and down and down into this launch.

When the ship steamed away she saw the black and brown humps of Mount Camel:

I was so thankful to see something that was steady and solid and looking as if it was never going to go away.

She struggled to get a sense of place – geographically and personally:

I didn't know that I had another Granny and Grandad. I thought that everybody just had one set of grandparents. My Grandma Thomas and my Grandpa Thomas. So we arrived at the little jetty and there was great excitement as far as my Dad was

Alice (standing), with her sister Val.

concerned because he was meeting up with his brothers again. And then we were brought up to the house to meet Granny and Grandad Wagener.

I hadn't seen a big house like that in my life before and I wondered what on earth it was we were coming to. But we came in through the gate and my feet scrunched over the shells as we came up the path. Then I saw people standing at the front door. My Granny was standing there and she looked to be altogether different from Grandma Thomas. She was very stiff and straight and she had a sort of tight-lipped face and her hair was dragged back. She had drab clothes on and I had a vision of my grandma in Auckland who was such a different, soft and cuddly sort of person.

Anyway, I came forward with my eye glued on

Grandad Wagener and Granny Wagener who left the young Alice with indelible memories.

everybody else and fell over the step that has had so many other people coming in and out of it in the ordinary way. If it had been my Grandma Thomas, she would have picked me up and given me a cuddle. But Granny just said, "What's the matter with you? Get up." And I knew from that time on that my Granny was that sort of person. She always expected you to just get up and go again and make the best of whatever happened to you.

In the meantime, I was told that this was my Granny. And there was another person there I hadn't taken all that much notice before, but I suddenly looked and saw this man with a round face, pink cheeks, very blue eyes and a white fringe of whiskers and a bent back – I was sure he must be Santa Claus. He looked exactly like him but they said it was Grandad Wagener.

It was Alice's introduction to another world, and although she stayed there only briefly at the beginning, she was to return many times to be with her new and sometimes forbidding Granny. Slowly the two grew together:

She used to be amused by what they told me were the quaint things I said. I didn't know I was any different from anybody else but I can remember I was very anxious to know who I was, what I was here for and what I was likely to do with myself. I was only little at the time and they said, "Oh, you're just a little girl made of sugar and spice." And I can remember protesting very loudly and calling out that I didn't want to be a bun for the rest of my life.

That seemed to amuse Granny and she used to talk about this child who said she didn't want to be a bun.

I used to run away all the time and Granny was always making me come back again…. I actually scolded her one day for making me want to come back. She used to say she liked kids with a bit of spunk in them, so that was evidently the first sign of softening.

Her Granny kept hens and chickens and Alice often wondered what the little three-cornered boxes were outside the house:

She said they were for chickens – and I wanted to hold a chicken. The first time she let me hold one of those little yellow chickens I felt how soft it was and I could see that she and I had something in common…. Granny and Uncle Fred and Grandad seemed to rattle round in the house. It was a bare place. It wasn't like our house in Auckland which was typically Victorian. There were bare boards with just rugs on the floor and everybody seemed to be scrubbing floors. There was no wallpaper – it wasn't a homely-looking place, but it always had a great air of mystery.

Alice's parents settled in their home at Pukenui where she lived most of her young life, but during the holidays they would return to Granny's Houhora homestead:

The Wageners' Houhora homestead.

Granny used to want my sister and I to sleep out in the bedroom off the front verandah – there was no power, just candles, and we didn't like being out there. But she used to give us our candle at night and Val and I would go out through the front door and then head for the room on the verandah known as Uncle Percy's room. Granny would turn round and come back inside, and we were just left there.

Outside, the young girls would be frightened by the noises of the night – sounds from the movement of big gum trees nearby as the branches moved against each other, shadows thrown by the flickering candles, and wails from Mount Camel:

There were a lot of goats on the hill and the little kids used to call out... they sound exactly like a baby crying. We used to worry about these babies that might be crying over there on Mount Camel.

And there were penguins – lots of penguins were down here just under the cliffs and they made a most mournful sound. If we had been at home in our own place, we would have just simply left where we were and gone into our mother and said, "We don't like being out there." But Granny didn't let you do that so we just had to put up with being there.

But we were always quite glad to get up very early in the morning and come back into the old kitchen. Granny would always be up very early and she used to have only a colonial oven to use for cooking. She used to call it "that demon" because it was... there was a lot of black wood and big black pots to handle

– she never seemed to think she had enough wood to keep it going.

She wouldn't give us our breakfast until we'd all gone outside with a big flax kit and gone round the paddocks to pick up pine cones and bring them in for her to use as extra fuel for the fire. And when all that was done and she was satisfied, she used to send us off down to the blacksmith's shop to where the well, the trough and the pump were. There was a stand beside the pump with a piece of yellow soap and the water was always very cold. But we had to pump the water up into the basin and every now and again tadpoles would come up through the pipe. And one morning this awful frog suddenly leapt out of the end of the pump and landed on my chest....

We weren't allowed to have warm water or anything like that unless we were sick. And then here in the house, there were always big jugs and basins and we might be allowed to have a little bit of warm water there.

Then we all lined up at the great big old table out in the kitchen and there was a big form behind it – it was better to use a form because you could get more kids sitting along one. Grandad had cut a blue gum stump in a big thick round slice... the littlest one always had to sit on this blue gum stump and of course always wanted to get big enough to get off the stump and sit on the form with the rest of us.

Granny used to make us eat porridge. I didn't like porridge but we had to have porridge in these great big old dishes. It was so thick, we used to cut cracks in the top of it with a knife or a spoon and pour the condensed milk in through these little cracks.

It was very, very plain food. We had a lot, a lot of fish – they caught it of course. And Granny made her own bread so she had to have her own yeast. In those days they made potato yeast and it was very potent stuff if it wasn't tied down properly. So Granny had this great row of bottles with corks and string going across the top of them lined up in the cupboard alongside the colonial oven. And one thing we had to be very careful about was not to stamp too hard past these yeast bottles in case we loosened the string and the cork and they blew up as we went by.

As time went by, Alice discovered that a love of music was another thing that she and her Granny had in common:

I was just a little girl and I couldn't play the piano. But she used to let me come and put my fingers on it. Uncle Fred used to play with one finger and as he played, he would hum the tune. He always opened and shut his mouth all the time. Nobody told me that when you played the piano, you didn't open and shut your mouth all the time to go with your fingers, so I used to do that. Everybody was amused because that was the way I played the piano – like Uncle Fred. Later on I began to take music lessons and Granny used to buy me music. She and I used to play duets.... She loved music and they used to have a lot of singing in the evenings, community sings and so on. Granny was always very keen to know of anybody that had a really good voice.

The extended family on a picnic – Alice is pictured sitting (centre) in the front row with relatives and friends.

Alice was not at the house the day her grandmother died because by then she had left home to become a teacher. But even after death, music still bound them together in an eerie coincidence:

I didn't know she died because at that time I had grown up and gone away and had become a teacher. I'd had a very bad experience which left me with what they used to call a nervous breakdown. I was at home and I didn't know. They wouldn't tell me that she had died. But another cousin of ours, Kewpie Steed, was staying at the house with Granny and was looking through a lot of old music. She was curious to know what some of the music was about. She said to Granny, "This is all about a barn dance... and here's something about quadrilles." She asked: "What were they?" Granny said, "Oh, I'll tell you." She was seventy-five I think, and very, very stiff and rheumaticky by that time. They tell me that she decided to give Kewpie a demonstration. So she got up and prepared to do a barn dance round this room and then went and sat down at the piano to play the music, and just fell forward over the keys.

But the coincidence of the link I had with Granny was that although I didn't know until after her funeral, I alarmed everybody at home by getting up in the middle of the night and going to my piano, which was then in our house at Pukenui, and playing one of Granny's tunes.

It's a tune I still like to play on that piano. It's an old thing called "Myosotis" which means Forget-Me-Not, strangely enough.

Granny's been dead for many years now, but when I visit the old house the tyrant clock still stands on the Old Henry Cupboard, needing only winding to clang out its summons once more.

Alice wrote later in her book Mount Camel Calling:

And can Granny be far away, when there on the window ledge behind her treadle sewing machine rests a faded pin cushion bristling with pins, a threaded needle, a thimble inverted on a hatpin, Uncle Percy's First World War badge?

When in the colonial oven, her bread tins wait as if just placed there to dry out? And in the set-in cupboards by the fireplace are her potato yeast bottles, the corks tied down with string? Instinctively I still tiptoe past that potential arsenal, obedient all these years later to Granny's urgent instruction: "Look out for my yeast bottles".

Sources: Edited Ninox transcripts from Our People, Our Century, 1999; and Alice Evans, Mount Camel Calling, Hodder and Stoughton, Auckland, 1981. All photographs from the Alice Evans Family Collection.

Chapter 2

1910

1920

Disease & Strife

**MORE MONEY FROM
YOUR DAIRY HERD**

There was a yawning gap between promise and reality for many early settlers. The bucolic cover to the catalogue for dairy equipment (above) is no more than a dream for farmers like the one at Mangaonoho, Rangitikei (right), living in often primitive conditions while they burned off and cleared the land.

At the Edwardian era's close, New Zealand was a contented and prosperous producer. In 1910 Mother England took 84 per cent of our exports and we were richer by more than £22 million. But not everyone could claim to be part of the new prosperity and despite the optimism about our progress, New Zealand remained in many ways a society of unequals.

No language or vocabulary has yet been invented to capture the unique New Zealand balance of equality and inequality, freedom and constraint. The poor and unskilled were more likely to die early, go to prison, or be unemployed. Battery hands at the Waihi Gold Mine Company's works were, on average, forty-seven years old when they died. Members of Dunedin's elite Fernhill Club on average lived to be seventy-two years old.[1]

Many Kiwis reached for the dream of equality but still found it elusive. Workers perceived a decline in their standard of living. In Auckland and Wellington the cost of living – fuel, food, clothing and housing – was rising while there was little or no real growth in workers' incomes between 1901 and 1914.[2] Take-home pay also fell as the average working week shrank from 54 hours to 48. Workers were not prepared to stand by and see their conditions worsen year by year and union membership rose sharply, mainly in the transport, mining and building industries. At the same time, tough new union leaders emerged. Among them was a young Australian, Michael Joseph Savage, who would become one of the country's most loved leaders.

In 1910, a Liberal Party veteran, Sir Joseph Ward, held the high office Savage would one day occupy. Ward was a publican's son and messenger boy who had risen to become the country's Prime Minister despite bankruptcy, political scandal and his religion (Ward was a Catholic in very anti-Catholic times). But he did not have Richard Seddon's force of personality or political talent for holding together the Liberal Party's many factions. His new policies alienated first the conservative, rural wing and then the urban interests and radicals. His strong imperialist stance was the only safe political ground at a time when Germany's military expansion caused mounting tension in Europe.

The conflicts of interest in the Government's broad coalition mirrored the country-town split within the nation. As numbers grew in the agricultural and industrial organisations, the gulf between them widened. Most militant were the Farmers' Union and the Federation of Labour (FOL).

The New Zealand Farmers' Union began as a forum to improve farming practices, but soon became a political lobby. Its most fervent members were the growing numbers of small North Island dairy farmers whose livelihood was barely at subsistence level. In contrast, city dwellers were dismissed as:

... parasites, living off the farmers' sweat, contributing little to the Dominion's wealth, and fermenting undesirable, anti-British beliefs in socialism, radicalism, and in the trade unions.[3]

The farming community demonised the union movement and in particular the FOL, the "Red Feds", founded by the coalminers of the West Coast. The unionists, like the dairy farmers, felt excluded from their fair share of the wealth earned by New Zealand products overseas. The upsurge in labour militancy during this period was part of a world-wide trend. Within the local

ATL G-21520-1/1 (F. J. Denton Collection)

A festive meet at the Wanganui races. The racecourse was the pride of every town, large and small.

Many diggers in the Northland gumfields were immigrants from Dalmatia. Abandoned diggings scarred the region.

G-11220-1/1 (Northwood Collection)

Ngawehi Jim Mikaere
Growing up in the Manaia Valley

Ngawehi Jim Mikaere was born on 31 August 1910 in the Manaia Valley in the Coromandel. The Mikaeres are Ngati Pukenga with affiliations to most of the Tauranga and Hauraki iwi, the most important with Ngai Tamarawaho hapu of Ngati Ranganui, Tauranga Moana. They were a big family and when Ngawehi was a little boy he spent two years living with his elderly grandfather, Mikaere Taoki.

We had a tin shack, me and my grandfather, and we got on very well. He said one thing I remember, "Fight in the mornings, argue in the mornings." He had a habit of getting up in the morning and lighting his pipe and smoking tobacco he made himself and man did it stink. He was an old man then. He used to be a gumdigger up in Northland.

Life for Maori of that period was only just beginning to change, influenced by the growing number of European settlers. Ngawehi was one of a family of 16. Their house was "just one big hall" with an earth floor, "in those days a wooden floor was very rare", and a drain dug round the outside to help keep the ground dry. The house was thatched with nikau palms and Ngawehi's youngest brother, Slim, born in 1929, recalls that in heavy rain the water used to work its way through the thatch: "So we had a little spade there and dug a drain so the water ran out the front door. We only had one door." They cooked on an open fire and spread their sheets and blankets on beds made of vines gathered in the bush and packed into bags. Transport was by horse and they rode into Coromandel township to sell kauri gum and buy groceries. Food staples introduced by the Pakeha – flour, salt, sugar and tea – had quickly become indispensable to Maori as well. Ngawehi remembers:

We had very little money. The old man used to work, bush work and the road, and then there was a lot of gumdigging done. What money we had, we spent on groceries. To survive one had to do a lot of gardening. After school we used to go down and weed the gardens and we had big gardens. And Saturday and Sundays we used to go out fishing and up the bush hunting wild pigs and pigeons. We never had a fridge. We salted everything. We used to half cook the meat and pour fat over it, cover the whole with pig fat, and that keeps it, preserves it.

Then, as now, the area was a fertile provider and Slim Mikaere recalls growing and storing the year's supply of vegetables:

Each family had at least a two-acre garden. You grow spuds first, and then they used to grow the kumara between the rows of spuds. And any spare lots they had, they grew cabbage, silverbeet. My dad used to store the spuds, and the kumara too, in a pit, about three feet underground. And then we used to go up into the bush and get a plant there called a waikahu. That's to cushion them, you know, to keep them warm.

The sea completed their diet. They fished with hand lines and gathered shellfish from the beach.

We used to like to get shellfish. Sometimes you used to cook the water on a fire out there at the beach and sometimes we'd eat one mussel, just half would be thrown away, and they used to growl at us, man! They didn't like us wasting food. And we only took back home what was required. No more.

When Ngawehi Jim Mikaere was 13, he left school and the valley and went to work with his uncle cutting flax and working in a flax mill on the Hauraki Plains. It was 10 years before he returned home to Manaia.

Source: Edited Ninox transcripts from *Our People, Our Century*, 1999.

labour movement were some who were extremely ideologically driven and in contact with the latest developments in European and American socialist, anarchist and syndicalist thought. But the majority were not driven by theory or doctrine, but by pragmatism and the desire to prevent the great inequalities of the Old World.

> [I]t is not socialistic doctrines which inspire them…. They reck [care] little of general ideas and great principles…. More than anyone, they have the art of taking questions successively, and they are only interested in solving them as they arise. Under such conditions there is little room for socialistic doctrines.[4]

In the 1911 general elections, Ward and the Liberals lost their huge majority. The next year they fell from power altogether, and ended 20 years of Liberal rule. Enter William Ferguson Massey, the Reform Party leader. He was a bluff, Ulster-born Protestant who had farmed in Mangere.

> According to tradition, Massey was building a haystack on his farm… when a telegram arrived asking him to stand for Parliament. The message had to be handed up to him on a pitchfork. Had Massey been a radical, some farmer would have remarked, instead, on the symbolic fact that "mangere" is the Maori word for "lazy".[5]

In the next two years he presided over the worst violence since the New Zealand Wars as the Government, the employers and the "cow cockies" sought to crush the "Red Feds". A number of large unions had joined the powerful West Coast coalminers and the watersiders in the FOL. Moderate Wellington tram drivers had gone on strike and won; "wilder prophets of class war, preaching sabotage and violence, could be heard".[6] But when the miners at the Waihi quartz goldmine went out on strike in May 1912, the industrial landscape was about to change dramatically, and for that change Massey was largely responsible.

Massey and the Reform Party, strongly supported by the rural vote, were fiercely anti-union. Reports that the miners in Waihi had celebrated the death of King Edward VII and lamented the coronation of George V disgusted him. Like the farmers he regarded them as irreligious, anti-British and, with the "Red Feds", a threat to social and economic stability. Now, in the Waihi strike, he also saw an opportunity to broaden his party's support and strengthen his precarious hold on power.

The Government ordered armed police from all over the country to Waihi to enforce "law and order" and protect workers from newly formed unions that had split from the FOL – "arbitrationists" or "scabs" depending on the speaker's political point of view – who were starting work at the re-opened mine. Over 60 FOL miners were arrested for obstruction and sent to Mt Eden prison after refusing to pay fines. Fights and fires broke out regularly. Violence reached its peak on 12 November when a group of new unionists and their police escorts provocatively paraded past the miners' headquarters, and then stormed the hall. In the ensuing fight shots were fired. Constable Gerald Wade was shot in the stomach and a striker, Frederick Evans, was beaten to death. The strikers and their families were forced to leave town, many hunted through the streets by armed mobs. When the strike ended on 30 November the mining company refused to re-hire them.

Despite the Government's heavy-handed intervention in Waihi, there were a

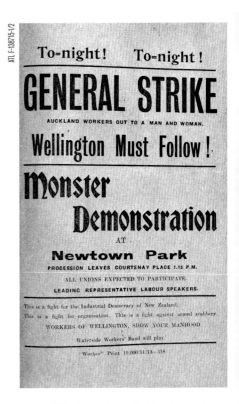

In 1913, strikes in the Huntly mines and on Wellington's wharves escalated into wide industrial action and culminated in some of New Zealand's worst industrial conflict.

Opposing Voices from the Waihi Goldminers' Strike

Thomas Johnston, arbitrationist, describes events on the day the Miners' Union Hall was stormed:

... We fell into rank, the Waikino boys intermixing. No time was lost, as each lot dismounted we fell into rough order, as soon as the last brake discharged her cargo we proceeded.

I had hardly reached the pavement when I heard the rumour, that, as the Waikino boys proceeded to the Hall the night before, with the intention of dealing out to the strikers, a charge of gelignite was thrown into their midst, from a window of the Hall....

As we proceeded, I noticed the Verbo Arbitrationist busy talking to a striker outside the Hall. When I was within a few feet of them another worker G— stepped up and ordered the striker off the footpath. He did not do so. G— seized him by the two shoulders and dumped him across the footpath, we stepping aside to let them through. This worker never even waited to see him land but rushed away. On looking to see where he was making for, I noticed a boot and one half leaf of the door which opened into a passage being closed. My one thought was, it was a trap, and that some of our boys might have been fool enough to follow the strikers in, who had been outside, and in all probability were being dealt to in a similar manner to that which we dealt to their boys yesterday.

This worker G— and another F— were in the recess of the doorway, one at each leaf when I reached them. They tried to pull them open but failed. One of the workers struck the door with his baton. The other and I tried to force it.

[On] our first trial we opened it about a foot, both of us were jammed behind, and the pressure inside was too strong. It was pulled back instantly. We tried a second time. No sooner had we grasped it, but it opened easily. As soon as I felt it coming, I sprang back sideways, with the intention of rushing in, and so we wouldn't be jammed behind the door way....

No sooner had I sidestepped than what I saw made me immediately jump sideways and backwards instead of forward. While I was in mid air I felt a lightening thud together with a lightening [sic] channel cutting sensation in my leg. Instantaneous with the report, I struck the asphalt with my feet, my leg with my hand and cried out "I'm shot," being conscious also of a gap in my rear, back to the footpath.[i]

Charles Tierney, a striker, arrives at the Miners' Union Hall to find himself in the midst of the arbitrationists:

When I got to the middle of the road in front of the butcher's shop, Delaney came across the street and caught me by the coat and threw me down.... The scabs were all around me by this time and they lifted me up and beat me and I fell down again.

After being knocked about by the crowd, I got into the butcher's shop; how I don't know. I was dazed and the next thing I remember was that the police were holding me up inside the shop. The police threw me on the floor again. I was on my back and a constable kicked me on the thigh saying, "Get up you mongrel and fight now."

I said, "I can't fight; I'm not able to fight." I was still on the ground between the constables in the shop. At this time there were about half a dozen police in the shop and others at the window. Some of them wanted to cart me round the back, and one constable of tall build and fair hair, whose name I do not know but whom I could identify, picked me up in his arms and said to the others, "You've done enough to him now; I'll look after him."

...Then the constable outside the window sang out that I had been in the shooting in the hall, the constable who was protecting me said, "No he hasn't. He's just come from home."

The outside constable replied: "Oh, before that he was shooting in the hall." They grabbed hold of me and said, "Search him for firearms."

I had none. A constable said, "Will you leave the city?"

I said, "I'll leave anywhere if you'll only get me out of this."

They said, "Go then," and as I got to the door of the shop a constable from behind kicked me in the thigh. I fell down and said, "You've broken my leg." They pushed me on to the centre of the road and Constable Skinner and another mounted trooper got each side of me and rushed me across the street to Wood's chemist shop.[ii]

[i] Thomas Henry Johnston, *Account of the Waihi Strike*, Manuscript Collection, Alexander Turnbull Library, pp. 185, 195-197.
[ii] Charles Tierney cited in Stanley Roche, *The Red and the Gold: An Informal Account of the Waihi Strike, 1912*, Oxford University Press, Auckland, 1982, p. 128.

record 35 strikes in 1912 – New Zealand had become one of the most unionised countries in the world. Militant unionists and extremist elements associated with the American-based anarchist organisation, Industrial Workers of the World, now wanted to take on the Government, the Employers' Federation and the Farmers' Union in a class war. But the FOL leaders who had sought unity with more moderate unionists after Waihi were very aware of their weaknesses. Nevertheless, that record of industrial unrest made Massey, his Reform Party and its backers even more determined to break the "Red Feds". Massey introduced legislation to curb unions' rights and proposed to make it almost impossible for any union outside the arbitration system to strike.

In October 1913 the miners at Huntly went on strike just as a dispute involving Wellington shipwrights suddenly escalated. Within 10 days most miners were on strike and the Dominion's ports were closed. The Government saw a serious threat of civil disorder and disruption to trade and called for volunteers to help maintain law and order. The response was overwhelming, from town and more especially the country. The Farmers' Union rode in to the cities to save their livelihoods, and to smash the "Red Feds" and the union movement forever:

> *The time has arrived when the farmers should stand up for their rights, and if others would not help them shift their produce then they must do it themselves.*[7]

Armed special constables known as "Specials" or "Massey's Cossacks" converged on the two main port cities. Strikers also armed themselves. Marines from two British ships paraded with drawn bayonets on Auckland's wharves in the wake of street riots and arson. A lawyer, returning home from duties as a special constable in Wellington, insisted his young daughter leave the turbulent city: "My father came

ATL F-80609-1/2

Invention and new technologies excited and transformed the new century. The capital city's GPO (above) was illuminated for the coronation of King George V in 1911. The previous year the country's first coin public telephone was installed in Wellington and by 1919 a growing number of affluent homes had their own phone.

ATL G-16292-1/1 (Tesla Studios Collection)

Strikers and protesters scatter as mounted police canter up Wellington's Featherston Street during the 1913 general strike.

ATL F-160127-1/2

back in a frightful state and said, 'This is the French Revolution all over again and you must be sent away to the country.'"[8]

The rhetoric certainly had the flavour of revolution. The capital city's evening paper reported Harry Holland of the FOL, later the first leader of the Labour Party, saying that "nothing could be too bad for a man who plays the traitor to his class in a strike"; and quoted another FOL leader and future Labour Prime Minister, Peter Fraser:

> As long as there was no attempt to take the bread away from the workers' wives and children there would be no violence, but, if an effort was instituted to work the cargo by scabs then it would have to be prevented even if everyone of the strikers was shot dead.[9]

On 8 November 1913, 1,600 Specials and police charged and seized the Auckland wharves. "Massey's Cossacks" opened Wellington's port by force, firing guns and batoning anyone in their paths, innocent or otherwise. *The Sydney Morning Herald* described it as a kind of civil war between town and country. The strikers and unionists used another term, more familiar in the Old World:

> … [I]t was a class war – worker against employer, farmer against townie – an uneven conflict well exemplified in the potent images that survive in the photographs of the time, of special constables on horseback and strikers on foot.[10]

Captain Scott Sails for Antarctica

Robert Falcon Scott's ill-fated expedition to Antarctica cast off from Port Chalmers at half past two on a sunny afternoon in November 1910. The people of Dunedin turned out to farewell them with sirens, whistles, detonators and rockets and in a fleet of pleasure craft and ferries. They believed they were witness to the start of another great triumph for the Empire – winning the race to the South Pole. The next morning, 30 November 1910, the *Otago Daily Times* described the *Terra Nova*'s departure.

> … *Captain Scott, equipped with his powerful binoculars, stood holding on by the maintopmast backstay talking happily with the people on the Plucky's bridge, and as absolutely unconcerned as if he had nothing to do with the matter. He spoke, however, of the call the* Terra Nova *would make at the Campbell Islands, and of the stormy 2,000 miles which just at present separated her from the great ice barrier; of the wonderful luck that Sir E[rnest] Shackleton had in discovering the pass leading cross-country to the great plateau. The passengers on the Plucky stood on the hatches and seats and absolutely feasted their eyes on the decks of the* Terra Nova, *where all the most interesting things in the world seemed to have been compressed. The dogs looked down upon the water, away to the green receding shores, and then at the people in the tug, with a wave of the tail.*
>
> *But it is hard to say good-bye. It was a case of aching hearts and smiling faces. Ladies on the tug were pressing mementos, brooches, and small trinkets upon the blue-jackets who leant over the bulwarks and pinned the keepsakes on the great burly bosoms. The sailors gave in exchange cap ribbons and the like. It was wonderfully simple, homely, and earnest, and, for that very reason, powerfully tragic. Every farewell is a tragedy….*
>
> *Every eye watched her till she vanished round the headland. Later in the afternoon she was seen a speck on the horizon, and this gave place to a wisp of smoke, which was soon lost in the haze of a summer's evening.*[i]

Scott and his party reached the South Pole on 17 January 1912, 35 days after Amundsen. Scott perished with four of his companions on the return journey to base camp. A month later the *Terra Nova* sailed into Oamaru and New Zealanders were the first to hear the news of their deaths.

---

i *Otago Daily Times*, Dunedin, 30 November 1910 cited in Robin Bromby (ed.), *An Eyewitness History of New Zealand*, Currey O'Neil Ross Pty Ltd, Victoria Australia, 1985, pp. 102-3.

Union response to the take-over of the wharves was immediate – the Seamen's Union ordered its members out and in Auckland 14 more unions went on strike, including the newspaper boys. The country's largest city ground to a halt. Incredibly, one of the British ships returned to port and trained its guns on the city. "Red Fed" leaders, including Holland and Fraser, were arrested and charged with inciting violence and sedition. Holland was jailed for a year. But Prime Minister Massey was warned to stay out of the conflict. Both sides wanted a fight to the finish and a clear victor.

The police and Specials soon won control; ships were loaded and sailed for Britain. After 58 days, the strike was over. It was the worst industrial conflict the country had known and while the level of violence was far less than other countries had experienced, it still did not sit comfortably with many workers. They had been intimidated by both the Specials and the "Red Feds". Others were more afflicted by apathy.

One may sum up the public opinion of the country by saying that it is temperate and reasonable rather than enlightened and foreseeing. In domestic affairs it thinks of comfort first, tolerates abuses, is glad to throw responsibilities upon Government, prefers to mitigate the consequences of political evils rather than exert itself to remove their causes.... [11]

Although the unions were beaten, they had not been destroyed. The FOL lost two-thirds of its membership but overall union numbers remained roughly the same. However, their leaders realised they could not win an industrial confrontation against the combined forces of Government, employers and farmers. Their tactics would have to change – they would have to win political power to achieve their goals. In 1916, the United Labour Party and the Social Democratic Party, together with a range of moderate and radical unions, came together to form the New Zealand Labour Party. It would become the longest-surviving political party in the country.

While New Zealand recovered its equilibrium, Europe was fast losing its stability. When a 19-year-old terminally tubercular, Bosnian Serb nationalist stepped out into a Sarajevo street on 28 June 1914 and shot the Austrian archduke Franz Ferdinand and his wife, Sophie, he not only killed the heir to the Austrian throne, he precipitated the First World War. The assassin wanted Bosnia, at that time part of the Austrian-Hungarian Empire, to join Greater Serbia. Austria was convinced the Serbian Government was involved and declared war on Serbia. By 4 August, most of Europe was at war.

The assassination was all that was needed to start a conflagration that had been in the making for years. The four principal fuels were nationalism, imperialism, militarism and a system of alliances which ensured almost all the main European powers would be involved – Great Britain, France and Russia against Germany and Austria-Hungary. Aligned with Britain were her dominions, the most loyal of which was New Zealand. Charles Plunkett, a young Auckland seaman, feared the worst when he heard news of the conflict's spread at church:

Sunday. At 11am Mass and to Vespers in evening. Announced from Pulpit, Germany had declared war against Russia. Fine sermon on Peace by Reverend Father O'Donnell from Victoria. Fear we are in for bad times, and glad it's come before I started building, money is sure to be tight – [and] business bad if England is embroiled which seems inevitable. [12]

Whakatane District Museum & Gallery Collection, F469-1

In September 1914 an explosion on White Island spewed out a great lahar which completely overwhelmed the island's sulphur works. The ten men working there vanished, along with the factory, living quarters, boats and wharf. Rescuers searched in vain beneath the active volcano in rubble that was still hot and full of boulders. The sole survivor was one of the island's five cats. He lived out his life in Opotiki, the reputed father of at least half the town's cats and named, appropriately, Peter the Great.

ATL C-21991-GT

LIBERTY LOAN.

MEN AND MONEY.

NEW ZEALAND HAS THE MEN and they have proved themselves equal to the world's best and bravest soldiers. NEW ZEALAND HAS THE —— MONEY, without it we could not provide for the men. ——

BOTH ARE NEEDED TO WIN THE WAR.

You must, however, put your money into action, and each help according to his means.

WAR LOAN CERTIFICATES

—— ENABLE ALL TO DO THIS. ——

for 13s.	you can buy a £1 Certificate.	for 16s.	you can buy a £1 Certificate.
for £6 10s.	you can buy a £10 Certificate.	for £8	you can buy a £10 Certificate.
for £65	you can buy a £100 Certificate.	for £80	you can buy a £100 Certificate.
Repayable in TEN Years.		Repayable in FIVE Years.	

For those of small means there will also be issued POST OFFICE WAR BONDS bearing interest payable half-yearly at FIVE PER CENT. per annum. These will be £100 each, and the revenue from them will not be free of income-tax.

You Help Your Country—You Help Yourself
and by doing so you will materially HELP TO BEAT THE ENEMY.

LET YOUR ACTION BE PROMPT

I am relying on every man, woman, and child to do their best.

JOSEPH GEORGE WARD,
Minister of Finance.

Wellington, 15th August, 1917.

War brought out the best and worst in the country – fierce patriotism and loyalty to Britain, self-sacrifice, bigotry, sectional jealousies and a manic and petty xenophobia which led to people of German origin being hounded, stripped of their citizenship and imprisoned. Families of northern European extraction were abused and harassed because of their suspiciously foreign names, the word "Holstein" was deleted from the official name of Friesian cattle, and "Rangitikei Lutheran congregations, whose sons served at the front, were accused of observing the Kaiser's birthday and their children's school rail passes were withdrawn".[13]

A new strain of fanatical anti-Catholicism promoted by the Protestant Political Association linked peace sermons in some Catholic churches with the Pope and socialism, and claimed they were all in league with the enemy, Germany. When the Mayor of Auckland, Mr Gunson, formally welcomed the visiting Papal delegate, the Loyal Orange Lodge No.70 issued a pamphlet attacking him:

It is time to wake up to the menace of Romanism. It is time to make men like the Mayor realise that we regard them as betrayers. It is time to investigate the place and power of Rome in our Police and Civil Service. It is time to deal with the anti-Protestant Press. It is time to repudiate with scorn any suggestion of welcome to the representative of the friend and Ally of Germany. It is time to fight for our Liberty and our Country.[14]

ANZAC soldiers at Gallipoli, Turkey. The miseries of trench warfare became emblematic of the First World War.

Auctioning tickets for a concert in Nelson to aid the war fund, raising money and spirits at the same time.

The Mayoress, Mrs Gunson, was castigated for visiting Mother Mary Joseph Aubert's nursing home where the poor, the slum dwellers and indigent received free, badly-needed care.

New Zealand rushed to support England and Empire and within days Britain asked the Government if it could send a force to seize control of the German colony of Western Samoa, 2000 kilometres north-east of Auckland. Just over 1400 men sailed two weeks later and took the islands without a shot being fired, the first German territory to be occupied by the British Empire in the war. These were the first of more than 100,000 men to leave the country to fight in a war many believed would soon be over but which was to last four grim years.

I was walking through the country... and the people cheered. You could understand it – a long period of what was comparative prosperity... no great events happening for a long time... everybody rushed of course to enlist. That was the spirit. A lot of folks sang patriotic songs and they cheered. Folk talked about the great sacrifices of young men that would be made.[15]

The rate of sacrifice was more than anyone could have imagined – 42 per cent of men between the ages of 19 and 45 were in active service overseas; 16,781 New Zealanders lost their lives abroad and another 45,000 were wounded, a huge 58 per cent casualty rate.[16] The memory of war lingered for years in the figures of thousands of permanently disabled and sick ex-servicemen.

The first public euphoria dissipated rapidly during the New Zealand Division's first long and doomed engagement at Gallipoli. The casualty rate was an almost unbelievable 88 per cent. A survivor later described the muddled landing in the early hours of 25 April 1915:

> *… the carnage was indescribable. Many were gunned down while still in the water…. Corpses lay in rows on the sand or half way up the cliffs, men lay about cut, bleeding and dying… the Turks had held their fire until the boats grounded, then they let loose a fusilade…. That night on Anzac beach conditions were worsened by a steady drizzle which chilled the [troops] as they stumbled among the scores of wounded lying on the beach.[17]*

After eight months of hellish fighting with the unbearable heat of summer giving way to winter blizzards, and with the campaign's goal of clearing the Dardanelles no closer than when they started, the Allied troops were evacuated. It was the only part of the entire enterprise to be carried out successfully.

Although they had not thought it possible, conditions worsened when in April 1916 the troops moved to the Western Front and began two and a half years of trench warfare in France and Belgium. There, at a front line that often moved only yards at a time, backwards and forwards, they experienced mud that sucked like quicksand, winters of snow and ice, the stench of men and animals left too long unburied, and war's newest and most silent weapon – poisonous gas.

> *[It] looked as though a herd of prehistoric monsters had chewed and rooted up the earth for miles around. Not a sign of anything green and not a chance for anything to grow. It was part of the Front that had been taken and retaken so often that it presented an appearance of indescribable chaos. Everywhere there was mud and slush and men always floundering through it by tracks and duckwalks that were always being blown up. It was told that a million men had fallen there…. It was still being shelled and the yawning mouths of the countless shell-holes were ready to suck in the living men who moved day and night among them like maggots in the slime.[18]*

As the fighting continued, the death toll rose… and rose. It becomes easy to see why at its end people talked about the Great War and, more hopefully, "the war to end all wars". How could a small country survive such casualties – at the Somme, in a single month in

ATL G-1791-1X8

Soldiers commemorate All Saints Day at a church in Selle, France.

ATL G-1806-1X8 (R.S.A. Collection)

New Zealand artillery in action, New Year's Day, 1918.

ETTIE ROUT

In 1916, a young socialist journalist from Christchurch described the conditions of the Wazza in Cairo where Kiwi soldiers went looking for recreation when on leave from war:

The streets and alleys were filthy with offal and the stenches abominable, but they were crowded with men in khaki. There were several drinking shops and dancing halls quite open to the streets, and hundreds of soldiers were in these. Outside notorious brothels long queues of soldiers waited their turn. One open door revealed a stairway with lines of soldiers going up and down... Bedizened and lustful women thronged the streets and doorways, many of them being embraced by soldiers.[i]

Ettie Rout (centre) with the first group of the New Zealand Volunteer Sisterhood to go overseas.

Ettie Rout had gone to the Middle East as a volunteer nurse and social worker to set up a canteen and the Volunteer Sisterhood to inspect brothels and instruct and issue the soldiers with prophylactics (condoms). By 1915 a number of Kiwi soldiers had caught VD. In fact, the first casualties to return from the war were those wounded in "horizontal combat", sent home ignominiously to be placed in isolation on an island in Otago harbour.

Rout lobbied the politicians and military authorities to authorise the free distribution of condoms to the troops. The authorities prevaricated, fearing that if women found out they would try to stop their husbands and sons from joining, and slow recruitment. They also were concerned that it would appear they were condoning and even encouraging such behaviour. When news of Rout's work leaked out, a group of women, led by Lady Anna Stout, an early member of the National Council of Women, petitioned the Government to order her home immediately.

The problem was never officially dealt with but Rout continued to distribute information and condoms. Later in the war some senior officers organised condoms for their troops and the incidence of VD dropped significantly. Nevertheless sexual infections from returning soldiers had a detrimental effect on the health and fertility of women at home.

---

[i] Ettie Rout cited in Michael King, *New Zealanders at War*, Heinemann Publishers, Auckland, p. 95.

1916, 1,560 Kiwis dead; 3,700 casualties at Messines; 640 men from the New Zealand Division killed and 2,100 wounded in the space of a few hours in one battle at Passchendaele.[19]

Soldiers of the Pioneer Battalion in hot weather kit.

It was a pitch dark night, with a drizzling rain falling, and the trench we were holding was a series of shallow shell-holes, hastily connected by strenuous digging, in ground which had been so constantly ploughed by shells that it had become "yeasty" in texture. The crumbling, rain-soaked sides of the trench came sliding down each time a shell landed near, and the only respite for the sentries was strenuously shovelling out the sticky soil. We had waited impatiently for darkness to fall, so that the stretcher-bearers could work on the slope behind us, where a line of khaki figures, some moving and crying pitifully, stretched to the trench where we had started the attack.... I shivered in my soaked clothes as I floundered and squelched about the muddy ditch with sparing shots from my flare-pistol, occasionally squatting down to clumsily and laboriously peel a flare-cartridge, which had become wet and too swollen to fit in the barrel.[20]

H-474

New Zealand soldiers on the frontline
on the Somme in April 1918.

Enlistment was voluntary initially, but in August 1916, as losses mounted in France and volunteer numbers dropped, enrolment for military service became compulsory. A national register of all men eligible to serve had revealed that of the 196,000 available, 33,700 did not want to take part in any kind of military service and 44,300 said they would only serve in New Zealand. Conscientious objectors were treated increasingly harshly, charged with sedition and thrown in jail for the duration of the war. Some were sent to the frontlines of the Western Front, and condemned to what the army called No.1 Field Punishment:

[The poles] were willow stumps, six to eight inches in diameter and twice the height of a man, and [he] placed me against one of them. It was inclined forward out of perpendicular. Almost always afterward he picked the same one for me. I stood with my back to it and he tied me to it by the ankles, knees and wrists. He was an expert at the job, and he knew how to pull and strain at the ropes till they cut into the flesh and completely stopped the circulation. When I was taken off my hands were always black with congested blood.

My hands were taken round behind the pole, tied together and pulled well up it, straining and cramping the muscles and forcing them into an unnatural position. Most knots will slacken a little after a time. His never did. The slope of the post brought me into a hanging position, causing a large part of my weight to come on my arms, and I could get no proper grip with my feet on the ground, as it was worn away round the pole and my toes were consequently lower than my heels ....

A few minutes after the sergeant had left me, I began to think of

DOMINION OF NEW ZEALAND.

MILITARY SERVICE ACT, 1916.

ENROLMENT OF

EXPEDITIONARY FORCE RESERVE

BY PROCLAMATIONS dated respectively 1st and 2nd September, 1916, the enrolment of the Reserve is directed. Enrolment MUST be made not later than 15th September (First Division) or 16th September (Second Division).

RESERVISTS' OBLIGATIONS.

The Reserve consists of men not less than 20 and under 46 years of age.

THE National Register is the basis of the Expeditionary Force Reserve Registers.

Men **not already registered** must supply enrolment-card not later than 16th September, 1916.

Men already registered need not supply an enrolment-card, but must, not later than 16th September, 1916, **notify present address** if place of abode has altered since registration.

Men **reaching military age** or **arriving in Dominion** after 16th September, 1916, must supply enrolment-card within fourteen days thereafter.

After enrolment every reservist who **changes his place of abode** must notify new address within fourteen days thereafter.

The Act makes the reservist's obligation to do any of the above things **a personal one**, and he is not relieved by information previously given to recruiting officer or committee.

REMEMBER!

IT IS YOUR DUTY
TO ENROL.

For the Protection of Reservists, certificates of enrolment will be issued as soon as practicable after receipt of application on form provided.

Voluntary Recruits not accepted for service will have this fact recorded in the Register on supplying proof to the Government Statistician that they have volunteered.

REMEMBER!

YOU MUST DO
YOUR DUTY.

Enrolled men have the **chance of the ballot.**

Men not enrolled may be sent **straight into camp.**

Employers are **forbidden to employ** men who are not enrolled.

Men who fail to notify change of address may become liable on a **charge of desertion.**

EMPLOYERS' OBLIGATIONS.

Employers must not employ a reservist who is not enrolled.
Penalty on conviction—Minimum fine, £20.

Employers must not employ a deserter.
Penalty on conviction—Minimum fine, £50, or imprisonment not exceeding three months.

ONUS OF PROOF in every case is **ON THE DEFENDANT.**

Call at nearest post-office For cards, forms, information, and assistance.

(By Order.) **MALCOLM FRASER,**
Government Statistician.

New Zealand troop transport
in Palestine.

In the Nelson Red Cross Depot piles of hospital
supplies wait to be packed and sent to Egypt and
England during WWI.

the length of my sentence and it rose up before me like a mountain. The pain grew steadily worse until by the end of half-an-hour it seemed absolutely unendurable. Between my set teeth I said: "Oh God, this is too much. I can't bear it." But I could not allow myself the relief of groaning as I did not want to give the guards the satisfaction of hearing me. The mental effect was almost as frightful as the physical. I felt I was going mad. That I should be stuck up on a pole suffering this frightful torture, a human scarecrow for men to stare at and wonder at, seemed part of some impossible nightmare that could not continue. At the very worst strength came to me and I knew I would not surrender. The battle was won, and though the suffering increased rather than decreased as the days wore on, I never had to fight it again.[21]

Anyone speaking out against conscription was also charged with sedition and several Labour politicians including Peter Fraser and Robert Semple were jailed. But despite the losses and the carnage, the protesters were a distinct minority. Duty was due England and we were not ready to question it or count the cost: war on the Western Front killed 13,250 men and wounded 35,000 more.

Yet for many men, the battlefield was also where they first realised that New Zealanders were not carbon copies of the British, that they had their own national characteristics. It was at the Battle of the Somme that the distinctive "lemon squeezer" hat was issued for the first time; and it was in France that the ANZACs – the Australian and New Zealand Army Corps – became known as "digger". From within those years of terrible warfare New Zealand (and Australian) troops discovered the first indicators of a sense of nationhood, distinct from the "mother country".

Meanwhile the New Zealand Rifle Brigade was in the Middle East fighting the Turks and defending the Suez Canal. Their desert environment was as much an enemy as the men they were fighting and hostile in a totally different way to the Western Front:

As the day advanced the fearful heat wave descended on us and our drinking water soon gave out and our food [from] our camel train got cut off and there was only the evil-smelling brackish well water in swampy spots.

By now the wind was like a blast furnace and men began to double up... many collapsed and in the middle of this prostration the Turks were announced. The men were swaying about as they tried to mount the guns on the horses, for escape was the only thing to attempt. Fortunately, it was soon apparent that the Turks were suffering from heat too, and after a few shots they were seen retiring.

Then I fell off my horse and for some hours men kept pouring well water over me and the others who were down, and ultimately pulled us round.... As soon as the fierce sun went down and the blast furnace of red hot sand cooled off we mounted our horses and rode home still very thirsty and feeling rather sorry for ourselves.[22]

A Maori Prophet in Zion

The First World War brought the Maori tribes and leaders who were struggling for internal autonomy into conflict with the Government and with Maori MPs and leaders who had been educated by Europeans. This second group saw the war as a chance for Maori to prove themselves and their loyalty by signing up to fight for Britain and the Empire and they worked hard to get Maori to enlist. Opposition to Maori conscription was centred on Waikato leaders Te Rata Mahuta and Te Puea Herangi and some Tuhoe and Taranaki leaders. The Maori King insisted none of his people should be conscripted or volunteer until land confiscated during the reign of his great-grandfather had been returned.

Rua Kenana Hepetipa emerged as a visionary leader of the Tuhoe in 1905 when the tribe was fighting to retain control of its land which although promised to Tuhoa had been opened up illegally to prospecting. Rua founded Maungapohatu, his Zion and City of God on earth, and built there a huge round wooden temple and parliament. He proclaimed himself the predicted successor to Te Kooti, and identified with the Israelites. He preached everlasting life for Maori who joined him and the eventual removal of Pakeha from New Zealand. By 1909 he had more than 1,000 followers and his message of self governance had earned him the dislike and distrust of Pakeha and Maori parliamentarians.

In 1916, the Government re-issued old sly-grogging charges on which he had been tried previously. Rua refused to answer the summons. In reality the Government wanted opposition to Maori recruitment out of the way. It also wanted to put an end to any promotion of Maori independence. At the beginning of April, 60 armed police marched to Rua's settlement in the Urewera and forcibly arrested Rua and 31 of his followers. In the confusion and violence they shot and killed two of his people, one of them his son. Four policemen were injured. The confrontation has been called "the last shooting in the Anglo-Maori wars".[i]

Rua (fourth from left) handcuffed to his son Whatu and under arrest.

Rua was charged with sly-grogging and making seditious comments and after the longest trial in New Zealand up until 1977, he was sentenced to 12 months' hard labour followed by 18 months' imprisonment. The judge made only too clear the real issue – Pakeha authority:

> Now you learn that the law has a long arm, and that it can reach you however far back into the recesses of the forest you travel, and that in every corner of the great Empire to which we belong the King's law can reach anyone who offends against it. That is the lesson which you and your people should learn from this trial.[ii]

Many of Rua's followers believed he also had been shot and when he returned to his people in 1918 some regarded the fact he was still alive as proof he was the son of God. However, over the following decades people drifted away from Maungapohatu and although he continued to lead a smaller group until his death in 1937, any serious talk of autonomy and independence for Maori was over.

[i] M P K Sorrenson, *Maori and Pakeha*, in Geoffrey W. Rice (ed.), *The Oxford History of New Zealand*, Second revised edition, Oxford University Press, Auckland, 1992, p. 161.
[ii] *New Zealand Herald* 4 August 1916, cited ibid., p. 294.

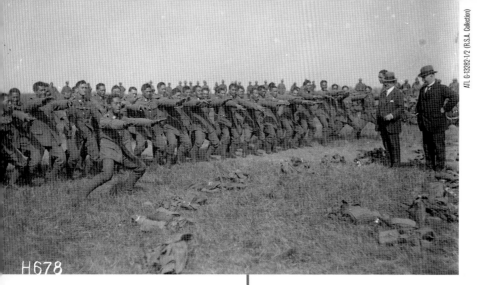

France 1918: the Maori Battalion welcomes
William Ferguson Massey and Sir Joseph
Ward with a mass haka.

Home from the horrors of the Front, wounded
soldiers practise the more gentle skills of needlework.

Nursing staff and soldiers take time out from
hostilities in a tug-of-war at Etaples, France,
a few months before the end of the war.

When the Mounted Rifles finally sailed for
home in June 1919 they left behind 500
dead and had counted 1,200 wounded in
three years. Looking at our casualty rate,
one of the highest in the Empire, soldier,
writer and politician John A. Lee considered
the cost of such loss to a young developing
country: "Further away from the war, with a
greater percentage of casualties, greater
blood sacrifice, you realise what a terrific
blow it must have been.…"[23]

At home, Massey and Ward, unlikely and reluctant partners
in a wartime Coalition Government, had spent their time
shuttling between London and Wellington to represent New
Zealand interests, domestic and frontline. Like the fighting men,
they too had experienced a similar but much less vivid sense of
separation from our traditional "Home". But at the same time,
economics was binding the country more tightly to England.

Britain's prewar recession had been pushing New Zealand to
break our export dependence on her and start looking for new
markets. But within weeks of England going to war the
Government signed a deal committing all the country's meat,
wool and dairy products to Britain's needs. Prices were set for
the duration of the hostilities.

As this "war to end all wars" dragged slowly to a close, it
loosed a final scourge, a world-wide epidemic, carried home by
returning soldiers. Disease, and death from disease, were still
prevalent in the 1910s, especially among the poor and Maori.
There were 11 cases of plague in Auckland between 1910 and
1911, and two deaths. Typhoid rates were high and the mortality
rate was climbing steadily. For the first time more people died of cancer than
tuberculosis (TB). Between 1912 and 1921 official statistics recorded thousands of
Pakeha deaths – nearly 6,000 from pulmonary TB, 415 of typhoid fever, 258 from
scarlet fever, and 1,282 from an increasingly virulent strain of diphtheria. The largest
recorded outbreak of smallpox in New Zealand, brought into the country by a
Mormon missionary, occurred between 1913
and 1914. Maori settlements in the Auckland
province were most affected and it was
estimated that over a hundred Pakeha and
almost 2,000 Maori were infected, and some 55
Maori died. Fear of the disease was widespread.

*… I rode on into Whananaki, to be greeted by
the news that all the Maoris were down with
the dread disease. The storekeeper kindly
offered me a bed for the night, and he and his
big family made me very comfortable. The
way he served out stores was as follows.*

A Maori would come along and stand by a certain post some distance away, and shout out what he wanted to buy. The storekeeper would call out the cost, and the Maori would hold up each coin, then drop it into a jar of strong disinfectant. The goods would then be tied to the end of a long pole, and poked out to the buyer.

When morning came, I was feeling rather afraid of my coming visit to these Maoris, but it was impossible to turn back, so on I went.... Oh, will I ever forget it. Little children, men and women, all covered with smallpox and horrible to behold. Men so bad that they could not bear tight clothing, just wearing a shirt and a sheet draped around their legs. Little children crying out as they tried to stand on their sore feet. These people asked me to stay the night. I could not. They prepared food for me, and I could only bear to eat fish, because it was boiled and there was little fear of infection in it.[24]

Tahupotiki Wiremu Ratana (left) was faith healer, religious founder and political leader at a time when the fortunes of Maori were at a low ebb – ravaged by diseases such as smallpox and influenza, poverty, lack of education, superstition and the continuing loss of land. He began his faith healing after WWI and was so successful thousands sought his help. A settlement, known as Ratana Pa, grew up around his house. He established the Ratana Church and within a few years it had 22,000 members. (In the early 1980s it was the seventh largest church in the country.) In 1928 he turned his attention to politics and by 1943 all four Maori parliamentary seats were held by Ratana candidates.

But all of these outbreaks were completely overshadowed by the 1918 influenza pandemic which came in two waves. The first began in July 1918, reached its height in September and then began to ebb slightly in October. This was a mild strain of influenza. The second wave exploded suddenly and with shocking strength in November and infected 40 per cent of the population, as the indefatigable diarist Charles Plunkett noted:

November 10 Sunday. No Mass anywhere today, chopped on account of epidemic. At various cases with Aunty and want assistance badly. Aunty stayed the night at Bartletts (bad case). In to Newmarket for drugs and hard to get.[25]

Schools, shops and industry closed; public transport almost stopped running.

My clearest memory of those weeks of dread is of a November morning, warm and still, when I stood on the edge of an empty street and watched a lorry, piled skywards with unvarnished coffins, lurching towards an undertaker's yard around the nearest corner.[26]

Public meetings of any kind were prohibited and pubs were closed by the Public Health Officer. Ida Reilly, an 18-year-old at the Auckland telephone exchange where 80 per cent of the staff went home sick, was one of the few who worked right through.

It was a terrible time. You just didn't know who was going to die next. It was very noticeable that in times of trouble everybody tried to help, and you were just glad to speak to anyone, friend or foe.... All you saw on the streets were sad and solemn people, hearses and ambulances, and that terrible lost and lonely feeling....[27]

During November and December 6,700 died from the Black Flu. That was more than that had died

Desperate times, desperate measures. An inhalation chamber set up by the Public Health Department in Christchurch to try to fight the 1918 influenza pandemic by disinfecting throat and lungs.

A Rowdy Night at Tolaga Bay

Florence Harsant was a young temperance worker who travelled the upper half of the North Island on horseback, setting up Maori Women's Temperance Unions and preaching abstinence to the Maori. She recalls:

There was a bad typhoid epidemic raging in the settlement, so I had to choose between a hotel or private Boarding house. I chose the latter. After making arrangements for a meeting to be held next day, I had my tea and went to bed in a small room on the ground floor, taking the precaution to lock my door and barricade my window, having been told that Tolaga Bay was a wild town. About 2 a.m. I was wakened by a man rattling my door handle. He fell down outside. Another came along, swearing horribly, fell over the first man, tried my door. He finally found an open door across the hall, and dragged his mate there with him. After an hour of comparative quiet, I heard a fearful row upstairs, and peered out the window. Three men were fighting and snarling like dogs, just above my room. Then a woman appeared on the scene, screaming and shouting at them. She drove them out on to a small landing leading to an outside stairway, and was hitting at them with a broom. Finally she drove one of the men down into the wet yard. I barricaded my window a bit more, but was unable to sleep again. Soon the noise subsided into mumblings. Early in the morning two young men were using the bathroom just next door to me, and I could hear them discussing the night's performance. The combatants were the landlady, her drunken husband and his two drunken companions. They chuckled over her appearance in bedraggled dressing gown, oversize slippers, hair in curlers, and armed with the broom! When I thought all the men had dispersed, I opened my door. Straight opposite I could see a man lying, his head on one stretcher, his feet on another, his body suspended between, and his mate curled up on the floor. I went to the sitting room – a drunk occupied the sofa; the dining room – full of drunks. I proceeded to the kitchen to pay for my bed. The landlady suggested breakfast but I told her I could not leave quickly enough. She assured me such a thing had never happened before, but I was told later that her house was the weekend rendezvous of all drunken bushmen.
I bought some buns and a glass of milk at a dairy for my breakfast.[i]

---

[i] Florence Harsant, *My Everyday Life as Travelling Organiser for Maori Women on Behalf of the Women's Christian Temperance Union*, Special Collections, Auckland City Library, pp. 75-76.

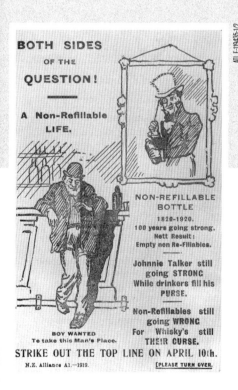

ATL F-119435-1/2

from influenza in New Zealand since figures showing the cause of death were first compiled 46 years earlier. The exact number of Maori deaths is unknown but it is estimated that 2,160 died, 4 per cent of the total Maori population, a death rate twice as high as that of Pakeha.[28] A Royal Commission blamed poor housing and badly serviced subdivisions as major causes for the spread of the disease, but influenza took rich and poor alike. Auckland was the worst affected, so much so that official celebrations to mark Armistice Day on 11 November 1918 were postponed until the following year; Dunedin suffered the least. The virulent strain spread from Auckland to Western Samoa, where one quarter of the population was killed by the disease, the highest national death rate recorded during the pandemic.

The re-integration of 70,000 men, almost half of them wounded, back into the civilian population produced all kinds of strains. In 1919, divorce rates soared, and women's expectations plunged. Women who had left home life for the first time to replace men in the paid workforce now found they were expected to return home. The war years had sent contradictory messages to women and women themselves responded in two distinctly different ways. Those women who took the opportunity to go out to work moved into the growing area of clerical work, became shop assistants and, briefly, joined the Public Service. Unlike other countries, male unions ensured women were shut out of skilled trades. Even more women believed their role was to "keep the home fires burning" and restricted their war efforts to cooking, knitting, sewing and raising money for the fighting men.

The war gave added impetus to the movement to reform women's clothing: the need for simpler and more practical styles for women entering the workforce or active in fund-raising, fewer servants to take care of the elaborate clothes of wealthier women, and the shortage and rationing of materials. The new freedom of movement that came with shorter skirts, simpler clothing styles and the loss of boned corsets was welcomed. Much to the alarm of the older generation, young women began to wear lipstick and some even smoked. But sexual stereotyping of appropriate male and female roles had actually strengthened.

The decade ended very differently from the way it began. It was an uneasy peace in which New Zealanders and their Government sought to keep the country safe from contamination by an outside world filled with political, social and artistic revolution. New Zealanders were worse off economically than they had been in 1910 or 1914. After all they had been through, they did not expect a recession and few understood that with the end of Britain's guaranteed purchase of our agricultural products, they would no longer receive the premium prices they had been earning in British markets.

By the end of the decade, the countries involved in the Great War had realised that the losses of life and property and the decline of wealth and prestige were far greater than any had anticipated. Postwar settlements left few of the combatants happy. The French writer Romain Rolland wrote, "Sad peace! Laughable interlude between the massacres of peoples!"[29] Twenty years later his words would seem a prophesy.

ATL G-22163-GT

Prime Minister Sir Joseph Ward wanted every working man to own a motor car. There was a growing range of makes on offer.

ATL F-710-1/2-MNZ (Making New Zealand Collection)

A rough road through the King Country, photographed on the first trip by car from Wellington to Auckland via Taihape, Taumarunui and Te Kuiti, in 1912.

Maori images were used increasingly on material to promote New Zealand and its attractions and the country was widely referred to as "Maoriland". The postcard below shows a "Maori maiden" in an artist's classical interpretation of traditional dress beside a picture of the Victoria Bridge in Christchurch, ca 1910.

The legend of Hinemoa was the inspiration, and title, of the first locally made feature film featuring Hera Tawhai Rogers as Hinemoa. It began playing at the Lyric Theatre in Auckland in August 1914. The film has not survived.

Stills Collection, New Zealand Film Archive

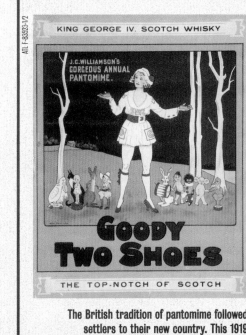

ATL F-85623-1/2

The British tradition of pantomime followed settlers to their new country. This 1919 production toured Australia and New Zealand. Theatre, vaudeville, musicals, concerts, ballet, visiting star performers and shows by enthusiastic amateurs were still the main entertainment. The arrival of "talkies" at the end of the 1920s would kill off vaudeville completely and put theatre into decline.

The Elworthy Family
Down-to-earth Gentry

If there is a name synonymous with the land, farming and Cantabrian gentility, it is Elworthy. Edward Elworthy first began farming in South Canterbury in the 1860s, sharing a leasehold on a farm called Pareora with another settler, David Innes. Gradually he bought the other half of the farm, now known as Holme Station. By 1890 Edward and his wife Sara had transformed Holme Station, with its mix of hill country and flat land, into a run of about 100,000 acres. Edward died from a heart attack in 1899, aged 62, and obituaries were full of praise for his contributions to the land and the community.

In his will, Edward provided legacies for his four daughters, Maude, Edith, Ethel and Muriel and left an annuity for his wife Sara. He carefully planned the subdivision of his estate between his three sons. His eldest, Arthur, was given the homestead block, which retained the name Holme Station and was sold in the 1940s. Herbert inherited Craigmore, and Percy was given Gordon's Valley.

The Elworthys continued to have strong links with the Mother Country, and sent sons there for their education.

Between them, the families of Herbert and Percy produced two down-to-earth knights: Percy's son, Sir (Sam) Charles Elworthy who went on to become Lord Elworthy of Timaru and the County of Somerset and eventually, Governor of Windsor Castle; and Sir Peter Elworthy, Herbert's grandson, the prominent businessman and former President of Federated Farmers.

It all began on the land, which is where it continues for some of the Elworthys today. One of them is Sam's son, Chris, who manages Gordon's Valley, but owns a quarter of the land and half the farm in partnership. He recalls the way his grandfather Percy stirred his interest in New Zealand:

I'd always been interested in farming.... Always been fond of animals and even as a kid I can remember going down to the local dairy farm and being allowed to milk a cow.

When my grandparents came over to England, my grandfather would tell stories about Gordon's Valley and about farming in New Zealand and I used to think it sounded a pretty good life.

Grandfather Percy was a hunting-fishing-shooting type, who married the youngest daughter of New Zealand's Archbishop Julius, Bertha Julius, a well-educated and very musical woman. During the First World War Percy fought with the Life Guards, in France.

Edward Elworthy's legacy — his children and their partners. From left, back row: William Bond, Ella Julius, Herbert, Francis Baber and Alice Maude. Middle row seated: Ethel, Arthur, Granny Elworthy (Edward's mother) and Edith. Front row: Muriel and Percy.

Bertha and Percy in later years.

His family lived in London while he was away fighting and at war's end he returned with them to the peace of Gordon's Valley, where Percy's sons were tutored:

When they reached the stage of going to secondary school, they were both sent to Marlborough, which was a well-known English public school in Wiltshire. Then my father went on to Trinity College, Cambridge, where he did a law degree.

In 1936 Sam married an Aucklander, Audrey Hutchinson, who was on her OE. She had completed a degree in English at Auckland University and was chaperoned to England by one of Sam's cousins, John Elworthy, who introduced them.

The couple had two boys, Tim and Anthony, in the next four years, as the clouds gathered ominously over Europe. Worried about the possible invasion of Britain and knowing his parents lived in the safety of Gordon's Valley, Sam Elworthy thought it would be a good idea to evacuate the children. In 1940, both boys travelled by ship to live with their grandparents. Their mother arrived early in 1946 to pick them up, and had Chris here before returning to the UK that year.

Long before Chris' birth, his father Sam completed his degree and decided to learn to fly. He took out a short commission in the Royal Air Force — and stayed for the rest of his career. Chris recalls:

It was really circumstances. The Second World War broke out and he flew as a bomber pilot in the early part of the war, flying in Blenheim bombers and commanding 82 Squadron. The attrition rate was huge. I think life expectancy in those days was a little more than a fortnight for bomber crews.

He was very fortunate and lived through it. He always said, probably quite modestly, that it wasn't so hard for him to get to the top because a lot of his competitors — a lot of the people who could have got there — were killed.

Sam eventually became Chief of Defence Staff and, watched by some of his children, was knighted at Buckingham Palace in 1959. He later went on to become a life peer. He returned to Gordon's Valley in 1976 and, although no farmer, took a lively interest in what was going on around him:

The P. A. Elworthy homestead at Gordon's Valley.

Chris Elworthy.

Percy with his children (from left) Janet, Sam, Anthony and Anne in London during the First World War.

At shearing time he would always come down and talk to the shearers and ask about the wool. He would spend hours in the trees pruning them... he was a very outdoors sort of man and enjoyed physical exercise.

Audrey Elworthy died in 1986 and in the last few months of his life Sam Elworthy turned to Chris to ask:

"When I've had it, what are you going to do with me?" And I said, "I don't know Dad. What would you like us to do with you?" And he said, "Oh, I'd like to be buried on the valley." So I said, "That's fine."

Chris suggested a nice spot set on a plateau behind the homestead where there were views back to the bush gully and across to the sea:

And he said, "Oh, that sounds really good." So I said, "What we'll do is go and get a nice lump of local limestone and put you under that." And he said, "I'd like that. That'll be great."

"Now," he said, "Mum's ashes are still in the bottom drawer down at Gordon's Valley. I think I'd like you to mix her ashes with my ashes and we can both be there."

His father died in 1993 and the family, arriving from all over the world, decided to carry out his wishes together.

We came up here one evening, a beautiful evening, and mixed the ashes together and my brother said,

"You're the farmer, you dig the hole." So I dug the hole and we buried them here and decided we'd have a plaque put in place to commemorate the spot on the rock.

When he died, my father had thirteen cases of gin in his possession. He wasn't an alcoholic or anything but he was fond of having a gin or two in the evening. And so we thought it was very appropriate to bring up a bottle of his gin and we had a gin and tonic right here when we buried them.

Chris and his wife Annie both relish farm life despite its vagaries. She grew up on a farm about 20 miles south of Gordon's Valley at Hook, just north of Waimate:

My father was a Romney sheep breeder and I used to help him a lot on the farm. I was on the payroll during the school holidays and I used to love being outside with him working with the sheep and cattle.

Chris had worked on farms in Kenya and France before starting work in the Hawke's Bay as a cadet farmer. He married Annie, came to Gordon's Valley in 1975 as a shepherd and, after a few years, took over management of the property. If there's one thing the land has taught him it is to be more philosophical about its unpredictability.

If you are going to be a farmer, you just simply have to have that ability to deal with it.... I tend to get agitated and if the weather's bad at lambing time I can be up during the night sticking my head out of the window to see if it's clearing or if there's any chance of clearing. Whereas I have friends who are far better adjusted and they just say, "Well, I know I can't do anything until first light in the morning, so I'll just sleep." That's not really my way.

When you work on the land it's not like an office job. You can't leave your farm always nice and tidy as someone would perhaps leave their office at 5 o'clock on a Friday night. Farming isn't like that....

Annie supplements the family income by selling for Avon Cosmetics in Timaru:

A lot of it is telephone work and I can do that from home and juggle it in between the times that I'm helping Chris on the farm. I'm very lucky... I can do this in my time. As long as I meet deadlines, I can work in with the farm work which always has top priority.

Like other farmers in the 1980s, the couple struggled as the Labour Government removed subsidies and provoked farmers into protest action. Chris recalls that the protests happened at about the same time as the sharemarket was booming.

Wedding day for Chris and Annie.

I remember several people in Wellington that we met saying, "Why don't you sell your farms and put your money into shares?" And I'd like to meet those people today. I could give them the answer.

When they removed the subsidies [SMPs] I suppose in some ways there was a sense of relief because all my friends in town couldn't tell me any longer that I was being subsidised by them. In fact, we all know that SMPs weren't sort of put into huge piggy banks.

I can understand the rationale behind subsidies being removed from the farming industry but there was an expectation that this would go along with perhaps a more level playing field.

We were promised in return that there would be strenuous efforts made for better access for our products to world markets.... The suggestion was that trade barriers were going to be broken down and a lot of farmers pinned a lot of hope on that.

We now know that that hasn't happened and so when the Minister of Finance at the time told the rest of the world that New Zealand farmers didn't need subsidising, we believed it because we thought, "Well, there's a better future for us. We're going to have better access to markets."

In fact, what happened was that we saw the sheep farming industry go into decline and it's a decline in my opinion that is going on to this day.... I fear that what was once the envy of the world – the best pastoral sheep farming business in the world – is in danger of collapsing. That is a great shame because all New Zealanders benefit from a strong sheep farming or strong farming economy in New Zealand.

I'm saddened that this has happened because it's quite evident to me – and I dare say to most farmers – that we're not going to see the breakdown in trade barriers that we expected.

It's politically unachievable in my opinion, and so we're going to be in competition with industries which are highly subsidised. I think more than 80 per cent of the British farmer's income may be in the form of subsidies. Here in New Zealand it's nil. That makes it a pretty tough road for the New Zealand farmer.

Chris says farming is going through difficult times at the moment. 1999 was the first time in 90 years that Gordon's Valley did not sell sheep at the annual Holme Station sale in February. The previous year Chris sold 900 sheep at the sale – in 1999 he is not selling or buying any.

If the farm is sold he says he will be saddened. Part of the joy of farming is simply working a beautiful plot of land with its crisp air, the song of bellbirds in the mornings and the history in all the trees planted by his grandfather. However he is philosophical about the farm passing out of family hands:

As long as a property is looked after and in good hands, I feel quite happy about that....

Sources: Edited Ninox transcripts from *Our People, Our Century*, 1999. All photographs from the Elworthy Family Collection.

1920

Chapter 3

1930

All Dressed
Up and...

In the Roaring Twenties, image always triumphs over substance. Yes, there were Flappers, the Bright Young Things of the social set; rising hemlines to match falling waistlines; new diversions quite literally in the air, in the form of radio and flight. But in the shadows of the high life lay growing unemployment, more bankruptcies, moral panics, and not one but two depressions. The second of these threw the entire world into economic chaos, that environment so conducive to the absolute certainties of totalitarianism. While the fresh new music of George Gershwin, Noel Coward and all that jazz enriched the period, upstart political agitators tried hard to give it the blues.

Nelson Provincial Museum (Chittenden Collection)

Freewheeling Flappers posing on, if not riding a motorbike.

In 1922 the Fascist leader Benito Mussolini was appointed Italian Prime Minister in a bid to prevent a Communist revolution, and later assumed dictatorial powers. The following year, an obscure and moody German ex-corporal with a demagogic gift railed prophetically at a gathering in Munich:

We are now met by the question: Do we wish to restore Germany to freedom and power? If "yes", then the first thing to do is to rescue it from the Jew who is ruining our country.... We want to stir up a storm. Men must not sleep: they ought to know that a thunderstorm is coming up.[1]

At the time, Germans, beset by the hyper-inflation which had wiped out savings and made their currency almost worthless, had more important things to consider than this rabble rouser, Adolf Hitler. As he did time in jail for his role in the 1923 Munich coup, the major world powers began to come to terms with a threatening new reality: Soviet Communism.

The "war to end all wars" did not succeed in ending war, but it did sweep away many barriers and conventions and, as a result, the Twenties was a decade of cultural and political ferment. Art, literature and music all experimented with new forms which often provoked shock, censure and, sometimes, downright confusion. Cole Porter wrote his song *Anything Goes* in 1934, but it captures the creative nihilism of the Twenties perfectly:

In olden days a glimpse of stocking
was looked on as something shocking
now heaven knows,
anything goes.
Good authors too who once used better words
now only use four letter words
writing prose,
Anything goes....

Extract courtesy of Warner/Chappell Music Australia Pty Ltd.

Every fashion-seeker should own one – the very latest in men's underwear.

The best in fashion at Tahuna beach in Nelson.

ATL F-55193-1/2

Swag on the shoulder, billy in hand – one of the vanishing breed of swaggers on a backcountry road.

Surveying the decade and its values in New Zealand, historian Keith Sinclair found few Flappers, but noted a rapid uptake of material possessions, and some improvements in living conditions. He added:

> *Yet wherever one looks at life in New Zealand during the 1920s there is evidence of a loss of confidence, hesitancy, disillusionment. Life seemed more circumscribed than at any time since the Eighties. These were years of loud talk and little faith.*[2]

He attributed much of the pervasive insecurity of the period to uncertain prices for the country's primary exports. Four years of war barely changed New Zealand's economic patterns. Although factory workers increased in number from 42,000 in 1910 and 1911 to 63,000 in 1920 and 1921, New Zealand remained a pastoral plot in the South Pacific. Four commodities – wool, butter, meat and cheese – accounted for 80 per cent of exports by value of products.[3]

But the war had changed the economy in other ways. The national debt soared by 70 per cent between 1914 and 1919 and this was worsened by more borrowing in the 1920s. In the brief post-war boom the Government spent most of the borrowed money on settling returned ex-servicemen on farming land it had bought – often at inflated prices.

It then offered substantial loans to buy and develop the land and prices rocketed as about 22,000 returned servicemen joined what became a speculative land rush. It has been estimated that just on half the occupied land changed hands between 1915 and 1924.[4]

When the bubble burst in 1921 and 1922, many new farmers were left with mortgages and interest rates based on boom prices, forcing some to walk off the land. Often they were inexperienced but, equally, the land the Government had bought was sometimes of dubious quality for farming.

The rate of failures prompted the conservative Reform Government to establish boards to investigate the causes:

> *The boards established that half the farms they inspected were either outright failures or temporarily unsuccessful. In 1923, the Government set up a revaluation board and 5,347 soldier-farmers applied for mortgage assistance or relief.*[5]

These were bitter days for the soldier-farmers, and the situation was worsened by a widening gap between town and country. As the towns grew in size and importance, farming publications lampooned bludging "townies" who were carried by productive farmers.

But the mood of the country slowly began to change as it prospered and modernised, enthusiastically embracing the many new and exciting material innovations of the age. One of the most exciting was radio,

Nelson Provincial Museum (F.N. Jones Collection)

Damage following the Murchison earthquake which measured 7.75 on the Richter scale and claimed 17 lives.

The Wins:
Walking off the Land

The Win Family Collection

Don and Vera Win, with Pat, Matiri Valley, Murchison, 1926.

In the early Twenties, a young, recently married couple settled with high hopes on a piece of land near Murchison in the South Island. Don Win and Vera Bastin had married in 1921. For the next year they lived and worked on the Win family farm at Dovedale, north-west of Nelson. Don's and Vera's eldest son, Pat Win, says:

The boys, all his family – and there were quite a number of them – worked for nothing on their father's farm. But when the time came for them to start out, their father purchased a block for them. This was the way Dad was paid for all his years of work at home. In 1922, they decided to go farming and purchased a block in the Matiri Valley. Grandfather George Win put down the £500 towards the farm. The rest was paid by mortgage.... It was virgin country, mainly in bush, trees or regenerating scrub. They milked by hand. But they were only two generations from the pioneers so they were still pioneers really. Grandfather George Win had plans to shift his mill on to the property and mill the timber for sale. The price of butterfat was reasonable and, as my mother once told me, things looked very prosperous and promising... Mum was quite an ambitious person, very forward looking. Dad was certainly a very handsome young man. And I think they saw themselves as having a lot of prospects. I think they also worked extremely hard on the property.

Roger Win, his brother, agrees: *I'm pretty certain until 1926 they thought the world was their oyster. They had a rosy future. Dad no doubt expected to be able to break in his land and bring it to full production like his father had, and like his grandfather had. And they'd got themselves well enough established to avoid financial disaster. But not in 1926, 1927. Income didn't pay out-goings, and that was it.*

In 1926 commodity prices collapsed. Butterfat prices halved. George Win decided there was no gain in milling the timber on his son's farm. Dennis Win, Don's youngest son, remembers the effect on the family.

It was a world-wide phenomenon, but the effect here in Murchison was that the price for cream in the dairy factory dropped from tenpence a pound to fivepence a pound. Their income was insufficient to pay the mortgage and the groceries. They soldiered on for a few months until all of Mum's savings were used up and then they just packed up. Dad had been in Murchison to buy groceries and talked to Mr Hodson the storekeeper. He told Dad that in his view a really bad time was coming and it might be a good time for a chap to get to Nelson and find a safe job.

And a bad time was coming – the stockmarket crash and Great Depression. Don and Vera Win left the farm. When they arrived in Nelson all they had left was one pound. Don Win got a job as a carpenter's labourer but was laid off when the effects of the Depression took hold. He kept himself and his family by odd jobbing for his brothers and cousins round Dovedale. Pat says:

I believe that having to walk off the farm began to disrupt their relationship. As Dad said, he lost five hundred pounds and five years' hard work. And I don't think he ever really forgave the system. He blamed the politicians, the bankers, the people like lawyers, because for some reason he was forced into bankruptcy. And for that he never forgave himself.

Dennis adds: *Dad felt they'd been dealt with fairly hard, because returned servicemen and farmers who had owned their properties for a long time and were settled in were able to get financial help. But not farmers starting out like him. That hurt him quite badly – that he didn't get a fair go, as he hoped all New Zealanders would. Mum was philosophical I think. She would have been very disappointed but she would never have dwelt on it because it wasn't in her nature. What was past was past. She used to say, "So that's that" and she'd change the conversation and get on to something else.*

In time Don Win revised his feelings about losing the farm. Pat explains: *Just before his death, he said to me one day, "The best thing I ever did for you kids was going broke in Murchison." By that he meant that coming to live in a bigger centre gave us far more opportunities than we could have enjoyed there.*

Source: Edited Ninox transcripts from *Our People, Our Century*, 1999.

A family eagerly gathered around
the cold fire of radio.
....

....
Pioneer radio operator Professor Robert Jack.

a new medium whose impact on the lives of listeners was almost as great as television when its first pictures came to living rooms.

The world's first radio station, KDKA, opened in Pittsburgh in 1920. In the same year Dame Nellie Melba broadcast from the Marconi Company in Chelmsford – thinking that the louder she sang the further her voice would travel.[6] And in 1922 the British Broadcasting Company began a regular radio service with a very British dress code for its announcers: when they were reading the news, they had to wear dinner jackets.

New Zealand began its experiments with radio early in the decade and could have been transmitting sooner but for an unsympathetic Post Office which was concerned about interference to shipping communications. Otago University's Professor Robert Jack had been working on radio since before the war and in 1920 won the necessary authorisation from the university to buy transmission equipment. On 17 November 1921 he made his first radio transmission from the physics laboratories of the university and included a popular song, *Hello My Dearie*.

The music was one of a number of gramophone records supplied by a local music store, which made more records available for future transmissions. The two-hour broadcasts went to air on Wednesdays and Saturdays each week until Christmas Eve. In Wellington Post Office worker Clive Drummond, who was to go on to become a broadcasting celebrity – "the voice of 2YA" – picked up the broadcast.

> *I used to listen for three or four minutes every quarter of an hour, night after night. So one night I started at half past eight and heard "Come into the Garden Maud". I can't tell you what I said, but I nearly went through the roof, as you can imagine. All the sound you ever heard was morse and static, but to hear a voice – well!* [7]

Dr Jack had stimulated curiosity and demand – enthusiastic reports of reception came in not just from Wellington but as far north as Hamilton. In 1922 Dr Jack went on to found the Otago Radio Association whose station, 4XD, is the oldest in the Commonwealth and still broadcasts in Dunedin. Broadcasting, as governments all over the world realised, was too powerful to be left to its own devices. The New Zealand Government gazetted its first broadcasting regulations in 1923.

Broadcasters had to satisfy the Government of their good character; they had to give priority to religious subjects for at least three hours on Sunday; restrict all broadcasting to programmes of:

> *... an educative or entertainment character such as news, lectures, useful information, religious services, musical or elocutionary entertainment and items of general interest that might be approved by the Minister from time to time.* [8]

So the first, crude concepts of public service broadcasting were elevated and the market was outlawed – advertising was banned.

In these early days, the new medium came to homes through earphones and a huge horn of a loudspeaker atop the set. Manufacturers subsequently put the speakers inside large and often ornate cabinets, designing them to become part of the living room furniture.

Radio gave its eager listeners more than music. It took them to rugby and racing – though the press box at the Canterbury Jockey Club in August 1926 was a haystack; it brought them live broadcasts of royal tours, children's programmes, and stories from both European and Maori cultures.

Listeners began to share the big moment and learned that this new medium could also transform them into silent witnesses to both tragedy and triumph. In 1927, American aviator Charles Lindbergh made the first solo flight from New York to Paris and became an international hero. Less than a year later, in January 1928, two young Kiwis, Captain G. Hood and Lieutenant J. R. Moncrieff, attempted the first trans-Tasman flight from Sydney. They took off in a flimsy monoplane fitted with an automatic radio transmitter, and held a nation spellbound for hours.

Its single note, fading, faint, but audible, was a link that kept the waiting crowd in suspense all day long. The country's 38,000 radio licence-holders sat by their loudspeakers, their number swelled by family, neighbours, friends – even gatecrashers.[9]

The aviators were expected to land at Trentham racecourse near Wellington at about 7pm – their signal had been heard two hours earlier. But then, both the monoplane and its signal vanished. Eager anticipation gave way to foreboding and, finally, the realisation that the attempt had failed, tragically. In September that year, though, Charles Kingsford Smith and C. T. P. Ulm did cross the ditch, flying from Sydney to Wigram airport and maintaining radio contact throughout their historic flight.

4 ATL F-51215-1/2 (New Zealand Freelance Collection)

Hood and Moncrieff about to climb into their cockpit for their ill-fated trans-Tasman flight.

Waiting for their aviator-husbands – Mrs Hood, pointing, and Mrs Moncrieff. Both men vanished on their attempt to fly the Tasman.

ATL G-5962-1/4-EP (Evening Post Collection)

Kingsford Smith's "Southern Cross" in a crush of the curious after landing at Wigram, Christchurch, 1928.

If radio transported the imagination, then flight realised our age-old imaginings. For some, speed and the sheer thrill of being airborne was simply intoxicating, as *Vogue* told its readers:

> *Click goes the safety belt. Click goes the throttle too. Then down goggles, a last wave towards the poor stay-at-homes and off you go – bump, bump – down the long rutted field. Faster, faster, with the propeller making a whirring mist in front of you and the wires jerking like mad – faster – faster – round a bit to get the wind – faster! Can you ever put it into words, that thrilling moment when for the first time you felt no ground under your wheels? An aeroplane doesn't rise all at once, like an automobile growing wings. It takes little shivering trial flights, an inch or so from the top of the ruts. But the first time it does the trick, you feel it down in the bottom of your triumphant soul. It isn't fear. It isn't even surprise. It's a lift of the heart, a catch of the throat, a drumming roar in your ears that chants, "I knew it – I knew it! This is what I have always wanted. I was born for it. I can never do without it again."[10]*

In the 1920s women were not only encouraged to fly, but to buy their own planes – with matching hair colours. *Vogue* suggested that the two-seater Oriole was especially recommended for brunettes whose colouring would contrast agreeably with the orange fuselage.

A long way from this high society, Tuakau's Beryl Rushworth (later Ley) had misgivings about flight. After tumultuous welcomes throughout the country, Kingsford Smith visited Tuakau.

> *Afterwards all and sundry who had the courage went off to take a flight of a few minutes for one pound from Barnaby's paddock where the* Southern Cross

Kingsford Smith and crew after arrival at Wigram.

could land. I wanted to go very much but I was scared and I could ill afford to part with a pound. It was a voluptuous Maori woman who provoked me into going for a flight in the Southern Cross.... She came into the store and said "You been up in the plane missus?"

I said, "No."

"Py korry, it's good you know. I spent four pounds, it's beauty, worth it all. I only wish I had more money. Surely you're not scared missus?" That last remark fixed me – I must go too. The Vicar and I journeyed to Barnaby's paddock only to be told "No more flights today". Of course after having made up our minds to go we were bitterly disappointed so when they said "We'll take you to Mangere for a pound" there was no holding us.... The trip to Mangere took us exactly seven minutes and the trip from Otahuhu to Tuakau via Pukekohe [by bus] one hour and forty-five minutes! [11]

Ford announces its new 5-seater touring car.

Vogue believed planes could be useful for dropping in on friends by landing on their ample lawns without disturbing their garden parties. In New Zealand, back on the ground, more and more Kiwis satisfied their need for speed behind the steering wheels of the wheezing, backfiring buggies of the time. Between 1920 and 1925, the number of cars in New Zealand rose from 40,000 to 71,000. Austins and Standards from England vied for popularity with ubiquitous Fords and other US models, though British cars dominated our roads. But travelling conditions for motorists were truly rugged.

Even in Europe, at the beginning of the decade, there were few asphalt roads. Luggage in the open tourers had to be strapped outside and whipping along at 25 miles an hour, the speed re-configured coiffures and hats in unmentionable ways. But at least the problems the fashion-conscious faced there were cosmetic. In New Zealand's backblocks, the obstacles were more fundamental. The lack of purpose-built roads meant that there were often no bridges for cars, so motorists sometimes shared bridges with rail, had to ford rivers themselves, or be carried across on barges.

Muddling along in the mud – motoring was often arduous in the Twenties.

Beryl Rushworth had a truck to deliver goods from her store door-to-door weekly to surrounding country districts. Preparation for making the deliveries resembled gearing up for mountaineering: "The roads were long and unsealed, in fact in many places pure clay. Chains, ropes and spades, plus a tomahawk and sacks were essential equipment for a delivery." Roading was improving throughout the decade, however, and the Government was actively involved. The 1922 Main Highways Act established 22 highway districts and designated main highways, largely funded from a tax on tyres, motor vehicle registration and, later, fuel.

The travail of travel was at least lightened by the friendship of small communities. Help was always available – and, often, so too was a pot of tea and hot scones, or freshly made bread at a farmhouse. Cars offered speed and convenience, but in their early days at least, left intact the traditions of country hospitality.

Car rescued from Oreti beach by a "motor ambulance".

New Zealand in the Twenties was homely, and far removed from the revolutionary cultural innovations in fashion, art, music and literature in Europe and prohibitionist America. Nightlife was, like the national emblem the Kiwi, almost impossible to spot, but there was a common thread in fashion.

The 25 December 1924 edition of New Zealand's *Illustrated Sporting and Dramatic Review* said:

> *Paris decrees that black stockings are to be fashionable again this season and she is making them of the finest silk, so that they are quite transparent. Satin shoes are popular, too, for the daytime....*

Meanwhile, in London, the magazine noted a "perfect craze for pink... that reproduces the texture of the English Flapper's rosebud complexion". Fashion produced outfits for flying and motoring as well as the famous and flimsy drop-waisted dresses of the decade. In New York and London those dresses were often knee high and swirling on dance floors to the Charleston or the Black Bottom.

Miss Andrews of Wellington — the complete Twenties girl.

J. W. Chapman-Taylor — an Architect-Craftsman

Some of New Zealand's great private houses were built in the first three decades of the century. There were an increasing number of local architects, often trained in England, who brought back design principles from the Arts and Crafts movement or from British architects and designers such as Sir Edward Lutyens. Back home they adapted them to local life and terrain. Some of the best known were Basil Hooper in Dunedin, R. K. Binney and Gerald Jones in Auckland, and Samuel Hurst Seager and J. W. Chapman-Taylor in Christchurch. Chapman-Taylor was one of the most interesting of the group with a clearly defined philosophy of architecture:

> *The art of building is so subtle because it has to do with human moods and should influence them for the better. Are we dull? White walls will cheer us. Are we fearful? Thick walls and high set windows guard us. Do our hearts feel cold? A generous fireplace and red curtains warm our spirits to a glow again. Sentiment attaches itself to permanent homes and around them patriotism and public spirit grow and thrive.* [i]

It is easy to recognise a Chapman-Taylor house.

> *Their trowel-stroke finish, hand-adzed front doors and windowsills, squared chimneys with side vents, cottage-like proportions and generally rustic appearance make them look as if they have grown out of the ground. Chapman-Taylor, never a man given to false modesty, wanted them to look as though they would endure forever. This he believed was the supreme test of architecture.* [ii]

[i] J. W. Chapman–Taylor cited in Peter Shaw *New Zealand Architecture*, Hodder and Stoughton, Auckland, 1991, p. 80.
[ii] Ibid., p. 83.

"THE DESERT SONG"

Slinky style in Wellington's Grand Opera House programme cover featuring "The Desert Song".

In New Zealand the beat was weaker and Flappers fewer, but the Dixieland Dance Hall in Auckland held dances each night after 8pm. And Bert Ralton's Savoy Havana Band played at His Majesty's and was "ovated" nightly during its visit, said one critic in the *Illustrated Sporting and Dramatic Review*.

It was, he added, "the very essence of jazz itself" and among its popular songs was *Horsey Keep Your Tail Up*. However, it was difficult in a nation newly wedded to the idea that its pubs should close at 6pm for any real nightlife to flourish the way it did overseas. In the mid-1920s a young Royal Navy officer Thomas Woodrooffe noted: "... I caught the Remuera or Onehunga trams to one party or another. I danced at the 'Cabaret', so called apparently because there wasn't one."[12]

If he had ventured into the country he would have witnessed a backblocks dance the way former swag Bob Edwards saw it:

People at that time didn't go to a dance simply because it was a break from their working-day life. They went there because it was a chance to be with people. A chance to feel the warmth of human companionship …. People had nothing as far as money was concerned, but the women would knock up a few cakes, and if you were lucky there might be a few sausage rolls and that sort of thing…. There were the odd times when there was some booze, and generally there was a good scrap – you could just about bank on it that there would be a couple of good scraps.

… in those days the women would be waiting for a dance, but the blokes would be gathered out the back, arguing the toss about who could swing an axe best, or who could ride a horse best.

… a man… maybe wanted to do a line with a sheila, and again he felt self-conscious, because he always felt that the bloke that was the best dressed had the best show, you see.[13]

Music also broke free and increasingly "negro music", along with jazz, entered the mainstream. George Gershwin and Irving Berlin added their melodies to the syncopation of the era. In the eclectic Twenties, audiences in England and New Zealand alike flocked to see Eastern exotica in performances of *The Desert Song* or *Chu Chin Chow*. There was a fascination with things Eastern – Auckland's famous Civic Theatre, built in 1929 with ornate minarets and domes, was emblematic of the preoccupation.

Part of the fascination with Arabia grew from the medium of silent movies in which heart-throb Rudolph Valentino rode through desert sands to rescue damsels in distress and left women swooning in their cinema seats. The cinema patrons returned, though, for lighter moments – watching Charlie Chaplin in films like *The Gold Rush* and in 1928, giggling at a new comic creation, Mickey Mouse. A year earlier Hollywood had produced the first talking movie, *The Jazz Singer*, and actor Al Jolson wisecracked prophetically "you ain't heard nothin' yet". From that moment on, silence was no longer golden and the curtain came down on the era of silent movies.

Rudolph Valentino woos Vilma Banky in the "Son of the Sheik" and wows female cinema-goers.

All lit up, the Tivoli Theatre Christchurch. Theatres like this sprung up over the next few years.

Courtesy Collection, New Zealand Film Archive

On the set of "The Birth of New Zealand". Director Harrington Reynolds shot most of the film around Howick, outside Auckland. The first screening was in Palmerston North in February 1922.

Throughout the decade, New Zealand was a gauche and awkward innocent, but her freshness delighted visitors like Woodrooffe:

I walked up to the bows of the [Devonport] ferry for my first sight of Auckland. There were no terraces or rows of houses. Each red-roofed white house stood apart in its own garden. From the wooded hills above the masts and cranes of the docks, they looked out clear across the harbour or down the gulf where the sea and sky became one. In the rain-washed air the place looked fresh and clean with plenty of room. This was no begrimed and sooty seaport. It was where the countryside met the sea.[14]

Others like *Punch* writer Sir Alan Herbert who visited in 1925, declared New Zealand "a darling". He sensed but could not have known how thoroughly egalitarian it was, as this Kiwi diary shows:

The Hokitika Stay
… I met in Revell Street one day, "Donald", the Hokitika chimney sweep and incidentally the showpiece of the town. One eye – one nostril – a cleft palate – he looks a most unfinished piece of humanity. But, for all his difficulty of articulation, has excellent manners. He is an uncanny "calculator". Quite defective mentally in other respects (he could never pass the second standard in the public school), he can do instantaneously the most extraordinary calculations. Give him your age and the date of your birthday – he tells you at once on what day of the week you were born. He multiplies billions by millions in his head in a few seconds.…

Called on Johnny Breeze… who cobbles in his little shop, mends your boots while you wait, and meantime talks philosophy and belles-lettres. He recites for example the whole of the Rubaiyat – fond of Tennyson – proud of the opportunities his cobbling gives of meeting interesting people in his shop. Quite the best-read man in Hokitika.[15]

Bilingual greetings to the Prince of Wales, 1920.

And later the writer, Supreme Court Judge O. T. J. Alpers, mentioned in a letter that a former classmate, Sir Ernest Rutherford, was in New Plymouth staying with his parents while he, too, was in town. Alpers visited, but seemed more impressed with Rutherford's 83-year-old mother than the man many regard as the father of nuclear physics.

Society may have been vigorously egalitarian, but just as oaks grew faster here than at "home" in England, so too did authoritarian Puritanism. Behind the roar of the Twenties was the lash of censure.

Even children like Nancy Sutherland growing up at French Pass, an isolated settlement on Tasman Bay, felt it early:

We weren't supplied with adventure playgrounds or jungle gyms or whatever. We climbed trees, and we were forbidden. And we climbed up on the roof and fell off and broke arms, and would be forbidden. You know, forbidden, forbidden all the time, so that in fact the thing to do was really to do the thing you were forbidden to do. We were not allowed to walk on the wet beams under the wharf; we were forbidden – so we walked on the wet beams....[16]

Ernest Rutherford
The Father of Modern Nuclear Physics

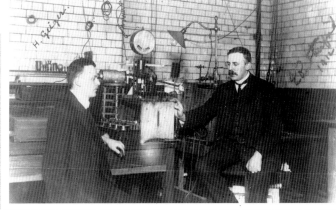

AIL F-60890-1/2 (Ernest Marsden Collection)

Ernest Rutherford (right) and Hans Geiger in the physics laboratory, Manchester University, England.

Ernest Rutherford is to science what Sir Edmund Hillary is to mountaineering. Born in 1871, at Spring Grove in Nelson, he was educated at Nelson College and Canterbury (University) College and went on to become one of the world's most famous scientists, as some of the descriptions of his work indicate: "... the greatest physical scientist of his age"; "a physicist who obtained the highest prizes in life, who ranks among the greatest scientific men of all ages"; and "the greatest experimental physicist since Faraday".

He began his research career at Cambridge in 1895 and was the right man in the right place because this was an exciting new era for the physical sciences. Between 1895 and 1897, scientists discovered x-rays, radioactivity and the electron. Among his many other achievements, Rutherford made four outstanding discoveries in the field of atomic physics – any one of which was enough to win international fame.

In 1903 he advanced the revolutionary theory of spontaneous disintegration to account for the newly discovered phenomena of radioactivity. In 1908 Rutherford was awarded the Nobel Prize for his "researches on the disintegration of the elements and chemistry of radioactive matters". Five years later he investigated some extraordinary effects observed in experiments on the bombardment of metal foils with the alpha particle emitted by radium, and concluded that the atom – that minute unit believed to be part of all materials and previously thought to be indivisible – was in fact very complex. He propounded the nuclear theory of the atom, in which he envisaged this tiny unit as a collection of still more minute particles, behaving like planets (the electrons) revolving around a central sun (the nucleus).

In 1919 he succeeded in detecting the transmutation of one elementary material (nitrogen) into another (hydrogen), a process induced artificially when the former was bombarded by the natural alpha particles of radium.

In 1932, working with two other scientists, Rutherford took the idea of transmutation further. Their work showed that artificial transmutations could be accomplished by using as projectiles for the bombardment, particles of hydrogen which had been artificially accelerated to enormous speeds under the influence of a new type of electric machine they had developed and called a proton accelerator.

This last stage of research and discovery paved the way for spectacular future developments concluding with the release on an industrial scale of the enormous energy latent in radioactive materials and harnessed in atomic energy power stations.

Sir Ernest (Baron Rutherford of Nelson) died in 1937 and his ashes were interred in Westminster Abbey alongside other greats of science such as Newton, Faraday and Darwin. Rutherford was respected among his peers for more than his scientific discoveries. Lord Baldwin wrote of him:

His refreshing personality, his dauntless spirit, the merry twinkle of his eye, the exuberance of his ever-youthful, ever-joyful enthusiasm: how can they be recaptured? One can only say... he was a peer among men.

Sources: A H McLintock (ed.), *Encyclopaedia of New Zealand*, Government Printer, Wellington, 1966; and Ray Knox (ed.), *New Zealand's Heritage: The Making of a Nation*, Paul Hamlyn, Wellington, 1971-78.

Trust and young people remained strangers. In 1924, Principal Mrs M. McLean had this advice to parents:

Don't give your girls too much liberty. Remember that these girls are not ready for it. They are just like an untutored people – not ready for self-government. The girls need restraint. When they leave school, be their guardians as well as their parents.[17]

Mrs McLean and others, like the Church and the Government, had sensed that the decade's new freedoms threatened their positions of power and control. In many ways, the Twenties represented a cultural faultline where the values of liberal secularism collided with the well-worn plates of religious orthodoxy.

In America in 1923, strong movements were under way in 15 states to enact anti-evolution laws prohibiting public schools from any teaching which conflicted with the biblical story of Creation. In one state, Tennessee, it was already law and a young schoolteacher, John T. Scopes, was charged in 1925 with breaking the new measure. The famous Scopes "Monkey Trial" followed, and though the teacher was found guilty and fined $100, the State's Supreme Court later reversed the decision on a technicality.

The spirit if not the letter of the Religious Right was infectious. In the new era of broadcasting in New Zealand, radio initially met the demands of its listeners by covering racing. Coverage continued until 1928, when the Racing and Trotting Conferences suddenly passed resolutions prohibiting any further direct broadcasts from tracks they controlled:

They offered a pious hope that this might discourage illegal betting and expressed concern at the "disadvantages to the business community" they might have been responsible for unwittingly by condoning widespread listening to race commentaries. [18]

Broadcasters adapted, covering events using stepladders, "Scotsman's stands" and anything which gave them a view. The racing authorities remained adamant and the ban lasted four years.

Other media suffered at the hands of our unduly sensitive censors. In 1923 Customs banned Ettie Rout's book *Safe Marriage* which advocated contraception as a protection against the spread of venereal disease. Three years later the Censorship Appeal Board, comprising two librarians and a bookseller, banned Jean Devanny's novel *The Butcher Shop*. Australia also banned it – along with James Joyce's *Ulysses* in 1929 – and it was on the Australian prohibited list until 1958.[19]

Devanny's story of lust and jealousy on a sheep farm was also considered dangerous not only for those reasons, but because of its robust promotion of freedoms for women. In a society whose newspapers ran advertisements telling nursing mothers that the future of the Dominion lay in their hands, it's not hard to see how parts of the book sparked indignation. The heroine also nurses her baby – but simultaneously seeks sex outside her marriage.

In 1926, the Government was warned of its impending release in a cable which read:

Jean Devanny, author of the banned novel "The Butcher Shop".

Instruct watch for new novel entitled Butchers Shop [sic] *by Jean Devanny Wellington lady Publishers Duckworth, London, alleged depiction station life New Zealand disgusting indecent communistic.*

The censors agreed:

The Board considers this a bad book all round – sordid, unwholesome and unclean. It makes evil to be good. We are of the opinion that it should be banned.[20]

Censure was not limited to literature. At the highest level it caught up with no less than Auckland's Catholic Bishop James Liston, who was tried unsuccessfully for sedition in 1922.

Katherine Mansfield

ATL D-P01801I-CURIO-CT

Katherine Mansfield became an icon and example for those New Zealanders who longed to leave the cultural poverty of home in the first decades of the century for the cosmopolitan and stimulating literary worlds of Britain and Europe. She was the first native-born writer to earn international recognition for her work.

She was born Katherine Beauchamp on 14 October 1888 in Wellington, the third child of a well-to-do bank director and importer. She left New Zealand twice. The first time, at age 14, she was away three years at Queen's College in London with her two sisters. She returned to her home country but chafed against its lack of intellectual and creative stimulation:

I am ashamed of young New Zealand but what is to be done. All the fat framework of their brains must be demolished before they can begin to learn. They want a purifying influence – a mad wave of pre-Raphaelitism, of super aestheticism should intoxicate the country.

When she left again for Europe at 19, it was for the last time. While she mingled in the leading literary circles of the time in England and Europe, her writing was rich with the memories of her childhood growing up in New Zealand. Her work became renowned for its revealing detail and the nuances of social stratification in a supposedly egalitarian society:

... the school the Burnell children went to was not at all the kind of place their parents would have chosen if there had been any choice. But there was none. It was the only school for miles. And the consequence was all the children of the neighbourhood, the Judge's little girls, the doctor's daughters, the storekeeper's children, the milkman's were forced to mix together. Not to speak of there being an equal number of rude, rough little boys as well. But the line had to be drawn somewhere. It was drawn at the Kelveys. Many of the children, including the Burnells, were not allowed even to speak to them. They walked past the Kelveys with their heads in the air, and as they set the fashion in all matters of behaviour, the Kelveys were shunned by everybody. Even the teacher had a special voice for them, and a special smile for the other children when Lil Kelvey came up to her desk with a bunch of dreadfully common-looking flowers.[i]

Before her early death in 1923 after a lengthy struggle with tuberculosis, Katherine Mansfield had become a recognised master of the short story.

[i] Katherine Mansfield, *The Doll's House*, cited by P. J. Gibbons, The Climate of Opinion, in Geoffrey Rice (ed.), *The Oxford History of New Zealand*, second revised edition, Oxford University Press, Auckland, 1992, p. 317.

When lemonade was home-made.

He had inflamed Protestant opinion that year when, in a speech at the Auckland Town Hall, he referred to those who had died fighting for Ireland since 1916. He then included a reference to 57 people including three priests who had been "murdered by foreign troops" – the infamous "Black and Tans", demobbed British soldiers sent to bolster the Royal Irish Constabulary. [21]

The jury may have found for him but it added its own reprimand by way of a rider:

We consider that Dr Liston was guilty of a grave indiscretion in using words capable of an interpretation so calculated as to give offence to a large number of the public of New Zealand, and we hold that he must bear the responsibility, in part at least, for the unenviable notoriety that has followed his utterance. [22]

In the climate of censure schools became part of the battleground. Through the decade the number of pupils had risen from 199,802 to 222,467. By 1924, 93 per cent of pupils attending state secondary schools were receiving free education, according to the 1925 Yearbook. Their education was also secular – a fact which leading Anglican clergymen found unpalatable. Along with others they joined in the "Bible In Schools" crusade and were resisted by an equally passionate Rationalist movement.

In this era of new temptations where outrage lay close to the surface, even something as innocent as playground swings could be seen as evil. A deputation from the Thames Ministers' Association approached the Thames Borough Council in January 1930 to demand that playground swings and other attractions be locked up on Sundays. The Council decided that there was nothing in the playground that would corrupt a child's morals and thought it best to leave the decision up to parents. [23]

For all its freedoms, the era was harsh on dissent over issues like Compulsory Military Training. A brave young Auckland theological student, Alan Richards, was the first resistor since the war. In 1927 he was fined and lost his civil (voting) rights for ten years. Joined by two other friends he lost them again in 1928 and 1929. [24]

Throughout the Twenties, Labour continued to win support. The farmer-supported Reform Party had won the elections in 1922 and in 1925, when party leader William Massey was succeeded by Gordon Coates.

Coates began a pragmatic extension of the role of the state and while his policies had similarities with both the Liberals and, later, Labour, they eventually alienated businessmen who branded him a socialist. His record included borrowing money for public works, building state-owned highways, a network of hydro-electric stations with electricity sold by elected boards, and centralising the control of exports for primary products. [25]

In 1927, a conference of businessmen met in Wellington and, according to historian Bill Sutch, demanded that Coates keep the Government out of any activity

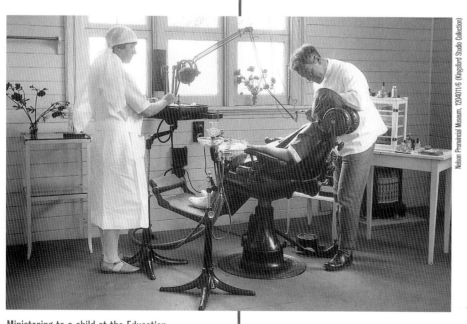

Ministering to a child at the Education Board Dental Clinic in 1928.

which might bring profit to private enterprise. "The movement, which became the '1928 Committee', decided that reducing state activity meant eliminating Coates as the parliamentary leader." [26] Coates was not helped by what historian Keith Sinclair described as "one glorious last error" from the "very decrepit financial wizard Sir Joseph Ward". He was now the leader of the United Party which had risen from the ashes of the Liberals.

> *In a famous speech he promised a Vogel era of progress based on a £70,000,000 overseas loan. Later the party explained that he had meant to say £7,000,000 for ten years* [which was no more than Reform had been borrowing], *but the conservative Press which persistently ridiculed his original grandiose proposal, kept that tempting "seventy million" dangling before voters' eyes. Droves of them, believing the newspapers' figure, returned to the Liberal* [now called "United"] *fold, hoping nostalgically that the pastures would be as lush as when Seddon had been the shepherd.* [27]

United, supported by Labour, took the Treasury benches. This was to be a lame Government headed by the ailing Sir Joseph Ward. Still, for business in 1929 there was good reason to look ahead with confidence. No less than the *New York Times* predicted good tidings ahead in an editorial on 1 January 1929 saying:

> *But it will be hard to get people to think of 1928 as merely a "dead past" which we must make haste to bury. It has been a twelvemonth of unprecedented advance, of wonderful prosperity – in this country at least.... If there is any way of judging the future by the past, this new year may well be one of felicitation and hopefulness.* [28]

New Zealand's business leaders may have been satisfied that finally less government had arrived in the form of United. In fact, never would less come to mean more, as jobs and business empires alike disappeared into the vortex of the Great Depression.

ATL F-117814-1/2 (Gordon Burt Collection)

NEW ZEALAND LABOUR PARTY

THE BASIC WAGE

The Basic Wage fixed by the Arbitration Court is £3 17s. 0d. per week. On September 18, 1925, (six weeks prior to the election) the Court announced that, owing to the increased cost of living, the rate for future Awards would be £4 0s. 8d. per week.

Could *YOU* keep a Family like this

IF YOUR WAGES WERE ONLY £3 **17 0** PER WEEK?

LABOUR'S POLICY
is to make the Minimum Wage sufficient to ensure a reasonable standard of comfort FOR EVERY FAMILY

VOTE LABOUR

New Zealand Worker Print

Labour's pitch to the working family. The party's support grew throughout the Twenties.

Note the furs – women shopping inside a department store, 1920s.

The Edwards Family
Waiting for the Revolution

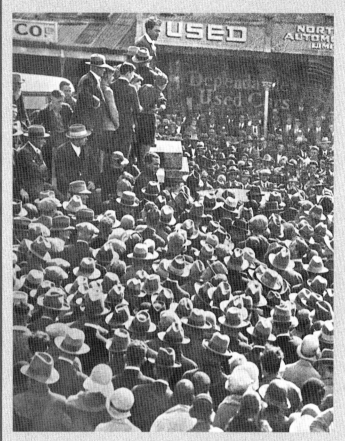

Jim Edwards addresses a demonstration by unemployed workers in Auckland, Wednesday 13 April, the day before the Queen Street riot. His son Jim leans out over the crowd below them.

I heard someone cry, "They've killed Jim Edwards! They've killed Jim Edwards!" You can imagine how I felt: they'd killed my father? I didn't know what to do. I was caught suddenly in a crowd that had literally gone mad.... I'm only a kid, I'm not yet quite 14 years of age. I don't know what's happening to my father. Is he really dead? I'm bewildered, I'm afraid, I've tears.

It is the evening of 14 April 1932, outside the Auckland Town Hall. The Great Depression has reached its nadir. And the story-teller is Jim Edwards, a schoolboy named after his father who was described

in newspapers of the time as a mob orator, a communist and firebrand agitator.

Jim Edwards senior had arrived in New Zealand 19 years earlier. He was a Londoner, son of a printer and one of six children. He joined a ship in the Blue Funnel Line in 1913, and worked his passage to Wellington as an assistant steward. He disembarked in the middle of the bitter 1913 waterfront strike, knowing no one and without work. But there were jobs on offer everywhere. He took one and so became a strike breaker, a "scab". In later years he wrote:

I can only say that I was young and ignorant. I am older and wiser now. I have learnt a bit about the world and I kick myself every time I think what a young mug I was. In that 1913 strike it began to dawn on me that I was on the wrong side, a traitor to myself and to my class. I began to do a bit of thinking for myself. And in 1914, I joined the Socialist Party.

It was the beginning of many years of political activism. In 1917, during the First World War, he was jailed for the first time after speaking at an anti-conscription rally. In Wellington's old Terrace Prison he was befriended by Peter Fraser, a Labour politician and another anti-conscription campaigner, who would later become the country's second Labour Prime Minister. Fraser continued Jim Edwards' political

Nellie Douglas later in life. She eventually walked out on Jim Edwards when she discovered he was having an affair. They both re-married and their son Jim says, "She did eventually find real happiness, and so did Dad."

Jim Edwards leaves Auckland Central Police Station after giving himself up the night before. He had been on the run for six weeks.

education, loaning him books on socialism. Always a prolific reader, Edwards began reading the works of Jack London, Upton Sinclair, Theodore Dreiser and, inevitably, Karl Marx.

A month after his release from prison, he married Nellie Douglas. He'd met her at one of the Bible classes he ran for the Salvation Army. He was 25 and an active officer in the Salvation Army; she was 20, a pacifist at heart and against the First World War. It was she who encouraged him to join the Socialist Party, persuaded him not to enlist when war broke out, and to oppose conscription. Jim, the eldest of their eight children, was born the following year:

Their relationship from what little they ever told me about it was quite a stormy one. They, in many ways, were not compatible. Right from the start my father was not a ne'er-do-well, but a most unreliable man. But my mother always accepted Dad for what he was. My father's passions were many and varied. He was a romantic. He had a passion for music. He had a beautiful baritone voice. He sang in church choirs. He sang on Scrim's Friendly Road programme. He sang for old people. And he was a wonderful actor. He played in some working class dramas. A lot of these working class plays were put on in theatre by the Workers' Educational Association.

Jim remembers his father as a well–intentioned man who was a disaster as a breadwinner, a Mr Micawber character who told his wife:

"Look, Nell, and you kids, don't worry. Everything will turn out all right. You know, something will

turn up." And then Mum would say to him, "Jim, the only thing that's going to turn up for you are all these unpaid bills." And that was so true. They did. I remember one occasion he came in, he'd been somewhere or other and he'd had a few beers. There they were – "love letters" the bailiff who delivered them called them – a big pile of bills. And my mother confronted him with these and he picked them off the table, ripped them up into pieces and just threw them in the air, and said, "For Christ's sake, put a bloody record on and forget them."

It was Nellie who kept the family together through increasingly hard times. Her eldest son remembers:

My father was always a door-to-door man, a commission man. As he said, he would never ever, and never could be, an eight to five man. He used to work for photographers and he'd go out knocking at the doors of people and persuading them to buy a coupon to get their picture taken at a special cut rate price. He sold colour enlargements, insurance, encyclopaedias. He went door-to-door changing gramophone records. In those days people just had gramophones and they'd get tired of their old records so you'd go round and change them.

We lived in Newton, I should think in as many as a dozen different houses, mainly because we couldn't pay the rent and because he didn't bring enough money in. And yet ours was not an unhappy house with all the kids crying and all hungry. My mother had this miraculous ability to always see that there was something in the pot. I don't remember ever going hungry even though there was no money sometimes and the rent was unpaid. We would always make it, one way or another. In spite of the soup and broken biscuits and the rotting fruit, there were times when the money did come in. Then there were lovely roast dinners and Yorkshire pudding because my mother could make a superb meal if you'd give her the goods.

And I think he said sometimes to Mum in her moments of consternation, "Look, I know how it is for you, I know the kids have to go and do this door-to-door thing, and I know what you do, I know how supportive you are. But I've got a greater responsibility because there are so many people out

Jim Edwards is arrested by police during the Norfolk Street evictions. His son Jack is on the far left.

there that are worse off than we are…. There's things I'm just obligated and have to do."

Chief amongst those obligations was Jim Edwards' work for the unemployed. As the Depression deepened, he had left his family in New Plymouth and moved to Auckland, hoping to earn more money. He took lodgings in The Rooms in Victoria Street in the city. This was his introduction to more radical politics.

This place was run by an ex-seaman, a fellow called Bill Tovey, and he had all sorts of odd people staying there. And these were all people involved in one way or another in what they believed was the coming revolution. And they influenced Dad. Some of them were communists, some called themselves anarchists, all sorts of things. He was right in the heart of "the movement" as he saw it. He thought the only way was the way of the revolutionary elected. Not in throwing bombs around or violence, but the transition from capitalism to – never used the word "communism" much, it was always "socialism" that he talked about.

In 1931, his family with him again, Jim Edwards joined the Communist Party and helped set up the Unemployed Workers Movement. Nellie Edwards had no patience or interest in his love of theatre or music. But she was totally supportive of his political work, even though it took him away from home and stopped him earning desperately needed money. She coached him for his speeches to his Sunday Quay Street meetings, smoothing the edges of his Cockney accent, polished his worn out shoes and made sure his shirt was always washed and ironed. Sometimes she went with him to meetings and took up collections for the UWM.

After the first major clash between the unemployed and the police in February 1931, Edwards was arrested and served a month in prison. In October he was back in prison for his part in the protest against a Norfolk Street eviction. By now he was generally recognised as a spokesman for the unemployed. Their numbers were climbing steeply. The marches and protest meetings increased, along with frustration and anger at the Government's failure to alleviate conditions for the unemployed and low-paid workers.

In April 1932, all these pent up emotions boiled over. On Friday 8 April, the Government announced that it proposed to cut civil service wages by another 5 to 12 per cent – they had already been cut by 10 per cent – and to reduce interest rates, rents and pensions.

That same day in Dunedin, crowds rioted, attacking the Mayoress's car and smashing the windows of the relief depot. Three days later they tried to storm the hospital board office for food, but were driven back by police with batons.

The Post and Telegraph Employees' Association organised a public meeting at the Auckland Town Hall for Thursday 14 April to propose a general strike. That evening an estimated 15,000 people converged on the Town Hall. Jim Edwards junior, playing truant from school, remembers it began very quietly:

We set off in an almost ominous silence and as we walked along I remember watching people on the pavement. And some were looking at us I think with contempt. Others with a sort of toleration. But among some of the faces that I still recall... were the faces of women who were crying. It was pretty depressing: just the sound of feet, an eerie silence almost, apart from that. But my father, determined to enliven proceedings, ran ahead of our section and stood on the tram zones, megaphone in hand calling out, "Are we downhearted?" and a great cry would come back "No!" "Are we going to the slave camps?" "No!" "Are we going to fight for our rights?" "Yes!" And all these resounding shouts echoed in Queen Street.

When the unemployed marchers reached the Town Hall they found their way barred by a police cordon. The marchers were told the hall was already full. They did not believe the police. Jim Edwards led his group round the side to the back doors, but these too were locked:

Then suddenly it seemed there was a flaring of anger, a flaring of frustration, and some of the section in our lot made a mad rush back to the front doors. Dad, anticipating trouble I think, ran beside them, telling them to get back into ranks. He was ignored. Those who had led the on-rush were confronted by the police who now had drawn batons. Dad, obviously seeing there was to be trouble, turned his back to the police and put his hands up in a gesture of restraint. He put his hands up and with that he was heavily batoned from behind and fell to the ground. And then I lost sight of him. But I heard someone cry, "They've killed Jim Edwards", a woman's voice....

It was like a spark that ignited... this frenzied screaming, shouting, people rushing across the road to the City Mission and taking palings from the church fence. And all of a sudden there was this confrontation between rioters and police, and it was all on. I can't get to him because by this time I'm packed in closely by a surging crowd. A mounted policeman rode through the crowd, turned the horse and its flank hit me and pushed me hard up against the side of the Town Hall.

And then suddenly, miraculously it seemed to me, there he was being assisted up on to the balustrade of the Town Hall. In the street light I can see blood running down the side of his face on to the collar of the shirt Mum had washed and ironed for him that morning. And he called out to the crowd, "If the police do that again, surround them. Take the batons off them. But for God's sake no violence." Someone assisted him down and I lost sight of him. Well once I knew Dad was alright, I mean alright enough to be able to stand up and talk, all I wanted to do was to get the hell out of it and get home. But getting through a crowd wasn't exactly easy. I literally fought my way out of the place.

Jim Edwards' father arrived home later that night, his head roughly bandaged and soaked with blood. Warned that he would be blamed for causing what had become a full scale riot which smashed through Queen Street, he was convinced to go into hiding. He left the house just before the police arrived to arrest him. He was on the run for six weeks while his head wound – a gash requiring 30 stitches – healed and emotions cooled. Then he gave himself up. He was charged with inciting lawlessness and taking part in a riot. Tried twice in the Supreme Court before an unsympathetic judge, Mr Justice Herdman, he was found guilty by the second jury and given the maximum sentence – two years' imprisonment with hard labour.

Sources: Edited Ninox transcripts from *Our People, Our Century*, 1999; and Jim Edwards, *Break Down These Bars*, Penguin Books, Auckland, 1987. All photographs from the Edwards Family Collection.

8   THE AUC

QUEEN STREET RIOT

MOB SMASHING AND LOOTING

SEVERE CLASH WITH POLICE

SCENES ALMOST INCREDIBLE

CASUALTIES   NUMBER   OVER   TWO   HUNDRED

STRONG GUARD ORGANISED FOR TO-NIGHT.

Riotous scenes without precedent in Auckland were witnessed in Queen Street last evening. Trouble commenced with stone-throwing by processionists in Queen Street. It developed into severe rioting in the vicinity of the Town Hall, where, amid pandemonium, batons and sticks were used, and it spread over the greater length of Queen Street, where shop windows were shattered and stock looted. It was a startling instance of mob impulse and the lawlessness and abandon that is bred of contagion.

For over two hours sporadic raiding went on over a big section of Auckland's main shopping area amid the cries of excited people and the tinkle and crash of breaking glass. The police were hopelessly outnumbered. A naval detachment was sent over to the city from the naval base, special constables were hurriedly sworn in and at the height of the trouble the Fire Brigade turned out. The members of the St. John Ambulance worked at peak pressure to rush casualties to the Auckland Hospital, and over 200 cases—several of a serious nature—were dealt with.

For nearly three hours Queen Street was more or less in the hands of a lawless crowd bent on destruction, while thousands of citizens helplessly and amazedly looked on. The grip of authority tightened slowly but effectively, but it was a late hour before the situation was well in hand. Broken plate glass windows were a common sight, and broken glass was littered everywhere. This morning citizens were shocked on realising the amount of wanton damage that had been caused, and to-day special steps were taken to deal with any further trouble that might arise.

Close on 250 plate glass windows were smashed, and the damage runs into many thousands of pounds.

Full arrangements have been completed for the guarding of the city to-night. The Mayor strongly advises all citizens, if not on special duty, not to loiter in the city after shops and theatres have closed.

Auckland Star, 15 April 1932

Chapter 4

1930

1940

Depression & Deliverance

The Thirties were a decade in which the impact of foreign political and economic events shook the country. It opened on a growing world financial crisis and closed at the start of a conflict which would become the first truly global war.

A day at the races. With the Thirties, curves returned to women's fashion.

ATL F-49804-1/2

When the Depression hit, it was no ordinary setback. This was "the Great Depression" and its title was well deserved – a global phenomenon which destroyed individual livelihoods and social structures alike. Its impact conditioned an entire generation and led to the creation of the modern welfare state.

The bitter experience of the Great Depression also left its mark on children:

Depression is an ugly word. It's uglier still when you know what it means.... People who talk of a Depression don't remember, and have no concept of, what the Great Depression was like, or why it rates a capital letter.

In a Depression there is a constant stream of people at the door, trying to sell anything they can carry with them. A Depression is soup kitchens, lines of hungry unemployed, hunger marches, riots and looting; happy employers able to pick and choose workers and drive them to the edge of rebellion, knowing they won't complain. A Depression is many wives and daughters on the streets, selling their only asset in exchange for a few pence for food and clothes. A Depression is hopelessness, yet working to help your neighbour, and pulling together.

A Depression is a time when the best and worst of human nature comes to the fore. Only a war is a more testing time, a time when you find just who your friends are. In a Depression you have only one pair of shoes and one set of reasonably good clothes in which to seek virtually non-existent jobs. It's when you walk rather than take public transport, when you know what bread and dripping tastes like, when your meals – usually irregular – are mainly potatoes, pumpkins, turnips, tapioca, sago, anything that fills an empty belly.

A Depression is when you don't see food scraps thrown away, when people don't feed the birds, can't keep pets; when free concerts, community singing, free milk at schools, health camps for children are not subjects for remark.[1]

Children's gala in 1932.

Nelson Provincial Museum 1/2 44 (F. N. Jones Collection)

Childish Pastimes

Life for children in the 1930s was still influenced by mores of much earlier eras. In 1933 women's groups were petitioning the Government to raise the marriage age for girls from 12 to 16. The school year finished early in 1936 and opened late in 1937, but the prolonged summer holidays were spent mooching about the family backyard while yet another serious polio epidemic raged – almost 900 notified cases and 46 deaths.

But there was always time for happier pursuits:

Numerous small children soliciting "pennies for the guy" were again abroad in the city last evening. The parties of weirdly attired children included several girls with their faces liberally daubed with charcoal.

Besides singing popular songs a troupe at the corner of Victoria and Queen Streets showed considerable originality by staging impromptu gymnastics....

However, the sight of numerous small boys standing on their heads in the direct path of motor traffic in Victoria Street also drew the attention of a patrolling policeman, who good-humouredly shepherded them from the danger zone. Undeterred, the troupe continued merrily down the street to fresh haunts.[i]

[i] Gil Dymock (ed.), *Good Morning New Zealand: News Stories of the Day* from the 1930s, Moa Publications, 1990, p. 41.

"A fine sample of the crop of winter gooseberries [kiwifruit] grown by Mr. H. Wright at Avondale, near Auckland." Hayward Wright's development of the "Goldmine" nectarine, "Paragon" peach and "Hayward" kiwifruit were of worldwide importance. His kiwifruit selection was the most important fruit cultivar ever developed in this country. He provided the seedlings for the first local commercial planting of "Chinese gooseberries" in 1937. A ban on fruit imports during WWII boosted the fruit's popularity in New Zealand. The first kiwifruit were exported to England in 1953.

Dominion

...Consider the curious fate
of the English immigrant:
his wages were taken from him
and exported to the colonies;
sated with abstinence, gorged
*   on deprivation,*
he followed them: to be confronted
*   on arrival*
with the ghost of his back wages,
*   a load of debt;*
the bond of kinship, the heritage
*   of Empire.*[1]

A.R.D. Fairburn

[1] A.R.D. Fairburn, *Collected Poems*, Pegasus Press Ltd, Christchurch, 1966, p.23.

Photo credit: Hort Research, Auckland, (New Zealand Smallholder Collection)

1930-40

In the early 20th century, the world was divided into two groups – countries that were sustained economically by industrial production and those which provided raw materials or food for the first group. New Zealand, with over 90 per cent of its export earnings derived from agriculture, was part of the latter; and in 1930, as the world economic situation deteriorated, demand for agricultural produce collapsed. The effect on this country was catastrophic, and unforeseen.

As a society, we had become accustomed to routinely shipping our agricultural produce to Britain, but we had failed to diversify in what we produced or where we sent it. Against earlier proofs to the contrary, we continued to believe as long as we carried out these "ritual acts" that "... New Zealand could stand aloof or not as we chose from international affairs, whether they were political or economic.... It was a form of reverse cargo cult and was similarly without substance."[2]

In the midst of the growing gloom, this racing-mad nation still had its heroes, and few were bigger than Phar Lap or "Big Red", the Kiwi horse which made Australian competitors look like also-rans:

> *Striding away from the pacemaker, Temptation, at the top of the straight, Phar Lap drew right away to win the Melbourne Cup this afternoon with ridiculous ease from Second Wind and Shadow King.*
>
> *... Phar Lap's Cup will always be remembered as one of the most sensational, as on Saturday an attempt was made to shoot him.*[3]

In 1932, now racing in America, his career came to an abrupt end when he was accidentally poisoned. At the time, New Zealand was at its lowest ebb in the 20th century. Once famed as a "social laboratory", by 1930 we had fallen behind many other countries in provision of social services.[4] The country carried a large debt and more and more money from a shrinking government purse went on servicing it; in 1933, 40 per cent of the Government's total expenditure went in interest payments.[5] At the same time, between 1928 and 1932, export returns fell by 40 per cent and wool prices by a staggering 60 per cent. Farmers' net incomes dropped into the red as their costs outweighed their earnings.

In 1928 and 1929, there were 4,500 registered unemployed; by December 1930 the numbers had more than doubled to 11,000. Ten months later they had climbed to 51,000 in a population of 1.6 million. And they continued to rise until they peaked in 1933 at approximately 81,000. However, these numbers do not include women out of work or Maori – "by 1933 three-quarters of the adult male Maori population was registered as unemployed."[6] The Great Depression confronted many of those who lived through it with "conditions they thought they had escaped from".[7]

As if to demonstrate that misfortune never travels alone, natural disaster added to growing economic hardship. On a February morning in 1931 Wellingtonians sensed an eerie stillness:

> *Then the dogs began barking, howling, and we knew the quake was getting ready to strike....*
>
> *The air became more oppressive, and the groups along the road stopped talking. There was complete silence except for the dogs....*
>
> *Suddenly out to sea, we heard a low rumbling, which rapidly increased in intensity. Mother grabbed me with one hand, the gate with the other. Next*

moment there was a violent shudder on the earth beneath our feet, and the electric wires along the poles in the road began to swing violently. Then, noise. I remember someone along the road screamed, which didn't seem to do a lot of good. The shuddering kept going, it seemed for minutes, but in reality probably only for seconds.

The shuddering stopped, then began again. Out over the bay several big waves raced ashore, crashing on the beach with tremendous noise. Then it all stopped, and there was silence again.[8]

What they didn't know then was that Wellington's experience was mild. The quake's epicentre was in Hawke's Bay, registering 7.9 on the Richter Scale, and it was not until 10 o'clock that night that the first definite news of what had happened in the worst-affected area reached the rest of the country. The commander of a Royal Navy sloop now aground in Napier's inner harbour reported that virtually all the stone and brick buildings of the seaside town had been destroyed, many were blazing furiously and hundreds of wooden buildings had been wrecked. There was no water and so the fire brigade was unable to do much more than watch their town burn. The navy had set up a food depot, temporary hospitals and a shelter for those women and children who were now homeless.

That night in Napier, 17-year-old Rona Lawrence, her sister and their widowed mother laid out a mattress for her badly injured brother in an empty section along the road from the ruins of their home:

10.50am, 3 February 1931. Against a background of dust clouds and smoke, a fireman picks his way down Hastings Street, Napier, 30 minutes after the Hawke's Bay earthquake.

ATL F-139885-1/2 (P. T. W. Ashcroft Collection)

Napier — After the Earthquake

When Napier was officially declared a city in 1950, it held a competition to choose a motto for its new civic coat-of-arms. The winning entry, "Faith and Courage", came from Rona Lawrence who had been 17 at the time of the 1932 earthquake. Four years after the quake, she described what it had been like in the days that followed:

There was very little to eat so I thought I would go over to the town and try to procure something. It was a nightmare of a journey, and at one stage the road was completely blocked. I tried a different route and on my way passed the nurses' home at the hospital, which had fallen down like a pack of cards, killing several night nurses who were asleep at the time. Patients from the collapsed wards and injured people from the town were taken to the Botanical Gardens nearby where beds were placed beneath trees.

Houses and lamp-posts were tilted at the craziest angles, and from one home a woman ran out screaming. Evidently the strain of further quakes had proved too much for her.

A little later I was in the town itself and I could only stand and gaze uncomprehendingly at the ghastly scene. Fires were smoldering in every direction, and weary, smoke-grimed firemen were struggling desperately to stem the shooting flames. Great heaps of blackened masonry thrust gaunt shapes against the grey sky.

I wandered on, and came to an area which so far was free from the flames. Here a butcher had a temporary stand and was serving meat to any who cared to purchase it. I bought some chops and with a few stale buns headed home.

I arrived back eventually at our small camping area to find that most of the women and children were preparing to leave the town. The probability of an epidemic through lack of water and the destroyed sewerage system was an ever-present menace.[i]

---

[i] Rona Lawrence cited in *The Daily Telegraph 120 Years: Double Diamond Jubilee 1871-1991*, Daily Telegraph Co., Napier, 1991, p. 17.

The night seemed endless, and the full moon was blood-red from the reflection of the fires. The ground trembled with shocks of varying intensity. The dawn came and revealed in all its starkness the utter desolation.[9]

The *Dominion* newspaper's reporter described the scene next day:

Napier as a town has been wiped off the map. To-day it is a smoldering heap of ruins, the sepulchre of a prosperous port and the gaunt remains of a beautiful seaside town.

Its people are wandering the streets hopelessly, yet with a fortitude born of extreme adversity. Before them the seafront has receded perhaps a hundred feet from the famous parade that itself has risen from eight to ten feet. Behind them the whole town is a reeking mass of ruins with not one building standing in the centre part....

The face of the Bluff has come down across the road to Port Ahuriri and blocked access to it by land as well as by sea.... Streets have been torn up like billiard cloths ripped with a sturdy cue, and telegraph poles have been thrust at a crazy angle over every road with wires tangled and hanging from wrecked buildings like charred serpents suspended from the last branches of a brick and concrete forest.[10]

Police recover bodies from the rubble outside Bestall's Building in Hastings Street, Napier.

Hawke's Bay Museum 7182 (Collection of the Hawke's Bay Cultural Trust)

Hastings and the smaller towns of the region were also heavily damaged – 900 chimneys came crashing down in Waipukurau in a few seconds and the brick fronts to many shops crumbled; in Wairoa shop fronts and buildings collapsed and the bridge across the river was destroyed. All communications – roads, rail, bridges and telephone lines – were badly disrupted. The quake left 256 people dead and caused over £5 million worth of structural damage alone (over $300 million in the currency of the late Nineties), an impossible burden in an already bleak economy at a time when there was no general insurance against earthquakes.

Through necessity, the re-building of Napier and Hastings went against the Depression's plummeting building statistics: in 1930 nearly 4,000 building permits were issued, but in 1933 there were less than 1,000.[11] Napier, the worst hit, took the opportunity to completely re-design and extend the central business district. By 1940 the city was transformed. Some of the new buildings were modelled on the "Spanish Mission townscape" of Santa Barbara in California which had been devastated by a severe earthquake in 1928, but the majority owed much more to a design movement popularly known as Art Deco, which had its origins in the 1925 Paris *Exposition Internationale des Arts Decoratifs et Industriels Modernes*. Napier, and Hastings to a lesser extent, remain the only extensive examples of the Art Deco

Election night ritual – the crowd outside the offices of the "Evening Post" in Willis Street, Wellington, to watch the results of the 1931 election come in.

ATL G-4500-1/1 (W. H. Raine Collection)

Unemployed men and boys on relief work at the "Kindle Club", chopping and bagging kindling wood, August 1932.

movement in New Zealand. Even while the Napier quakes continued, other cities were being rocked by civil unrest. The years 1931 and 1932 were ones of protest and riots. Frustration and hunger spilled over in spontaneous outbreaks of anger. The writer John Mulgan, a university student at the time who served as a special constable during the riots, wrote later of his experience of the Queen Street rioters:

> *They were the swift runners and the leaders who went first and broke everything they saw without caring. To them it was the releasing of accumulated desire, a payment for the long weeks and months of monotony and weariness and poverty and anxiety that could be satisfied like this in a few moments of freedom and destruction.*[12]

Miner's housing on the Howard goldfields. A desperate Depression Government gave some 250 unemployed spades and pans and sent them in search of gold.

The Government's response was to dismiss the protesters as trouble-makers and agitators, not the "real" unemployed, and to hastily draft the "specials" again to patrol the streets:

> *I went that night into the streets of Wellington and saw volunteers armed with batons and wearing metal helmets from Army stores. Each patrol had a single officer in a trench coat as they marched along one footpath and down another, watched mostly in silence by crowds who came in from the suburbs to sense the crackle of electricity which might at any moment become a further outbreak of looting…. Soon afterwards… I was regularly a spectator at Lancaster Park. A few players, until then idols of the*

The Woman at the Store

crowd on the Bank, had been identified as Special Police during the riots, and as they ran on to the field were greeted raucously with jeers strange to hear in that place and time – "Tin Hat! Tin Hat!"[13]

The Coalition Government voted in to deal with the economic crisis had become obsessed instead with balancing the budget at a time when "the country was flat on its back".[14] There was a school of thought within Government that events such as the Depression were like "natural disasters to be endured rather than human activities to be managed".[15]

The charitable aid organisations, church missions and the hospital boards could not cope with the demands now made of them and in any case had little sympathy with the able-bodied man out of work – traditionally regarded as the least deserving supplicant. In 1931 and 1932, hospital boards provided relief to 93,800 men, women and children, nearly 20,000 receiving continuous relief for six months or more. Conflicting government demands of the country's hospital boards to assist the unemployed while reducing hospital expenditure caused over 40 per cent of the boards to exceed their income that year. In a single day in April 1932, the month of the worst riots, the Auckland Board had 800 applications for relief.[16]

The Government's reluctant contribution to the many in need was subsistence unemployment relief raised by a compulsory tax on all workers, male and female, but available only to Pakeha men, on condition they worked for it:

I was on relief work – I would get for myself, my wife and child, 27 shillings a week. Now if I was sacked off relief work, which we very very often were… we went on sustenance which only entitled me to 13 shillings and 6 pence a week and so we had relief depots… where we were trying to provide some sustenance for unemployed workers and their families.[17]

Beryl Ley owned and ran a country store and like many small traders had a better idea than most of the personal and financial situations of those in her community. She drove mothers to Auckland to hospital when they had no transport or money for a taxi when their children were seriously sick. Occasionally she tried to get families in dire need to accept a free food parcel. She watched extreme poverty bring great strains to some family relationships and breed resilience in others. In every case, the children were the most vulnerable:

Though the Depression was beginning to ease, its effects were still with us. Quite a number were still out of work, others were on charitable aid where the breadwinner was in poor health, and housing conditions were often bad. Family sickness without Social Security could become a grievous burden. One of our customers with a large family lived at the quarry at Pukekawa on the Waikato River and called fortnightly to pick up the order. Almost each year there seemed to be a new baby and one Saturday I noticed that the baby looked pretty sick.

"Is the baby alright?" I asked.

"Oh yes," said the mother, "but when I picked her up for her early morning feed today there was a rat in the cot and it had chewed a piece off her ear."

I felt really ill but the mother remained calm since there was no money for unnecessary trips to the doctor anyway.[i]

[i]Beryl Ley, *Life and Work in a New Zealand Country Store*, Manuscript Room, Auckland City Library, p. 38.

Hunger marchers arriving in Wellington from Gisborne in 1934.

ATL F-29261-1/2

The Wageners & Edwards
The Flour Power Generation

Being young in the Depression meant different things to different people, but in the country it represented a kind of wild freedom, living off the land, and never wasting anything. At Pukenui in the Far North, Roy Wagener was one of eight children whose mother also ran the local Post Office.

She was a master, I think, of making a little go a long way because I don't recall any occasion when we were really hungry. We had the benefit of living right on the harbour. There were shellfish and fish… an abundance of it. If mum wanted something for tea, if she wanted a fish, then it was just a matter of catching one. If she wanted pipis or something like that, we could do that too.… Ninety Mile beach was full of toheroa. You could go and dig a sack full and bring it home if you liked. There was no restriction on it and it was a great day to walk five or six miles to the beach and cart home a great heavy load of toheroas. We used to eat them for our lunch over there.

Roy Wagener (centre) and his brothers
Bill (left) and Brian (right).

Fish was a staple and meat was also on the menu when the family could afford it. It arrived not by refrigerated truck but from the district's butcher, delivering on horseback with a basket in front of his saddle. Groceries came at least once a fortnight – on a boat, so Mrs Wagener had to plan and order ahead. She also made her own bread twice a week and found new ways to recycle the used flour sacks.

Before my time, as well as the Post Office, she looked after a little store. Flour for our bread came in 100lb bags and we got around with Northern Roller Mills written on the seat of our underpants and singlets, such as they were, because Mum made them.

There was no natural larder for city kids in those hard times. Jim Edwards and his younger brothers were still at primary school in Auckland when they started contributing to the family purse.

We were door knockers. We were among an army of people who went round knocking at the more wealthy people's doors to sell them anything that they'd buy. All sorts of things were sold door-to-door, but we sold home-made bath cleaner. This was put into treacle and golden syrup tins that we scavenged from the rubbish dump. We boiled the labels off them and then filled them up with a mixture of grated sand soap and borax, a bit of Tannerwell soap and water. And this was our magic cleaner that my father maintained would clean anything but the conscience.

There was no car and often no tram fare so their father, Jim Edwards, walked from Newton to Remuera or Epsom or Herne Bay to do his selling; and in winter he'd sometimes come home soaked to the skin. Eventually he became very ill with pneumonia and pleurisy.

So this is when my brother, Jack, and I and my much younger brother Brian – I think he was only about five – began to help in the family budget. Now Jack was an incredible story teller and he was always very very good at selling this cleaner. Sometimes he and I would go out together. He would do one side of the street, and I the other. And sometimes when I got to the end of my side, I would have maybe not even sold a single tin. He would come with an empty sugar bag. Sold all his tins. I thought this was incredible, you know – What does he say? I thought I was a better talker than him. Anyway, I sneaked up behind him one day, to have a listen to his sales patter. The gist of his story was there was a family of eight children – he was only a little boy, remember, younger than me – and we're out selling these tins of cleaner to help Mum to get food and things. And my Dad is ill in bed with double pneumonia and pleurisy. But the thing was, Jack was telling this story six months after Dad had fully recovered. I was never a good liar, you know, but Jack was. But he was an incredible salesman.

Source: Edited Ninox transcripts, *Our People, Our Century*, 1999.

ATL F-49826-1/2 (Evening Post Collection)

For the poor and out of work, the Great Depression meant queuing — for food, for unemployment relief, for medical assistance. A crowd builds up along Wakefield Street, Wellington, outside NZ Smith Family Joy Spreaders, probably to collect second-hand clothing.

There was no relief for working women who increasingly lost their jobs to men, and a much reduced payment to Maori men who were expected to get food from traditional sources.

Meanwhile, the Government made swingeing cuts – closing kindergartens, taking 5-year-olds out of school and lowering the school-leaving age, sacking teachers so that the median class size rose to 60, closing two teachers' colleges, stopping the school dental service, pressuring hospitals to release patients earlier and provide fewer meals, cutting pensions, ceasing work on major public works projects and firing the department's workers only to swell the ranks of unemployed and re-employ them on relief work carrying out cheap and often pointless make-work schemes such as sweeping footpaths and weeding streets. No area was sacrosanct – payment for the upkeep of overseas cemeteries for New Zealand's war dead was stopped; and no saving too small – the budget for milk for the cats that kept government buildings free of mice and rats was halved.

Against economic and employment trends everywhere in the industrialising world, including New Zealand, the unemployed were encouraged to seek work in the country although by 1932 "half the farmers were reported to be bankrupt".[18] Work camps with primitive conditions were set up in isolated places to carry out public works and plant trees and, perhaps most importantly of all, keep angry men out of the cities. In early 1932, hungry unemployed had revolted in Dunedin. Far worse rioting and looting took place in Wellington and Auckland:

Thursday 14 April 1932... Phone from Muriel 11 Pm saying serious rioting taking place in City, mob in full control!!!

Friday 15 April Rioting in City last night! Very serious. Not unexpected by me. Perhaps people in N.Z. will concern themselves with N.Z. affairs now & not elsewhere....

Saturday 16 April More serious rioting in Newton last night, the mob have got the "Powers" and "authority?" on the run and anything may happen. Muriel came up in Pm & think she is not too happy being alone in house.[19]

The "anything" anticipated by Auckland diarist Charles Plunkett didn't happen although the Government, believing revolution was at hand, ordered weapons removed from military stores in Auckland and machineguns mounted in Basin Reserve after banning a public rally there. The positions and attitudes of the Government and the unemployed hardened:

You asked me what my feelings were that night – it built up an intense hatred for the system that provoked it. It made me and those like me very bitter towards the police when I saw some of them... indiscriminately lashing out at anyone near.[20]

The riots also provoked shock and less easily defined feelings in the population:

A few days later we went into town and I clearly remember seeing dozens of

Depression Life

The *Weekly News* described the shocking conditions at a work camp at Aka Aka, south of Auckland:

... the floors of the tents are earthen, uncovered by boarding, and on Wednesday many of them were dampened by rain soakage. The surroundings of the camp were very muddy. The men bathe in the drains, wash in horse troughs, and if it rains have to don wet clothing next day.... Men recently arrived at the camp and unused to navvying may earn only 5 shillings a week, but as they become used to the work and more experienced, their earnings become

Police arrive to carry out the Norfolk Street eviction.

proportionately greater. There is, in addition, a free issue of candles and soap. Men who arrived in the camp without blankets have been supplied with bedding, which they pay for at the rate of 1 shilling a week. Damp clothes constitute an ever-present problem at Aka Aka. The men work all day widening drains, nearly always they are ankle deep and knee deep in water and often waist deep.[i]

Back in the cities families unable to keep up their rent payments were regularly evicted. Efforts to stop the evictions became part of the on-going battles with the police:

The anti-eviction campaign was an on-going thing and almost a daily occurrence. Whenever the members of the unemployed workers' movement got wind of a pending eviction and understandably some relief workers were a bit reluctant to inform us – they weren't all as militant as we were – and there was some reluctance to let us know and as a result a lot of people got evicted from their homes which we could have possibly prevented. However, when we were notified we rallied as many troops as it was possible and we picketed the house. The highlight of course was the Norfolk Street eviction which took place over about three days. Mrs Martinovich, "old Marty" as we called her,... she barricaded herself and kids inside and she was joined by a number of the unemployed. The rest of us took turns to picket outside. There was, you know, a lot of the leading lights – Jim Edwards – he was coming backwards and forwards and haranguing the crowd, you know and what have you.... I was outside. We were taking it in shifts. Blokes that were inside of course they had to stay there. There was no point in them coming outside.... When the police finally decided to storm the house it was quite an affair – a number were arrested – ... he was waving a lump of timber; he was prepared to use it too... anyway he dropped the lump of wood but they still... used it against him in evidence. Sheer weight of police numbers forced us to retreat. And they got inside the house, and you know the police took control of the house itself.[ii]

[i] *The Weekly News* 27 April 1932 cited in Stephen Barnett (ed.), *Those Were the Days: A Nostalgic Look at the 1930s from the Pages of the Weekly News*, Moa Publications, Auckland, 1987, pp. 14-15.
[ii] James John Mitchell, Papers, Manuscript Collection, Alexander Turnbull Library.

shop windows still boarded up all along [Lambton] Quay, the shops closed. Groups of silent police stood on street corners and people walked past them without looking at them.[21]

The Government's response was the Public Safety Conservation Act. The Act, one of the most undemocratic of the period in the western world, allowed the Government to declare a state of emergency and withdraw civil rights if public order or safety was deemed to be in jeopardy.

There was little tolerance for opposition of any kind – political, philosophic, cultural… or criminal. Flogging was regularly added to sentences of imprisonment for crimes such as robbery as both punishment and deterrent. Society was considered to be jeopardised by any criticism of Government's actions (or inaction), protest, non-conformity and "unapproved" ideas and philosophies. "Moving pictures" were banned on Sundays unless a special permit had been granted by the local council, concert programmes had to be approved and a department store manager was fined £5 for selling an "indecent document", the magazine *Gangster Stories*, which the judge deemed would "deprave and corrupt minds". A writer at the time noted that "they are almost all alike in their habits and views... and they persecute fiercely those who are different".[22] This lack of tolerance for the unorthodox was often remarked on by visitors:

For originality there may be a small place. For eccentricity, there is practically none at all, which is unfortunate. We haven't even… tolerance of harmless Bohemianism.… A woman who doesn't kill herself with housework and die before her gas stove baking her last scone is morally frowned upon. A man who fails to keep his garden in order is regarded as a dangerous character. And keeping one's garden doesn't merely mean surrounding oneself with an agreeable profusion of herbs and shrubs and trees. It means plastering the paths with concrete and torturing the earth into heart-shaped beds.[23]

Tongariro was New Zealand's first national park.

The Raurimu Spiral – promoted as a touring attraction.

When Rail Was King

The great days of rail travel. At least five of the six Fell steam engines specially designed in England to traverse the Rimutaka Range power the royal train carrying the Duke of Gloucester during his visit in 1934. The Fell had an extra engine to drive horizontal wheels that gripped a central third rail in the railway track. On the downhill run, special brakes were needed to keep the speed to 16 kilometres per hour. Trains had more to deal with than just the Rimutaka's steep gradient. The range's ridges were extremely windy: in 1880 several carriages were blown off the line, killing three passengers. The 1930s and 1940s were the golden age of rail in New Zealand, although the system continued to expand until the Fifties.

Beach Treasure

Perhaps the greatest indication of the times, and one of my longest memories, was the time my mother found a halfpenny. I was eight at the time. My mother... and I were walking over the sand hills which then stretched unbroken from the Lyall Bay bathing shed, the only one on the beach, to the rocks at what is now the southern end of Wellington Airport's runway....

We carried as always a sack each, into which we put anything which would burn. Sea-coal – coal which had drifted ashore from the bunkers of coal-burning ships – was a bonus, but many people were on the lookout for it and finding any was a red-letter day.

We had found a small lump of dried seaweed and were putting it into one bag when mother exclaimed, and into her pocket put a halfpenny she'd found beneath the seaweed. It was worth two "specs" – two slightly shop-soiled apples – at the greengrocer and was therefore a worthwhile find.

Later, after we had unloaded our bags at home, mother took out the halfpenny from her pocket. She was about to put it into her purse when she looked again at it. I recall clearly her odd expression as she pulled out the cake of Monkey brand sand soap from under the wooden bench and began to scrub at the coin under the cold water tap – the only tap. Slowly the seawater and sea air coating disappeared and it began to gleam.

It was a silver coin – a whole shilling. Ten cents today, worth in fact nothing. To us it was, with care, two meals. It was a fortune.

A farmer would sell you a whole sheep for that coin if you were lucky enough to have transport. Of course to us in the heart of the city that was impossible. But eked out with lots of potatoes and gravy, and a good soup before it, the meat it would buy might even cover three meals.

My mother put the sand soap away, put the gleaming shilling on the table, and without a word burst into tears.

I think that was the moment when I realised we were poor – but poor proud.... Mother's wedding ring had long gone to help keep us afloat, gone to that busy "second hand shop" as it was euphemistically known, in Kilbirnie. The "gold" band she wore to her death 50-odd years later was brass. I don't think my father ever knew. I had the impression that after the Depression she kept it as a reminder of those grim days, a sort of indication that she had been so far down, the only way from then on was up.[1]

<hr />

[1] Colin J. McKay, *The Silver Halfpenny*, Manuscripts Collection, Alexander Turnbull Library.

Currency of the 30s

A specifically and distinctively New Zealand coinage was not introduced until 1933. Prior to this, we had used British coins. The first local coins in circulation were the Threepence, Sixpence, Shilling, Florin and Halfcrown. All were of an alloy containing 50 per cent silver. Copper Pennies and Halfpennies, dated 1940, were not introduced until December 1939. There was also a commemorative Crown (five shilling piece) that was originally planned to be issued with the other silver coins in 1933, but design delays meant it was not issued until 1935. This coin is the world famous "Waitangi" Crown and is the key to the whole New Zealand series. Bank notes issued by The Reserve Bank of New Zealand in August 1936 replaced all notes issued up until then by each of the private trading banks.

Literature classed as radical was suppressed – men were jailed for publishing a book about Karl Marx and a lecturer who protested publicly about such censorship was dismissed from his university position. George Bernard Shaw, the British writer who visited the country in 1932, was asked what he thought of Victoria University which forbade discussion among its students on sex, religion and a number of other subjects. He replied tartly: "Where there is any such place it is not a university. It is a contradiction in terms if there is a ban on such subjects. That is what universities are for."[24]

In the very worst days of the Depression, a publication more in sympathy with the New Zealand ethos was launched. The first issue of *New Zealand Woman's Weekly* was published on 8 December 1932 and proclaimed:

> *The New Zealand Woman's Weekly is born with a definite mission and a definite objective. It is to go forth among New Zealand women – rich and poor, young and old – and preach the gospel of usefulness, cheerfulness and happiness. Its mission is to teach, to entertain, to assist and to amuse; its objective, to become a national family journal in the truest and fullest sense of the word.*[25]

As might be expected, the magazine had a rocky first year, changing hands a number of times; but it survived to achieve its objective and become the largest-selling weekly magazine in the country.

With 12 to 15 per cent of the workforce unemployed, and a Government failing to address the problem, the stresses of life turned sectors against each other. In the country, where farmers paid their rates by labouring for the council and with their families ate "cocky's joy" (boiled wheat and treacle), town dwellers were once again regarded as parasites as they queued for food and hospital aid, protested in growing numbers, or went on the road as swaggers. The new, quasi-fascist, ultra-conservative New Zealand Legion, opposed to any government intervention, quickly gained 20,000 members, including two future Prime Ministers, Sid Holland and Keith Holyoake. The Communist and Labour Parties set up competing organisations to support the unemployed.

The Depression had also masked the growing impact of mechanisation and specialisation on both the urban and rural workforces. The number of apprenticeships was cut by 26 per cent between 1926 and 1936 while the male workforce increased by 15 per cent.[26] Concern about the rising number of people, particularly unskilled workers, for whom there was no longer work was forgotten in the more pressing concerns about the sheer numbers of Depression-unemployed.

But the Depression wasn't bad for everyone. The overall retail price index dropped by 20 per cent, the average price of food fell by 27 per cent and rents by 24 per cent. There were those who profited from cheap labour. There were some who continued to lead privileged lives, taking trips back "home" to England, attending the races in furs and formal suits, going to parties and balls, and buying the latest car, electric stove, water-heater or radio from an expanding range of products. There was no appreciable fall off in demand for consumer goods. For middle class families where the father (and sons) kept

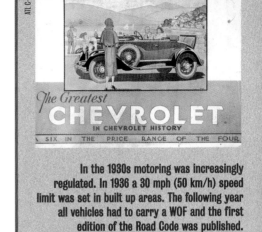

ATL G-22218

The Greatest CHEVROLET IN CHEVROLET HISTORY

A SIX IN THE PRICE RANGE OF THE FOUR

In the 1930s motoring was increasingly regulated. In 1936 a 30 mph (50 km/h) speed limit was set in built up areas. The following year all vehicles had to carry a WOF and the first edition of the Road Code was published.

NZM Archive

Cover of the first issue of the "New Zealand Woman's Weekly". In the decades that followed, the magazine became a Kiwi institution.

Beneath the soft bias-cut dresses of the Thirties, foundation garments of whalebone and steel, and the new elasticised girdles, roll-ons and step-ins in Lastex, reintroduced curves, carefully controlled, of course.

Nelson Provincial Museum 10018 (F. N. Jones Collection)

their jobs, life was still manageable if lived more quietly and frugally. Glamour and plenty were provided instead at the picture theatres where Hollywood produced fantasies, stars and songs to help Depression audiences forget the cold and mean reality outside the cinema doors.

The year 1935 was to prove a turning point for New Zealand; yet its beginning was far from auspicious, with a series of almost biblical plagues and infestations – swarms of stinging flying ants, plagues of rabbits, and ravening caterpillars which infested farm lands in Northland.[27] The Coalition Government had delayed the election a year, but it could not be postponed again.

In this country at least, the very worst of the Depression was over. Prices for our exports were rising faster than for the goods we imported. However, there were still nearly 36,000 unemployed; and the last five years had shaken people free of their old political mindsets. Finally the Labour Party was perceived as a real alternative and not a fringe party of radicals:

There was a good spirit abroad that it was going to happen and with the enthusiasm being whipped up by Scrim and others – propagandists – it became infectious. When the Friendly Road Radio Station was jammed by Adam

In a by-election in 1933, Elizabeth McCombs became the first woman elected to the New Zealand Parliament, following the death of her husband. He had held the Lyttelton seat since 1913. Elizabeth was a feminist and prohibitionist. When she died in 1935, her seat was won by her son, Terence.

A young woman – "Miss Twenty One" – has her named checked on the electoral roll before voting for the first time in the 1935 general election.

Labour Wins Its First Election

I will never forget that election night as we watched in our thousands outside the Auckland Star office, as the results were being displayed. Pandemonium reigned when it was obvious the hated Forbes Government was out. People sang and danced in Shortland Street and even though I knew there were some characters who had been elected on the Labour Party ticket who had not the slightest interests in the principles of socialism, it was impossible not to be caught up in the enthusiasm. I also saw members of the Communist Party who had made the disastrous mistake of telling the workers not to vote Labour, themselves cheering each Labour Party candidate that was being victorious.... They completely miscalculated the feeling of the working class.... There was this feeling abroad, how people, workers, were telling the guard he no longer was boss of the train, and all this kind of thing, you know. It was anybody in authority. This was our Government now and you'll do what we're going to say... which to me I think at the time anyway symbolizes the atmosphere that was prevailing.[i]

[i] James John Mitchell, Papers, Manuscript Collection, Alexander Turnbull Library.

Hamilton [a Government Minister], *to us it was obvious that the hated Forbes Government was out.*[28]

Labour's win on the promise of state intervention to control prices, foreign exchange and credit, and the better distribution of production and services to ensure that everyone willing and able to work could be ensured of a decent income can be seen as part of a world-wide movement away from the old laissez-faire policies. The failure of that doctrine to combat the effects of the Depression had caused a loss of credibility. Right across the political spectrum, governments increased control over their economies, from anti-democratic dictatorial and totalitarian regimes headed by men such as Mussolini, Hitler, Franco, Stalin and many eastern European leaders, to democratic governments in Scandinavia and France and the United States where Franklin D. Roosevelt's "New Deal" won him the 1933 elections.

In New Zealand, the new Prime Minister, Michael Joseph Savage, and many members of his Cabinet were men who had stood beside, fought beside and represented the workers for more than two decades. The "radicals" had captured the Treasury benches and not everyone was happy. The new Government would find some of its reforms blocked by two powerful groups: the banks here and in Britain, and a professional union – the British Medical Association. But those troubles were still in the future when Savage and his Cabinet took their first decisions as Government. There was a Christmas bonus for the unemployed while relief workers got seven days' paid holiday. In a move rich with symbolism, all Labour MPs, Cabinet Ministers and backbenchers alike, pooled their salaries and redistributed the money much more equally. For many New Zealanders it seemed that the Depression song *Happy Days Are Here Again* had come true. Savage said that Labour "intend[ed] to begin where Richard John Seddon and his colleagues left off". He was "among those who believe that, in a fertile country, the standard of living of the people... should not be influenced by any external factor whatsoever".[29] This insulation would never be totally successful.

Many of Labour's early actions restored cuts made by the previous Government. Five-year-olds went back to school, the teachers' colleges were reopened and the school dental service bolstered with more dental nurses. A small independent scheme providing free milk in schools which had started in Wellington during the Depression was applied nationally. A report published in 1934 found that seven out of ten school children in Auckland had physical defects and more than 1000 in Wellington were suffering from malnutrition. In Canterbury more than 600 children did not have enough clothes and over 200 were malnourished.[30] Peter Fraser, the Minister of Education, displaying a Scot's passion for education, made state-funded secondary schooling available to everyone up to the age of 19:

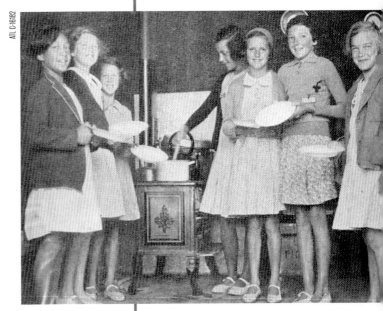

ATL C-16182

Breakfast of champions – the line for porridge at a Christchurch health camp. Six weeks of vigorous exercise and plain wholesome food in a country or seaside setting was the prescription for poor and sick city children.

Suit and tie always required, even at that great Kiwi outing – the picnic.

Nelson Provincial Museum 1/2 17 (Miscellaneous Collection)

Early State houses favoured an English rural cottage style, to the extent that even the high casement windows were more appropriate for an English climate. Despite original intentions that every house be slightly different in design, State housing suburbs soon came to have a uniform look. Above, a family at the front steps of their State house in Naenae, Lower Hutt. Below, Housing Under-Secretary John A. Lee (third from left in centre) watches Prime Minister Michael Joseph Savage carry furniture in to the first State house, in Miramar, Wellington.

Politics never change – an election poster in the 1938 campaign. Labour was returned to power with an increased majority.

The Government's objective, broadly expressed, is that every person, whatever his academic ability, whether he be rich or poor, whether he lives in town or country, has a right as a citizen to a free education of the kind for which he is best fitted, and to the fullest extent of his powers.[31]

Teachers were better paid and better housed. The curriculum was broadened and towards the end of the 1930s adult education was piloted.

Housing conditions for the poor, especially those in cities, were even worse after the building hiatus of the Depression. A government survey revealed there were 27,000 houses that needed to be demolished immediately and 55,000 in urgent need of repair.[32] The Department of Housing Construction was established and photos and newsreels showing Savage and other ministers carrying furniture into the first State house in the Wellington suburb of Miramar boosted the new Government's popularity. In the first three years nearly 3,500 State houses were built – four out of every ten new houses. They were New Zealand-designed, constructed with local materials, placed on sections to catch the maximum sunshine, with spacious modern kitchens and a separate indoor lavatory, a luxury for many who had only known the discomfort of the outdoor privy up until then.

In the country, the small dairy farmers who had suffered from falling prices and a flooded market during the Depression became unexpected supporters of the Government after the introduction of the Primary Products Marketing Act which gave them a guaranteed price. The dairy industry represented significant support: by 1935 almost half the country's nearly 85,000 farms depended on dairying while only 20 per cent relied solely on sheep.[33] The Government was both purchaser and seller of New Zealand butter and cheese. Its critics dubbed it "the primary products pirating bill" but by 1949 the Stabilisation Account held £12 million to cushion the industry against future falls in prices.

In towns and cities factory workers welcomed the introduction of the 40-hour week and civil servants in many government departments began working five instead of six days a week. The new Government made union membership compulsory and re-introduced industrial arbitration. The basic wage rate was set at what was considered sufficient for a man to keep a wife and three children "in a fair and reasonable standard of comfort".

For the first time, all benefits available to Pakeha were now available to Maori. Savage and his Government's strong support for biculturalism and equal rights for Maori and Pakeha, albeit with a paternalistic cast and an underlying belief that European ways were innately superior, was the beginning of a long alliance between Labour and Maoridom. One Maori leader in particular expected a more sympathetic ear from Labour. At a meeting between the Maori leader and prophet Ratana and Michael Savage, Ratana laid out a potato, a broken gold watch, a greenstone tiki and a huia feather before the Prime Minister. Savage studied them carefully:

> *"Brother," he said, "they're speaking to me. I can just hear what they're saying. Yes, they're speaking, but I would prefer you to tell me."*
>
> *The Mangai [Ratana] acknowledged the tribute to his Mana and then explained the meaning of the symbols. The potato was the ordinary Maori needing his lands, for a potato cannot grow without soil. The watch had belonged to his ancestor Ratana Ngahina and it was broken. So was the law relating to Maori land. Only machinery could repair the watch, only the law of the new Government could correct the law of the old. The greenstone tiki represented the spirit in Mana and the traditions of the Maori people. If Mr Savage would save them he would earn the right to wear the huia feather, the sign of the ariki, the paramount chief of Maoridom. He would become the father of his Maori people.*[34]

The race which at the turn of the century had been predicted to disappear now had a natural rate of increase three times greater than the European, but the number of full-blooded Maori had dropped to around 50 per cent[35] of a population now numbering more than 82,000.

In the 1938 elections, with the benefits of the new Social Security Act tantalisingly set to come into force early the following year, the country returned the Labour Government with an increased majority. The social security package drew previous pensions together, substituted a contributory scheme for a non-contributory one, provided for a free universal health system, a means-tested pension for those aged 60 and universal superannuation at 65, and introduced new benefits for sickness, orphans and widows without dependent children, as well as an emergency benefit. It was a defining piece of legislation for the nation and for nearly 50 years it was the basis of government policy and the New Zealand way of life. However, fierce

When Tame Horomona Rehe (Tommy Solomon) died in 1933 aged 50, the last of the full blooded Moriori died. A few of today's Chatham Islanders are descendants of those Polynesian people who settled there about 800–1000 AD.

At the funeral of Te Rata Mahuta, the fourth Maori King in 1933; (from left) Tonga Mahuta, Gordon Coates, Henry Holland, Frank Langstone, Sir Apirana Ngata and Tumate Mahuta at the graveside.

The Argentinians called her clavel del aire – flower of the air, the British Sportsmen's Club, "Our Little New Zealand Lamb". In 1933, Rotorua born Jean Batten bought a plane once owned by the Prince of Wales and began a series of record breaking flights across the world.

opposition from the British Medical Association, which argued that the Government's "state medicine" was interfering and interposing itself in the doctor-patient relationship, prevented the full implementation of free hospital and medical services.

A fresh optimism percolated its way across all aspects of life. In 1935 British coins finally ceased to be legal tender in New Zealand and the specifically local currency introduced two years before became the only currency accepted. At the carefully stage-managed Berlin Olympics in 1936, the New Zealand runner Jack Lovelock won one of the glamour races, earned New Zealand's first gold medal in a track event and set a new world record for the 1,500 metres. Optimism was also in the air. Commercial aviation expanded rapidly both internally and internationally, transporting passengers, cargo and mail. Aviatrix Jean Batten set a number of records flying solo between Britain and Australia and across the Tasman. Everywhere she landed, the small stylish woman in her distinctive white flying suit and helmet was mobbed by enthusiastic crowds.

But such freedom for a woman was the exception. At the same time, the medical adviser to the hugely influential Plunket Society was warning that "modern" education was ruining women.

> One hundred years ago women fought for equality with men and demanded the right to sit for the same examinations, he said. They confused equality with identity, and this had led them to the present system of education totally unfitting for womanhood.
>
> "The women demanded it and they got it. Now they can see where it has led them. Empty cradles and a distaste for housekeeping and motherhood; flats instead of homes, books instead of babies. We blame our bright young things for their feverish desires and their immoral outlook. What chance have they had? – a life spent in school books from the age of five, and then grown up in a night; one moment a schoolgirl, the next a belle at a ball."[36]

Another quite different woman, whose message Plunket would have found more acceptable, was Mrs Maud Basham, "Aunt Daisy", whose weekday morning programme began broadcasting on the new government-owned commercial radio station 1ZB in 1936. For more than 25 years its opening theme of *A Bicycle Built for Two* and Aunt Daisy's cheery warble, "Good morning everybody, good morning, good morning, good morning!", was one of the most familiar sounds on a medium that was expanding in every direction. The business of Parliament was now broadcast from the House of Representatives; a weekly programme on the blues, jazz and swing, *Rhythm on Record*, began a 40-year run; quiz shows appeared; and a slew of recorded radio serials, local, Australian and British, became essential listening for families – *Easy Aces, Dr Paul, Portia Faces Life, Big Sister, Officer Crosby, The Lone Ranger, Dad and Dave, Dr Mac, Fred and Maggie Everybody* and *Life with Dexter*.

But in other countries, these were more troubled times. Throughout the Thirties international tensions and conflict were increasing. Germany and

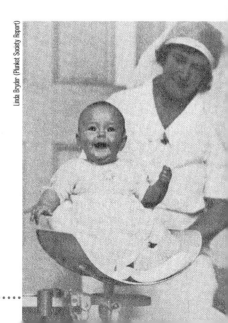

"Dorothy Ann", granddaughter of the founder of Plunket in Auckland, Mrs W.H. Parkes, stars in the twenty-fifth annual report of the society's Auckland branch in 1933.

Mr Dallimore Comes to Town

The popular interest of Auckland changed from wrestling to faith healing with the arrival of a Mr Dallimore who preached and laid hands on people in its town hall. Always he had a couple of assistants ready to hold up those smitten by the cataleptic property of his hands. Truth *newspaper didn't seem to like him, writing about him in a hostile kind of way, but* Truth *was also a bit of a racist in those years, pretty hard on Chinese herbalists suspected of aiding abortion. I had made friends with a young Englishman from Devon where my father's family originated.... Together we attended one of Mr Dallimore's meetings. Judging by outward appearance the man was all right, and his woman companion had a very pleasant face. After we had sung some hymns he made a short address ending with, "My friends, please don't come up on this platform just to see whether I can make you fall down." Soon people started going up, women easily outnumbering men. Each he laid hands on, uttering at the same time a healing prayer. It was the women who fell over mostly, some having to be held up for about a minute, other people recovering after a few seconds, a number remaining firmly upright. I was surprised to see my companion fall backwards into the hands of Dallimore's helpers. When my turn came I remained upright, though for a moment experiencing a tingling sensation in the part of my body where I suspected intestinal sluggishness.*

"You must have felt a shock," I said to my friend as we strolled Queen Street later. "Not at all," he answered. "I had to fall back to stop myself from laughing aloud." "That was silly of you," I retorted. "You should give the man a fair chance." Many others spoke well of him. The warehouse senior said his rheumatic aunt had gone up on the platform, felt a click the moment Dallimore touched her and started to walk more easily at once.[i]

<hr />

[i] James Gidley, Manuscripts Collection, Alexander Turnbull Library.

ATL F-29331-1/2-MNZ ('Evening Post' Collection)

Wrestling was a national craze. Local hero "Lofty" Blomfield (on top) wrestling Don Noland at the Wellington Town Hall while referee Alf Jenkins calls the count.

Japan both had expansion in mind, the former driven by the ambition to create a great German empire and the latter to acquire both territorial and economic security. Great Britain, France and the United States, still war-weary and concerned with their own economic problems, were reluctant to do anything concrete to stop German or Japanese aggression. The Soviet Union was more willing, but not prepared to stand alone, although Stalin provided some help to China against Japan's relentless invasion. The huge differences in ideologies and mutual mistrust between the western democracies and Soviet Russia also stopped them banding together against the aggressors. However, the politics of denial came to an abrupt end when Stalin unexpectedly signed a pact with Hitler effectively dividing Poland between them. German troops crossed the border to attack Poland on 1 September 1939. The policies of appeasement had not worked. Two days later Poland's western allies declared war on Germany. It was the start of the Second World War.

Prime Minister Savage had been warning the country of the possibility of war for several months. After scathing public criticism on the sorry state of the nation's armed services by the "Four Colonels" – a group of former brigade commanders who had been effectively demoted in an army restructure in 1937 – the Government began rearmament and recruitment programmes... after posting the uniformed bearers of the bad news to the retired list. But like Britain, New Zealand was still militarily unprepared for war. Nevertheless, there was no hesitation in joining Britain in declaring war on Germany and her allies. A state of emergency was declared and on 5 September the country's radios carried the solemn announcements:

Summer pastimes, 1930s style.

Nelson Provincial Museum 163327/6 (Kingsford Studio Collection)

That evening we heard… Chamberlain saying that Hitler had not responded to the ultimatum and therefore a state of War exists between Britain and Germany. Immediately following this announcement from Britain our Prime Minister Michael Joseph Savage came on the radio… and made his famous announcement – Where Britain goes – so do we, and we are therefore at war with Germany and her Allies…. Then followed stirring patriotic music e.g. Land of Hope and Glory and Oscar Natske the NZ bass, singing There Will Always Be an England.[37]

There were none of the celebratory parties which had greeted the First World War, still fresh in too many people's minds. Rather, the excitement of the young at the chance for travel and adventure was tempered by a sad sense of déjà vu amongst their parents and grandparents. Monty Holcroft remembered that just for a moment life continued as before:

Lovelock Wins!

On 6 August 1936 at the Berlin Olympics John Edward (Jack) Lovelock won the 1,500 metres and knocked a full second off the old record to set a new world record of 3m 47.8s. He was 26 years old, born at Crushington near Reefton and educated at Timaru Boys' High School and Otago University before going to Oxford University as a Rhodes Scholar in 1931.

On the afternoon of the race, Lovelock was the last of the competitors to arrive at the track, shortly before Hitler. The race had been scheduled to start after the Führer's arrival and began just before 4.30pm with a field of 12. The race and Lovelock's progress were described in detail in the British press:

He was gliding along, moving with beautiful grace and power. Suddenly, with half a lap to go, we saw Lovelock lengthening his stride. Away he went, past Beccali, past Cunningham, ahead of the field and round into the last bend. Veteran journalists leapt to their feet and bellowed…. Into the straight, and Lovelock's slim figure moved with exquisite rhythm and certainty towards the finish. On the main terrace a group of New Zealanders, their voices cracking in the excitement, rose to shout him home. Herr Hitler, who had half risen, sat back in his seat. New Zealand voices were hoarse.

So too was the BBC's radio commentator Harold Abrahams, the great British runner and a long-time friend of Lovelock, who gave his listeners a breathless and exhilaratingly partisan description of one of the great Olympic races:

Cunningham's fighting hard, Beccali coming up to his shoulder. Lovelock leads! Lovelock! Lovelock!…. Come on, Jack! My God he's done it. Jack! Come on!…. Lovelock wins… five yards… six yards. He wins! He's won. Hurrah!

The *Manchester Guardian* summed up:

A race magnificent beyond all description. It had all the elements of greatness – wonderful speed, wonderful tactics, constant fluctuation and all the romance of the great race that these men have been running in the past few years, through which they have been making history. And it was Lovelock's day. His mood was on him. He was running in a rapture, and no human being could live with him….

Lovelock himself wrote later in his training diary, "It was the most perfectly executed race of my career." On 28 December 1949, at the close of the first half of the century, Lovelock collapsed on a platform at Brooklyn's Church Avenue station in New York, fell beneath a moving subway train and was killed instantly.

Source: Don Cameron (ed.), *Memorable Moments in New Zealand Sport*, Moa Publications, Auckland, 1979.

Only a few hours after New Zealand entered the war... footballers ran on to Lancaster Park, and all other grounds, to play their matches, amid the cheers of onlookers, as if nothing untoward had happened to affect their concentration. Young men who played in those games were soon to be on active service and many would die: but on a Saturday afternoon, the turf springy beneath their feet, and crowds on the bank urging them on, war was still remote and not fully understood.[38]

The year 1939 and the decade closed in a jumble of images. Twenty-one days after war was declared, 11 men died of asphyxiation in the Huntly mines. After an extraordinary winter in which regions as unlikely as New Plymouth, Wellington and even Auckland experienced snow, the decade rolled over during the long, hot summer that followed. The year 1940 would mark a hundred years since the signing of the Treaty of Waitangi. As if to put the troublesome Thirties behind it as soon as possible, the nation began celebrations early, on 8 November 1939, with a huge ball to mark the opening of the Centennial Exhibition in Wellington.

Then, on 17 December 1939, Germany experienced its first setback of the new war when the captain of a badly battle-damaged and trapped pocket battleship, the *Graf Spee*, scuttled it just outside the South American harbour of Montevideo. The crew of the *Achilles*, one of the three British cruisers that had hunted down the German boat, were mostly New Zealanders. In the preceding battle the New Zealand ensign had been raised for the first time in a naval engagement. It was the perfect Christmas present for a young country intent on celebrating nationhood in the lull of a war not yet fully engaged.

ATL F-2746-1/2-MNZ (Making New Zealand Collection)

Sunlight League OF NEW ZEALAND
RULES FOR SUNBATHING

WARNING TO SUNBATHERS—The eyes and back of the head should be protected, when sunbathing in the hot sun, to *AVOID THE RISK OF INJURY TO THE EYES OR SUNSTROKE.*

DURATION OF SUNBATH—Those about to commence sunbathing must remember that the skin is unaccustomed to light, and therefore they must begin very slowly. For a dark-skinned person in bathing suit a sunbath of 15 minutes, 7½ minutes to the front and 7½ minutes to the back, is amply sufficient to commence with. A fair-skinned person in hot sun should commence with much shorter time. Gradually increase the sunbath by 5 or 10 minutes each day, up to 2 or 3 hours. The ideal to aim at is a gradual tanning of skin, without peeling or blistering.

THE BEST HOURS for sunbathing in mid-summer are before 11 a.m. and after 3 p.m. The reason is that at mid-day the infra-red or heat-rays predominate over the ultra-violet rays, and these ultra-violet rays have the beneficial power of producing chemical action in the skin. Infra-red rays in excess make the sunbath an exhausting steam bath, instead of the stimulating light bath it ought to be. Even on sunless days ultra-violet rays are present to an appreciable extent.

"SUNBURNING IS NOT SUNBATHING."—Coco-nut oil or olive oil are good to rub into sensitive skins *before sunbathing.* More benefit is obtained by moving about and allowing the air to reach the skin, than by lying on the hot sand.

WARNING TO PERSONS IN POOR HEALTH.—They should not in any circumstances undertake sunbathing without first consulting a physician.

TEST OF VALUE OF SUNBATHING.—Has the sunbath left a feeling of stimulation and exhilaration? If it has, all is well. Has it left a feeling of lassitude and weariness? If it has, then it has been too prolonged, and is a clear warning to take shorter ones. *COMMONSENSE MUST BE USED,* as individuals re-act differently.

RESULTS OF BATHING in Sunlight and Sea are:
1. Higher resistance to bacterial infection and to colds.
2. Increase of lime, phosphorous, iodine and iron in circulation.
3. Improvement in muscular development, bone and growth, and production of a perfect neuro-muscular balance without excess of muscle or surplus fat.
4. Better digestion, keener appetite, and increase of joie de vivre.

Enquiries regarding the Sunlight League's activities in the Health Camp Movement, School Dental Scheme, Smoke Abatement, Diet Reform, Milk Experiment, Heliotherapy, Tramping, and the Youth Hostel Association of New Zealand, will be welcomed by the Hon. Organising Secretary, Miss CORA WILDING, 58 St. Martins Road, Christchurch.

Join the Sunlight League
Annual Subscription 2/6, payable to Mr. C. G. McKELLAR, Hon. Treasurer, 80 Hereford Street, Christchurch.

ATL F-126064-1/2

Sir Apirana Ngata, MP for Eastern Maori and ardent defender of Maoritanga, leads the haka at the centennial celebrations at Waitangi, 1940.

The Edmonds Family
The Rise and Fall of a Dynasty

At the end of the 1870s, a 21-year-old Londoner and his wife emigrated to New Zealand in search of a new life. Jane and Thomas John Edmonds settled in the port town of Lyttelton. They opened a confectionery business, then a grocery store. But trade was slow, and Thomas Edmonds moved his business, wife and nine children to Christchurch. To bring in a little extra, he began making baking powder. The first batch of 200 tins, mixed at the back of his shop, sold quickly.

Keen to expand sales throughout Canterbury, he gave away free samples and when one of his customers asked whether his baking powder would improve her scones he replied that they were "sure to rise". The phrase appealed and he designed the now-famous rising sun trademark to accompany it. By the turn of the century Edmonds baking powder had become a national brand. The *Edmonds Cook Book*, full of recipes using his product, was first published in 1907 and Thomas Edmonds liked to send copies to engaged and newly married couples. It was clever promotion. By 1912, Edmonds had sold a million tins of baking powder. It was the foundation stone of what would become the country's most successful and best known line of baking products.

Two of Thomas Edmonds' grandsons remember him as a kind, retiring man. David Cropp, born in 1914, recalls:

He was a quietly spoken man. He had a very clear complexion and he didn't smoke and he didn't drink, and he didn't talk much. He was quiet and very private. He was a soft touch. If anyone wanted money, they would ask him. He didn't care. But on the other hand, he lived very frugally. I can see him opening a [wooden] case and he took the nails and straightened them out and put them into a glass jar. I remember thinking as a boy, "My goodness, why?"

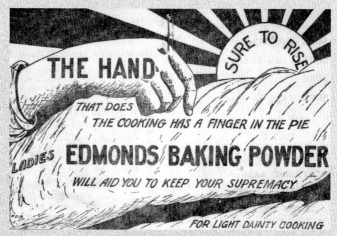

Edmonds advertising appeals to members of the country's "kitchen cabinets".

But it was a way of life with him. I knew my grandmother much better than I knew my grandfather. She had a restricted education, as most people had in those days. She was inclined to embrace religion, not that she was unpleasant with it – she wouldn't try to proselytise – but she got a lot of comfort from it. She would get hold of mediums. I remember there was one in particular who said she could get grandma in touch with T. J. [after he died], and she was very pleased with that one.

Murray Edmonds was born in 1926 and remembers his grandfather as "a genial, white-haired man who seemed to be eternally busy":

I recall one time in Latimer Square being invited by him to step into his electric car. This car had a control tower on it like the airport control tower, just a glass canopy, and it was steered with a tiller. I remember that it made a whirring noise. It was amazing because we are talking about probably one of the first electric cars in New Zealand. It was like being asked to go for a ride in a spaceship.

In 1922 a new factory complex was built on Ferry Road in Christchurch. It housed the latest machinery and baking equipment. The Edmonds rising sun and "Sure to Rise" sign overlooked the factory's gardens, which consistently won prizes throughout the 20th century. Murray Edmonds remembers them when he was growing up:

The Edmonds factory was a much visited place. My recollection of it was the begonia houses which were simply superb and I often moved with large crowds of people through there in the weekends. The scents and the sights and the skill of the full-time gardener in those gardens and in the begonia houses were quite remarkable. They stood out in those days because there wasn't a lot else to interest the population.

The familar Edmonds slogan and trademark rise above the old factory buildings and gardens.

Thomas Edmonds' son William managed the business from 1904 to 1914 when Thomas Edmonds' son-in-law Albert Cropp, David Cropp's father, took over. The company's success in the early part of the century was considered by *Manufacturing New Zealand* to typify "both the growth of a robust young country and faith in its economic future". Edmonds was regarded as a good employer and many workers joined from school knowing they had a job for life. The local newspapers regularly ran stories about long service awards to Edmonds' staff.

The company made its founder a rich man and at his death in 1932 his children shared the wealth. Although Murray Edmonds' parents divorced when he was eight, he remembers some of the family lifestyle:

My father, George Edmonds, was a son of T. J. Edmonds. He designed and built a house at St Albans that was typical of the sorts of homes built by all the T. J. Edmonds children: large enough in which to develop their many hobbies and interests, and also for their social life. The homes were built to almost a standardised plan for wealthy people in those days. They had to be two storeyed, spacious inside, with many rooms and always with an overhanging archway or a portico which cars drove under to let people out in inclement weather.

I recall the house mainly as a place to visit on the weekends when I came home from boarding school, or in the holidays when I used to help my father with his woodwork. Because he was originally a carpenter, he had an interest in woodwork of all sorts. He built, for example, the model of the T. J. Edmonds factory for the Centennial Exhibition. He also designed and built items which he found in Popular Mechanics of those times, including large motorised surfboards. He gave one to the South New Brighton Surf Club. He made his own billiard tables.

When he inherited the money on my grandfather's death, he faced a life where he no longer had to wait for a pay cheque once a week or once a fortnight, or whatever it was. He and his brothers and sisters all then proceeded to lead a life where selective entertainment was their main preoccupation. But I don't think that in terms of today's wealth, he was a wealthy man. He had sufficient to indulge his hobbies. He had sufficient shall we say, at the age of about forty, to adopt the lifestyle of a retired person. But he was energetic.

He used some of his inheritance to buy cameras. He flew the Southern Alps with V. C. Brown, a well-known photographer. He was a very close friend of George Regels, a Christchurch photographer, and he and Ernest Adams were both keen collectors of cameras. He developed and printed his own photographs, always in black and white in those days. I can remember my father went off many a time in an open-type car with the canopy folded

In 1936 the production line in the custard powder filling department could handle 4,000 tins an hour.

down at the back and three or four men, all packing their photographic equipment into it. They would head off over towards the West Coast on shingle roads. Extra tyres were strapped to the side of the car and puncture mending gear always accompanied them, extra water, extra fuel.

When he stopped work he took up an invitation from a friend to travel the world. This gave him the chance to use his photographic skills. So off he went by ship, as they all did in those days, on a two-year trip. He took huge quantities of 16mm film, carting a large tripod and a very heavy camera. I remember seeing a film that he took of the Hindenburg. He was there when it caught fire and crashed; and he had

footage of it falling to the ground with people leaping from it, in flames.

My father didn't do a lot of socialising in the house. There was a large tennis court and pavilion and there were many parties there, everyone in the correct attire, and with the appropriate sort of cocktails and festivities that went with parties in those days.

The evening social activities of the Edmonds families were held by my father's sisters. They were great entertainers and very capable hostesses. The lifestyle of these folk was quite dissimilar from that of people today. Even you and I dine out. If they wished to dine out, it had to be a formal occasion and reserved at one of the two or three hotels which existed. They did this perhaps two or three times a year. As a result, they tended more to have catering in their own homes and the wives usually were excellent cooks.

I can remember going to many of their homes and the feasting was quite considerable. The tables always laid in the best quality silver and crystal glasses. They therefore regarded the ultimate in entertainment as going out to someone else's home for an evening.

The women of the family, Thomas' daughters, were patrons of the arts. They were also exponents of the arts. The younger daughter, Irene Ballantyne, was an extremely fine pianist, a concert standard pianist, and frequently used to entertain visiting artists from overseas. One of them was Noel Coward. I can still see him standing at my Aunty Rheen's grand piano and singing, holding a glass of wine, and elegantly dressed. That was a highlight of the year.

George Edmonds' contact with the firm increased after his father died. He called in several times a week. Murray Edmonds says:

He talked with the workers. They knew him well; he knew them well. He was interested in what they did because he had a working background himself. He

Shortages of food ingredients during the Second World War forced Edmonds to use a cheaper substitute, Acto, instead of cream of tartar in their baking powder. The label carries a recipe for scones and an All Black-like fern leaf.

was close friends with the engineers who maintained the machinery in the factory. It was all fabricated on the factory premises by two engineers with a complete metallurgical workshop. As my father took a greater interest in it, he moved back almost into a working style. He developed the jelly crystals ["Sure to Set"] and the custard powder ["Sure to Please"] there. This gave him an intense interest and the products started to go nation-wide very successfully.

By this time David Cropp's father was managing and running the company after his brother-in-law William died. It was a major change of direction for Albert Cropp. David Cropp remembers:

When he, of all the family, was asked to take over he didn't know anything about business. He was making money in shows, singing, and he was also working in the Bristol Piano Company, but he was just the "boy". I remember him telling me what a thrill he got when he learnt double entry book-keeping. I used to visit the place until about 1932 when I finished school; and the next year I went down to Dunedin studying medicine.

Medicine had been David's father's idea. He saw it as a safer occupation for his son than business. In 1932 and 1933 the Great Depression was at its worst, although David Cropp says the Edmonds family was not affected

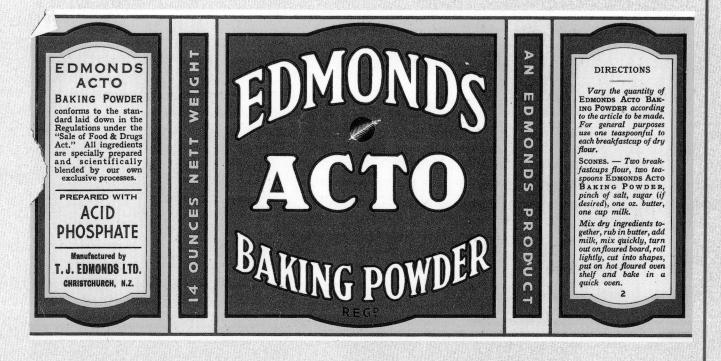

A postwar window display at Beath & Co. in Christchurch reminds housewives why it's worth paying a little more for baking powder made with cream of tartar.

by it. 1928 had been one of their best years ever – they sold two and a half million tins of baking powder:

We were conscious that there was a Depression on but it never hurt us. In fact we prospered in the Depression, which was rather unusual. No one was put off because of it. That was before redundancy. I don't think they knew the word. The company did well because of the habits of the New Zealand housewife.

Murray Edmonds agrees:

The housewife baked. In those days you didn't go out and buy sandwiches and cakes and pies or stacks of fish patties or whatever from the supermarket. There

weren't any. If you wanted to fill the tins at home or provide a meal, you baked or cooked – mince or a stew.

Murray remembered his father taking huge bowls of homemade soup down to the queues at the soup kitchens – "He felt he was doing a social good. It made him feel good." He says the factory kept its workforce by reducing wages or halving working days. It was during the Depression that Edmonds became the first company to introduce the 40-hour week. Albert Cropp was congratulated by Michael Joseph Savage for this innovation but his son, David, says there was a practical reason for it.

We used to fill the tins in the morning and label them in the afternoon. And if you filled them in the morning, and Saturday morning, and you were not going to be there on Saturday afternoon, it was a bit of a muddle. So my father decided that they wouldn't come back Saturday morning. Mr Savage told him it was very enlightened; but it was only convenience.

Albert Cropp was to be the last member of the family to have hands-on management of the company. After 1942 the family presence in the business started to decline, although Thomas Edmonds' sons and daughters remained shareholders. Murray Edmonds and one of his brothers worked there for a time – Murray in his holidays from teachers' training college – but the new manager, Frank Taylor, made it clear there was no place or future for the family in management. The family lost interest in the business as they followed their own careers. Murray Edmonds says now:

They just spent their income and gradually dwindled their fortunes away. The old man made a fortune, his sons and daughters spent it, and the grandchildren had to go out to make a living, and it's just as well we did. It was no good hanging around in those days thinking, "Oh, I'm going to reap a fortune" because we saw it rapidly disappear in front of our eyes during our parents' lifetime. They can't be credited with either abusing or disabusing their money. The men themselves didn't really know what to do with it. It was like winning the lottery.

David Cropp and William Edmonds' son, Keith, remained on the board of directors. David was aware after the Second World War that the company could not continue to rely on its original products. It needed to diversify:

We were the only country in the world that had a high profile baking powder like "Sure to Rise" was. It was going to strike difficulties later obviously. You could see the habits of housewives were changing, even in the Fifties. After the war, the housewife started playing tennis and golf and if she wanted cakes, she would buy them on the way home. And the cakes that were made professionally were not made with cream of tartar [as Edmonds Baking Powder was]. They were made with a ferro phosphate. Something had to be done about this change, and we tried all sorts of things. We associated with White Wings. They were making cakes. And Oxo, cake mix and pickles. We tried everything. And then of course we struck the venison business and that's when the trouble started.

1979 was Edmonds' centennial year, and their last good one. They received an export award. During that 100 years the laboratory staff at Edmonds had produced more than 200 products for local and overseas markets. There was also a factory in Parramatta in Sydney manufacturing cream of tartar and tartaric acid.

The crunch came soon afterwards. The company had began to shift many of its operations to Auckland to cut the hefty transport costs of moving bulk products like self-raising flour to the much larger northern market. Successive managers had also channelled money into other ventures, unbeknown to the family. David Cropp still remembers the family business's sudden demise:

There's a lot that I don't know and can't know, it happened so quickly. One minute we seemed to be going on as before, and then suddenly the manager told us everything had collapsed. Everything seemed to fold at once. I think the other members of the family felt they had been let down. I kept out of everybody's way. I knew I was held responsible in some measure and I hadn't been. It was just as big a shock to me as it was to them.

I never went down when the factory was being demolished. I felt so ashamed.

Thomas John "T. J." Edmonds in 1931.

Murray Edmonds was sorry to see the gardens and the distinctive "Sure to Rise" sign disappear from the old factory site. It marked the end of his grandfather's great endeavour. But he is also philosophical about it. All credit for the company's prominence remains, he says, with its founder:

The presence of Thomas Edmonds in New Zealand came about as a result of his and his wife's courage in leaving the home country. Things were not easy and I admire him for the move he made, just as I admire people I know today who left Europe and settled here and made a good life for themselves. Some brought great skills with them. Others have had to learn skills in New Zealand; and I think that my grandfather learnt the art of selling. He was motivated to move his cart around the streets and approach people face-to-face, like the early insurance men. But it worked. Without his willingness to go that extra step beyond his shop, he possibly would have faded into obscurity.

Edmonds products, including the original baking powder, continue to be manufactured by Bluebird Foods in Auckland.

Sources: Edited Ninox transcripts from *Our People, Our Century*, 1999. Photograph on p. 106 from the Alexander Turnbull Library (C-22361); portrait of T. J. Edmonds on p. 111 from Canterbury Museum (H. H. Clifford E86-1/2); all other photographs from Bluebird Foods (The Edmonds Collection).

1940

1950

Chapter 5

War and Its Aftermath

When the Second World War began, the Labour Government was still smarting from diplomatic hostilities with Britain over the question of loans. England disliked its debtor's unorthodox "socialist" policies and struck a hard deal. How the Government should respond to this pressure opened a rift in the Labour Party. But the whole issue was rendered obsolete at a stroke, by war.

Within days, just as in the First World War, Britain commandeered New Zealand produce at a good price, although below world market levels. Already long established as Britain's farm, we would continue in that role for the war's duration and nearly 10 years beyond. It was a timely solution for the immediate problem.

Burial at sea after the battle of Kolombangara in the Pacific. The HMNZS "Leander" was hit by a massive Japanese torpedo; 35 crew were killed or injured.

Royal New Zealand Navy Museum

Conscientious objectors in the detention
camp at Hautu in November 1943.

By 1945 the Government had paid off almost all
overseas debt and was even in a position to make a gift of
£10,000 to a devastated England, by then worse off than
during the war. But it made us even more dependent on
a single market, seeding problems for the future.

Labour had no reservations about fighting this war.
The idealists and conscientious objectors of the First
World War now ran Cabinet and the country and "had
come increasingly to the idea of force as necessary to
restrain evil".[1] A couple of years earlier Peter Fraser had
told a Labour Party conference they must be ready to defend and even die for
"Labour Democracy", asking "Do you think we would get any mercy from Mussolini
or Hitler?"[2]

What was less expected was the way they treated anti-war protest. The declared
state-of-emergency authorised censorship and the Emergency Regulation Act gave
the Government enormous powers to monitor and control what people said, wrote,
saw and did. The men who had spent time in prison for their beliefs and opposition
to conscription some 20 years before now brooked no interference in their plans and
preparation for war. Communist and Christian pacifist papers were closed and
protesters arrested. During the next five years about 800 men – dubbed conchies or
shirkers – were locked up in special camps nicknamed "funk holes" for refusing to
serve in the armed forces. One of the best known was a First World War hero and
Methodist minister, Ormond Burton. He was already incarcerated in Wellington's
Mt Crawford prison when the first soldiers sailed for the Middle East:

> The great ships passed immediately below the prison garden. Some twenty-five
> years before I had been with the cheering transports that swung out from
> Mudros to the beaches of Gallipoli where the gallant companies were torn to
> bloody shreds by the bursting shrapnel and the hail of machine-gun fire.
>
> In my mind's eye I could see the battles that were to come and how the
> strong and exultant young men who crowded these decks would be broken
> under the barrages. I found it very moving, as one always must when one senses
> the willingness of men to suffer and die for a cause that seems to them right.
> So, standing in the garden in my prison dress of field grey, I gave the general
> salute with my long-handled shovel – very reverently.[3]

But the first public mourning of loss was at home, when the Prime Minister,
Michael Joseph Savage, died of cancer. The people's hero, whose portrait hung in
the front room of workers' homes like a talisman, was given a huge funeral. The train
carrying his casket from Wellington to Auckland was met at every station by silent
mourners, before he was buried on a headland overlooking Auckland harbour. Kiwis
in their tens of thousands turned out to farewell him:

> … silent crowds thronged every section of the route, waiting, many of the men
> with bared heads, to pay a tribute of respect to the memory of a man admired
> and respected by all sections of the community. The warm autumn sunshine
> poured down on closed shops and public buildings and the half-masted flags
> hung limply, scarcely stirring in the faint breeze. The drawn blinds in the

"Playland"

The Centennial Exhibition was the last of the great exhibitions, and the biggest. Built on land adjoining Wellington's Rongotai airport, it had a central Art Deco tower with 219 steps to the top, 15 acres of display parks, reflecting pools, fountains, man-made waterfalls, two sound shells, a cabaret, creche and hotel, and a 10-acre amusement park, "Playland". In one of the courts, model-makers had constructed 10,000 miniature buildings representing major New Zealand cities, in another a replica of the Waitomo caves with electric glow-worms. Robots like "Dr Wellandstrong" conducted visitors through the Health Department exhibit and two master carvers, Pine Taiapa and Hone Metekingi, could be watched at work. A huge sculpture of Kupe and his whanau by the Christchurch sculptor William Trethewey is one of the few exhibits to survive and now stands in Wellington's Winter Show building. Australia, Britain, Canada and Fiji all had extensive displays and about 250 businesses and other organisations were represented.

For many visitors the most memorable part of the exhibition was "Playland", the largest amusement park New Zealand had seen, and particularly lively at night. There was the "Laughing Sailor", a mechanical barker, Rosie the fat girl who was reputed to weigh 54 stone, an ice ballet, crazy houses, a ghost train, miniature racing cars and, most exciting of all, the "cyclone ride" roller coaster – the largest in the Southern Hemisphere – which provided hair-raising rides at 70 miles per hour.

Despite the war the exhibition was a stunning success. When it closed on 4 May 1940 nearly 2,650,000 people had attended, a staggering million more than the entire population of New Zealand at the time.

ATL G-17266-GT

ATL F-36214-1/2 (Eileen Deste Collection)

Centennial

In the year of centennial splendours
There were fireworks and decorated cars
And pungas drooping from the verandas

But no one remembered our failures.

The politicians like bubbles from a marsh
Rose to the platform, hanging in every place
Their comfortable platitudes like plush

Without one word of our failures.[1]

Denis Glover

---

[1]Denis Glover, 'Centennial', *Selected Poems*, ed. Bill Manhire, Victoria University Press, Wellington, 1995, p. 37.

Government Buildings, the absence of traffic noises, and the bands playing funeral music added to the solemnity of the scene....

More and more people hurried to join the waiting thousands along the route. Most of the men and many of the women wore dark clothing and some had badges with Mr Savage's picture on them, adorned with black ribbon....

The tops of buildings and other vantage points were black with people, and others stood on chairs and stools in shop doorways to catch a glimpse of the procession.[4]

The man who succeeded him, as Savage himself had ensured, was his deputy, Peter Fraser. Fraser never inspired the love accorded his predecessor but he was a tougher politician and tactician, described by a senior civil servant as astute and far-sighted with "breadth and enlightened humanitarianism".[5] His deputy was Walter Nash, the Minister of Finance, who was to spend a large part of the war in Washington looking after the country's interests. Fraser was determined that despite the war Labour's political reforms would continue. In September 1939, 19,000 men were still on benefits or in subsidised work. Constant pressure from the opposition to form a coalition government was rebuffed. During the next five years, except for a brief period, a War Cabinet of three Labour and two Opposition MPs handled the business of war. The National Party's new leader, Sidney (Sid) Holland, ran a constant attack on Labour "claiming that there was a second war on the home front where the Government was implementing socialism".[6]

The funeral cortege of Labour Prime Minister Michael Joseph Savage moves slowly through crowd-lined streets on its way to Wellington railway station to begin the journey home to Auckland.

A few families and young men reluctant to enlist received white feathers, but nothing like the numbers which had silently accused men out of uniform of cowardice 25 years before. The practice was condemned by the Queen and MPs of all parties. Fears of a "fifth column" caused harassment of foreigners, including those fleeing Hitler's Germany. All "aliens" had to register with the police and Somes Island out in Wellington harbour became a barren, windswept detention centre for 86 men of various European nationalities. But for most of the ordinary civilian population, life changed little at first as they got used to being at war:

For most people there was nothing immediate to do. With some people, self-interest balanced fervour and they began at once to hoard food... they bought tea, sugar and flour in panic quantities.... Tinned fruit and fish were also bought up by those who could afford them, while in drapers' shops the belief that reels of cotton would be scarce made the demand so strong that they were scarce indeed.[7]

The Elmwood Home Guard at the ready, as Japanese forces race down the Pacific, set to dig air raid trenches for the ex-servicemen in the Rannerdale Home in Papanui Road.

Petrol rationing was introduced early, private cars were commandeered for defence use and over 2,000 drivers adopted an alternative gas fuel powered by small burners carried on the back bumper or running board, which ran for a smoky short distance. But as rubber and tyres and spare parts were soon almost impossible to get, many cars spent most of the war off the road.

Milking time for a member of the Women's Land Service working on a farm in the Rotorua district.

The Land Girl

Mine is the wind, and mine the sun,
The rain, the clouds, and every one
Of those pale stars at dawn.

Theirs is the house, and theirs the land,
These hills are theirs on which I stand,
And theirs my bed and board.

But I, I own the whole wide sky,
This lusty wind that rushes by,
And this old huntaway.

Mine is the work, and theirs my keep,
Mine is this horse, and theirs the sheep
I muster from the hills.

The horse, the dog, my soul are mine,
The work I love in wet or fine,
All these and life are mine.[1]

Mary Guthrie

[1] Mary Guthrie, "The Land Girl", *New Zealand Farm and Station Verse 1850-1950*, ed. A.E. Woodhouse, Whitcombe and Tombs, Christchurch, 1950, p.161.

Almost 60,000 men had volunteered for armed service when conscription was introduced. From then on all Pakeha males aged 18 to 46 were eligible for service in the armed forces at home or overseas. During the course of the war, two out of every five men served their country in uniform. Home Guard numbers climbed to a peak of 124,194.[8] The remains of Depression unemployment evaporated and women began to move into essential industries to replace the men leaving for war. Over the next five years they became posties, train guards, railway porters, tram conductors, policewomen, jurywomen, factory workers and the mainstay of shops and schools. Over 4,500 enrolled in the Women's Auxiliary Army Corps, others served with the air force and navy. The Women's Land Service put over 2,000 "land girls" onto farms.

Mary Guthrie, who wrote the poem "The Land Girl", had grown up on farms and worked as a land girl during the war:

> *I drove a tractor, baled lucerne, stooked the oats and wheat, foot-rotted sheep, lambed the ewes and plucked dead ones. Mustered, sweated in the shed, and sometimes cooked for the shearers. Cut out cattle, milked four cows.*[9]

She at least had some experience and knowledge of farm life. Young women from the towns and cities often found the experience far less bucolic.

The real war was moving closer. A German ship laid mines in the approaches to Auckland harbour; days later they claimed the mail steamer *Niagara*. The BBC radio news broadcast each night became essential listening. In the Battle of Britain, some 100 pilots were New Zealanders[10] and aircraft from No. 75 (NZ) Squadron took part in the first large-scale attack on Berlin in reprisal for German attacks on civilian Britain.

Everything changed in 1941. That year Kiwis in great numbers met the reality of war for the first time. In April and May, the New Zealand 2nd Division was blooded, first in Greece and then in Crete. Losses and casualties were high. Both battles were lost and New Zealand soldiers experienced one of the first attacks by airborne troops:

ATL F-14389-1/4-DA (War History Collection)

A bad beginning to the war – Bill Crawley and Phil Tritt after their car had been dive-bombed and machine-gunned during the retreat from Grevena, Greece, in April 1941.

> *… someone gave an exclamation that might have been an oath or a prayer or both. Almost over our heads were four gliders, the first we had ever seen, in their silence inexpressibly menacing and frightening. Northwards was a growing thunder. I shouted: "Stand to your arms!", and ran upstairs for my rifle and binoculars. I noticed my diary lying open on the table. Four years later it was returned to me, having meanwhile been concealed by some Cretan girl.*
>
> *When I reached the courtyard again the thunder had become deafening, the troop-carriers were passing low overhead in every direction one looked, not more than 400 feet up, in scores. As I ran down the Prison road to my battle headquarters the parachutists were dropping out over the valley, hundreds of them, and floating quietly down. Some were spilling out over our positions and there was a growing crackle of rifle-fire.*[11]

For the next four years, families with men fighting overseas dreaded the sight of the telegram man coming up the front path with the official notice of death or missing in action:

> *I remember going into people's houses whose sons and brothers had been killed and it's an aspect of the war that's been forgotten largely, the gloom that's cast through the house, the special kind of grief. Because there was no body, nothing to concentrate the grief on. It was a lost grief. It was an appalling experience.*[12]

A bomb casualty at Alamein during the North African campaign.

Newspapers carried lists and photos of the dead and missing along with reports of battles long since fought. The soldiers themselves were also coming to terms with the business of war:

> *I go to ground like a rabbit and press myself deeper and deeper. And so it goes on for 20 minutes and I see one poor bloke 10 yards away get it in the back. It's a very peculiar experience being machine-gunned. You get a cold feeling in the stomach when first they come along – then you get extremely annoyed and, when you're certain they will get you, you feel resigned about it and begin wondering what it will feel like. Then off they go and you feel rather exhilarated and a bit dry.*[13]

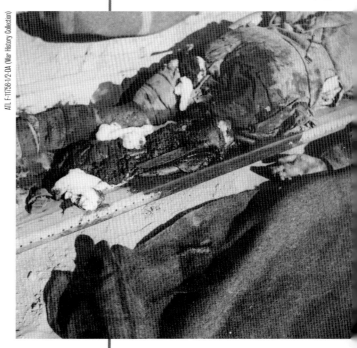

ATL F-11758-1/2-DA (War History Collection)

It was a sign of the change in government thinking and in New Zealand's international status since 1914 that Fraser appointed a

Lilian Wagener
The Postmistress and the Law

Consider the Postmistress in the days when the Post Office was the hub of community life. Lilian Thomas (later Wagener) ran the Pukenui Post Office with its responsibility for bringing not just good, but deathly news. Her son Roy recalls:

In World War One she received every telegram that came from the War Office for people wounded, people missing, people killed, including her own brother. And then in the Second World War, she went through it again with three sons overseas. But she carried on.

Apart from war casualties, there were times when a local child died in hospital and the message came through to the only telephones in the district, at the Post Office. When this happened at night, Lilian would have to go through the rutted roads of the district to break the news.

During the Second World War, Lilian watched one day as the military police pulled up outside her little Post Office trying to find the address of a neighbour. Roy recalls:

House and Post Office at Pukenui in the 1940s.

Lilian Thomas (left) and older sister Maud.

He lived just down the road on the only farm. He had a young wife and I think he had two children and no money. He was trying to break in a farm and he got conscripted into the Army. His wife was heavily pregnant with, I think, their third child. He came home on leave from the Army and they had no water supply so he decided he'd dig a well. They had only had an open fire.

The place they lived in was a shed that was made out of rolled out 44-gallon steel drums. And there was hay stacked in one end of it. So he got to work to dig a well and do some other things for his wife because she had to carry water along the road in a four gallon tin.

When the police arrived Lilian asked what they wanted with him and was told he had gone AWOL (absent without leave) from camp. They were there to pick him up and take him back, but Roy remembers that his mother had other ideas.

She said "You can't do that!" And they said, "Oh yes we can. Why can't we do that?" And Mum promptly jumped up and down and said, "Well look, he's digging a well for his wife. His poor wife's heavily pregnant and she's carrying water along the road in a four gallon tin to wash the other children, and to cook with. She's got no decent fireplace... you can't take him back because he hasn't finished."

They said, "Well, the regulations say that he is AWOL and has to go back." So she told them what she thought about it all and said, "Surely the war, with all the thousands of people they've got in a war on the other side of the world, they can do without one person for a couple of weeks and let him finish the job."

Eventually they decided that that's what they'd do and said, "Well you keep your eye on him, and when the well is dug and when the other jobs are done, you go and tell him he'd better come back to camp or we'll pick him up. We'll jack it up the other end." And that's exactly what happened.

Source: Edited Ninox transcripts from *Our People, Our Century*, 1999.

British born, New Zealand raised, First World War VC winner and professional soldier, Bernard Freyberg, to lead the NZ 2nd Division. His appointment was intended to ensure ultimate New Zealand control over our forces under British command. Neither man was afraid to challenge the High Command in the interests of their soldiers. After the debacle of Greece and Crete came the Division's longest-running campaign. The "Div" joined British and Commonwealth forces to push the Germans and Italians from North Africa. Those cited for daring acts became household names – Hinton, Hulme, Upham, Elliott, Ngarimu and Manahi.

On 7 December 1941, as the battle lines swirled back and forth across the desert, Japan entered the war with a series of attacks across the Pacific, including the infamous attack on Pearl Harbour – its own version of "blitzkrieg". Now there was a seemingly unstoppable enemy in our home sphere, "this sense of a tide racing down towards us at extraordinary speed…."[14] Even as the country tensed to face this new threat, New Zealand suffered its largest single loss of naval personnel of the war. *HMS Neptune* was sunk by mines in the Mediterranean and most of the 150 Kiwi sailors in the ship's crew of 750 lost their lives.

When Singapore with its expensive and supposedly impregnable defences fell to the Japanese, any remaining hopes that Britain would defend us were ripped away.

> *In the second year of the second Pakeha century the settlers faced their grimmest threat, that of a Japanese victory in the Pacific, and were taught that the British, in whom they had trusted for the first century, were no longer reliable.*[15]

Suddenly New Zealanders felt terribly exposed. A Japanese plane made reconnaissance flights over Wellington and Auckland; Darwin was being bombed almost daily. The fighting men were off in the European theatre of war. The Home Guard was poorly equipped and made up of men too young, too old, or rejected by the services as unfit for a fighting war. There were only four anti-aircraft guns to defend the entire country. Although the chiefs of staff concluded quite early that New Zealand was very unlikely to be invaded, on civvy street the danger appeared very real. People talked about "when the Japs come" not "if the Japs come".[16]

Networks of tunnels and trenches to provide air raid shelters for up to 10,000 city workers were built in the main cities while the bigger buildings adapted their basements to house their staff. Shelters were also dug in backyards, slit trenches in school playgrounds, the children had regular air raid drills and there was a new "baddie" at the Saturday pictures in the serials and propaganda films:

> *Children make wonderful victims for the propaganda machine, so we got a lot of films about very, very goofy foreigners. All the Germans were methodical, they clicked their heels and said "Heil Hitler", but they were easily outwitted by the quick-thinking Englishman or American who tangled with them, even though they were always outnumbered. And, of course, the Japanese were shown to be idiotic. They were extremely idiotic in fact, and so we always jeered and shouted at these people.*[17]

When the Japanese bombed Pearl Harbour, they brought the United States into the war. This marked the beginning of a new relationship for the New Zealand Government and its people. The "Yanks" and not the "Poms" were to be our saviours, and seducers. In the

ATL F-6037-35MM-DA (War History Collection)

Commander of the 2nd Division, Major General Bernard Freyberg, with Prime Minister Peter Fraser during his visit to "the Div" in Italy.

New Zealanders in 485 Squadron, Royal Air Force, in front of one of their Spitfires.

Battle of the Coral Sea and the Battle of Midway they finally stopped the Japanese juggernaut and its rapid spread across the Pacific. It would take three years of grim and bloody fighting to push the Japanese back to their home islands.

On 12 June in Auckland, and then 14 June in Wellington, the first US Marines disembarked.[18] By the war's end, 120,000 American servicemen had passed through New Zealand,[19] using it primarily as a training base and for rest and recuperation. The excitement of their arrival was tempered by the introduction of serious rationing. "Managing" became a lot harder. Ration books were issued and queues became part of life. There were strict limits on eggs, meat, butter, sugar, tea, household linen and hosiery. Double blankets were a thing of the past and knitting wool was in short supply. Those "knitting for victory" learned to unpick old jerseys and woollens and reuse the wool. Cooking for parcels to be sent overseas to those fighting or in prisoner of war camps was more and more of a challenge. People became very creative in getting what they needed:

> *Occasionally we would get a little low on funds and ways and means of extracting extra cash from long suffering locals had to be devised. One ploy backfired and nearly caused a lawsuit. The idea seemed simple enough but oh, boy!! A portrait of a very ugly man was drawn on a blackboard, a man's name appended with an invitation for him to replace his name for another on payment of 2 shillings, 6 pence. The name of the local "Mayor" was given the honour of first place, but when notified, his sense of humour completely deserted him and he threatened prosecution. His name was hastily removed, another husband's name substituted and we were in business. This proved a very profitable money spinner.[20]*

The Women's Institute and other committees and groups throughout the country baked fruit cakes and biscuits, knitted natural wool jerseys and socks, scarves and balaclavas with wool often recovered from farm fences, collected fat and copper and seeds for Burma. Sewing bees made clothes for displaced people in Britain and Europe. They made swabs and dressings and rolled bandages. Women joined the St John Ambulance and became drivers after getting their First Aid certificates; they collected books to send the troops and made toys for refugee children. They held farewell parties and later welcome home parties for local servicemen. In one district every departing serviceman was given a wallet.

We became a nation of collectors and savers and recyclers – bottles, all kinds of rubber, string, tin, almost anything you can think of which could be fed into the industrial maw and reinvented as goods for war. The recently launched magazine *New Zealand Listener* reported:

> [Aunt Daisy's] *Yale Key Campaign which was inaugurated in connection with the "Weapons from Waste" drive, closed... with a total of more than*

School girls knit for victory while wartime paper shortages reduce the "Woman's Weekly" to fortnightly publication.

25,000 keys; to say nothing of the enormous quantity of good brass candlesticks, ornaments, trays, vases and bells, besides brass fitting of all descriptions.[21]

Many women were learning to manage a family and finances alone for the first time in their lives – "I never thought of myself as a solo mother, but that's what we were."[22] War brides often had a tough time:

She must bear most of the social, spiritual and frequently the financial responsibility of a home. If there is a child she has to bring it into the world and care for it alone. She must be husband and wife, housekeeper, breadwinner and handyman – and pretend that it's easy. Considering how many brides are barely out of rompers, this is a tall order.[23]

In the past, those women who could afford them had been able to get domestic servants to help. But domestic work was classed as non-essential and the new jobs offered women at least twice the rate of pay, and weekends off. Between 1936 and 1945 domestic servant numbers dropped from over 29,000 to 9,000 – a 70 per cent reduction. The war effectively put an end to the profession.

Wartime and essential industries were now at full stretch and more was needed. Food was required for the Pacific theatre of war as well as Britain; and the Government was determined to put a New Zealand Army Division into the Pacific as well as air force squadrons and New Zealand Navy ships and minesweepers. They wanted to ensure our territorial interests and a voice in Allied councils. It proved impossible; there simply were not enough men to fulfil all the demands now being made on the country. With reluctance Fraser informed the Americans

ATL F-66941-1/2 (Evening Post Collection)

We weren't fighting at home, but the war made itself felt in all sorts of ways. Right, schoolboys proudly display some of the bottles and scrap metal they have collected as part of the war funds effort in Miramar. Below right, women pack and wrap food parcels for troops overseas. Below left, during 1944 refugees from war-torn Poland – 82 adults and 755 children – arrived from holding camps in Europe to begin a new life in a strange country.

ATL F-36291-1/2 (Joe Pascoe Collection)

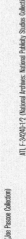

ATL F-34240-1/2 (National Archives: National Publicity Studios Collection)

A wounded soldier of the 30th Infantry Battalion, 3rd NZ Division, waits to be taken off Nissan Island in the Solomons.

that the 3rd Division would have only two brigades instead of three. Under their commander, Major General Harold Barrowclough, they entered the Pacific arena, "just a tiny drop in the great American sea".[24] Bad though physical conditions were for the 2nd Division in Italy, conditions on the ground in Guadalcanal, Vella Lavella and the Green Islands proved equally gruelling. A few soldiers experienced both:

We had been trained but it was still pretty horrific. You had to learn a lot of things, like snipers. They tied themselves to trees and you could be walking along, looking everywhere else but up. They would let a patrol go by, then cheat on you from behind, from up top of the trees. That took a bit of getting used to. It was bad on the nerves, what with crocodiles, lizards, poisonous spiders, land crabs and mosquitoes. In the jungle, particularly at night, you didn't know what was going to happen, if anything. You were tensed up, really nervous, and your ears were tuned all the time to any sounds, like clanking….[25]

While their men fired the guns, women made bullets, grenades and bombs. During the latter years of the Second World War, four out of every 10 factory workers were women.

Between March 1942 and January 1944 all women between 18 and 40 and all men aged 18 to 59 came to be "manpowered" in stages into essential work.[26] Essential industries claimed 40 per cent of the workforce. Maori women initiated the first wave of Maori away from the land to urban areas. There, they too went to work to support the war effort in essential industries. Many of their men, never subject to conscription, were fighting abroad as volunteers in the army in the Maori Battalion, and in the navy and air force. The number of women in industry rose from 180,000 in 1939 to 228,000 by December 1943 – 45 women to every 100 men.

A growing number of women with children also wanted to work but, unlike in Britain or the United States, no thought or provision was made for childcare. For many women the reasons were financial – it was up to their husbands in uniform how much of their pay was allotted to their families at home and for some it wasn't enough. Others wanted to take the new opportunities offered, to do their bit in the war industries to support the fighting men, or to escape the terrible loneliness and lack of adult companionship at home. Government and Establishment propaganda exhorted otherwise, selling motherhood as an essential industry and patriotic duty:

Motherhood can be declared the first essential industry in any country. Women must realise that their primary place is in the home. The majority of women have their highest ambitions wrapped up in a happy home life.[27]

It is not surprising then that the Playcentre movement began during the war. The first Playcentre's aims were "to provide leisure time for mothers, and opportunities for the social development of the pre-school child". Those involved were only too aware of what later would be termed "suburban neurosis" and believed:

[Playcentres] *did something towards curing this by bringing women out of their homes and making them feel they were part of a community group that was doing something more than just minding children.*[28]

Meanwhile, the Americans were making their presence felt. It wasn't just that they arrived in a country which had been drained of most of its best and most eligible young men. They were different. They were more outgoing than the average Kiwi male, they brought gifts and a whole range of things in short supply – cigarettes, sweets and chocolates, silk stockings, hair shampoo. They gave women flowers and talked to them and enjoyed women's company; and their uniforms were better tailored. They brought their music and big bands with them. In the golden age of movies, the age of the matinee idol, it was as if Hollywood had come to town, an altogether powerful combination:

Social life became a lot more interesting with the arrival of "the Yanks". US servicemen fraternise with the locals at the Majestic Cabaret in Wellington.

ATL F-164516-1/2 (E. M. Alderdice Collection)

ATL F-37429-1/2

In a referendum held at the end of the 1940s, 6 o'clock closing for pubs, introduced during the First World War, won resoundingly. The drinking hour from five to six, at the end of the working day, was appropriately dubbed "the 6 o'clock swill".

Before the war, Auckland was a sleepy main street where people gathered in knots and talked. It was six o'clock closing of course, so there was virtually no night life. But the Auckland I found when I arrived in 1942 was totally transformed. The streets were full of Americans. There were things like "hubba dubba ding ding" and "hey man" being shouted, there were strong smells of aftershave, and the American uniforms were so strikingly different from the uniforms of our own servicemen. Everything was so jazzed up and so foreign.[29]

The pleasures taken were innocent and otherwise, but despite dire warnings the illegitimate birth rate only rose from four to six per cent. Adoption rather than fostering began to be encouraged. However, there was a sharp rise in abortions – an estimated 15,000 to 20,000 a year during the war compared with an estimated 6,000 a year during the Depression.[30] There was harsh criticism of engaged or married women who fraternised with the visiting Americans. The Auckland university paper *Craccum* was perhaps the bluntest:

Any married or engaged woman who cannot wait till a man returns from overseas to settle her emotional problems has about as much stability as a prostitute.[31]

Of course, not everyone liked the new "cousins". There were those who considered the Americans flashy and arrogant and agreed with the Australian doggerel:

They saved us from the Japs
Perhaps
But at the moment the place is too Yankful,
For us to be truly thankful.[32]

There were occasional confrontations but the only serious conflict came at the so-called Battle of Manners Street when, after a disagreement in one of the Wellington servicemen's clubs, a pitched battle developed between American servicemen, Kiwi servicemen and civilians – about 1,000 people.

War began to take its toll at home. At the POW camp in Featherston, Japanese prisoners attacked their guards with disastrous results – 48 Japanese died and 61 were injured. One guard was killed and 11 injured. The first soldiers in the 2nd Division to leave for war came back on furlough at the successful end of the North African campaign. They saw able-bodied men earning good wages and striking for even better money and conditions and when the time came for them to return to the Div hundreds of them refused. No one should be asked to go twice, they said, when there are those who still haven't been at all. In the midst of all this were elections, already delayed by two years because of the war:

A Tangi in Italy

We entered the house, coming into a large room empty of furniture except a bed. On it they had laid the soldier, a fine young man of the Ngati Tuwharetoa people, looking in death the young chieftain he was. A grey blanket covered most of his body and beside him were his rifle and his steel helmet. Seated beside him was his platoon commander and close by were officers of the company. The company commander sat with bowed head on the far side. Standing against the walls or seated on the floor were his comrades, their rifles or light machine guns in their hands, grim, silent. I think of how young we were. And yet that was the age at which many of the warriors of old laid out their dead and mourned for them on the field of battle.[i]

[i] Harry Dansey cited in Michael King, *New Zealanders at War*, Heinemann Publishers, Auckland, 1981, p. 228.

... this time the number of votes cast against the Internal Marketing, the cost of living, the return of the Furlough Draft, congestion on tram-cars, no bananas, and every form of vexation, great or small, may make a considerable difference.

The two Parties have been going at it hammer and tongs now since the beginning of the month. A sort of free enterprise versus free beer campaign has been waged by the nationalists and our old friend the slump has not been neglected by Labour. [33]

Labour was returned to office at the end of 1943 with a majority of 12 seats. Many of the furlough men stayed, discharged from service; over 500 others were dismissed with the loss of civil rights and pensions, although these were reinstated at the end of the war. But there were those who returned to their mates and the Div, this time to the hard slog of the Italian campaign. It was a different climate and terrain and so a different kind of warfare. The battle for Cassino was among the worst:

First light broke on a ghastly scene. Huge railway engines, boilers with jagged holes, twisted rails, dragging telegraph wires, crumbled building and masonry, surrounded us. The dead lay everywhere. The wounded were being taken to the rear.... A pall of smoke hung over everything and the smell of gunpowder and blood was sickening.

Our chances of survival lessened as the sun rose in the sky.... The Germans realised our predicament. Encouraged, they closed in on us and by nine o'clock we had lost half the station and our line was a mere loose circle. Inside that huge shell of a building, Ngapuhi and Arawa lay side by side and died.... Tommy guns spat and grenades exploded and screams curdled the blood.

At about 4.30 in the afternoon the Germans withdrew and we heard the unmistakable noise of tanks moving from their lines.... We ran or staggered until we reached the safety of our lines. Of 175 men who had set out the night before, 40 came back. [34]

ATL F-12430-1/2-DA (War History Collection)

Graves of soldiers from the 26th Battalion after the Div's unsuccessful attempt to take the town of Cassino in Italy.

The Maori Battalion moves to the line in the Faenza sector in Italy. Jack (Hakirau) Love carries a mortar gun (front right); behind him is Hapurona (Ronald) Rangi of Ngati Haupoto, Taranaki iwi.

ATL F-7880-1/2-DA (War History Collection)

VJ Day "Peace Comes to Town and Kicks Up Her Heels in a Clothing Factory"

While people all over the country sang, danced and drank in the streets and in offices and at home when the sirens blew at 11am on VJ Day, a young *Woman's Weekly* reporter, Jean Wishart, invited herself to one of Auckland's largest clothing factories:

… my office was in an uproar. Dozens of faces, half of which I had never set eyes on before, had glued themselves to my window, while any unattached papers on my desk were torn to ribbons, and fluttered out of the window on to the pavement below.

I grabbed my hat and coat and was gone….

The scene at the clothing factory when I finally arrived was everything I had expected it to be – and a lot more. As if by magic, the cafeteria had been transformed into a jungle of red, white and blue streamers and flags, and while the piano churned out the Hokey Pokey, hundreds of young people sang and danced, their feet scattering the carpet of confetti on the floor.

The employees at this factory were celebrating peace with the same energy with which they had worked during the war. For years they had toiled over khaki fabric which went with our men into battle in the far corners of the earth. It had made them feel close to the war, and there is no doubt about it that, together with thousands of other workers in similar factories, they played an important part in New Zealand's war effort. In one of the departments they had formed a Soldiers' Club which sent comforts to overseas servicemen. This small band of workers had every right to be proud of the fine total of 900 parcels which they dispatched.[i]

Nelson Provincial Museum 160683/6 (Kingsford Studio Collection)

At 11am on 15 August 1945 the sirens sounded and New Zealanders took to the streets to celebrate VJ Day and the end of the Second World War.

---

[i] Jean Wishart, NZ *Woman's Weekly*, 30 August 1945, cited in Janet Blackwell (ed.), *NZ Woman's Weekly: The First 60 Years, 1932–1992*, Moa Beckett Publishers, Auckland, 1992, p. 37.

In April 1945 Hitler committed suicide. When Germany finally surrendered to the Allies a month later in May 1945, the Div was in Trieste in a stand-off with Tito's Yugoslav partisans. As one war ended, the shadow of another, the Cold War, was already forming.

Peace in the Pacific took longer, as the Japanese fought on and on, with the New Zealand air force and navy involved right up to the end. And the end came with what would become the emblem of the 20th century – the atomic bomb. It had been developed in the "Manhattan project", an international undertaking that included several New Zealanders. Dr Ruth Flashoff, working at army headquarters in Wellington, claimed she knew what was planned six weeks before the bomb was dropped… but had no idea how lethal it would prove:

The atomic bomb… what does it mean? It means more to a younger generation because they have seen the effects of it. We hadn't. We didn't know what it would do. It was just something that was ghastly, just like those prison camps in Germany where they had gas chambers and everything. We were just horrified.[35]

New Zealand sailors on the HMNZS *Achilles* went to see the devastation in Nagasaki for themselves, and heard grim stories from others:

> *When they got there, the dogs from the outlying districts were eating the cooked flesh of the humans, the Japanese civilians, at a hospital. They were cooked on steel bed frames.*[36]

> *We were taken out by bus to see the actual site of the atomic bomb. It was amazing. The bomb apparently exploded over an earthquake-proof building which, remarkably, still stood, but everything around it was laid waste. We had a good look at this atom bomb place, never of course giving any thought to fallout. It wasn't mentioned in those days. We saw nobody in the city.*[37]

It was a shocking end to a shocking war. VJ Day (15 August 1945), when the Japanese capitulated, left a nine-year-old boy with a lasting memory:

> *I will never forget those crowds. Public displays of joy were never common in New Zealand and in my short life I had seen nothing like this (I was on a farm on VE Day). Everyone kissed everyone or danced in conga lines, waving beer bottles, or hung off trams and sang, waving beer bottles, or just stood, waving beer bottles. To me everyone seemed instantly drunk. One woman had a rat in a cage with a ribbon around its neck and a big label "Tojo" – the Japanese war prime minister. "Things are soon going to get back to normal," the woman in the cake shop told my mother. "Getting things back to normal" had been the dream of every New Zealander since 1939.*[38]

But they didn't. And they couldn't… just yet. Approximately 140,000 men and women had served overseas; 11,625 of them had been killed.[39] Over the next few months, as shipping became available, servicemen and women returned from all over the globe. They had fought in every theatre of war and seen and experienced things that would stay with them forever. The death camps and concentration camps of Nazi Germany were found to have their Asian counterparts. The inhumane conditions and sadism of the Japanese captors had a profound and lasting effect on the prisoners who survived, and those who freed and nursed them afterwards:

> *… the Japanese prisoners of war, most of them were moving skeletons, and we thought they would just crumble and break. We were terribly careful with them…. [They] were so emaciated and*

TO ALL ALLIED PRISONERS OF WAR

THE JAPANESE FORCES HAVE SURRENDERED UNCONDITIONALLY AND THE WAR IS OVER

WE will get supplies to you as soon as it is humanly possible and we will make arrangements to get you out. Because of the distances involved it may be some time before we can achieve this.

YOU will help us and yourselves if you act as follows :

1. Stay in your camp until you get further orders from us.

2. Start preparing nominal rolls of personnel giving the fullest particulars.

3. List your most urgent necessities.

4. If you have been starved and underfed for long periods do not eat large quantities of solid food, fruit or vegetables at first. It is dangerous for you to do so. Small quantities at frequent intervals are much safer and will strengthen you far more quickly.

   For those who are really ill or very weak fluids such as broths and soups, making use of the water in which rice and other foods have been boiled, are much the best.

   Gifts of food from the local population should be cooked. We want to get you back home quickly, safe and sound, and we do not want you to risk getting diarrhoea, dysentery and cholera at this last stage.

5. Local authorities and or Allied officers will take charge of your affairs in a very short time. Be guided by their advice.

Nothing in their previous experience of caring for prisoners of war had prepared liberators and medical staff for the appalling effects of Japanese POW camps.

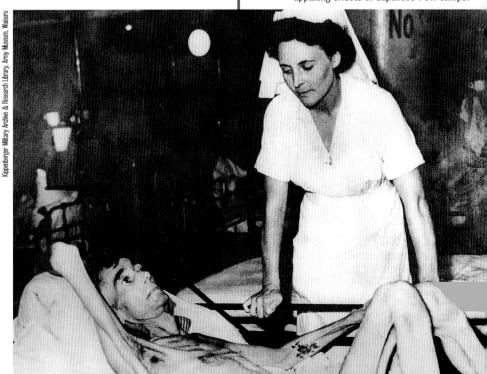

Kippenberger Military Archive & Research Library, Army Museum, Waiouru

Fatal Fires

Two of the country's worst fires occurred during the 1940s.

The first, in December 1942, happened at the isolated Seacliff Mental Hospital 30 kilometres from Dunedin. Patients had been locked in their wards for the night and were trapped when the fire started in Ward Five. Thirty-nine of the 41 women in that ward died. The fire prompted an overhaul of fire regulations to prevent another such tragedy taking place.

The second fire took place in Christchurch in November 1947 in the Ballantynes department store. It began in the afternoon, while the store was open, and those who died – 41 in total – were all staff who were trapped in offices and workrooms on the top floor of the three-storey building. The fire had started in the basement among highly flammable furniture and spread with unexpected and deadly speed throughout the building.

The Dunedin *Evening Star* described the scene at the King Edward Barracks where all 300 employees had been asked to report at 8pm to establish the number of casualties and missing people.

In the great, cold, empty arch of the King Edward Barracks were heard the deep sobbing of parents whose daughters had not come home, the lighter, easier weeping of girls who sought but could not find their workmates, and the voice of the police sergeant with a soft gentle touch of brogue to it saying, "and the address if you would please".[1]

The inquiry that followed found that there had been a delay in calling the fire brigade and that the brigade themselves did not realise at first just how serious the blaze was.

[1] Robin Bromby (ed.), *An Eyewitness History of New Zealand*, Currey O'Neil Ross, Victoria , 1985, p. 204.

weak that they didn't really want to talk much, but the ex-German POWs were quite angry and had much, much more spirit. I found it very hard to take. Quite honestly, those of us who nursed them on the first day sobbed ourselves to sleep that night.[40]

Returning servicemen were given free travel warrants for holidays, low-interest loans to help buy houses, assistance into businesses and retraining for professions, free tertiary education; there were extra ration coupons for those getting married and cash payments to help them buy furniture… if they could find a house and the goods to purchase as rationing and shortages continued. They were older, sadder, in some cases embittered, and only too aware of the depths to which human behaviour could sink. The country they returned to was not like the ones they had been fighting in and it was not the one they had sailed from to go to war:

We came home to Christchurch, Lyttelton, with a few hundred New Zealanders, and it was Labour Day and nobody wanted to meet us…. The war was over… and I don't know what the troops expected would happen, but we certainly didn't expect to find that the wharfies wouldn't tie the ship up. I can feel a bit offended about that. I can remember driving up through Featherston and thinking this is not at all what I've been remembering for the past five or six years…. The country was so empty, there didn't seem to be anybody; it made a big impact. Nobody on the roads; this was a big contrast to Europe. It wasn't a very happy time really.[41]

It was not just the empty roads that differed from Europe:

I think some of us were a little disillusioned about the peace-time world in New Zealand initially, because we were told how badly everyone had suffered, but we couldn't see any signs of it particularly. We'd been in the middle of a country [Italy] that had suffered the most severe rationing and bombing and hardships, and seen so much of it in a worse climate. To come back to the sunshine in New Zealand and see everybody healthy, and learn about the rationing here which was fairly mild compared with what we'd seen….

We were a little unsettled and trying to get back, as so many had, into their education or jobs wasn't easy. You might have a 25 or 23-year-old Squadron Leader who'd had quite a lot of responsibility and status, had been an apprentice electrician before he went away, and found that some 19-year-old kid was now senior to him in the old firm. Many of them were quite disillusioned.[42]

It was also difficult for the women and families they were returning to. Women welcomed home "men who couldn't sleep, had nightmares, mood swings, anxiety attacks or, in some cases, were in deep depression" or "who would have outbursts of rage for many years to come".[43]

The women had changed as well – they had got used to life on their own:

We'd both grown up a lot in the intervening years and we'd changed a lot. We were different people. I was pretty independent, and Stan was not in good health for some time. He was exhausted and not ready for the irritations of family life. He'd been the captain of an aircraft and the crew had responded to his orders without question. He soon found out that a family can't be run that way, especially with a stroppy co-pilot.[44]

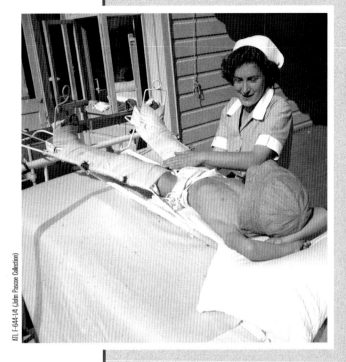

ATL F-641-1/4 (John Pascoe Collection)

The *Woman's Weekly* ran articles advising women on how to help their men through this transition period. The basis was always the same – the subordination of themselves and their needs to their men. W.B. Sutch cast a jaundiced but by no means inaccurate eye on the respective and divergent centres of their lives in the coming years:

> *… the lonely suburban home with the mother usually setting the pattern of daily conduct;… the other the town pub, associated with guilt, concentrated beer drinking and fairly excessive male heartiness.*[45]

As in the First World War, those women who had tasted the freedom and stimulation of the paid workforce were expected to go back home to make way for the returning servicemen. Many did, but not all. While political parties and the Establishment idealised and romanticised family life, and the postwar baby boom began, women had a firm foothold in the working world outside the home and from now on it would only increase.

Polio epidemics continued to strike periodically and the young were the most susceptible. In November 1947, all North Island schools were closed because of an outbreak of polio and did not reopen until late March 1948.

The Grant Family Collection

Dorothy Grant

Dorothy Grant
A Stranger in a Strange Land

Dorothy Grant left New Zealand in 1942 and spent three years as a voluntary nurse, serving on the hospital ship the *Oranje*. When she returned home she found both she and her homeland had changed.

It was a different place when I came back. I mean, the American invasion for one thing. I came in and I felt a stranger in a strange land. It just didn't seem like home. I mean, I was in uniform and people treated me in a way quite different to when I was living here as a civilian. Everybody wanted to do things for you, to shout you drinks and so on. I suppose the returning hero, or something like that. So that was strange in itself.

But the place had changed because people I knew suddenly had totally different lives, especially women. A lot of them had moved on from being just a housewife. They'd found they had other skills and it was different.

When the boys did come home it became accentuated because they found things different too. I know of at least one family where the marriage never succeeded after the war. The man who came home just could not accept that the baby he'd left at four months was this lovely little girl of five and he just ignored her completely. And that was terrible, but he couldn't adjust. Then his wife of course couldn't either. There were lots of cases like that. It didn't always just work out.

A man came home to find that his wife now was an independent person with a life of her own. And he had visualised her, I suppose, as still being at home preparing the meals, perhaps going to look after her, the new family and so on. Lots of women were very happy to go back too, but some weren't. They felt they'd achieved a new kind of lifestyle by working.

Source: Edited Ninox transcripts from *Our People, Our Century*, 1999.

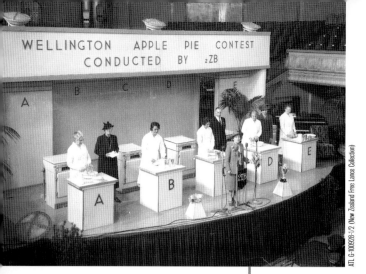

Picture this – the Radio 2ZB Apple Pie Contest staged at the Wellington Town Hall, Mistress of Ceremonies, "Aunt Daisy", at the microphone.

Swimwear was gradually becoming skimpier. In the 1940s, the backless one-piece led to the "midriff" two-piece, the precursor of the bikini.

Unlike most other Allied war-time leaders and governments, Fraser and Labour were returned to power in the first postwar elections – but only courtesy of the four Maori seats. The austerity measures of the war years persisted, in order to help Britain. It would be mid-1950 before all rationing ended. Fraser continued to develop the welfare state and to nationalise a number of concerns: the country's principal trading bank – the Bank of New Zealand, the mines and the new and rapidly expanding airlines. The Minimum Wage Act provided a national standard rate for all employees and a minimum wage that employers could not pay below – 5 pounds, 5 shillings a week for adult men and 3 pounds, 3 shillings a week for women. A universal family benefit paid to mothers replaced a means-tested benefit and was payable on each child. Dental benefits paid dentists in private practice to treat children up to age 16.

In towns and cities new sounds mixed with the old. The rattle of passing trams was about to succumb to the whoosh of trolley buses. New battery-powered portable radios took the call of cricket and rugby commentaries out into backyards and gardens. You could still hear the cry of the food vendors round the neighbourhood, but not for much longer:

> ... the rabbito and the whitebait seller and the clip-clopping hooves of the milko's horse-drawn float – as the milk wagon was called – or the baker's cart. (Few would mourn the passing of midnight clatter and horse hooves of the night-cart, servicing the still large number of suburban homes without sewer connections.)
>
> Rabbits were 1 shilling, 6 pence each and whitebait was 3 pence a glass. The baker, who would carry his basket of breads and buns round to the back door of the house for the housewife to make her selection, charged by the week, as did the milko and the butcher, who still delivered his wares either by van or by means of a butcher boy with his delivery bicycle. Grocers, too, made home deliveries.[46]

New subdivisions spread out in ever-widening circles but housing shortages remained so great that transit camps were established in the cities to provide temporary housing for returning soldiers and their new families and the refugees arriving from a war-devastated Europe. A letter to the Editor in 1949 described the plight of many:

> "Next Time Lucky" has my sympathy. My daughter is a fourth-generation, true-blue New Zealander and lives in one room in a condemned hovel (all she could get) with her husband and 14-months-old baby, and has another one coming. The window is jammed and only opens one-third up, and the door must be kept shut... or! The conditions she exists under would not be believed if printed, yet she is told that

The Farmers free tram was superseded by the Farmers free trolley bus in 1949. Later that year trolley buses replaced trams on the city's Herne Bay run. It was the beginning of the end for trams.

Visual Arts
The "Modernist Revolution" Begins

Although the voices of writers and poets in the 1930s and 1940s were beginning tentatively to seek out a cultural nationalism, developments in the visual arts of that period were much more dramatic and radical. At the forefront were four painters, each with a very different style and vision, each to achieve a substantial reputation – Colin McCahon, Toss Woollaston, Milan Mrkusich and Gordon Walters. W. H. Oliver says of the works exhibited at the end of the 1940s:

McCahon's quest for archetypical symbols, Woollaston's delight in colour and form, Mrkusich's movement into pure abstraction, and Walters' surrealism with its hints of his later abstract manner, all indicated that the modernist revolution in New Zealand had at last begun.[i]

"The Promised Land", 1948, by Colin McCahon.

For those involved in the art and literary scenes, it was a time of great excitement; but public sentiment was not so enthusiastic. Many people were not impressed by modern art's new directions. Some were positively aggravated. The following letter to the Editor expresses sentiments which would be heard increasingly in debates on what constitutes "good" art and painting over the following decades.

Sir, – In your issue of October 8 [1948] appeared an "ink drawing" by M. T. Woollaston, alleged to be a pictorial representation of his mother. If this is the best he can do, no doubt many other readers besides myself are wondering why a whole page of The Listener should be wasted upon extenuation of sheer rubbish. There is a small clique of misguided persons in this country which tries to impose upon the intelligent majority a perverted view of art, in the shape of sham music, sham drawing, sham painting, sham literature and poetry. The Listener could render a real service to the community by ruthless exposure of such charlatanry.
    L.D. Austin (Wellington)
    (We gave our space because we are not quite as sure as our correspondent seems to be that everything had been said in literature, music and painting, before the death of Queen Victoria,—Ed.)[ii]

"Mount Arthur, Nelson", 1945, by Sir Tosswill Woollaston.

[i] W. H. Oliver, The Awakening Imagination 1940-1980, in Rice (ed.), *The Oxford History of New Zealand*, p. 549.
[ii] Crockett, Little and Snow (eds), *The Listener Bedside Book*, p. 52.

thousands are much worse off than she, therefore she cannot get a State house. If that is true, New Zealand ethics are criminally shaky. Her husband would make a garden paradise out of a stony wilderness – but all doors are slammed in their faces because they are parents.[47]

Although a record number of State houses were built in 1949 – just over 4,100 – there were still more than 52,000 applicants waiting to be housed. Like rationing, the transit camps were to remain far longer than was ever intended. The last, behind Auckland's War Memorial Museum, was finally closed and dismantled in 1964 after 19 years in existence.

Increasing numbers of Maori were among those looking for houses and jobs in the city. The urban drift, begun during the war, continued. In Auckland, a community centre established in an old cargo shed for the 10,000 Maori who now lived in the region was a forerunner of urban marae. Maori and Pakeha came into greater and closer contact and revealed a lack of racial tolerance not obvious before:

It was when I started school that I learned I was "different".... It meant that I was questioned, out of curiosity by some children, as to why I was brown.... I found that being "different" meant that you could be blamed – for a toy gun being stolen then thrown into a drain, for neighbourhood children swearing, for writing appearing on walls, for a grassy bank being set on fire. Being "different" also meant that there was a low expectation of me by some teachers, and that I was continuously having to prove what I could do.... I had a few neighbourhood friends too, mainly those who attended the same school as me. But it was in that mainly working class, but upwardly mobile, neighbourhood that I came in for a rough time. What I disliked most was being told I was dirty and that I needed a good scrub. (I tried the scrubbing.)[48]

Labour had done much to help Maori since 1935, both by improving work opportunities and economic and social conditions, and in giving Maori equal access to the benefits of the welfare state. Improved health care and housing had dramatic results – the death rate from tuberculosis fell substantially, infant mortality rates fell, typhoid declined and life expectancy rose from 46.6 years for men and 44.7 for women between 1926/27 to 57 and 59 years, respectively, in 1956/57.[49] The Government attempted to settle long-standing land claims and paid compensation, arranged for Maori electoral rolls to be compiled (and to include Maori of half-European extraction if they wished), introduced the secret ballot for Maori electors, and appointed the first Maori welfare officers. Peter Fraser was the Native Minister as well as Prime Minister after 1946, and totally committed to Maori welfare and to special provisions where needed. Historian Michael King says:

... [although he] was known to some as a man of frightening calculation and expediency, this was rarely his approach to Maori matters [and] he was received by Maori with an affection not accorded any Pakeha leader since Coates.[50]

A totally New Zealand invention, marching girls received their first official mention in 1901 during the visit to Dunedin by the Duke and Duchess of Cornwall and York. By the late 1920s, it was an organised sport in Otago. Numbers expanded rapidly during the 1930s and in 1941 the New Zealand Marching Association was established. In 1944 it laid out a code of rules. By the early Fifties some 3,500 young women belonged to marching teams.

ATL C-23002

One of Fraser's secretaries said:

Fraser governed with his heart rather than his head. He had never forgotten the experience of the crofters in Scotland.[51]

Fraser appointed the first Maori Under-Secretary of Maori Affairs, Tipi Ropiha, and substituted "Maori" for the word "Native" with its suggestion of racial inferiority, in all official papers and correspondence. The symbolic importance of both actions was understood and appreciated by Maori. His stated goal was:

… an independent, self-reliant and satisfied Maori race working side by side with the Pakeha and with equal incentives, advantages, and rewards for efforts in all walks of life.[52]

Amongst Maori themselves, the debate was growing on how best to survive the increasing contact with the dominant Pakeha culture – assimilation or separatism. Sir Peter Buck had seen the "fusion" of Maori and Pakeha as inevitable. But other leaders such as Maharaia Winiata did not believe that cultural conformity was the same as racial equality. Sir Apirana Ngata and Te Puea Herangi were among those who preached the value and importance of Maoritanga and the need to keep the Maori point of view before government and those in power. The basics of bi-culturalism were already being promoted:

Nelson Provincial Museum 160970/6 (Kingsford Studio Collection)

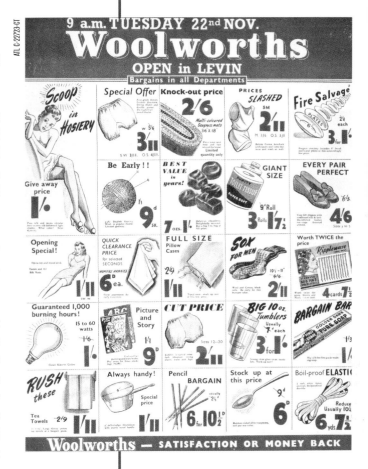

Old style wooden surf boards and muscle line up at Tahuna Sands.

The language, history, crafts and traditions of the Maoris should be an essential part of the curriculum throughout the country.... Unity of Maori and Pakeha can only grow from each sharing the worthwhile elements in the other's culture.[53]

As growing numbers of Maori left (and lost) traditional land for the siren call of city life, the debate would become increasingly urgent. For the moment, however, over 70 per cent of Maori still lived in the country.

The rural sector was experiencing its own boom. The Government had set aside carefully selected land for rehabilitation farms and arranged loans and training to assist returning servicemen, usually with some farming experience, to settle on them. Over a 10-year period, some 10,000 took up the opportunity. Even while the war had raged, experiments in agricultural management and methods were sparking a revolution in farming. Returning pilots would get work sowing grass seed and spreading fertiliser from the air, turning thousands more hectares into productive land. There were powerful new weedkillers like DDT, which would only reveal their darker side decades later; light tractors such as the Ferguson which revolutionised heavy farm work; the introduction of spray irrigation and rotational grazing. Despite this boom, numbers working in manufacturing overtook those working in primary industry for the first time.

Wild New Zealand was being explored, and developed too. The returning servicemen took to bush and mountain to rediscover their homeland. Hunting, tramping and mountaineering grew rapidly in popularity. The early skifields were developed. The country's third national park, the Abel Tasman National Park, was established, and conservation became an issue. When logging threatened a Northland

"The Wasps Are Coming! The Wasps Are Coming!"

The cry might have been heard in any Auckland suburban street on the morning of 1 April 1949. Phil Shone, the 1ZB breakfast session announcer, had just put over a special bulletin: "A swarm of wasps has been sighted moving east of Papatoetoe. It's reported to be one mile wide and several hundred yards deep, and it's being kept under observation to give fair warning of the direction it takes as it approaches Auckland city."

Between records and commercials from then on, for about half an hour, Phil Shone kept listeners informed of the progress of this extraordinary invasion. Housewives dutifully heeded advice on anti-wasp precautions. "Smear jam or honey on bits of paper and leave them outside the door. Close all windows. Wear protective clothing." Excitement and apprehension were intense – until Phil gently reminded everyone what day it was and admitted he had been pulling their leg.

His little joke had a mixed reaction. Laughter, relief, annoyance, chagrin at being made to look foolish – Aucklanders remembered (too late) that Phil Shone had caught them before on April Fool's Day. Only one man failed to see anything funny in it at all, the Hon. F. Jones, Minister of Broadcasting. In a statement to the House he condemned such irresponsible behaviour, such a wicked hoax. Later he informed members that steps were being taken (ominous phrase) to ensure that nothing like it would happen again.

Memories of the panic caused by the broadcast of the War of the Worlds in America ten years earlier may have moved the Christchurch Press to tut-tut disapprovingly at the "danger that can be done" and to comment that "an important question of broadcasting ethics has been raised". The New Zealand Herald thought otherwise – " ... simply good fun... a little nonsense now and then is good for everybody".[1]

[1] Peter Downes and Peter Harcourt, *Voices in the Air. Radio Broadcasting in New Zealand: A Documentary*, Methuen Publications in association with Radio New Zealand, Wellington, 1976, pp. 151-52.

forest, 50,000 people signed one of the biggest petitions to Parliament at that time, and won. The forest became a reserve. And a bird believed to be extinct, the takahe, was re-discovered in the Murchison Mountains west of Te Anau.

The decade's end brought with it the end for Labour and their 14 years in power. Shortages, rationing, insufficient housing and National Party accusations of stifling bureaucracy whittled down Labour's slender majority. Fraser and Nash, sitting at conference tables overseas, heard and understood the growing international fears of a new war against our recent ally, Soviet Russia. However, the introduction of compulsory military training in the new peacetime lost the Government traditional Labour supporters. Labour was increasingly authoritarian and tired; National was no longer attacking social security and the welfare state. The Holland National Government swept to power with 46 seats to Labour's 34. The House also had its first Maori woman MP, Iriaka Ratana, representing Western Maori. It was the end of one of the most significant eras in New Zealand history.

At the close of the 1940s, New Zealanders could truly join writer Robin Hyde in saying:

Iriaka Ratana, talking with Peter Fraser, became the first Maori woman MP in a 1949 by-election following the death of her husband, Matiu Ratana. She had been preparing for political life since her youth. Iriaka Ratana represented Western Maori until 1969.

> [I]n our generation, and of our initiative, we loved England still, but we ceased to be "forever England". We became, for as long as we have a country, New Zealand.[54]

Power to the People

From the late 1930s, the Government began a series of major construction projects for road and power schemes. The first motorways appeared in Auckland and Wellington and secondary and country roads were upgraded. Massive hydro-electric power project developments began after the Second World War. Since the mid-Thirties, rapid increases in the demand for power had created shortages, and by the mid-Forties power cuts were a common factor of life. In 1946, the Government established the State Hydro-electric Department, later the NZ Electricity Department. The following year the power station at Karapiro on the Waikato River began operating. The completion of a number of huge power stations, in particular Roxburgh in the South Island and a whole series of dams along the Waikato River, finally ended power shortages in the late 1950s.

The Maraetai hydro-electric station under construction on the Waikato River near Taupo. It began generating power in 1953.

Sonny Sewell
(Rangi te Puru Waretini)
The Legend of the Lizard

During a lull in the Battle of Crete in the last World War, Sonny Sewell was chatting with his mates when he glanced down at something moving on his boot:

It was a lizard, and I let it play around in my hand a bit and one of my uncles came along and asked me what I had. And I said "Look" and he said, "We're saved... we'll survive this war." When I asked why, he said: "That's our guardian. That's our taniwha, that one there. He'll look after us."

Sonny came from a family whose traditions included belief in a spirit guardian in the form of a lizard:

Now this lizard, wherever it's seen by any of our family, is a sign of good tidings. Something good is going to happen to us – our guardian has come along to look after us and uncle and I both came home. He was unscathed. Not a mark. I had a few superficial wounds that haven't affected me.

Sonny, whose Maori name is Rangi Te Puru Waretini, was raised in Auckland and Rotorua by doting grandparents and a big, ever-expanding family:

Around Christmas there'd be anything up to 50-60 members of one family just running around there... everybody knew each other. And when we went to war we knew everybody. My particular platoon for example came from one village of Whakarewarewa.

In Rotorua Sonny and his friends would dive for pennies, play in rivers or just sit and sing the school songs they had been taught by the headmaster at the local school:

He was a great person for choir music. And the songs of those days, they're still sung in the village now. If anybody of that age dies, you'll find that during the

Sonny Sewell back on civvy street.

morning of the tangi, just before the burial, those attending will stand up and sing all these old songs they used to sing together... like Annie Laurie, *and* Softly through the Meadow.

In 1939 Sonny was working as a forestry cadet 40 miles from town. He did not get to Rotorua often, but one day in September his sister wrote to ask him if he could come for a weekend. She told him the locals were preparing an away sports trip to play basketball, rugby and hockey with teams at Cape Runaway. Sonny joined the trip and left with the others on their bus:

Preparing a hangi in the Western Desert.

We were going through Opotiki and stopped for a meal because we had another hundred-odd miles to go. And I remember this quite clearly as if it was yesterday. I went into the shop to get some fish and chips, and I spoke to the chap there and he says, "Shhh, I'm listening to the news — something important's coming over." Well, nothing was more important to me than eating at that time. So I said, "Well, how long are you going to be?" He said, "Here it comes now." And it was a Declaration of War.

So I went out and I told the rest of the people on the bus. I said, "War's been declared." And me being the youngest on the bus, they didn't take much notice. I said, "No, this is dead right."

So the bus driver went in, came out and said, "That's it. We're turning back. We're going back to Rotorua." And the people said, "What for?" He said, "I want to enlist." They said, "There's plenty of time for us. We've got the whole weekend. The war is going to wait... the war will wait for you. Don't worry about it."

So, when we came back on the Monday, all the eligible males and I — eligible in the sense that they were eligible to go to war — went in as a body and enlisted.

This keen body of volunteers was however advised by elders to hold off, while prominent leaders like Tai Mitchell and Sir Apirana Ngata met. Sonny recalls:

It was sort of a hush-hush meeting and the outcome was that they would approach the Government to form a Maori Battalion — a special unit composed entirely of Maoris. They would offer the unit to the Government to fight the war.

Sonny was 16 when he first tried to enlist "... but the guy who ran the recruiting office knew me and told me to go home. Then one day I heard he was sick, so me and my mates raced down and enlisted." Eventually one of his uncles heard about it, marched him back home to his grandmother, and told her Sonny had enlisted:

She looked at me and I looked at her, and we sort of shrugged our shoulders at each other. She said: "Do you understand what you're doing?" and I told her that I thought so. She said: "All right then."

His mates were 14 and a half and 15 years old. Whether they all enlisted because of boredom at home or the adventure ahead is still not clear to Sonny:

... People were just coming through the Depression then and the only work that you could get was labouring in the forestry and that sort of thing. It could well have been that a man needed a change from that.... The Maori race is a martial race... a very warlike race... we felt that in the light of our traditions as a martial race, we had to be involved.

But involvement was painful for both the newly enlisted and those they left behind, as Sonny discovered when he left Rotorua for training and, eventually, battle:

We had been sort of congregating in the local hostelry, I suppose you might call it, prior to the buses coming to pick us up to take us to the station. We had about two hours to spare. I had already said goodbye to my grandmother and the rest of my family and I was waiting outside the pub for the rest of them, and I thought "Oh blow it. I'll go inside." So I went inside, sat down and everybody was singing and having a great time.

I heard this wailing in the distance and wondered what it was. I put my head out the window of the hotel and it was my grandmother. The gestures she was making while she was wailing were the same gestures they make when the body leaves the meeting house to go to the burial ground.

There's a tradition among Maoris, when they feel they need to go to war, they say, "Don't come back. We don't expect you back. You go there, you fight and you die. You die on the battlefield." And it was these very selfsame actions that she was giving to me as I went. In other words, she was saying "Go to your destiny. That's your destiny. You go." This was all in Maori of course. But that is

The Maori Battalion march to.... Among the ranks of faces is the young soldier Sonny Sewell.

the tradition within Maoridom.

But that was a very emotional moment, that. So I ran across the road and I gathered her up into my arms – she was only a little person. I gathered her in my arms and said, "I'll be all right. Don't worry about me."

But she stayed there and I was told she was still there two hours later, after the buses had gone. Because my uncle and I were both on the same bus. That was probably one of the worst moments I've ever faced I think. But I wouldn't have been the only one. I suppose that particular scene would have been repeated all around the place. I still feel it. I can still see her there.

In May 1940, Sonny and other recruits boarded the vessel *Aquitania* in Wellington and were farewelled by about 80 to 90 Ngati Poneke. Throughout the night they sang and performed hakas. As the liner pulled away, a band played *Now Is the Hour*:

There were very few dry eyes and then to make matters worse we were only about two hours into the strait and everybody on board was seasick.

Initially Maori were not allowed to land at Cape Town, but after New Zealand protested, this was reversed:

We spent about three to four hours ashore, cooped up in an old place where they fed us on boiled eggs and chicken sandwiches. The natives there were treated like dirt. They were elbowed off the footpaths and everywhere you saw notices saying "black, white". You couldn't use the same toilets or restaurants....

From England in the Blitz, he went to Egypt for training and Greece where he joined in the Allied retreat. There, he saw among other things, an ingenious Kiwi cocktail:

We found about 30-40 barrels of cognac and it was raw... like drinking barbed wire. Some of the trucks had run out of petrol so they poured this cognac into them and they went. Mind you, the engines were a mess by the time they finished but they managed to get them mobile. We were told we had to destroy the vehicles anyway, so what better way than putting this stuff through it? And we got a ride as well as a drink when we wanted it.

But his next destination was Crete, where there was little time for wartime amusement as German paratroopers fought Kiwi soldiers at Maleme airfield:

We could actually see into the plane and see them walk out and jump out. To be perfectly honest it looked like a game until somebody said, "We'd better shoot some of these characters...."

You know, we'd just put our arms down and we were watching them, until we realised they were serious. Because they'd come down firing with little, short Tommy guns. They'd come down, firing at us and I said, "Oh heck, better get out of here or get somewhere where we can't be seen."

But their initial draft [of paratroopers], they were just annihilated. They had everything firing at them. Even the cooks were coming out of the cook houses firing.

At that time Sonny was the company runner, which meant he was with the OC of the company all the time and took his messages out to the platoons. As the battles intensified he witnessed two bayonet attacks:

I was involved to the extent there were chaps on either side of me and just in front of me bayoneting people. I had a pistol. I didn't have a rifle and bayonet. So I had an excuse. But I never ever, ever want to see anything like that again. It was just slaughter. When you see a guy's face... and you see it when something that long is going straight into his stomach, you never want to see that look on anybody's face again. But that's war, you've got to put up with it.... It lives with you for a long time. I think I've got over it now, but it took a long time then.

Tending to the wounded was the job of stretcher bearers behind the troops but frequently they could not reach them because of the intensity of the fire. They were, says Sonny, the real unsung heroes.

Sonny spent a year in various battles in the Western Desert before his uncles and officers pulled him out of the action and placed him in headquarters:

In a unit where you've got tribal representation, it's inevitable that you're going to have more than one member of a family in a unit. With the Maori Battalion, the special nature of it was that families all went together and it seemed all right at the beginning.

Now, it's all very well until one dies, one gets killed. Then whoever's at home starts worrying. Then if a second one goes, then that's where the real worry starts. From the point of view of the company commanders, it doesn't do a hell of a lot for the company morale, when they see that sort of thing. So what they're saying is, "Go and have a rest. We'll pull you out."

So back I went. But I wasn't the only one. It was general policy within our particular company. I don't know so much about the other companies of the battalion.

But with our particular company, that was one of the things that they said. "Well, there's enough heartbreak at home by people getting killed here, why give them more? We know that sure, it's inevitable somebody's going to get killed but why four in one family?" That sort of thing. That was the reason behind the policy of bringing them back.

Four years after he left home, he was reunited with his grandmother and his many relatives. Today, he is active in Maoridom and is President of the 28 Maori Battalion Association. He is also walking proof of the lucky, as in the legend of the lizard.

Sources: Edited Ninox transcripts from *Our People, Our Century*, 1999. All photographs from the Sewell Family Collection.

Sonny and his wife Nan after he had returned from war.

1950

1960

Chapter 6

She'll Be Right... Mate?

We said she'll be right, mate, and most of the time she was – we lived in the Fifties, with full employment guaranteed in a distant two-horse race called politics. This was the long, hot summer of the Cold War, when we swayed inside hula hoops and floated dreamily on lilos; when tar melted in the heat like TT2s – The Drink on a Stick; when hamburgers were hip; when hooray meant goodbye and Kia Ora was, for most, tomato sauce; when Opo the Crazy Dolphin swam with us at Opononi by the sea; when men were blokes and women sheilas; when we ground Springbok hopes into the mud of our own turf; when milk arrived daily at the school gate; when everything seemed free, innocent and everlasting.

Museum of New Zealand Te Papa Tongarewa f5010

Joining the bathers at Opononi – Opo the "crazy dolphin" whose friendliness and frolicking in the surf were legendary.

These were indeed our Golden Days, as the country finally lived up to Liberal Premier Dick Seddon's turn-of-the-century characterisation of it as "God's Own". The land was blessed with unprecedented wealth, which gave it one of the highest living standards in the world. There was a job for everyone who wanted one – and a joke that the unemployed were all known by name to the Prime Minister.

This was an orderly era in which everything and everybody was in their proper place. And so, out of sight, was the gallows on which eight men died inside the walls of Mt Eden Prison. Sequestered from our sensibilities in mental asylums, many, like author Janet Frame, were jolted into "normality". While the others had no voice, hers hums with the terror of the electric shock treatment she received:

… I feel myself dropping as if a trap door had opened into darkness. I imagine as I fall my eyes turning inward to face and confound each other with a separate truth which they prove without my help. Then I rise disembodied from the dark to grasp and attach myself like a homeless parasite to the shape of my identity and its position in space and time. At first I cannot find my way, I cannot find myself where I left myself, someone has removed all trace of me. I am crying…. I am wide awake and the anxiety begins to accumulate. Will I be for treatment tomorrow?[1]

Little of this was known or appreciated, for we seemed always to progress, moving from country to cities, from renting to proud home ownership. In the Fifties the proportion of houses owned rather than rented grew from 61 per cent to 69 per cent.[2] Increasingly, too, coppers and washboards, those twin racks of the wash-house, gave way to washing machines and other labour-saving devices in these modern homes.

Janet Frame – one of the most gifted of our writers.

Keri Kaa on her 21st birthday.

Kaa Family
Kumara Patch Lessons

Keri Kaa grew up on the East Coast, the tenth of twelve children. Her mother, Sophie Whaanga, was Ngati Kahungunu and Rongomaiwahine, her father, Tipi Kaa, Ngati Porou. At 12 she boarded at Queen Victoria Maori Girls' College. Her father, she says, was determined that all his children would get an education like his own, in the riches of two cultures:

Tipi was a nurturing father. He was the one who told us stories. He was the one who read to us. He was the one who corrected our grammar, whether it was Maori or English. He was quite proper, and fairly strict. He was very well educated, extremely well read. He had two hobbies, haka and moteatea, and he taught us to do the haka in the kumara patch, because it relieved the boredom and tedium of standing.

I don't know whether you've ever stood in the hot sun with a little hoe to make little mounds and get every weed. It's tedious work and we were small children. Everybody had a line of kumara each and you had to chip away at the weeds and things. And to relieve the boredom he would start a haka from wherever he was standing. And he would chant away, and then he'd point to some lucky child and you were expected to respond with the next line. And the only one who ever got all the lines right was Wi Kuki because he knew all those things. Wi just picked up stuff like that. And we would all do the haka in the kumara patch, cause it was a game, it was always a game. It was fun, very cunning teaching.

He'd recite stuff from Shakespeare, poetry round the table. I can remember him reciting what I discovered to be [Gerard Manley] Hopkins, you know – "I caught this morning, morning's minion…." He liked people like Oscar Wilde. He'd had an English classics kind of education. They all did, because in those days Ngati Porou invested heavily in education and people like our Dad and his brothers were sent away to school – go and seek the Pakeha's knowledge, the white man's knowledge. The assumption was that this would advance you in some way. And what it really produced was very sophisticated men who walked two worlds with ease.

Source: Edited Ninox transcripts from *Our People, Our Century*, 1999.

Yvette Williams, who won an Olympic Gold for the long jump, becoming our first female Olympic champion.

Nationally, export values trebled between 1945 and 1951 as the country rode to prosperity on the sheep's back. From 1948 to 1958 the total sheep population increased by nearly 42 per cent, from 32.5 million to over 46 million and sheep became by far the greatest export earner.[3]

The rural also fed the cerebral, and society, fenced in behind the rigid conformities of the time, provoked this mocking verse from poet A. R. D. Fairburn:

Oh, come to the Land of the Free!
You'll find that you're free to agree
with whatever conforms
to the ethical norms
of descendants of dumpers of tea.[4]

Fairburn wasn't the only writer to note and criticise Kiwi conformity. A writer for the French Journal *Realités*, visited the country in the mid-Fifties. Along with favourable comments, the anonymous writer made two strong criticisms – which did not appear in the English language translation. In the original, *Realités* published this finding:

It is not necessary to live long in New Zealand to perceive that there rules there an intolerant conformism, that the enterprising mind is stifled, and that any intellectual or artistic life is impossible there. Hence an atmosphere of gloomy mediocrity, depressing in the long run for whoever arrives from a Western country.[5]

Realités also pointed out tartly, in its French version, that the glories of New Zealand were really two sportsmen – Jack Lovelock, the 1500-metre champion in 1936, Edmund

Everest

The story of Sir Edmund Hillary's conquest of Everest is by now well documented. Not so well known is the perspective of his partner on the climb, Sherpa Tenzing Norgay, and this is how he saw things as they struggled towards the summit:

Sir Edmund Hillary portrayed by John Cecil Hill not long after his historic ascent of Everest with Sherpa Tenzing.

... at last we came to what might be the last big obstacle below the top... a cliff of rock rising straight up out of the ridge and blocking it off.... Now it was a question of how to get over or round it, and we could find only one possible way. This was along a steep, narrow gap between one side of the rock and the inner side of an adjoining cornice, and Hillary, now going first, worked his way up it, slowly and carefully, to a sort of platform above.... I belayed him from below as strongly as I could, for there was great danger of the ice giving way.... Hillary got up safely to the top of the rock, and then held the rope, while I came after....
On the top of the rock cliff we rest again... we are both a bit breathless, but after some slow pulls at the oxygen I am feeling fine. I look up; the top is very close now; and my heart thumps with excitement and joy.
... Hillary stepped on top first. And I stepped up after him... we were there. The dream had come true.... What we did first was what all climbers do when they reach the top of their mountain. We shook hands. But this was not enough for Everest. I waved my arms in the air, and then threw them around Hillary, and we thumped each other on the back until, even with the oxygen, we were almost breathless. Then we looked around. It was 11.30 in the morning, the sun was shining, and the sky was the deepest blue I have ever seen.... At that great moment for which I had waited all my life, my mountain did not seem to me a lifeless thing of rock and ice, but warm and friendly and living. She was a mother hen, and the other mountains were chicks under her wings.

Source: Tenzing Norgay and James Ramsay Ullman, *Man of Everest : The Autobiography of Tenzing*, Revised edition, Severn House, London, 1975.

Celebration and Tragedy
— the Queen and Tangiwai

1953 was a year of celebration and sadness for Kiwis. In May that year, Hillary had conquered Everest and a few days later the young Queen was crowned. On 23 December that year she became the first reigning Monarch to visit New Zealand and her lengthy journey through the country brought people to the streets in their thousands to catch a glimpse of her. From Auckland, where she landed, to Bluff, from where she left five and a half weeks later, the response was the same:

> *Queen Street became the scene of a triumphal progress. Folk who had come as bystanders found themselves participants in the greatest demonstration the city had ever known.... She looked across a sea of faces, and at this crowning moment the full emotions of the city were loosed in a resounding roar of acclamation.*
>
> *... At the southern tip of the country an estimated 20,000 people invaded Bluff to share in the final act of the tour.*
>
> *... the last Royal Guard of the Tour presented arms and, with that act of formal respect, a stillness fell on the watching crowd.... Unashamedly there were tears.*[i]

ATL F-42418-1/2 (National Archives; National Publicity Studios Collection)

In the summer sun and cheered by crowds that blocked the streets, the Queen saunters through Nelson in 1954, followed by the Duke of Edinburgh.

A day after the Queen's visit began, the worst rail accident in our history occurred at Tangiwai. One hundred and fifty-one people died on Christmas Eve, when their northbound Auckland express plunged off the Whangaehu River bridge.

Only moments earlier, the Crater Lake on Mount Ruapehu had unleashed a massive volcanic discharge. Thousands of tonnes of rock, ice and ash struck the bridge, whose concrete piers gave way. Five of the train's carriages hurtled through the void and into the floodwaters. A sixth teetered briefly on the edge long enough to allow some passengers to be saved by a guard and Cyril Ellis, who witnessed the disaster. Then it also tumbled into the river below. Earlier Ellis had run down the railway line waving his torch to try to warn of what lay ahead, but it was too late.

The tragedy shocked the country and in the days which followed, railway trucks marked with white crosses carried bodies to their hometowns. Prince Philip attended a mass funeral in Wellington for those who could not be identified.

ATL P-AG-4875-069-17 (Morrie Peacock Collection)

Rail carriages litter the Whangaehu River bank after the 1953 Tangiwai disaster which claimed 151 lives in New Zealand's worst rail accident. A huge volcanic discharge from the Crater Lake on Mt Ruapehu swept away the bridge over the river.

i John Hardingham, *The Queen in New Zealand*, A. H. & A. W. Reed, Wellington, 1954, pp. 68, 260 and 262.

FOL leader Fintan Patrick Walsh making a
point at a meeting in Ngauranga.

ATL C-23679 (Evening Post Collection)

Labour leader the Rt. Hon. Walter Nash
about to make a radio broadcast, 1954.

ATL F-60070-1/2 (Evening Post Collection)

attack. Internationally, the contagion of Communism provoked McCarthyism in the
United States and a variety of witch-hunts of the Left in other western countries. In
New Zealand, newspapers all adopted a hostile line to Communism and the *Otago
Daily Times* took particular exception to the appointment of Dr Harold Silverstone
as senior lecturer in Mathematics at Otago University in 1953.

Attacking the appointment, the paper said Dr Silverstone had been "a contributor
to the Communist *People's Voice* and had spoken in measured terms of the iniquities
of the capitalist system". The editorial went on to say that the people of Otago would
not want a Communist to receive a salary of between £1,000 and £1,250 a year. The
newspaper's editorial thus converted Dr Silverstone from an intellectual contributor
to a Communist – in a single paragraph. However, the editorial was not well received
by some readers and the *People's Voice* reported that the Editor recently "returned
from an indoctrination course in the US, found the witch-hunt methods of his hosts
despised by New Zealanders".[12]

What the readers of the *Times* and other Kiwis could not have known was the
concerted nature of our anti-Communist propaganda and its top-level backing in
Government. Author Redmer Yska detailed the way carte blanche was given to
backroom civil servants to extend covert anti-Communist activities:

> In a memo to the Prime Minister in June 1950, Cabinet Minister John
> Marshall said the Publicity Division's work would help keep the Cabinet
> informed of the activities of the Communist Party in and beyond New Zealand.
> He suggested a Cabinet Committee be established to direct the anti-Communist
> work undertaken by the section, an idea rubber-stamped by Cabinet in July
> 1950. "For some considerable time, the Publicity Division has been distributing
> anti-Communist propaganda. I am encouraging and extending this work,"
> Marshall wrote. "It is most effective when it is least obvious."[13]

The "work" involved government propagandists liaising with news editors to print anti-
Communist material which could be run in local newspapers or broadcast on the State-
run radio. Marshall was really only putting into practice what Labour leader Peter Fraser
and the top unionist Finton Patrick Walsh, vice-president of the Federation of Labour,
had already preached years earlier. Both men used anti-Communist fears to isolate the
radical left. When the FOL members called for better conditions and wages, they were
often branded "agitators" and "tools of communism".[14] In a country steeped in moderacy
this was perhaps not unusual. However, there was a dark side to our aversion to
extremism and it lay in an ugly simplicity: intolerance of anything different.

Historian Keith Sinclair noted how Kiwis struck some observers as more equal
than the English "but less free". He added:

> They have, over a century, valued equality and fraternity more than liberty. This
> is not to say they are undemocratic; but signs of undemocratic attitudes have
> not been uncommon, especially that intolerance of minority opinions or
> conduct which has often been interpreted as a by-product of equality.... Civil
> liberties remain more or less intact, but under serious threat.[15]

There was no better illustration of disregard for civil liberties than in the bitter 1951
waterfront dispute. As a group, watersiders were unpopular because of public

perceptions of over-manning, and high pay for low productivity. The watersiders, part of a breakaway umbrella group, the Trade Union Congress (TUC), banned overtime after the collapse of their wage negotiations early in February 1951. However, they told their employers they were prepared to work a 40 hour week. The employers countered by effectively changing their working conditions – work was offered "subject to the acceptance of normal hours of work including overtime if required". Watersiders regarded this as a lockout and throughout the country the men voted against a government ultimatum to return to resume normal hours of work.

Very rapidly a dispute over wages and conditions escalated into a dramatic confrontation with Government. Watersiders saw it as a fight for the working man – though many workers disagreed with their position. The Government viewed the dispute as a timely expedient to consolidate politically, while crusading against Communists and "wreckers". Its opportunism was helped immeasurably by the Federation of Labour, which wanted TUC workers back under its fold. The FOL abandoned the watersiders and, praised by newspapers, called for a return to compulsory arbitration.

When the Government finally responded to the watersiders' rejection of its ultimatum, civil liberties were no longer under threat – they vanished. On 21 February the Government issued a proclamation under the Public Safety Conservation Act 1932, declaring a state of emergency.

Traditional liberties such as the right of trial by jury could be curtailed by any regulations issued under the Act, and any existing Acts of Parliament could be suspended. No right of appeal existed.[16]

The next day the Waterfront Strike Emergency Regulations 1951 were issued giving the Government astonishingly wide powers to deal with the watersiders. To some these regulations were a breathtaking extension of the powers of Government without the sanction of Parliament:

Newsmedia, Auckland (Auckland Star Collection)

Police move deregistered watersiders and others from the corner of Queen and Customs Streets during the waterfront strike which saw civil liberties suspended in New Zealand.

Tempers flare between police and unionists in the bitter waterfront dispute of 1951.

Not only were they quite outside the British tradition, they violated the Declaration of Human Rights and the United Nations Charter... this was peacetime with tranquillity. Holland, however, had no background of thinking on civil liberties, and the political tradition of his party included the repressions of 1912, 1913, and 1932. He felt he needed no excuse. The aim was to destroy the effectiveness of the "leftist" unions which preferred direct negotiations with employers. The means were state power without the restraint of free speech, freedom of the press, and freedom of assembly.[17]

The new offences included making a report or printing and publishing a statement by anyone which might encourage a strike; being an officer in a union where another officer had committed an offence, or where a fifth of the members were striking. The armed services could be brought in to do any kind of work – as they were called on to do on 27 February when they arrived on the wharves to handle perishable goods; the police could search private homes without warrants.

Dick Scott, whose book on the dispute is unashamedly partisan, documented the way the raids were carried out in attempts to muzzle opposing viewpoints:

Invariably working at night in the classic Gestapo manner, always forcing entry without warrant, squads of plain-clothes men ransacked the houses pointed out by informers as uniformed police patrolled outside. As many as three and four homes would be raided in one night, sometimes a house would be fruitlessly searched, re-visited weeks later and searched again. No record of these raids was ever published, no report ever given to Parliament....[18]

It became an offence for any member of the public to help watersiders' families with food and clothing, but in spite of the regulations a massive relief effort provided clothing, vegetables and slaughtered stock. Scott, the Editor of the *Transport Worker* wrote that the Government had no stomach for a frontal attack on the relief organisations:

Shopkeepers, restaurant owners and businessmen were "warned" not to contribute... while relief workers were away, their homes were visited and their wives questioned, but challenged to conduct a test case over closing a depot in the Hutt, the Government retreated. It would go only so far as the cloak of the emergency regulations kept its actions from the public....[19]

Army trucks bringing non-striking workers to the waterfront to do the job of watersiders.

But official mean-spiritedness was often matched by private generosity. Kiwis sensed what was happening behind the gag and despite the regulations, some individuals and organisations contributed to the relief effort.

Newspapers seemed to want blood – which was what flowed in Wellington and Auckland after police baton charges on union marchers and bystanders alike. On 1 May, the *Auckland Star* urged the Government in an editorial to act rather than talk:

The Hamilton Jet

A final warning should be issued, and it should take the form of a ban, in the meantime, on any gathering in the vicinity of the wharves. The Government should announce that crowds on the waterfront will be dispersed without hesitation, and that in view of what has already happened The Police Will Be Armed. And the Government should make it known, before any further incidents occur, that should individuals or groups defy the ban and challenge the authority of the police, The Police Will Shoot.[20]

Observers as varied as historian Michael Bassett and Australian journalists criticised the Kiwi press for its inaction. Bassett offered his assessment in the measured tones of an academic, saying that in the moment of the country's greatest industrial crisis, they (newspapers) were allowing themselves to become virtual propaganda sheets for the National Government and the port employers.[21]

Some Australian journalists referred to the "gutless New Zealand Press". After the Cuba Street batoning by police, one wrote to the *New Zealand Journalist*:

The [Melbourne] Herald, radio-telephoned New Zealand and found a curious reticence. It was then that we decided to send our own man over to cover the strike. A number of papers, dissatisfied with the poor cover, had already sent men. These men found nothing but hostility in a number of offices, and a desire everywhere to play the events down.

The fact that important principles were involved meant nothing. New Zealand journalists had entered a conspiracy, willingly or unwillingly, to look the other way while the most important news they had had for years was breaking all about them. And they resented anyone pointing it out to them. They resented even more that the Australian papers were publishing stories that they could not.[22]

Though the press was hardly courageous, it sometimes had to work under the conditions of a police state. At the now defunct *Southern Cross*, a police sergeant entered the building and demanded, under the emergency regulations, to check the next day's editorial. He issued instructions that no advertisements were to be published about meetings that were banned. The unions concerned and the Labour Party were also refused permission for time on radio to refute what they considered to be one-sided government propaganda.[23]

Other dramas played out unseen as a result of the dispute and included at least one suicide. One watersider's wife wrote this impassioned plea to Opposition Leader Walter Nash:

Dear Mr Nash,
Why don't you stop this strike? Before this business we were a happy family. Now my husband has started hitting me and my kids.[24]

On 11 July, five months after the dispute began, the watersiders recommended a return to work, and acknowledged defeat. Other losers from their ill-fated intransigence included militant unionism and the Labour Party which lost a snap election called by Holland for 1 September – five weeks after the emergency regulations had been withdrawn.

The jet boat was not invented in New Zealand but refined by Bill Hamilton, a man who loved speed and the fast-flowing rivers of the MacKenzie country.

On land in 1925, Hamilton became the first Kiwi to do more than a 100 miles per hour in a 1914 Sunbeam. In 1928, his speed of 109 miles per hour set an Australasian record. Hamilton was the archetypal Kiwi do-it-yourselfer. When he needed to build a hydro plant to supply power to his homestead at Irishman's Creek, he developed a mechanical digger to scoop out the earth for the dam. He patented the machine in 1929 and it kept him in business during the Depression.

In 1951, when he was 52, he began to develop the idea of a boat which would travel rapidly upstream. He worked initially with Christchurch boatbuilder Arnold France, who suggested a jet unit for the shallow waters. The first prototype could do only 17 kilometres per hour on trials, but Hamilton's former apprentice Alf Dick came up with an idea. He suggested the jet unit should be mounted above the waterline, not below as had previously been the case. The boat's speed jumped to 27 kilometres per hour and it was successful in trials.

However, the real breakthrough came in 1956 when George Davison, a new engineering graduate from Canterbury University, worked with Hamilton and Dick and came up with a new approach. He suggested a two stage axial flow unit which was developed into the Chinook – the first commercially viable jet unit. Another improvement, in the form of a third stage, had the boat zipping along at speeds of 80 kilometres per hour, and the rest is now history.

Source: *Kiwi Ingenuity, A book of New Zealand Ideas and Inventions,* by Bob Riley, AIT Press, Auckland, 1995.

"The Group" Architects

In the 1950s a group of young architectural graduates from Auckland University set up in practice together with the intention of creating a revolution in New Zealand house design. They were challenging what one called "New Dreamland" and all those who lived there – "a bungalow bourgeoisie who don't give a damn for social or any other needs. We wonder how things will look to the neighbours. What will people think?" In the process they created an Auckland style, diametrically opposed to the "brick and tile" homes springing up all over the country, virtually the only ones that qualified for a State Advances loan. Jack Manning worked with Group Architects and remembers the first two houses they built on spec to demonstrate their radical principles:

> They were open-planned houses and they encouraged an informal and unpretentious lifestyle. They were timber houses – the timber was treated lovingly and it was also treated honestly by being exposed rather than hidden. But because the houses weren't designed to impress the neighbours, people thought they were cowsheds. They were disastrous from a commercial point of view. The miracle is that anybody ever bought them.

PUBLISHED MONTHLY UNDER THE AUSPICES OF THE N.Z. INSTITUTE OF ARCHITECTS

home & building

VOL. XVI, No. 5
OCTOBER 1 1953   A   1/-

Allan Wild/AGM Publishing

The interior of the Catley house on the cover of "Home & Building".

Almost 40 years later the Group's first clients still lived in the house they moved into in 1952, still unaltered except for new curtains. In 1991, Dorothy Catley recalled that their choice of home back then cost them in several ways: State Advances refused them a loan and there were social repercussions:

> In 1952, people were shocked by it. I lost a lot of my friends because of this house. My girlfriends wouldn't come up.... It was only after about six years that people began to understand the place and could see how it was the right kind of house to live in. No silly little passages... but good grief, where do you see a house with a living area which is nothing but two huge rooms? In another 40 years this place will still be modern.

Auckland architect Marshall Cook sees this architectural influence still at work almost 50 years on:

> The Auckland regionalist style looks totally back to The Group. One realised how competent their attitudes to planning were. How good their understanding of environmental issues about sun, shade, rain and wind actually was. They were against wanton display. We've been influenced not so much by the physical appearance of their houses but by the way they thought. They looked clearly at the way people lived and realised that Aucklanders are most comfortable in an easy social atmosphere.... Their socialistic ethic, their waste-not-want-not attitude to materials, their goodness and human purpose were admirable. Anyone who designs anything wants to have the basic anchor of a philosophy. The Group provided that for a whole generation of designers.

Source: Peter Shaw, The Group Architects and the Auckland House, Metro, June 1991, pp. 120-28.

Leaving behind the grim winter of 1951, we went into the lull of a long summer of canvas-covered dreaming. In our family jalopies, we pulled caravans and trailers to our favourite holiday hideaways where gimcrack baches of corrugated iron and Fibrolite were home. We pitched tents by sea and lake. As trampers, we refreshed ourselves in the cathedral calm of the bush. The French journal *Realités* recognised in this retreat to the countryside something special about the Kiwi character:

It is a happy country where one can experience that supreme blessing, henceforth denied to almost the whole of the civilised world – solitude at will. There is a strange feeling that anyone… may be off the next day in a small car or on horseback, or on foot, to some utterly lonely mountain or thunderous beach where a stranger is a rarity, or an inlet where you can play the hermit for a month.[25]

The writer found Kiwis rugged, unsentimental, disdainful of pretensions and suspicious of theories. Slowly, though, the make-up of New Zealand society was changing. In May 1950 the criteria for immigrants was relaxed with the age limits moved from 20–35 to 35–45. In addition, the ten pound contribution towards the passage paid by non-ex-service personnel was abolished. Free passages were provided for both single and married ex-personnel, including their families, and free passage was also offered to married non-ex-service personnel with up to two children.

Immigrant Poms were not so much discriminated against as tolerated. To Kiwis this was the land of milk and honey and complaints about oddities like old cars, and the social barbarism of the "six o'clock swill", were resented. Immigration was also opened up to some single non-British people and resulted in the arrival of Dutch, Danish, Swiss, Austrian and German nationals. If the English had earned a reputation among Kiwis for whingeing, the Continental newcomers had other cause to offend their hosts. They were, said Kiwis, too pushy, too hard-working in the land of she'll be right.

She'll be right often meant awful or non-existent service in hotels and shops. Kiwis almost prided themselves on their surliness and indifference to the service ethic. Barry Crump, who regularly trekked out of the bush to a favourite pub, noted a sign there

ATL F-27630-1/2 (National Archives: National Publicity Studios Collection)

Summers, the beach and invariably a beauty show whose merits were never questioned – though everyone had an opinion on the contestants.

British migrants on the "Atlantis" about to start their new lives in New Zealand, after docking in Wellington.

ATL G-100726-1/2 (W. H. Raine Collection)

A new migration – on the porch of the suburban Marae as Maori moved from country to town.

Selling the evening newspaper – young paper boys shouting their distinctive sales pitch to commuters before the sun began to set on the evening press.

A sign outside a pub in Auckland, not Alabama, in the Fifties.

which read: "Rangitaiki Hotel. Crook beer, dirty glasses, short change, incivility."

As immigrants tried to come to terms with these frontier attitudes to service, one more great Maori migration was taking place. This time it was driven by increased opportunities to work in the cities when fewer jobs existed in the country, by better education and the growth of manufacturing. In 1939 only 9 per cent lived in the towns; in 1956, the figure was 23 per cent. Just ten years later, nearly half of Maoridom lived in towns and cities.[26]

It was a mix which introduced new tensions to a society which had prided itself on its race relations, though traditionally the races had been separated by town and country. The real test of race relations was only just beginning and some failed at the first barrier, as the *People's Voice* reported. Under a headline which read "The 'Queen City' Stoops to Deep South Level", the paper ran a photograph of a sign above the door of the Kings' Arms lounge bar in Newton. The sign read, "No natives served in this bar – by order." A year earlier, the same newspaper named the Star Hotel in Albert Street for refusing accommodation to a Maori football team.[27] New Zealand was not immune to institutionalised racism, but it was a less virulent strain than the one being fought by civil rights campaigners in America's South at the time. Even so, the anxieties of discrimination at hotel dining rooms reached deeply into the lives of some Maori-Pakeha married couples:

It's terrible you know. On our way to dinner at a hotel we are all tense. This lasts right up until we're actually through the door and sitting down. Then we relax. It's not that we've ever been refused admission, but from what you read this sort of thing does occur and honestly, I just don't know what we'd do if we got knocked back.[28]

There were accounts of Maori wives of Pakeha men being refused a beer in bars while one was offered to the husband; at some rural picture theatres Maoris and Pakehas sat in separate sections. Despite our egalitarian ethic, minorities found the Fifties difficult because of the assumed superiority of WASPs (White Anglo Saxon Protestants).

Women were not a minority but their role was unquestioned – it lay in the home. The image of home-making was reinforced by recipe-led radio programmes like Aunt Daisy's, and in print by the *Woman's Weekly*, then a very different publication from the present-day version. A happy woman was a married women and spinsterhood with its cobwebbed connotations was to be avoided.

In a long *Weekly* article placed opposite an editorial slot headed: "Let's make a Hat!" (a perky pill-box), writer Peter Barttelott asked readers whether they were married to their jobs instead of a husband. He quoted American psychologist Beatrice M. Hinkle M.D., who believed one of the causes of spinsterhood was that women were in love with their fathers. He added:

Many women, particularly since women have become competitors with men in industry, art and commerce, choose a career instead of a husband. Why is it that they so often end up as unhappy spinsters?… Women do not function like men as far as jobs are concerned, unless they are of the abnormally masculine type.

Hanging — He "Died Game"

Capital punishment is an easy abstract but a sickening reality. The tensions leading up to the event and the hanging itself caused psychosomatic disorders in some prison officers.[i] On hanging day, they had to prepare elaborately for the event. The condemned man had to be weighed and a mock-up hanging staged with a sand-filled sack of exactly the same weight.

Reporters, too, witnessed hangings as public representatives; *New Zealand Truth* provided one of the most vivid descriptions of the hanging of 20-year-old Albert Black for the murder of another Auckland teenager in 1955:

He did not walk bravely, or imperturbably or any other way, to the scaffold. As they all do, he shuffled. He shuffled because the movement of his body was harnessed. His arms, at the elbow, were shackled to his body with broad leather straps, his crossed hands were strapped in front of him and his legs were pinioned above the knee.

Careful planning goes into preparing a man who is to be hanged. The idea is that he should be as near a rigid log of wood as possible when he is dropped. For this reason he is dressed in a stiff canvas coat, and steps out of his own shoes into a pair of heavy boots.

… the prisoner is given what a medical man would call "sedation" – what the layman would call a shot of dope. The party assembled along one wall facing the scaffold… a high steel structure. The platform, to which the condemned climb, is seventeen steps away from the ground. Canvas is lashed around the supports so that the space beneath the platform is concealed. The scaffold is lighted from overhead with a powerful electric bulb. The light shines on the white rope coiled beneath the metal gallows and on the noose hanging over the trap.

… Black came into the courtyard. He appeared, fortunately, to be composed…. Death comes to men in many forms. Black met death at the top of the stairs in the shape of a chunky figure dressed as if for a fishing expedition on a stormy day. This was the hangman. He wore a felt hat pulled down low over his eyes. To hide his eyes he wore sunglasses. His chin was sunk in the collar of a long topcoat buttoned all the way up the front. This garish figure waiting at the back of the platform looked ludicrously out of touch, like an actor in some fifth-rate melodrama.

He was properly clothed. So long as he is disguised, the hangman may wear what he chooses. There is no formal dress for the occasion. One New Zealand hangman favoured a skin-tight Superman-style black costume. Black turned from the hangman to face the sheriff and witnesses. He was asked if he had anything to say before the sentence was executed. Black looked down; wished everybody a Happy Christmas and a prosperous New Year. The warders closed around him. They pinioned his ankles, drew the noose down over his neck and placed a white hood over his head….

The warders moved away from Black. He stood alone. For a moment. The sheriff raised his hand carrying the warrant of execution. Death in dark glasses performed his office. Black was no longer there. The white rope was taut. The watchers winced from the thud of the trap as from a shot. The rope oscillated like a leisurely pendulum. The wind in the courtyard clutched at the canvas covering the bottom of the scaffold. In one corner it lifted. Nobody looked down twice. Had that been a boot-heel in view?

Two priests of the Catholic faith which Black had embraced in the last few weeks of his life prayed for him. The Superintendent went to the back of the scaffold; stayed there a short quarter-minute. It was finished. Nothing had gone wrong.

… It was agreed Black had "died game".[ii]

Frederick Foster (top), 26, hanged for shooting his girlfriend, 19-year-old Dorothy Skiffington, in Auckland during a jealous fit. Just before his execution, he was operated on for appendicitis and returned to prison where he was hanged — before the wound had healed.

---

[i] New Zealand Department of Justice, *Crime in New Zealand*, p. 70.
[ii] Extract courtesy of *New Zealand Truth* (14 December 1955 edition).

High fashion and old fashioned domesticity. As affluence spread, marketers continued to target women and introduced a range of improved labour saving devices. Despite the fashionable clothing, their place remained in the home.

Women give themselves over to their careers as completely as they give themselves over to the role of wife and mother in marriage. They in their jobs become as one and this leaves them no room for other relationships, particularly marriage. ... But for a man it is never too late to find a wife, especially if he has money. Marriage means a sacrifice for a man. For a woman, Dr Hinkle points out it is the missing of marriage that is the sacrifice.[29]

Some women did not need any persuading and in the magazine's famous *Over the Teacups* column, this contribution in the same issue spoke of domestic contentment:

I suppose I am just a sentimentalist at heart, but as I spent the three first and very important years of my married life in someone else's home, the true significance of this little verse will be appreciated by others as it was by me on finding the joys of owning and managing one's own home.

> POSSESSIVE CASE
> *I polish spoons until they shine,*
> *Contentedly, because they're mine;*
> *I wield a dust mop happily*
> *   because the floors belong to me;*
> *I iron and my spirit sings,*
> *   because I own these lovely things.*
> *There's joy in everything I do*
> *Because my heart belongs to you!*
> *– April[30]*

Visiting writers like novelist Eric Linklater also noted female devotion to domesticity and found women vying with their neighbours "to whip a stiffer, richer cream". But other women looked at Kiwi males and found them lacking in wit, grace and cultural refinement. One suggested that part of the problem also lay in the era's egalitarianism and materialism. She added:

... an alarmingly large number of cultivated and attractive young women in their twenties are making a discovery that is distressing both for them and for New Zealand's future. Though they wish to marry and have children, and though our society's mores are such that a woman who does not marry is made in a hundred ways to feel a failure, they are finding that they prefer to remain single....

*   Still, however, marriage is the most generally accepted criterion of feminine success....[31]*

The renewed battle for women's rights lay ahead. Kiwis had more immediate concerns about society and they lay in the dramatic rise of crime. Rape, as well as murder convictions, soared. Between 1920 and 1930, sixty-seven people were found guilty of rape, attempted rape, and assault with intent to commit rape. Between 1950 and 1960 the figure was 175 – a 161 per cent increase, while the population grew 52 per cent.[32]

The first Labour Government had suspended the death penalty in 1936, then

The Handleys
An Adoption

Adoption began to be pushed as an acceptable and eventually preferable alternative to fostering and orphanages in the 1940s. However, it was a stressful process fraught with hurdles and difficulties. Peggy and Jack Handley were among the thousands of couples who wanted to adopt a child.

Peggy and Jack Handley, 1939.

I was not able to have children. I had a surgery in 1942 and my surgeon joined the navy. When he came back in 1946 I went back to him. He said it hadn't been successful and if I really wanted a child I'd think about adoption. "But," he said, "I can't guarantee that you couldn't have a child because nature has a way of making liars of doctors, [but] I don't think it's very likely." And that's when we decided we would adopt a child.

We went to the Social Welfare and saw a social welfare officer and told him we were after an adoption. They asked whether we wanted a boy or a girl. Dot [Peggy's sister] had just had a boy and Jack's sister had just had a boy, so we thought maybe it would be better if we went for a girl, so there would be no sort of rivalry or anything like that. They said, "You will have something like a two year wait." They said, "We will have to investigate you. You will have to allow us into your house when we knock at the door. We will send the police up." And they did all that. The police investigated us. The welfare people would come in at any time and interview us and see us. And we waited about five months.

They were in a building at the lower end of Cuba Street [Wellington] and Jack would walk past it in his lunch hour every day – cheeky devil – and he would go up and see this lady and say, "What has happened to our baby?" One Friday he went up, and she said, "You have got a long wait ahead of you yet." He rang me up when he got back to work and told me he had done this.

Anyway, about 4 o'clock that afternoon I got a ring from this woman and she asked would we be prepared to take a baby on the Monday morning? I said, "Well yes, if a baby needs a home. We can manage something." She said the baby had been taken by a foster mother but she couldn't cope with it. So we tore around all weekend. Jack's sister came across with bassinets and layettes to clothe the baby, and all sorts of things. On Monday morning they rang and said that the adoptive father had been so annoyed and he wouldn't allow his wife to give the baby back. So we heard no more about it; that was that. I think Jack even gave up going in to see them. Susan was born on the 28th of August and this happened in September.

In November I got a ring from the welfare officer and she said, "Well it's not your turn Mrs Handley, but we feel this baby is meant for you." What had happened was the baby's health had deteriorated so much that the Plunket nurse went to the Social Welfare and the baby had been taken away from the mother and put into Karitane Hospital. When they got her back into good health and she was ready to come out, that's when they rang me up. This was the same baby! And that's how we got Susan.

When I first told my father [about the adoption], he was very much against it. But from the moment he saw Susan, that was it. He adored her. My mother knew an old Swedish lady, and when she met me with Susan she said, "You are foolish to adopt a baby. You don't know how that baby will grow up." I said to her, "Mrs Bernstein, do you think my mother knew how all we children would grow up?" And she never said anymore. But that I think was the times really. Most people didn't think like that. It is a risk you take of course. But you have to trust yourself to be able to bring up a child properly. Susan was lucky. She had lots of cousins. Jack's mother adored her, and his two sisters loved her, and my sisters loved her. And I don't think she ever felt that she wasn't part of the family.

Source: Edited Ninox transcripts from *Our People, Our Century*, 1999.

NZM Archive

Reelin' and a rockin' to the rhythms of Little Richard and Elvis; teenagers relished the freedom of rock and roll dancing.

In New Zealand, youth culture first shook up the establishment in the milk bar, like this one in Courtenay Place, Wellington. At milk bars, teenagers gathered to listen to Little Richard and others on the jukebox, and drink the Devil's Brew – milk shakes.

abolished it in 1941. In 1950, following a year which saw eight convictions for murder, National reinstated the death penalty, and eight murderers were executed between 1952 and 1957.

In the minds of many, rising crime was increasingly associated with the loose morality and the music of the young. As teenage teddy boys, bikies, bodgies and the female of the species – widgies – they scorned authority, flouted their sexuality openly, and trashed social norms. In the lineage of teenage culture they were *homo erectus* but then as now, it was the erectus which bothered parents. Their worst fears were realised by a former truck driver from Tupelo, Mississippi. In 1954, a year before he became a household name, a contemporary described his impact on young audiences:

This cat came out in red pants and a green coat and a pink shirt and socks, and he had this sneer on his face and he stood behind the mike for five minutes, I'll bet, before he made a move. Then he hit his guitar a lick, and he broke two strings. I'd been playing ten years, and I hadn't broken a total of two strings. So there he was, these two strings dangling, and he hadn't done anything yet, and these high school girls were screaming and fainting and running up to the stage, and then he started to move his hips real slow like he had a thing for his guitar. That was Elvis Presley when he was about nineteen, playing Kilgore, Texas. He made chills run up my back, man...[33]

In 1955 the rivers of rhythm and blues, country and rockabilly all joined and burst into the first torrent of rock and roll. Popular culture was never the same again. Bill Haley and his Comets took their form of rock to mainstream audiences with their song *Rock Around the Clock* in the 1955 film *The Blackboard Jungle*. Within a year Elvis, Fats Domino, Chuck Berry and perhaps the most colourful, Little Richard, all had chart toppers.

The raw sexuality of rock and roll offended the righteous and in America's South rock records were burned. In New Zealand, bandsmen played bland, sentimental music. If negro influences were the heart of rock and roll, then that pulse could best be felt with the beginning of the Maori showbands. At the Maori

Museum of New Zealand Te Papa Tongarewa, C-2739 (Gordon Burt Collection)

Phil Warren/NZM Archive

Community Centre in Auckland and in Wellington, the Maori Hi-Fives, and other bands with hugely talented performers, began their long play. But officially rock and roll was rationed on air, with the Broadcasting Service playing two to three "hit parades" a week. Instead of the rock revolution, young listeners got plenty of Mitch Miller's singalongs, The Ink Spots, and Rosemary Clooney.

At 1ZB, the programme organiser confiscated rock and roll records and hid them under the carpet in his office in an attempt to prevent breakfast host Buzz Perkins from playing them. Perkins outwitted him by buying multiple copies of records by Presley and other artists – although the organiser would hide these under the carpet as well. But when the organiser left the office and took the bus home at 5pm, Programme Department staff routinely broke into his office and removed all the rock records they could find. Between 5pm and 5.30 Elvis had bumper airtime on the station because the organiser was on the bus going home.[34]

Eventually radio stations bowed to the inevitable and introduced young on-air talent in the form of popular "deejays". Their relative brashness freshened the dull bureaucracy of radio. Predictably, older listeners despised them; just as predictably, teenagers adored them because at last they could hear more rock and roll. Its irresistible invitation to youth in stiff petticoats and stovepipe trousers was to dance.

By 1958 New Zealand had its first rock star, Raetihi-born Johnny Devlin, whose shirts were routinely torn off his back by hysterical teenagers. His first hit *Lawdy Miss Clawdy* received no air play, but teenagers queued to buy a copy – 2,000 were sold in Auckland alone in the first month of release.[35] The NZBS could no longer ignore "New Zealand's Elvis Presley" and those who followed.

NZM Archive

New Zealand's first rock star Johnny Devlin, is mobbed by fans and is about to lose yet another shirt off his back. After he performed fans often tore them off.

..it's a goal !

"RUGBY IN MY TIME"
by
Winston McCarthy
this week and every week in

THE NEW ZEALAND
LISTENER
ORDER YOUR COPY HERE

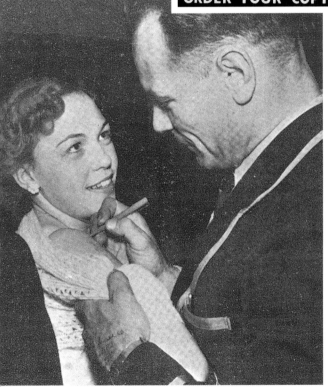

Rugby in the Fifties could not be complete without commentator Winston McCarthy (above left) with his clarion call: "Wait for it... wait for it... it's a goal!"

The man who usually put it between the posts from unprecedented distances was The Boot, legendary All Black fullback Don Clarke, pictured (above) holding a football.

Agape on the terraces – Aucklanders watch their team take on the Springboks, 1956.

Some people bring autograph books, but this young fan (above) prefers her shoulder. Springbok Chris Koch obliges by signing his name during the 1956 Springbok tour of New Zealand.

Politically, New Zealand's tastes changed – along with the way Kiwis paid their taxes. 1958 saw the introduction of PAYE (Pay As You Earn) income taxation which was backed by both parties – with some differences – at the 1957 election. On the political scene, Social Credit emerged as a third party and in its first attempt in 1954 won 11 per cent of the vote, but no seats. The contest was still between the two major parties. After eight years of National, voters took the Labour as opposed to the National electoral bribe, giving the party a two-seat majority.

Sid Holland had stepped down from National's leadership just before the 1957 election, handing over the top job to his deputy, Keith Holyoake. In the campaign which followed, neither party looked over its shoulder at the worsening economic conditions. One political scientist described the election as "an auction for the electors' votes".[36]

Among other things Labour promised – and later delivered – aid for lower income groups, a 50 per cent increase in the value of the family benefit and capitalisation of the family benefit to buy a home. However, after eight years of prosperity, Labour had inherited a major balance of overseas payments crisis. It took an unpopular course with stringent import controls and its 1958 "black budget". It raised indirect taxes on items like beer, spirits, tobacco and petrol rather than income tax. As such it was seen by many as an attack on ordinary (particularly male) workers – Labour's traditional supporters. Historian Keith Sinclair said these measures were largely responsible for Labour's defeat in 1960.

Imperceptibly, the economic noose was being tightened as we idled in the summer daze, convinced that she was right, mate.

National leader Sid Holland (right) with American President Dwight Eisenhower.

(Below left) In the electoral "auction" for votes in 1957, Labour won. Although the party delivered increased aid for lower income groups, it became unpopular because of its "Black Budget" which taxed beer, spirits, tobacco and petrol.

(Below) A final discussion between Prime Minister Walter Nash and his Finance Minister Arnold Nordmeyer, before Nash's trip to a Commonwealth trade conference in Montreal.

For your family's sake

VOTE LABOUR

The van der Poel Family
"It was just Fairy-tales...."

They sailed from Holland and expected their destination to be bush-covered and inhabited by natives. They thought they might have to live in a hut as they earned their way as new Kiwi farmers. But on January 18, 1954, after 35 days on an ocean liner, Kees van der Poel and his fiancee Riet entered Port Nicholson Harbour – to be pleasantly surprised. Riet recalls:

I still think that it's the most beautiful harbour in the country, in the world....

Riet and Kees in Holland before their decision to emigrate.

Like thousands of migrants before them, Kees van der Poel and his fiancee Riet leave Europe for New Zealand, and a new life.

She and Kees had come from a land where housing was predictable. What they saw from their liner was very different and delighted them as Kees recalls:

When we came to Wellington we saw all the different colours of houses, all the colours of the roofs... it was just fairy-tales.

Both came from the small town of Oude Ade in Leiden, near Amsterdam. Both left home for New Zealand with the traditional migrant dream – better opportunities for them and their children. They arrived in New Zealand with a few pounds in their pockets and with limited English. They found their way to the bus only after hearing a conversation between another English-speaking Dutch couple.

Kees' brother Koos had already immigrated and he took them to a farm at Rahotu in Taranaki where labouring jobs and accommodation were waiting for Kees and Riet who married shortly after arriving in the country. Kees had worked on a farm in Holland and was accustomed to milking by hand.

I never milked with a machine... in those days, just after the war, we had no tractors. Everything was still done by horse... everything was hand work – it was a big change for us here.

The couple worked on the Rahotu farm for just over three years, milking 180 cows before becoming sharemilkers at Hawera where they milked 110 cows and built a piggery on the farm.

Kees recalls that they often went without so they could afford to go sharemilking. To supplement their income they sold eggs to the local grocer and maintained a vegetable garden. He says:

We did all sorts of things to make money – we even skinned dead calves... we didn't envisage owning a farm because it was impossible [for us] to own a farm in Holland. When we got here and saw the opportunities, we understood it was attainable. Our boss gave us a very good start and honest advice and we found it easy to save money in New Zealand.

In 1968, 11 years after they began sharemilking, the couple bought their first farm at Ngaere, halfway between Stratford and Eltham. Early in their farming careers, the family shared the work – Riet and her eldest son Jim sharemilked 150 cows, while Kees redesigned the 203-acre farm. Kees recalls:

The farm was dry stock farm, flat and swampy. I had to build a cowshed and lay pipes. I bought it because it was cheap and isolated and initially I thought, "What a rotten place." We worked really hard for the first eight years. We had to get rid of tree stumps, and the boys and their school friends all helped.

He never insisted that any of his children follow his footsteps into farming although he knew his three boys were keen on the idea – son Jim had bred his own chickens and had ducks and guinea pigs.

Riet and Kees may have been stranded in their own paradise a long way from the familiar flatlands of Holland, but they immersed themselves in the Ngaere community, and also befriended other Dutch families in the area. Riet, who is Catholic, says:

We went to church to meet other people. When our children went to school there weren't many Dutch children and their teachers were intrigued with our accents and culture.

In 1979 they sold the Ngaere farm because they had a ready buyer and it was too big for Kees to run on his own. After a period sharemilking they bought a 178-acre dairy farm in Te Awamutu in 1980. Riet says:

Riet and Kees on their farm at Ngaere.

The day I came here I said, "That is it." I knew I wanted to be here and I loved the house.

Husband Kees recalls that among the reasons for moving to the Waikato was the warmer climate. But there were other attractions too.

We always liked the look of the Waikato – the tidiness of the place, but we have to be thankful for Taranaki because it made us what we are.

Ten years later Kees went into partnership with son Jim, each owning half the herd and half the farm. In 1994, Jim, who is a farming entrepreneur and now owns numerous farms in the Waikato and Ashburton regions, bought the entire herd. In 1999 Kees and Riet aged 70 and 68 are retired but still own part of the farm. They return to Holland regularly and their children Clazina, Deb, Jim, Kevin, Linda and John, all continue the farming tradition they began as eager migrants.

Sources: Edited Ninox transcipts from *Our People, Our Century,* 1999. All photgraphs from the van der Poel Family Collection.

Eldest son Jim feeds the chooks on the van der Poel property.

The MacGibbon Family
A God-fearing People...?

In the latter decades of last century, a steady stream of migrants from Scotland arrived in New Zealand. Among them were members of the Free Church of Scotland, breakaways from the Presbyterian Church. They saw themselves as the new Pilgrim Fathers, 19th century equivalents of the men and women who set sail on the *Mayflower* for the new world of America some two hundred years earlier. And their mission was similar: to set up a colony of righteous and God-fearing men and women, this time in the South Pacific, in Dunedin. The story of these families and their descendants is the story of the secularisation of great sections of New Zealand society.

Thomas and Isabella MacGibbon were among these new Scottish settlers. They raised their 11 children according to strict puritan ethics, with a strong emphasis on piety and the sacredness of the Sabbath.

Thomas and Isabella's great-grandson and the family historian, John MacGibbon, says:

Sunday was a day of great solemnity. Three services a day and the rest of the day was spent in very intense Bible reading, singing psalms, discussing the sermons. Till the end of Saturday night the children could play with their toys. They could read books. Then they would be packed away. All of a sudden on Sunday, they were things of evil. They could read Pilgrim's Progress. They could read the Bible; and they could read various religious tracts. No games whatsoever. Adults couldn't even go for walks for pleasure. They could walk to church.

When Thomas went to church — this would have been in 1909 when he moved to Dunedin — *he would head the procession of MacGibbons down the aisle of Knox Church. They'd get to the pew that the family had rented and he would stand at the outside, take his top hat off. The family would file past him. He would finally sit down, put his smoker's cap on. Then he would lean forward and pray vigorously.*

This first generation were strict adherents to the beliefs of the Free Church and then the Presbyterian Church — in October 1901, the Free Church had joined with the United Presbyterians of Scotland. Thomas and his brother John were also tireless in their work in the community. The family worked hard and prospered. It was a quiet, austere lifestyle. The one entertainment was music:

They let their hair down with a bit of music and dancing later in the century. They did like to sing the old Scottish songs round the piano. There was a lot of that sort of thing, and even dancing reels. My great-grandmother played the piano while everyone danced reels. So they weren't totally unbending.

Religious colonists: Thomas and Isabella MacGibbon with their children lined up for a family portrait at the turn of the century.

As time passed, Presbyterian attitudes and influence were gradually diluted by settlers of different backgrounds and beliefs:

Over the century they certainly became less puritan in their outlook, especially in terms of things like alcohol or even religion. These things changed because they met other people. It wasn't just this little Free Church community. For instance, in Dunedin the Anglicans were a great problem. They were known as the "little enemy" because they brought in other ideas and spoiled this little puritan settlement.

But there were influences even worse than the Anglicans – "Everyone knew the dangers of marrying a Catholic!"

Bruce MacGibbon, in front of his father Archie, with his mother Mary, brothers and sister, neat and tidy in their Sunday best, 1920.

Overseas travel during the two world wars brought sons and grandsons of the original settlers into contact with a whole range of beliefs and lifestyles, including social drinking. Men came home to Dunedin and Gore and Mataura with no intention of returning to the narrow old ways.

Bruce MacGibbon, John's uncle and one of Thomas and Isabella's many grandchildren, was one of six children. The influence of his grandparents' generation was still strong when he was growing up in the Twenties and early Thirties:

We read the Bible every Sunday night, that's for sure, and during the day. And of course we prayed at a church every Sunday morning. We had to clean our boots, lead them and everything, on Saturday in preparation to go to church on Sunday. You used to put your Sunday best on. I remember Dad used to have a bowler hat and a black cane with a top on it. It was a Sunday parade and we were all dressed up. We had the family pew in church and we all filed in.

Mother's mother used to come down the pew with us and she always had a bag of liquorice staples. She'd pass them along to us because Mother and Dad would be in the choir and it helped keep us quiet for the sermons which were rather long.

It was a busy day because we always had a very large dinner on a Sunday and mother used to cook up some beautiful feeds for us – jam tarts with the pastry criss-crossed over the base, and always a big bowl of soup, good vegetable soup. She was a very good cook. I can still remember her sitting with the crockery bowl in her lap, beating by hand, and the clink of her wedding ring on the side of her bowl. By Jove, she used to produce some great cakes.

But Bruce also watched the first loosening of the family's strict rules. His father was "a derivation" of the early Scots, canny in business dealings and with a streak of the "Bible banger" about him. Nevertheless, "… he wasn't as narrow in his attitude as my grandfather Thomas MacGibbon or my great-grandfather. But I still remember as kids we weren't allowed to read comics on Sunday".

Gradually his father loosened up until "… we were allowed to do practically anything. We used to swim down the river on Sunday. That was frowned upon in the early days." It was still not approved of by their grandparents and their visits put a temporary stop to such activities: "We didn't look forward [to their visits] with an air of expectation because we knew we had to toe the mark," he says now.

Music continued to be an integral part of family life:

Everybody would get round the piano and have a real singsong. Mother could play and so could my sister. So we had a lot of fun. We had a good family life, a good, wholesome, clean family life.

Wrapped up against winter – John MacGibbon with his mother, Marie, while brother Neil watches from the shelter of the car, Peel Forest, 1940s.

Music also began to spread beyond the family circle. Bruce's parents both sang in the local church choir in Mataura and his mother, a fine soprano, sang in oratorios around the district and down in Invercargill, her home town. Music had entered the MacGibbon blood. Bruce in his turn has long been a member of the Dunedin Male Choir. Conversely, his relationship with the Church and religion has become less intense:

I'm not a Bible banging type of person. I still respect the value of religion and I think it's got its place in the community, there's no question about that. I don't classify myself as a very good church person. I'm a fairly regular attender. Whether I go to heaven or not, that doesn't come into it. It's what I get personally out of going to church. I still get something out of it. Maybe it's an inner thing that

gives you satisfaction. It's probably inherent in me from way back. But I've got a much broader outlook on it than they used to have. I think people should have a certain amount of religion to get the values of life. I think it is very important the essential values are taught to children.

His nephew, John MacGibbon, grew up in the 1950s. The decade marked the rise of the first in a series of waves of change that affected all sectors of New Zealand society. Presbyterian Otago was no exception:

I think of those years I spent growing up in a place called Ardgowan, a country district out of Oamaru, between the ages of five and 17. It was a very narrow little Presbyterian district and one of the centrepieces of it was the little wooden church. I had to go every Sunday until I was old enough to say, "That's enough. I'm not going any more." We certainly were affected by the church. On the other hand, our parents couldn't be too strict about it 'cos my mother didn't go to church at all — though as a good community person she was a member of the Presbyterian Women's Mother's Union. My father went to church from time to time, but he was the local school teacher and I think he felt he had to put in an occasional appearance. When it came time for me to say "enough is enough", my parents didn't object.

Right from the start I found it exceedingly tedious. I just found it almost intellectually insulting to have to listen to a very boring minister pray "we have sinned", on and on and on. Then at the end of the prayer, beseech: "Forgive us, O Lord." Then carry on with a terrible hymn, and start the whole cycle over again. I just couldn't wear it at all.

The organisers of the North Otago Bible Class camps might have been disheartened to learn that their charges were not there for the good of their souls, or to improve their knowledge of the Holy Book. John says:

In theory we all went along to learn Scripture, but I didn't know anyone who went for that reason. It was really an opportunity to get away in the bush down at Glencoe and have a good time and meet the opposite sex, because we all went to single sex schools. I think there were some interesting encounters, although I'm sure that for most there was more talk than action.

Presbyterian values were not a bad way to lead your life but they were a little bit too restrictive. I've felt at times there were things I would have done differently without that bit of Presbyterianism in me. Not that I've been an active Presbyterian for 30 or 40 years, but there is an element that is part of my character still. In terms of basic values, I think they've remained fairly constant all the way through.

John MacGibbon's grandparents and great-grandparents might have been dismayed by his drift from church attendance and strict adherence to the tenets of the Presbyterian Church, but they would have been shocked by another of his life choices. For John did what to them would have been unthinkable – he married a Catholic. He and his wife, Liz Newman, raised their four children between the 1970s and the 1990s. By then values and the Church were almost totally separated. John says:

In terms of values instilled in our own children, we didn't try and use any religious justification for behaviour, but although neither Liz nor I went to church, we tended to follow the precepts of the ten commandments. I still have no problem with them, in general. So we tried to instill those ideas in our kids. Though we certainly wouldn't have gone through the individual commandments and said, "Thou shalt not ..." or "Thou shalt ...."

I guess in general we were pretty laid back with the kids. I think we trusted them to a fair degree and trusted they had a fair amount of common sense. We would occasionally step in and give them a few ideas and pointers, but basically we let them do it, and fortunately the kids never went off the rails.

Susannah MacGibbon is the second of their four children and their only daughter. The Sunday rituals of her parents' early years were completely absent from her and her brothers' childhood:

I've been brought up with no religion, pretty much. My [maternal] grandmother's Catholic. My mother was brought up Catholic. I've always grown up knowing that. And my mother rebelled from the Church quite a bit. So I've also grown up knowing its faults through her. I haven't grown up going to church, going to Sunday School. I have not grown up knowing Bible stories.

But the interesting thing is that since I graduated I've worked in a Catholic childcare centre in New Zealand, then in two Catholic schools in England. And over in England I had to teach religious studies, so I used to have to go home at night and swot up on the stories and on the things that we were going to be discussing and then present them. I absolutely loved learning these stories because all of a sudden things started having a bit more meaning. Pictures, paintings, all of a sudden I understood what the symbolism in them meant, and the story behind the picture.

So I think my generation has lost a bit, not having a great input from religion growing up, because we miss a lot of what's around us in terms of culture.

Sources: Edited Ninox transcripts from *Our People, Our Century,* 1999. All photographs from the John MacGibbon Family Collection.

The rituals of religion abandoned, Susannah MacGibbon with brothers Daniel, Stephen and Guy at Jindabyne, Australia, 1981.

Chapter 7

1960

1970

Breaking Out —
Twist & Shout!

The Sixties began with more of a lope than a swing, and at *The New Zealand Herald*, prophesy was alive and well. The newspaper's editorialists had seen the future, and it beckoned with riches and contentment:

No stubbies or indoor comforts for these "garden bar" drinkers in the Waikato.

Marti Friedlander

The country enters a new decade in good heart. The troubles which loomed 12 months ago have proved more psychological than real. Business is reviving from the economic setback caused by officially inspired gloom. Overseas reserves have recovered; full – indeed over full employment continues; and in the major export industries a brighter market for wool offsets a fall in lamb values.... Granted enterprise and co-operation this could be, locally and nationally, the opening year of a great decade.[1]

Nelson Provincial Museum 2023 FR 1 (Photo News Collection)

Equality in the flesh trade – a blokes' beauty contest – the 1962 Mr Tahunanui Contest. This was the matinee before the tobacco-sponsored Miss Craven A beauty contest.

There was, however, other officially inspired gloom in the newspaper that very day. Our cricket-loving Cassandra of a Governor General, Lord Cobham, had also looked ahead. He noted our material yearnings and in his New Year's message warned:

> It is the greatest mistake to imagine that mere material progress is getting us anywhere. On the contrary, the predominance of economic interests and motives in any civilisation is always the forerunner of moral decline and social disintegration.

Either way, the rhetoric went largely unnoticed in a society blinkered by affluence and comfort. We tinkered with old cars on new subdivisions and listened to trendy transistor radios on unspoilt beaches as we took a break from the pressures of the 40-hour working week.

For most Kiwis, the Sixties simply picked up where the Fifties left off – outwardly prosperous and cocooned in consensus of the kind preferred by new Prime Minister, Keith "steady as she goes" Holyoake. Few could have known the extent to which this was to become a watershed era for social experimentation and change. By the end of the Sixties we had swapped short back and sides for the radical chic of long hair; we made love free as if it once had a price, and war as if there was no cost; we met marijuana, farewelled the "six o'clock swill" – and welcomed that real sexual revolutionary – the Pill.

The Champions

Champion miler Peter Snell... "in his stride... was something else, a certain rapture" wrote one sports writer of his runaway style.

In the midst of the recriminations over rugby we also shared in the glory of other sport. In just one hour at the 1960 Rome Olympics two Kiwis, Peter Snell and Murray Halberg, won gold in the 800 metres and 5,000 metres events.

Considered a rookie, Snell powered his way to glory over a fancied field of runners in the 800 metres. Halberg, who had been toughened by defeat in the event at the Melbourne Olympics four years earlier, was determined there would be no repeat. Together, Snell, Halberg and their little known coach Arthur Lydiard, became more than household names. Their feats introduced the joys of jogging to a whole generation of Kiwis – but who was Lydiard? Journalist and broadcaster Gordon Dryden described him:

Here was a man who had taken us to the top of the world. A 44-year old former shoemaker pounding up to 40 miles a time around the streets of Auckland in the blazing sun to try out in practice his theories that were to re-write the record books.... Yet... he was so unappreciated in his own country that he had to work through the nights as a milkman to keep up the modest income that would enable him to take on the world. His runners in those days frequently helped him out on his rounds as part of their training....[i]

Arthur Lydiard, whose coaching helped take Snell and Murray Halberg (right) to the top. Lydiard also inspired a whole new generation of joggers.

Four years later, at the Tokyo Olympics, Lydiard's star protege, Snell, was considered by some to be below his best form. This time, though, he was determined to win not only the 800 but the 1,500 metres – and he did, with an ease which once again drew the admiration of some of the world's best sports writers:

In his stride was the crashing of tall timber, but there was something else, a certain rapture. Snell comes to life when he is running well. He looks alert and keen – his eyes seem to gleam. It was in this manner that he took a glance over his shoulder... ten yards away Davies, the Englishman, Simpson, and the Czech, Odlozil, clawed their way to the tape in a line, looking at each other constantly as they struggled on.[ii]

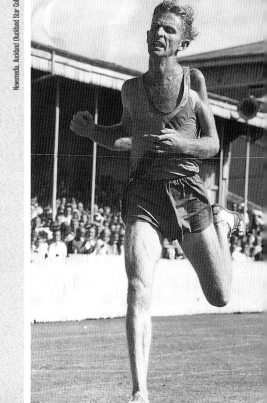

New Zealand came to a standstill for the 1,500-metre event. Parliamentary proceedings stopped as the news was relayed to MPs – there were only 18 in the House at the time, two short of a quorum. A 15-minute adjournment was called in the Wellington Magistrates' Court as Snell cruised to the tape. Once again two Kiwis stood on the podium, Snell to accept another gold and John Davies the bronze. By 1964, Snell held four world records, as well as three Olympic and two Commonwealth gold medals.

---

[i] Gordon Dryden, *Out of The Red*, William Collins Publishers, Auckland, 1978, p. 151.
[ii] Norman Harris cited in Don Cameron (ed.), *Memorable Moments in New Zealand Sport*, Moa Publications, Auckland, 1987, p. 173.

In many ways, the decade resembled the 1920s – both eras stood apart from others with their enduring labels: the Roaring Twenties and the Swinging Sixties. In both, the young pursued and celebrated image and personal freedoms with zest. The jazzy Twenties witnessed a sedition trial; the Sixties went hand in medieval mitt with a heresy case. Radio was the new voice of the Twenties, television the new cultural force of the Sixties. Both decades saw increasing sophistication of flight and the shrinking of distance. Both ended in increasing economic disarray.

In some ways, though, the *Herald* was right. Not only did the paper reflect a widespread smugness, but an optimism which seemed justified – the economic outlook was sunny. Never a supporter of the Left, the newspaper found comfort and stability in Holyoake, who went on to win four successive elections while Labour struggled to find new directions and leadership.

Aside from the calming influence of Holyoake at the helm, there was genuine evidence of prosperity of the kind the paper had predicted. In the opening years of the decade the high level of economic activity led to a heavy demand for imports and cars, household goods, new farm and factory machinery as well as luxury items which flooded into the country.[2] The country's farm exports continued to enjoy high prices and manufacturing expanded at a record rate during the first half of the decade. Real Gross Domestic Product rose by almost 25 per cent between 1960 and 1966, and this was accompanied by an improvement in our terms of trade.[3] We continued to thrive on the sheep's back – but that was part of the problem. For although manufacturing had grown dramatically, the New Zealand economy had not diversified rapidly enough.

Lord Cobham's cautions, thus, also came true. We were living in a material world and there was a price to pay for our prolonged indulgence. However, materialism was only one of our sins – another lay in our colonial mentality, according to Bill Sutch, a forceful advocate for increased diversification:

It is not simply because of high material living standards, or full employment and a good climate: these are but superficial explanations. It is rather because of our social heritage, of our patterns of thought and customary ways, and of our amiable inferiority. All of these stem from nineteenth century colonial society…. The crisis is one of attitude. It lies in a failure to understand fully the fact and nature of a crisis that has already arrived; and a failure to meet it quickly enough. It is also a crisis of dependence – a "decisive moment" for our future – colony or nation?[4]

By 1966, the economic indicators were all beginning to look ominous. The first chill of austerity hit the country the following year, as the economy spiralled into recession. For some historians and economists this first stumble was inevitable given the Government's inability to adapt away from the traditional export emphasis on primary products.

In the face of growing evidence to the contrary, many Kiwis felt Britain would continue to take our farm produce. But the UK, the market for 48 per cent of our exports in 1969,[5] was

Riding to affluence on the sheep's back – sale time at Coromandel.

Marti Friedlander

A Good Keen Man

Writer and quintessential bushman Barry Crump piggy-backing a dead tusker out of the bush.

In 1960 a bushman called Barry Crump introduced the country to the "good keen man" – a character not unlike himself, a professional hunter who culled deer and wild pigs from the rugged terrain of the New Zealand back blocks. *A Good Keen Man* was the first of 25 books which celebrated a character who had already been mythologised in Kiwi literature and pub tales for many years – the laconic man of few words living on the land, the loner, a successor to the pioneer-explorer:

By three o'clock in the afternoon the sky was starting to look angry about something and I wasn't sure I had enough ammunition left to be worth going right up to the tops, so we cut across to another ridge and hunted back towards the river. About halfway down Flynn got very interested in the wind and ignoring the heavy butt he suddenly charged into a narrow gully and set up a tremendous racket in the creek-head. I clambered along in his wake and found him with a young boar bailed up in the bole of a dead rata. It wasn't long since Flynn had been ripped by the boar at Te Puna and he hadn't forgotten it. Nothing would induce him to go in and hold and eventually I had to waste a shot on the beast which showed signs of getting bad-tempered.

Sleet started falling as we carried on down towards the river, and we hurried along with less caution than before. Nearly at the bottom of the ridge a hind leapt from a clump of crownfern and paused long enough for me to poke a shot at her. Flynn ran her down the side and was barking in the river before I'd picked up the trail of blood on the wet leaves. The deer was dead and the sleet had turned to heavy rain by the time I'd scrambled down to where Flynn was shaking himself on the river-bank. I stuffed the tail and back steaks into the pikau and squelched off happily towards the hut, thinking of a hot brew of tea and a woman I used to hang around with. Six deer and a pig were worth getting wet for, and at the hut there was a week-old hunk of venison hanging from a rafter and a couple of onions left in the bag.[i]

---

[i]Barry Crump, *A Good Keen Man*, Hodder Moa Beckett Publishers Ltd, Auckland, 1995 edition, pp. 123-4.

busy attending to its own future. And despite ties of blood and bonds forged in two World Wars, Britain's future lay not with what was left of the Empire, but with Europe.

In the late Sixties, the Holyoake Government lobbied the British intensively and, as an interim measure, managed to secure special arrangements for New Zealand. This was a reprieve and New Zealand, Britain's most loyal dependant, began to move towards a different destiny, with all the attendant discomfort.

We discovered, as we had done militarily in the Second World War, that we were vulnerable, a small primary producing nation of Anglophiles cast adrift by Mother England. We were up the creek in our *waka* with plenty of paddles but no navigation. Increasingly, economics began to direct our course. If in the Sixties the personal was the political in the domain of feminism and the growing protest movement, the worsening economy also began to set a social agenda. The emergence of a confrontational Minister of Finance, Rob Muldoon, and his devaluation of the dollar during the recession of 1967 were all harbingers of what was to come.

As the economy contracted, construction and road building were reduced. The cost of state services increased, the "milk in schools" programme was abolished, and there were reductions in essential services like health and education. Overtime fell and unemployment began to grow rapidly.

Prime Minister "Kiwi Keith" Holyoake, who tried to keep a "steady as she goes" course through the turbulence of the Sixties.

Commercial failures that year rose to 652, the highest since 1932.[6] For passionately pro-industry observers of the political scene like Sutch, policies like the abandonment of import licensing thrust New Zealand back to darker, Depression days:

New Zealand's main social contribution to the world up to 1967 had been its concept and practice of economic equality, seen in probably its most important form in providing, for all, the dignity of labour – a job. After 30 years this was suddenly no more. The poor and the unemployed were to be used as the stabilisers of the economy.[7]

Just as New Zealand's once healthy economy provided a comprehensive cradle-to-grave welfare net for Kiwis, its ailing successor began to raise questions about issues like full employment and the limits of the welfare state. Increasingly, consensus became an elusive ideal although "Kiwi Keith" Holyoake tried hard, in public at least, to maintain his bluff, good-hearted composure.

Holyoake often sounded pompous, but he tried desperately to minimise conflict and foster consensus in an age in which everything was questioned. Historian Barry Gustafson described him as one of the ablest politicians in our history and one who was always conscious of the effects of government policies on people. When those policies forced thousands to emigrate in what became known as the "brain drain", Holyoake publicly dismissed any such thing, but privately agonised over it. At an open air meeting in the Wairarapa in 1968, when a reporter asked him about the "brain drain", Holyoake paused – then, like a showman, drew the crowd's attention. Laughing, he clapped the young man about the shoulders in front of the National supporters and bellowed: "Listen people. This young man says we have a brain drain – what do you think of *that*?" More hearty laughter, this time with the crowd joining in. At that moment, the "brain drain" was a good joke and a bad story. Embarrassed, the reporter retreated towards his car. Minutes later a very different PM tapped him on the shoulder. "Listen," he said earnestly and in private. "We have got a brain drain. I don't know what we can do about it. Do you?"[8]

Holyoake pursued consensus, but it was 23-year-old Robert Allen Zimmerman – better known as Bob Dylan – who caught the spirit of the age when he wrote and sang *The Times They Are A-Changing*. The Sixties were characterised by many things, but the most common was the zest for challenge and change.

The first hints of the protest era were already clear as early as 1960. Churches, trade unions and others had all combined to condemn the Rugby Union's decision to exclude Maoris from the All Black tour of South Africa. Aware of the potential for damage, neither political party wanted to intervene and in Government, Labour defended the Rugby Union's autonomy. Kiwi protesters took to the streets in their thousands with their slogan "No Maoris, No Tour", and delivered a 153,000 signature petition to Parliament.

Even visiting American satirist Tom Lehrer

Decimal Currency

Decimal currency finally arrived in 1967, in a move which helped symbolise our shift away from Britain.

No more would Pounds, Shillings and Pence characterise commerce. It was farewell to the colloquial quid (one Pound), the flash fiver (five Pounds), those cousins in coinage a bob and two bob (one and two Shillings), the weighty Half-crown (two Shillings and Sixpence), and that cent-sized silver coin – the Threepence which could buy children endless sugary pleasures at corner dairies.

In place of the old coins came the rather more prosaic language of decimalisation. If some Kiwis had had their own way, our new currency might have been called, among other things, the Zeal – but for a change, our politicians did not pass the buck, and the unremarkable dollar arrived to stay.

Sporting contacts with South Africa increasingly became more than just a game as the anti-Apartheid movement pricked the nation's conscience.

ATL C-29494-GT

CITIZENS ALL BLACK TOUR ASSOCIATION

PROTEST MEETING

WELLINGTON TOWN HALL — WEDNESDAY 12th AUG. at 8 p.m.

NO MAORIS - NO TOUR

To fight racial discrimination in the selection of the 1960 All Black team to tour South Africa. This is an issue vital to every New Zealander. Racial discrimination must be fought right here in New Zealand.

Don't miss this meeting. Those coming in support from Hawke's Bay and North Auckland include:
GEORGE NEPIA and LOUIE PAEWAI
of the famous 1924 "Invincibles"
and VINCE BEVAN and M. N. PAEWAI.

ROLLAND O'REGAN, Chairman, C.A.B.T.A.

Marti Friedlander

Maori children playing in inner-city Auckland. Throughout the decade Maori came to cities like Auckland in increasing numbers.

Pat Hanly

"Figures in Light 17" by Pat Hanly is one of a series of paintings and prints shown originally at Auckland's Ikon gallery as part of the 1964 Auckland Festival. It was bought by Colin McCahon and presented to the Auckland City Art Gallery where according to art critic Hamish Keith it "just about doubled the colour intensity of the City Gallery". The Hanly and a Don Binney work acquired at the same time were both "figurative and use hard edge imagery to comment on the peculiar intensity of New Zealand light."[*]

[*]Hamish Keith cited in Russell Haley, *Hanly: A New Zealand Artist*, Hodder and Stoughton, Auckland, 1989, p. 144.

Auckland City Art Gallery

had his say on the issue. Lehrer, a professorial figure – lecturing in mathematics at Harvard – was briefed about the controversy by the *Auckland Star* show business writer John Berry. At the Auckland Town Hall on the opening night of his tour, he spoofed America's passionate preoccupation with gridiron and added, to a roar of applause:

At this juncture of this evening's symposium, I wish to pay tribute to the New Zealand Rugby Football Union – for not allowing a little thing like human dignity to interfere with the great principles of the game.[9]

Some of the protests foreshadowed the passion sporting contacts with South Africa could arouse. Just before the All Blacks were scheduled to leave, 2,000 protesters marched up Auckland's Queen Street and, afterwards, some decided on a different protest. Veteran anti-Apartheid campaigner Tom Newnham, who later founded CARE (Citizens Association for Racial Equality), wrote that there was no real feeling of defeat among the protesters although it was certain the team would go:

… all the talk was to the effect that this would never happen again. At the close of the meeting a student called for others to meet him afterwards to discuss their plans for the morrow. We had no inkling then that they were going to race across the [Whenuapai] airport tarmac and throw themselves bodily on the ground in the path of the departing aircraft which was taking off with the All Blacks on board.[10]

The All Blacks had been given a state farewell and flew off to the Apartheid state, returning to an unforgiving core of protesters. Off the field, the battle for the conscience of the country over this issue had begun in earnest. Increasingly, New Zealanders were being forced to confront uglier racial realities in South Africa – and, more disturbingly, at home.

The focus of protest may have been South Africa's Apartheid and our apparent connivance at its evils, but inevitably the movement began to turn inwards to examine our own proud boasts about race relations. Maori, especially, found a growing disparity between what was preached about race relations, and what was practised.

Like the debates over abortion, and to a lesser extent the Vietnam War, the issue of sporting contacts with South Africa lingered, bitterly dividing New Zealanders. A planned All Black tour to South Africa in 1967 was cancelled by the New Zealand Rugby Football Union because of the South Africans' continued refusal to allow Maori players. By 1970 Maoris could go to South Africa in the All Blacks, as "honorary whites". But a decade on from the failed petitions and pleadings of 1960 the temperatures quite literally rose. In May 1970 the headquarters of the Auckland Rugby Union were set on fire – apparently by a Molotov cocktail, an action condemned by CARE. At Lancaster Park Oval in Christchurch, a goal post was sawn down and anti-tour slogans were sprayed on the buildings. In Auckland in April, protesters sprayed anti-tour slogans on the hallowed turf of Eden Park. In Wellington, protest took to the clear blue skies; on a fine June day, sky-writer Mike Brannigan, who had been commissioned by CARE, wrote STOP THE TOUR over the city for lunchtime crowds and, more pointedly, for politicians.

In the end, neither violence nor imaginative protest succeeded, and when the aircraft carrying the team prepared for take-off at Rongotai Airport in Wellington, history repeated itself. A young, woolly-haired protester, whose perpetual smile had suddenly slipped from his face, leapt over the barrier and raced for the plane. Tim Shadbolt outpaced police pursuers, but was finally tackled by a rugby supporter. In court, he refused to pay his fine and went to jail for a month.

Students played a key role in anti-tour protests, just as they did with another internationally divisive issue – the Vietnam War. The universities became seed-beds of radicalism and nurtured the growth of movements as diverse as Maori nationalism and opposition to the Vietnam War.

When it came to fighting in far-off wars, Kiwis and their Governments were traditionally never slow joining in. New Zealand soldiers had been sent into Korea and Malaya as long ago as 1950. For many Kiwis, Vietnam appeared to be another Asian killing field – a defence of democracy against the encroachment of Communism. But Vietnam was different. Where both the Government and the Labour Opposition could agree on sending troops to Korea, no such consensus existed for this military venture.

The Government's decision in May 1965 to send an artillery battery to South Vietnam at the request of that country's Prime Minister, Dr Quat, was opposed by Labour. And on the streets, a small but determined group of protesters began anti-war demonstrations.

Yet our involvement was minuscule – no more than 550 men at any one time and a maximum of 3,500 between 1965 and 1972.[11] In 1966, US President Lyndon Johnson visited New Zealand and urged the Government to increase its commitment. After winning the 1966 election, partly over the Vietnam issue, the Government obliged and from 1967 Royal New Zealand Infantry Regiment companies were deployed in Vietnam.

In 1968, a year in which radical protest shook western governments around the world, Special Air Services flew to join the combat. In New Zealand the mood was still temperate as teach-ins like the "Peace Power and Politics" conference were staged, but in 1969 all that changed as protest leader Tim Shadbolt noted in partisan style in his book *Bullshit and Jellybeans*:

Newsmedia, Auckland (Auckland Star Collection)

Anti-war protests grew from a core of student demonstrators to encompass wider sections of society as concern grew about our involvement in the war.

Jungle warfare in Vietnam, and its victims.

Kippenberger Military Archive & Research Library, Army Museum, Waiouru

1969 saw a new element of protest evolve. Bombing…
Within 12 months there were thirteen bombing attacks on military bases and conservative establishments throughout the country.[12]

Vietnam protests grew not only in number but in size. The ranks of the original protesters – who had been abused and occasionally spat upon by bystanders as they marched down Main Street – were increasingly swollen by the middle class, often pushing prams. For Vietnam was the world's first television war and some of its dark images disturbed the comfort of the living room. Although NZBC coverage was nowhere near as frank as that of overseas broadcasters, it still helped to radicalise this first generation of television viewers.

Vietnam pitted our ancient fears about the Yellow Peril and Communism against humanitarian instincts: might against right. The United States was at war with the North Vietnamese but domestically was fighting for its soul. In March 1968, distinguished journalist Alistair Cooke could ask in one of his famous BBC Letters from America:

> *Was Vietnam indeed a crusade or a vast miscalculation? Was it the wrong war in the wrong place, or the right war in the wrong place? What matters, or will come to matter to most people, I think, is not any new balance we can strike in the old argument; but the realisation that America, which has never lost a war, is not invincible; and the very late discovery that an elephant can trumpet and shake the earth but not the self-possession of the ants who hold it.[13]*

National began our withdrawal in 1970, and by 1971 all New Zealand combat troops were home. Only training groups numbering about 50 men remained in Vietnam until 1972. Our commitment, described by its advocates as a necessary insurance premium for future security, resulted in 35 men killed. This is how one Kiwi soldier witnessed the death of his mate:

> *I was about eight or ten paces behind X when he stepped on the mine. It fucks me up to talk about this and I have nightmares about it fairly frequently, yelling out a warning to him not to move but no sound comes out of my mouth – the dream always ends the same way with a brilliant explosion and me waking up screaming.*
>
> *The mine was an M26 "Jumping Jack" and when it went*

On patrol in Vietnam – a war with no frontlines.

Kippenberger Military Archive & Research Library, Army Museum, Waiouru

up, the warhead actually propelled itself out of the ground up to the height of his balls… the mine blew the lower half of his body to pieces. His legs were separated from the rest of him and his balls were blown up on to his webbing.

We were all terrified that we were in the middle of a minefield and were pretty shaken up.

… as I watched the colour in his face drained and he slowly slumped on his side…. He bled to death before we could reach him.[14]

Evening Post

One hundred and eighty-seven servicemen were wounded in the war and many more were injured in countless other ways. They came home to indifference or antipathy and both cut deep, as one family member of a soldier who had died recalled:

Oh God how it hurt – not many people talked about Vietnam, the controversial war. Whether it was right or wrong made no difference to the pain, the awful pain of losing our brother. Whether it was right or wrong, he believed he was fighting for New Zealand….

Fifty-one lives were lost when the Inter-Island Ferry "Wahine" sank in Wellington Harbour in April 1968 in one of New Zealand's worst maritime disasters. The ferry struck Barrett Reef during a tropical storm. It drifted up the harbour, rolled over and began sinking.

Slim Mikaere
Working the Wharves

Slim Mikaere was born at the end of the 1920s, left school when he was 14 or 15 and, as he says now, never had trouble finding a job. He worked first as a shepherd on a North Island hill country farm before joining the Ministry of Works in Tauranga in a work gang. He moved north to Auckland and worked in a flour mill for six years; headed south again and joined the Mangakino dams project. Then at the start of the 1960s, newly married, he moved back to Tauranga and got a job on the wharves where he stayed for the next 29 years.

April the 9th, 1961, I think it was, I started on the wharf in Tauranga. And it was just a bare wage, for about two or three years, until Japan wanted logs. Well, as soon as the logs were brought on to our contracts, then we started to get a decent wage.

It was fifty-fifty I suppose, Maori and Pakeha jokers; and there was a lot of teachers, butchers and mechanics also. Their jobs weren't paying as much as the wharf was, so they decided to give up their trades and work on the wharf.

There was a school we had in Auckland that taught us how to handle cranes and forklifts and so on. At times we had to drive cranes on the big ships.

I enjoyed being on the wharf because you're not working with the same jokers all the time. They changed the gangs around. There used to be six in a gang, plus the crane driver.

It was good, man, because we were knocking out the shipping and we were breaking records loading. Even some of the stevedores would say it's a good thing we were breaking the records. But I think it got on to the public's goat because half of us were in town all the time, you know, instead of working. But we just had it worked out properly.

You really worked for your money then. It was good. When you got back at night and had a shower and you felt good. You feel good the next day too. Of course it was hard work, good hard work. Now it's all push button jobs.

Source: Edited Ninox transcripts from *Our People, Our Century*, 1999.

Easiest cooking   Easiest cleaning

Fisher & Paykel

The ultimate in ovens and fashion in the kitchen, 1965. In this attire and with this oven, women need no longer worry about tray "juggling" and turning. But wait there's more – sponges, cakes, biscuits and scones all bake evenly.

To MRS HOUSEWIFE M.H.B.
(Manager of the Household Budget)

ATL C-22353-CT

WE'RE HANDING YOU 2! IN A SENSATIONAL Triple money-saver!

Half-way through the Swinging Sixties and the woman's place was still the home. In this advertisement though, she has been awarded domestic credentials (M.H.B. – manager of the household budget).

The ultimate in modern kitchens in a house at Titahi Bay.

ATL F-1045-1/2-DW (Duncan Winder Collection)

Thousands of others fought for New Zealand in Vietnam, but you would never know. When they came home, they came quietly home, and no one said: "Welcome home".[15]

A long way from jungle tragedies another drama was unfolding, this time in the shadow of ubiquitous eucalypts, in the country's new and rapidly expanding suburbs.

New Zealand's suburbia has always attracted the attention of observers. In the mid-1950s author Eric Linklater saw in our houses and gardens evidence of concentrated domesticity. He also warned of the spread of housing which would transform green pastures into "vast archipelagoes of bungalow roofs".

The growing towns of New Zealand are designed to avoid pressure, they are suburbs gathering about a non-existent urbs, and the urbs is non-existent – even where some of it has been materially built – because social legislation has decreed that social life must stop at 6 pm.[16]

By 1967, six o'clock closing – the "six o'clock swill" – was an anachronism. In a referendum that year, Kiwis voted decisively to change to ten o'clock closing. And all the while the suburbs spread, prompting Austin Mitchell, the witty academic broadcaster and now an English Labour MP, to write:

Auckland... is essentially a main street surrounded by thirty square miles of rectangular boxes, covering as great an area as London to far less purpose.[17]

The rush to subdivisions accelerated in the Sixties partly because of a 1959 Government move which allowed couples to capitalise their family benefit. Children were quite literally an investment in the future especially when they attracted loans at 3 per cent interest. Fertility peaked in 1961, with 65,000 births. In Auckland the new harbour bridge opened up the North Shore for housing development, and throughout the country group builders offered cheap housing on the new subdivisions. Once ensconced on the bare clay of their new homes – the developers usually removed the topsoil for sale – the race to keep up with the Joneses began in earnest. Kiwis continued the spending spree they had begun in the previous decade.

The 1961 Census showed that more than half the country's households had electric stoves and more than three-quarters had washing machines, many of them the new-fangled semi-automatic tumble washers. These were accompanied by an increasing array of new appliances like electric frypans, food mixers and waste disposal units. All this gadgetry was designed for women. In New Zealand, Austin Mitchell described the Kiwi female:

Most countries have oppressed minorities. New Zealand has an oppressed near majority, sometimes called the New Zealand Woman, sometimes known by her Christian name, Sheila.... She needs little attention or maintenance: mumble at her occasionally... and you can ignore her for hours... what is her role? America is female dominated; France is male dominated.

From Corner Grocer to Supermarket

The first supermarket was developed in New Zealand by Aucklander Tom Ah Chee. Working from his produce store a kilometre away from Auckland's Newmarket shopping centre, he realised that distance mattered less than easy carparking.

He chose Otahuhu, near the planned new housing area of Otara, as the site for his first venture into supermarketing. But he could not have anticipated the reaction of shoppers when he opened his first Foodtown in 1958. The crowds were so big that radio had to appeal to people to visit the next day.

He went on to open other supermarkets in Papakura and Kelston in the early Sixties, his ventures illustrating the growing dominance of the car, one-stop shopping and increased expectations of choice.

After supermarkets came the first major malls. New Lynn Mall in West Auckland opened in 1963, and was followed in 1965 by the Pakuranga shopping mall which provided over 1,000 car spaces. The car ruled, but travelled less and less to the central city.[i]

[i] Paul Smith, *Twist and Shout, New Zealand in the Sixties*, Random Century NZ Ltd, Auckland, 1991, p. 22.

Clarkson's supermarket in Christchurch in 1965 when supermarketing was relatively new.

Serenading the shoppers – a rock band playing at the opening of Clarkson's supermarket in Christchurch.

Telly Like It Was...

When Peter Snell triumphed at the 1960 Rome Olympics, a Waiheke radio ham broke the news to Snell's parents in Auckland. At the time radio news was a pallid creature and television did not exist, except in experimental form. But when the new medium finally did arrive, it quickly began its transformation of society. In 1960 Prime Minister Walter Nash announced that television would be introduced to the four main centres, starting with Auckland. The New Zealand Broadcasting Service would run the commercial TV system.

The state's first test signals had, in fact, been beamed out in February the previous year from 1YA's studios in Shortland Street, Auckland. The first "official transmission" one night in May 1959 included a film on hydatids, a Health Department instructional film on eating houses, a Transport Department Film on road accidents, and a court case.[i] 1YA broadcast the first non-experimental broadcasts on 1 June 1960, and programmes included a documentary called *Your Children's Eyes*, episodes of *Robin Hood*, and the Howard Morrison Quartet live.

By January 1961, 5,000 Aucklanders could watch television for two and a half hours each night, seven days a week, for a licence fee of six pounds ten shillings.[ii]

In April 1961 television became commercial, to the annoyance of some who complained that the new service had breached its prime time limit of seven minutes' commercial time per hour. The responsible Minister flew to Auckland to investigate the issue, showing a government attitude startlingly different from that of the present day.

TV began in Christchurch in June 1961 and in Wellington the following month. Dunedin had to wait for a year before it could see the magic box. As it was introduced in the cities it proved such an attraction that some TV retailers provided benches outside their shops for the curious. There they could rest and view the limited, but still wondrous fare of *Laramie*, *Lassie* and a local production, *Fergie Fang*.

Our tastes rapidly became more sophisticated and at the same time television bred its first real celebrities in the highly popular *Town and Around* series which began in 1965 and ran for five years. The series illustrated not only a strong sense of regionalism but our joy in seeing our own stories told in the Kiwi vernacular. As *Town and Around* continued its run, more serious news and current affairs programmes like *Gallery* began to challenge politicians and their actions more directly. By November 1969, in time for the elections, the NZBC linked the country in its *Network News*.

At the other end of the television production line, entertainment programmes like *C'mon* flourished, while drama had more modest beginnings. And knitting town and country together was one of the longest-running series in New Zealand television – *Country Calendar*. Whatever the genre, this pioneering era of television was marked by resourcefulness and, often, untutored enthusiasm.

Television in the early Sixties mirrored the early optimism of society. It gradually changed the way we looked at both ourselves and the world, as it drew viewers into the visual mainstream of the global village. As it did so, another long-established institution, cinema, suffered. There were 545 movie theatres in the country in 1960/61; ten years later, only 210 still survived.[iii]

The biggest... the only rock show... on the only channel – "C'mon" where go-go dancers did their thing and local bands mimicked overseas trends.

An innocent age – cartoonist Lonsdale's early depiction of a square-eyed viewer, at a time when television viewing was limited.

[i] Robert Boyd-Bell, *New Zealand Television, The First 25 Years*, Reed Methuen Publishers, Auckland, 1985, p. 71.
[ii] Ibid., p. 81.
[iii] Gerald T Bloomfield, *New Zealand: A Handbook of Historical Statistics*, G K Hall and Co, Boston Massachusetts, 1984, p. 125.

New Zealand you have to accept as a world divided into "his" and "hers". The "his" compartment includes all the positions of power and the interesting jobs, all the folk heroes and all the dominant myths: sport, war and virility. Woman's role is to run the home, raise the children and make scones.[18]

Marooned in the new suburbia, often without public transport, social networks and sometimes basic amenities like footpaths, many young, well-educated mothers struggled to match their expectations of new home ownership with depressing everyday reality. For many, this was a fresh start away from old housing in decaying inner-city suburbs; for others, it was a nest of thorns. Having the latest sheer lines of a Leonard refrigerator, or the "Amazing Hoovermatic Twin Tub" failed to make up for their sense of alienation.

The landmark 1963 book *The Feminine Mystique* by Betty Friedan grew out of that same sense of isolation and frustration. In 1959 Friedan had a conversation with a suburban mother who spoke with "quiet desperation" about the anger and despair that Friedan came to call "the problem with no name" and a doctor dubbed the "housewife's syndrome".[19] For some New Zealand women, the ideal of owning a new home also turned sour. Margaret Shields and her family moved to Newlands, a new suburb outside Wellington, in 1963:

We were all supposed to be living happily ever after in these suburbs, but in reality the suburban dream was ghastly. Everyone was living in their little boxes and no one was connecting. There were all these hopelessly incompetent, inexperienced, very young women trying to do one of the most difficult jobs on earth alone, and without any support. I can still remember one woman in the street who used to walk up and down the street with her baby three or four times a day... finally I realised that the grocer was the only person she knew to talk to.[20]

By the mid-1960s, almost four times as many women as men were being admitted to mental hospitals with depression and nervous breakdowns. Twice as many women as men had tried to commit suicide.[21] Locally the US "housewives' syndrome" had a name coined by Kingseat Hospital psychiatrist Dr Fraser McDonald: suburban neurosis. Symptoms included a sense of inadequacy and a mis-match between expectations of motherhood and married life with their reality.

During the decade, women entered the workforce in greater numbers though rarely on wage parity with men. Even so, by 1969 one English observer commented that the average New Zealand woman seemed reluctant to shed the "petty confinement" of her life:

Why? Possibly because she is in her own home very much the boss, the matriarch. And, knowing little of any other way of life, she settles for the power and title of Queen of No. 1 Average Avenue.[22]

But that was before the Women's Liberation movement which came only a few years later, when many women swapped – or at least adjusted – their crowns for new roles.

Barren new subdivisions, old cars and young mothers. The suburbs which grew rapidly in the Sixties offered the promise of a better life but for many women resulted in a new medical syndrome – suburban neurosis.

Inner-city living at least provided a sense of community of the kind which was missing from the new suburbs, where women struggled on their own.

A Proud Tradition in Opera Singers

Since the beginning of the 20th century New Zealand has been the source of a constant and rich stream of singers who have left this country to fulfil their talents in the great opera companies and houses of the world. It is a peculiar irony; in their home country opera has had 100 years of struggle just to stay alive. As soprano Malvina Major once remarked, "Good heavens, in Italy we'd all be heroes!"

New Zealand's first internationally acclaimed prima donna was Frances Alda, who made her debut at Covent Garden in 1906. She became the Met's leading prima donna and one of the earliest recording artists after cutting her first disc in 1909/10 with Caruso. In 1925 she was one of the first singers in the States to sign a radio contract. She always included two or three Maori songs in her recital programmes.

Soprano Rosina Buckman made her debut at the Royal Opera House in London's Covent Garden in 1914. Her greatest success was in the lead role of Cio-Cio-San in *Madama Butterfly* and in 1924 His Master's Voice asked her to sing the part in its first complete recording of *Madama Butterfly*. Sir Henry Wood also chose her to be the soloist the first time his famous London Promenade Concert (later known as The Proms) was broadcast on BBC radio. Oska

Kiri before international fame – at the Ngaruawahia Festival of the Arts in December 1963.

Natzka, the first of a number of New Zealand bass singers, was granted a three-year scholarship by the Trinity College of Music in London. He became the first student to go straight from college to sing lead roles at Covent Garden after an opera director walking past the college heard him singing. Natska died suddenly at 39, at the height of his career.

Another great bass, only three years Natska's junior, began his career singing with Princess Te Puea Herangi's concert party and the Waiata Maori Methodist Mission Choir. Inia Te Wiata won a government bursary for singing tuition in London and made his debut at Covent Garden at the beginning of 1951. His versatile talent took him from opera to musicals to straight acting roles in two films, *The Seekers* and Disney's *The Castaways*. His other great love was carving. His special project was a 16-metre-high pouihi, a fully carved wooden pole, for the main entrance of New Zealand House in London. He died of cancer in 1971 in the midst of a busy schedule and a year later the pouihi was officially unveiled.

Bass Noel Mangin and Donald McIntyre, bass-baritone, both sang first as boys in church choirs and later travelled to Europe to train before embarking on illustrious international singing careers. Malvina Major and mezzo-soprano Heather Begg are two of singing teacher Sister Mary Leo's more famous pupils. Malvina Major won the Mobil Song Quest and Melbourne Sun Aria contest before heading for London. She broke her early career to return home and work with her husband on their farm and raise a family, singing occasionally for local audiences. She returned successfully to the international stage in 1986.

But without a doubt Sister Mary Leo's most famous pupil is soprano Kiri Te Kanawa. She has been called "quite simply one of the great singers of our age". She first appeared on stage at London's Covent Garden in April 1971 and only eight months later starred in her first major role as the Countess in Mozart's *Le nozze di Figaro*. She was acclaimed by audiences and critics alike. Andrew Porter, the doyen of critics, wrote:

The new star is Kiri Te Kanawa. For years we have been praising this young New Zealand soprano... yet the promise of her performances had hardly prepared us for... such a Countess Almaviva as I have never heard before... at once young, full-throated, a singer of great accomplishment and a vivid character.... She commands the stage, wears costumes well. She was a young, beautiful, dignified, warm-hearted and affecting Countess.

Te Kanawa says herself that this role was a breakthrough for her as well because, although her sudden rise to fame had its own stresses, it confirmed her career for her. "I never believed I had the voice for opera until I had sung the Countess at Covent Garden; and I had doubts for two to three years after that."

Te Kanawa broke through the New Zealand public's usual reserve about opera as no one else has since Frances Alda and Rosina Buckman. She has inherited the title bestowed on Frances Alda in 1927 during her only tour of her home country – "New Zealand's most famous daughter".

Source: Adrienne Simpson and Peter Downes, *Southern Voices: International Opera Singers of New Zealand*, Reed Publishing NZ, Auckland, 1992.

As the cracks in the Kiwi consensus widened, popular culture provided a fresh new cultural dynamic. In the early Sixties, Elvis was in the army and Buddy Holly was dead. The vigour of the first rock revolution seemed to have weakened and given way to fad dance forms like the Twist. In fact, it had simply found a new base – in Liverpool. There, groups like Gerry and the Pacemakers, who had been influenced by the music of Chuck Berry and Elvis, and the Beatles began to re-invent rock for a new audience and era. The Mersey sound, complete with the nasality of the North and its own sense of gaiety, reinvigorated youth culture.

Back in the Fifties, New Zealand had no television, and communications satellites were still to link the world. Nearly ten years on, when the Beatles led the second wave of musical change, television ushered them on to a world stage as the group triggered worldwide "Beatlemania". In Britain, the Beatles were introduced to television viewers in October 1962. It was a modest start for the four musicians but they were brought back to the small screen 11 times between April and December 1963 as they released hit after hit. They also impressed the *London Times'* music critic William Mann, who noted "the chains of pandiatonic clusters" in their compositions. A year later they arrived in New Zealand to an ecstatic welcome by 7,000 screaming Wellington teenagers – the vanguard of their often hysterical welcome throughout the country:

The dynamic Dinah Lee, one of the best female pop stars of the decade.

As the decade progressed, men's hair grew longer until it resulted in a musical, and fashions increasingly borrowed from the East.

> I can remember pleading and wanting to go, and Greg – who was 14 – wouldn't take me, because I was his ten-year-old sister and he didn't want to be seen dead with me. So Mum said, "Well, I'll take you then." We were at the back of the Town Hall upstairs, and I can remember Greg was sitting about three or four rows in front of us, horribly embarrassed that we were so close. Everyone was screaming and I can still see my mum with horrible black glasses which pointed up at the sides and she had cotton wool in her ears. She was paranoid about the noise.[23]

The "English invasion" meant more than the dominance of the Mersey sound in pop music. It coincided with the growth of "Swinging London" as a sometimes controversial fashion centre. Mary Quant was credited with introducing the first mini skirt which rose daringly above the knee. With the development of pantyhose, the hem kept on rising. Entrepreneur Bill Hall of Society Fashions was credited with introducing the mini to Auckland in 1963. When he tried to interest older buyers from established department stores in the skirt, they were not interested:

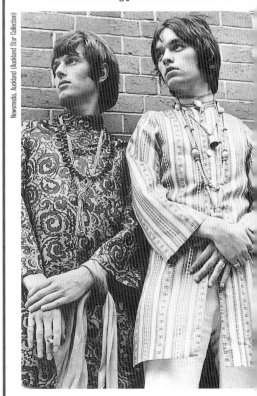

> They wouldn't buy it. They said it was indecent. We saw it and heard so much about it. We brought it out and we couldn't give it away. We were then doing a lot of business with a shop in Queen Street. He had a buyer who wouldn't take it. So we had a suit which was selling quite well and each time he ordered it, we shortened the skirt on it and they didn't realise it… in actual fact what we did eventually was to deliver him a mini. He said, "Christ this is selling fast."[24]

It was the beginning of a decade of self-indulgent decoration for both men and women. Although Chelsea and Carnaby Street first set fashion trends, they evolved in different ways to represent popular fashion:

Fashion became more daring in the Sixties. Skirts scampered further up thighs and see-through dresses like these laced and crotcheted examples were promoted.

One of our biggest and most durable international pop stars, John Rowles, featured in a welcome home concert at the Majestic Theatre, Wellington.

By the end of the decade the search for stimulation in style had seen the mini, the midi, toplessness, hairiness and hippiness. And that was just a sample. Fashion was so eclectic it rummaged successfully not just from the present but from the militaria of the Victorian past and from Asian continents thousands of miles away. If it felt good in the Sixties you did it. If it looked good, you wore it.[25]

Common to all of these trends were other signs of revolt – long hair, permissiveness and, increasingly, drugs. Youth mimicked the Beatles' mop hairstyle the way their predecessors had imitated Elvis, and the result at some schools was suspension. As late as 1969, a group of boys from Hamilton's Fraser Boys' High School were sent home to get their hair cut to a length conforming to the school's policy. Its standard was that boys' ears and collars had to be visible.[26]

Long hair and short skirts were symbols of defiance in a conformist society under rapid cultural change. During the Sixties, television, fresh freedoms in radio and increasing international air travel, brought new trends to the country without the time lag our past isolation had guaranteed. Traditional values were under siege, and if some schools imposed a hair code for boys, there was also a hem code for girls. At some schools, girls were asked to kneel – and passed the skirt test only if their hems touched the floor.

The oral contraceptive Pill and perceptions of openness in sexual relations earned the decade another label – the Permissive Society, although the reality for many was sometimes more mundane.

By the late Sixties, the optimism which had marked the early years of the decade had evaporated. President John Kennedy was assassinated in 1963; five years later, both his brother Bobby and Civil Rights leader Martin Luther King also fell to assassins' bullets. The Vietnam War divided opinion and created a counter culture; and spearheading some of the changes were the Beatles, who experimented with eastern music and meditation, to the dismay of many Indians:

The kings of Rock and Roll abdicated. To Ravi Shankar and the Maharishi.
As the sitar wiped out the split-reed sax, and mantras began fouling the crystal clarity of rock and roll lyrics, millions of wild-eyed Americans turned their backs on all that amazing equipment and pointed at us screaming, "You guys! You've got it!"
… Nobody wanted to shimmy. They all wanted to do the rope trick.[27]

As the most powerful nation in the world unsuccessfully unleashed its hi-tech assault on Vietnam, the anti-war movement grew all over the world. But if US actions in Vietnam often appalled other countries, its scientists – piqued that a Russian, Yuri Gagarin, was the first in space on 12 April 1961 – put the first men on the moon, in Apollo 11. In a "Moon Special" edition, on "Moonday", 21 July 1969, *The Auckland Star* recorded the event which was a television spectacular:

[Commander Neil] *Armstrong first appeared on the ladder outside the lunar module at 2.51pm – six hours and 33 minutes after it had landed on the moon. He asked Aldrin: "How am I doing?"*

Came the reply: "You're doing fine."

Minutes later Armstrong had climbed down the nine rungs and was standing on the porch outside the craft.

At 2.57pm, 17 minutes after he started opening the module hatch, Armstrong put his left foot on the moon… "One small step for a [sic] man; one giant leap for mankind".

In New Zealand, the decade ended with another election win for National although the party's support was declining. Garages in new suburban homes now often housed not one, but two cars. One-channel television linked us together as a mass, but our earlier consensus was disintegrating rapidly. It had been a great decade, but not in the sense *The New Zealand Herald* had intended in its first heady editorials. It had been tumultuous, exultant in its experimentation, and bloody.

It had seen a realignment of moral and political values and the beginning of the end of traditional ties with Britain. We had set a new course, buffeted by the turbulence of a range of movements including feminism and Maori nationalism. Increasingly, economic agendas began to dominate political debate – and led to the emergence of new market Messiahs.

Increased air travel both internally and internationally grew in the Sixties. In this ad, Mount Cook Airlines promotes its flights to the "scenic south" on its prop-jet 748.

When the Fab Four met the tangata whenua. The world's first super group arrived in Wellington in 1964 and were met by a Maori concert party which presented them with giant plastic tikis. When they played to a packed house at the Town Hall they were met by screaming fans and the hysteria which characterised their tours.

The Subritzky Family
Distant Cousins in Conflict

This is a tale of two Subritzkys: Michael, from a Kiwi family of nine children, was raised with the full knowledge of his Polish family background; Bill, a war child fathered by an American marine and deserted by his mother, knew nothing about his extended family in New Zealand, let alone his Polish whakapapa. Both served in the army without ever meeting each other. Bill saw action in Vietnam and Mike served in both the navy and the army, where he did 13 tours of duty, including a stint as a peacekeeper in Rhodesia.

What finally drew them together was not the cameraderie of the Armed Forces, but family. Mike had already absorbed his family's folklore and kept it alive by writing a book on the Subritzkys.

For his children's sake, Bill began looking into his family background when he was 50:

I never knew my mother... so I set about doing a little bit of research trying to track down my family and find out whether I had any brothers and sisters or whatever.

He had spent nine months finding his way through a cobwebbed parental past and it was not getting any easier. "It was brain-racking – sometimes I'd come up against a block wall and I just didn't know where to move."

He had, however, telephoned some Subritzkys and one suggested he should ring Joseph Subritzky:

So I managed to get him on the phone... and he says, "You're not the Bill Subritzky that was with 161 Battery?" I said, "Well, I'm one... there could have been some more." He says, "Oh no, there's only the one. You're William Dover Subritzky?" I said, "Yes." And he said, "We've been trying to track you down for a number of years now." And I says, "Well, that sounds all right but I really don't know you." And he said, "Well cuz, I am your cousin, you know?"

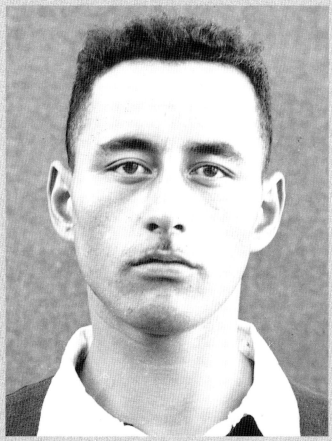

Vietnam veteran Bill Subritzky.

Bill accepted what he said but was still apprehensive because he wanted to find out whether he had any other living relatives, like sisters and brothers. Joseph told him:

"Give me five seconds." Then he had all the documentation right in front of him. "He says... you have a sister... two half-brothers." That was a shock for me, you know, because I had never ever met them. He was here the next day with all the documentation.

While Joseph was with Bill, Joseph's brother Michael called:

The only thing he could say on the phone was, "I've been trying to look for you all these bloody years, you bugger." He says, "I've got a present here for you." It was the Subritzky Legend book which I appreciated, you know? I feel very close to Joseph and Michael because of what they've done.

All Bill knew about his father was that he was a marine who died in the Second World War. His mother and her best friend worked at an ammunition magazine factory in Mount Eden in 1944:

When my mother went to work her friend would look after me. I don't think I was even 18 months old when my mother went to work and never came back again. So from that time on, this lady she left me with sort of took over the reins and brought me up... and did she ever remind me of that.

Jobs were easy to find in the Fifties and Sixties as a teenager, but Bill chose to join the army because of the security it offered. He became a gunner in 161 Battery which was sent to Vietnam.

Like other soldiers, he found the Vietnam heat unbearable and welcomed the relief of a cool spray drifting down from aircraft:

The minute we got out of the C130, it was like walking into a microwave – the heat coming off the tarmac and just coming into the back of that aeroplane was just unbelievable. I went over weighing twelve stone. Within two months I was down to nine. The sweat just poured off you continuously.

The clothes, your uniform just rotted off you. So when they talk about this Agent Orange spray that was coming over, we always looked forward to it because it was quite cool when they dropped it on you. It was like a shower. "Oh, here she comes, let's get ready boys" you know? And I thought nothing of it because there was no information on it at that time, you know, about this Agent Orange. But never mind, that's gone and past now.

Although Bill was a gunner, he once briefly swapped roles to become an infantryman and discovered the nightmares of a war without a frontline:

There was a time when we were stationed at Nui Dat... because the Australian infantrymen were lacking in jungle warfare. They approached a few of the Kiwis to see if we would do a one-for-one sort of a swap. Like we couldn't leave one man short on the guns so they were prepared to give one of the infantry men for one of us gunners. It wasn't an order given. It was more along the volunteer basis.

So me with five other stupid Maoris, we volunteered to go out and do just that... and this is when we actually got ambushed towards dusk. We had been following what we suspected were Charlies, Vietcong, for about three or four hours. Each time we got within range, they would disappear.

It was getting on to dusk and they just seemed to have vanished. Well, we decided that we'll rest up the night and head out again early in the morning, but just as dusk was coming down, we had incoming mortar fire. And it was at that time I just about became a contortionist and kissed my butt goodbye, because within about, oh, seven to ten minutes, there were about thirteen Australians splattered all around us. The mortars just took them out....

It's a terrible sound when you hear grown men yelling out for "Mummy!" you know? That's who they seem to want when they're... when they're going, is Mum.... Eventually whether we knocked the enemy out or not, I really couldn't tell you... it was really frantic at that time because we called in for helicopters to get the wounded out and everything like that.

There were other sights and smells he still finds hard to block out:

Like when you go through a village that the Americans had bombed a few hours before you arrived there, maybe an hour or so before. You'd see the planes coming in and dropping their napalm bombs and you have to go through the village and then you see the women, the children charred.

You can see that they'd been lying in the hammocks and it's just only the outer edge of the hammock and the bodies have fallen right through.

They're cooked and they're on the ground... and if they were left there for quite a while, you smell them before you see them because burning human flesh has a smell of its own.

When Bill returned home it wasn't to fanfare, but to a realisation that, in many eyes, Vietnam veterans were outcasts:

We heard about the Americans and all their public going on over there protesting against it, but we never got any feedback on what the public was doing back here. We thought they were right behind us in what we were doing.

It wasn't until I actually come back from my tour of duty that it hit home… it wasn't good to go out on the street in a uniform after we got back because we were called a lot of things, you know, like murderers. That's when reality hit us back here. I thought, "Why are we getting all this?"

Out of the security of the army and troubled by memories which often kept him awake, Bill drank more, found it hard to hold down a job and was often in trouble with the police. He became abusive physically and mentally towards his ex-wife, left the marriage partly for the sake of his children, and shifted to Australia where he lived for three and a half years before becoming sick. He returned to Auckland where doctors found he had tumours in his lower abdomen. He had tests and biopsies to confirm their suspicions about whether he had cancer or not:

I always got pains in my lower abdomen but after going through all the tests and everything in Middlemore five years ago, the doctor says, "Well, the tumours that were growing would have had to have been in there over twenty years ago." I just automatically said, "Would it be anything to do with Agent Orange – I was sprayed with the stuff." He'd never heard of it, and a lot of doctors today don't know what Agent Orange is. You know, you have to say, "Oh, it's a pesticide."

He and Michael had served in different parts of the world but both experienced the horrors of modern conflicts. As a peacekeeper in Rhodesia, Michael had to monitor the actions of the rival factions in the country. One day, while he was at a police fort, he had to fossick for ID through the blood-covered clothing on a man apparently killed in an ambush:

There was something telling me something was wrong here. So I looked at this guy. He'd been hit through the back and his entrails were hanging over his web belt and it sort of didn't look like enough to kill him. I sort of looked at his head and it seemed an odd shape. So I said, "Roll him over", and they said, "No, he's okay." I said, "Roll him over", so they did. And they had actually despatched him. They'd

Mike Subritzky on a peacekeeping tour (left). The face of war – despite the peacekeepers (top right). Mike Subritzky, standing centre, with others in the peacekeeping force in Rhodesia (bottom right).

put a pistol in his mouth and blown the back of his brains out... all his brains were in globules.

Mike knew this would have to be reported, but in the end after the commanding officer and the guerilla commander inspected the body nothing was said or done:

By that time he was covered with ants and bloody blowflies and eggs and shit... the smell was terrible so they just took one look at him and walked away. So I sort of had to live with that.

He cleaned up and later realised that it was lunch time and that he hadn't eaten all day:

I had this salad and got sliced meat and tomatoes and lettuce and all that and then at the very end, the cook, he flicked this bloody French dressing on to my food and it was exactly the same colour as his bloody brain globules, and I lost my lunch. From that time forth, I've never been able to eat mayonnaise or French dressing. In fact if my family have it, they put it out before I get to the dinner table and put it away....

The legacy of what remains with me from Rhodesia is I have nightmares at times. Sight and sound reactions, although that's diminishing. Another thing is that if I go to a restaurant or something like that, I'll always sit with my back to the wall.... I know it sounds stupid but I never sit over the wheels of a bus because those are the first ones to go up when a mine goes off....

The brutality of the things which both Bill and Michael witnessed changed them. They left as soldiers and came back if not as pacifists, then certainly as people with strong anti-war feelings. Bill says:

I wouldn't fight again if I had my time over. I probably would fight if I had to, but I would seriously look into it more deeply than what we did on this last one. But I'm sort of dead against war.... I think it's evil. I'm sure we can sit down at a table and compromise somewhere.

Michael found that the conflict changed old pastimes:

Danny Subritzky, left, with father Michael — maintaining a long military tradition.

One of the biggest changes when I came back from Rhodesia was that before I went I was an avid hunter – all my family were. But when you get out there in Indian country and the other guy is shooting bullets at you, you very rapidly lose all interest in shooting bullets at anything else.

Michael refused to sign the papers his son Danny brought him for recruitment to the army – so Danny took them to his mother, and subsequently served as a peacekeeper in Bosnia:

... as his father I'm very proud that he's over there. As his father I'm very concerned.... And I'm also very, very angry that he's over there, because I was in Rhodesia 20 years ago, and 20 years down the track the world hasn't changed and he's going to see exactly what I saw.... I'm very angry about that and there's no one to blame.

Sources: Edited Ninox transcipts from *Our People, Our Century*, 1999. All photographs from the Subritzky Family Collection.

1970

1980

Chapter 8

The Decade
of Protest

New Zealand in the 1970s was a nation fumbling for its future. The post-war generation grew up, and emerged out of the Sixties with a social conscience pricked by international and national affairs and fuelled by idealism. New Zealanders took to the streets in growing numbers in the Seventies. They marched in protest at wage and price levels and industrial conditions. They staged sit-ins to oppose the Vietnam War, nuclear testing and the bomb. They railed against apartheid in South Africa. They signed two of the biggest petitions ever received at Parliament, to save Lake Manapouri and repeal the Contraception, Sterilisation and Abortion Act.

In the 1970s, women demonstrated on their own behalf as well as for the wider community.

They wrote pamphlets and performed street theatre in support of women's rights. They occupied disputed land to uphold Maori rights. And they marched and called the new talkback radio and wrote letters to the Editor to protest against the protests.

Internationally, mayhem and protest grew on a murderous scale. Arab guerillas hijacked and blew up planes; Palestinian terrorists killed members of the Israeli team at the Munich Olympics; students "inspired" by Iran's new leader the Ayatollah Khomeini stormed the US embassy in Tehran and held 52 hostages for over a year; the Red Brigade killed former Italian Prime Minister Aldo Moro; and the IRA's fight for Northern Ireland closed the decade with the killing of Lord Mountbatten. Hundreds of thousands of people were killed in disasters, natural and otherwise – over 655,000 in a massive earthquake in China, and some 900 members of the People's Temple religious cult in a mass suicide in Guyana.[1] Across the world old leaders were deposed, often violently. In the United States, first the Vice-President, Spiro Agnew, and then the President, Richard Nixon, resigned in disgrace – the former after being convicted of tax evasion and Nixon for his role in the Watergate affair.

Newsmedia, Auckland (Auckland Star Collection)

The nuclear bomb became a local issue as French tests continued in the South Pacific.

A Soldier's Return from Vietnam

My family in New Zealand were eagerly anticipating my return home, and my mother sent me a letter tape with a recording of the song, "The Green, Green Grass of Home". This I would play over and over, increasing my own excitement all the more. I wondered if they would march us down Queen Street in Auckland when we got home. I could imagine the scene: the Vietnam heroes receiving a rapturous response, with bands playing, banners flying, marching girls.... I smiled at the thought, but felt that just to get home would be enough....

The aircraft touched down at Whenuapai airbase, just out of Auckland. We disembarked excitedly, then went through Customs and paraded. I could see my mother, my sister Adrienne and young brother Grant, standing and waving on the edge of the field.

An officer called us to attention, and gave us our final instructions. His words confused us.

"After you are dismissed, join your families and friends, and get out of your uniforms as quickly as possible. There's a strong anti-Vietnam feeling here in New Zealand. So don't be too vocal about where you have been, particularly when you're with certain groups. Stay out of trouble and report back for duty in four weeks as laid down in your documents. Attention. Dis—miss."

Colin Burgering, standing next to me, glanced in my direction. "What sort of a welcome home was that?"

"I don't know. Anyway, come and meet my Mum," I replied....

The next day was spent shopping and sightseeing in Auckland. While walking along the street, a car suddenly backfired; the next I knew I was looking out at Mum from underneath another vehicle that was parked. She was staring at me, with her head tilted to one side. "Are you alright son?"

I pulled myself from under the car, stood up and brushed the dust from my jacket. I smiled weakly at her and several curious passers-by. "Sure, just keeping my reactions in trim," was all I could think of.

Six months after leaving Vietnam, I was still having nightmares about the war, but by that time I was able to suppress any screams at the point when I woke up. This self-control saved me from having to make embarrassing explanations to my concerned family about the state of my mental health.[1]

[1] Colin P. Sisson, *Wounded Warriors: The True Story of a Soldier in the Vietnam War and of the Emotional Wounds Inflicted*, Total Press Ltd, Auckland, 1993, pp. 146-47, 149.

The Manapouri Debate

The nationwide fight to save Lake Manapouri in Southland marked the realisation by ordinary New Zealanders that the environment was their natural heritage. In 1960, the Government agreed to the raising of the levels of both Manapouri and Lake Te Anau to generate hydro-electricity for a proposed aluminium smelter. Manapouri, one of our deepest and most beautiful lakes, was to have its water levels raised by some 100 feet, linking it to Lake Te Anau which would rise about 25 feet. This greatly increased volume of water would pass through an underground power station into Doubtful Sound.

People were shocked that the lakes' position within Fiordland National Park did not protect them, and outraged by the proposed despoliation.

Conservationists warned that "the imminent destruction of the inlets, beaches, islands and forests of Manapouri and Te Anau... is not a transitory affair.... It is permanent".[1] By the late Sixties public opposition had reached an unprecedented scale. The Government agreed that the lake level should not be raised "in the meantime" but that did not allay public fears about future decisions. Their fears and the lakes' fate were resolved in the Seventies. In 1971 the Environment Council was established and in 1972 a new government portfolio for the Environment was created. The third Labour Government, which had campaigned before the 1972 election to maintain the lakes' levels within natural limits, set up the Commission for the Environment. The commission's role was to audit all projects involving environmental change and their impact on the environment.

[1] J. T. Salmon in Laurie Barber, *New Zealand: A Short History*, Century Hutchinson, Auckland, 1989, p. 179.

In New Zealand, three of the country's best-known leaders occupied the political centre stage in close succession. One of our longest-serving Prime Ministers, Sir Keith Holyoake, stepped down from office in 1972. That same year his successor, John Marshall, "Gentleman Jack", was defeated by Labour's Norman "Big Norm" Kirk. Labour's defeat in 1975, a little over a year after Kirk's sudden death, brought to power National and its new leader, Robert Muldoon. Just as Holyoake's "steady as she goes" approach had kept the country deceptively buoyant in increasingly stormy social and economic conditions, so too did Kirk's and Muldoon's strong personalities each mark the country and its increasingly turbulent politics and mood.

Historian Keith Sinclair was asked for his assessment of both men. He said of Kirk:

[H]e had a kind of natural dominance. When he walked into a room he immediately became its focal point... and I'm not just talking about size. There were some parallels with [Sir Walter] Nash. Both were intensely suspicious about those around them and didn't like delegating. Both, uncharacteristically for New Zealand prime ministers, were very concerned about foreign policy. In neither case did it turn out to be a very good idea in terms of electoral support at home.

He assessed Muldoon a year after he became Prime Minister:

He must be the most powerful political leader since Seddon. And there's one way in which he differs strikingly from former prime ministers. In this country the trend from the top is to try and dampen things down. Muldoon's tactic always seems to be to try to stir it up. I think he's an infuriating man. On the other hand, I'm sure he wants to be.[2]

The nation grew more and more urbanised – 75 per cent of Maori and Pakeha now lived in towns and cities, within a relentless suburban sprawl. The population continued to drift north. By the mid-Seventies, 73 per cent of New Zealanders lived in the North Island, a quarter in Auckland alone.[3] Four-lane motorways fed the growing number of cars in and out of metropolitan areas. Large parking buildings sprang up across towns and cities. We had one of the worst records for road fatalities and traffic accidents in the world; compulsory seatbelts in cars and crash helmets for motorbike riders made little impact on the road carnage.

Immigration from Britain and Europe fell sharply from the mid-Seventies. Instead, tens of thousands of men and women from Samoa, Tonga, the Cook Islands and Niue arrived to work. Auckland became the Pacific's largest Polynesian city with over 12 per cent of its population of Maori or Pacific Island extraction. The new immigrants came to fill a labour shortage in low-paid jobs, but their welcome was brief. In 1974, 2,000 Tongans were deported for overstaying their permits. From late 1976 the Government instigated dawn police raids on the homes of Pacific Island families, searching for overstayers. Maori were also arrested mistakenly, creating anger and bitterness.[4]

Education levels rose as more and more people stayed on to get secondary qualifications. The proportion of students going to university or polytechnic increased. At the same time, the population was aging. There was growing discontent with the health system, particularly hospital care and waiting times, despite vast increases in the health budget. By the mid-1970s, private insurance and medical care societies gave some 500,000 Kiwis quick access to private hospitals and partial reimbursement of their doctors' bills.

Six weeks before the 1972 elections the newly formed Values Party, the first New Zealand political party to make environmental issues its central concern, warned against materialism. The country was in the grip of a depression it said "not from lack of affluence but almost from too much of it. It is a depression in human values".[5] Inside the spreading suburbs was an emerging consumer society. "[C]lothing, hardware, electrical, and sporting goods stores, car sales and service firms grew in number and size."[6] Conspicuous consumption was measured by the affluence of households. In richer suburbs the trappings of wealth included two cars, a Hi Fi and the new colour TV (introduced in 1973), a dishwasher, swimming pool, skiing holidays and trips overseas, paintings and pottery by a growing number of local artists and crafts people, and "eating out".

But the suburbs also housed growing problems. As we strove for a "bourgeois equality"[7] and greater numbers moved into white-collar jobs, poverty was also increasing; by 1975 a government survey estimated that 18 per cent of the population (over 500,000 people) were living in poverty.[8] In the often arid and featureless new subdivisions, people talked about "the Otara syndrome" or "suburban neurosis". Youth culture explored different ways of living. Some left the city for ohus, to try living communally off the land. In Maori, "ohu" means either communal or group voluntary work. In the Seventies, the word became government policy as Labour sought to fill the spiritual aspirations of people pursuing an alternative style of life.

Marti Friedlander

Fletcher Challenge Archives (Arrowhead Collection)

In the mid-Seventies, the Fletcher Brownbuilt Pottery Award was established to encourage local potters "to expand their horizons". Winner in the second year of competition was Auckland potter Rick Rudd (above right) with the judge, Japanese potter Shigeo Shiga (centre) and Rudd's winning raku bottle.

A new generation went back to the land in search of a less materialistic and more communal way of life.

Seventies' fashion went to great (and
often unfortunate) lengths in its search
for something new.

Ohus were part of an official land settlement scheme which allowed alternative lifestylers a chance to lease crown land in rural areas. Prime Minister Norman Kirk hoped "kibbutz-type" communities would serve as an antidote to the materialism of society. His idea met with widespread interest and the Department of Lands and Survey began to look for suitable sites. In 1974, Minister of Lands Matiu Rata, explaining to an ohu working party why they were needed, foretold a monetarist future:

> The over-emphasis on the gross national product, perpetual greed, speculation, profiteering, unethical practices and the cult of individualism can only result in the further alienation of those who seek a return to community and group feelings. I share with government members the hope that ohu will, in some way, lead the way to a more concerned society and recapture anew the deep links of people and land.[9]

By the time ohu became part of government policy, many in the flourishing counter-culture of the late 1960s already had long experience of alternative living conditions which rejected society's materialism. They withdrew into a simpler existence, though by modern standards it was often a harsh return to the manual chores of another era:

> If the plumbing is unserviceable: avoid using it altogether. Washing up is more pleasant outside at a bench with a removable basin from which a thirsting summer garden can be dish-watered with the non-soapy water, for a vegetarian's dishes are few and ungreasy. From experience in the East we learned the benefits of shitting-in-squat, and composting excreta for at least six months with other vegetable and animal matter.... The Lady in the household has powerful conditioning to overcome. Because labour saving devices are labelled so by manufacturers, the absence of a device is not automatic drudgery. A furniture uncluttered house is easier to clean; with a well designed steam bench and/or copper and tub arrangement, washing clothing is a short daily chore; wood-fired cooking introduces a cherished skill to the kitchen and cooking realm....[10]

The youth of the Seventies continued to borrow the fashions, language and music of America and Britain. Experimentation with recreational drugs such as LSD and, more particularly, marijuana continued. Championing causes and stretching the generation gap even wider were all part of their experience. Maori and Pacific Island gang membership grew and so did crime, the two often interrelated.

Norman Kirk and Labour had swept to power in 1972 during a brief economic boom with a "programme for prosperity" and generous social reforms in keeping with the philosophies of earlier Labour Governments. But almost immediately pressures from outside began to have a negative impact. Britain had finally been accepted into the EEC and although New Zealand worked hard to maintain special access to our traditional markets for meat, butter and cheese, limits were being set. New markets developed slowly. New exports like kiwifruit, wine, berries, fish, timber, venison and deer velvet were not enough to replace what was being lost. Between 1973 and 1974 OPEC unexpectedly raised oil prices by 200 per cent and triggered a worldwide recession, and a new emphasis on energy issues. The search began off-shore for local sources of gas and oil.

Nevertheless, despite these economic pressures, Kirk believed it was possible to

base foreign policy on moral principle. He wanted a more independent position, less subservient than in the past to either Britain or the USA. Power bases and relationships among the major powers were shifting, the Cold War had been replaced by the ambiguities of détente, and "between the big fishes there was more room for small fishes to move".[11] Looking in new directions, he opened New Zealand embassies in Moscow, Vienna and Beijing. New Zealand also began to focus on its position and its relationships in the South Pacific.

In 1972, when Labour was still in Opposition, several private yachts had sailed in protest to the nuclear testing zone in French Polynesia. On board one of them was Labour MP Matiu Rata. Once in Government, opposition to nuclear testing became one of Labour's major planks in foreign policy. It was one of the defining issues of our emerging independence and Kirk was not afraid to stand against the opinion of much older diplomatic players, such as Britain and the United States. Together with Australia, New Zealand took a case against French testing in the Pacific to the International Court of Justice in The Hague. When the French signalled their intention to ignore the court's injunction against further tests, Kirk surprised the international community by sending the frigate *Otago* into the test area with Cabinet Minister Fraser Coleman on board:

In the early 1970s, leather and hair were big. Skirts were small.

> *We are a small nation but we will not abjectly surrender to injustice.... [The Otago is] a silent accusing witness with the power to bring alive the conscience of the world.*[12]

Partner not necessarily required at this dance competition — people danced together, in isolation.

For many Kiwis it was a moment of pride.

Later, as the French tests continued, Kirk was the prime mover behind a declaration condemning nuclear testing signed in Ottawa at the Commonwealth Heads of Government conference, much to Britain's displeasure. In June 1974, there was a small victory. France announced the end of atmospheric tests; they would continue underground. The following month the Minister of Justice and Attorney-General, Martyn Finlay QC, was again at The Hague, this time before the World Court to present New Zealand's case against nuclear testing. It was a stand that had significant support within the country and provided a foundation stone for the fourth Labour Government's anti-nuclear policies in the 1980s.

However, when the National Government took office late in 1975, such official protests ceased. Earlier, Jack Marshall had turned down Kirk's offer of a berth for an Opposition National MP on the *Otago*. Sending a frigate to the test area was, he said, "at best a futile and empty gesture". Plans for a nuclear-free zone were put aside. The new Prime Minister, Rob Muldoon, in seeking to strengthen New Zealand's relationship with America and our

An exhibition of French medieval art becomes political in light of France's continuing nuclear tests in the Pacific. Leading writers and artists protest outside the Auckland City Art Gallery, from left, Paul Haysom, Maurice Shadbolt, Michael Smither, Eric McCormick and Anthony Stones.

Norman Kirk sought to improve the existing order of society for the ordinary New Zealander.

place within ANZUS, welcomed the return of visits by US navy ships to our ports, despite their policy of neither confirming nor denying whether they carried nuclear warheads. As the Seventies progressed, anti-nuclear protests increased. A growing flotilla of craft greeted and attempted to impede the arrival of a succession of American warships in Auckland and Wellington harbours.

Norman Kirk's other significant stand was on South Africa. The 1970 tour by the All Blacks to South Africa had provoked widespread protests and was a harbinger of what would happen in the 1981 Springbok tour. Among the many troubled editorials that followed the team's departure, Alexander McLeod wrote in the *New Zealand Listener*:

There is plainly a gap between what we say in bodies like the United Nations and what we do within our deceptively secure frontiers. Many New Zealanders would like to take international opinion out of the argument and pretend that the tour can be justified on wholly domestic grounds. Even here there is naught for our comfort. We might, for example, wonder about a state of affairs in which Maori elders face the hostile condemnation of their brightest and best-educated children. We might steal a moment's reflection when it becomes necessary to mount heavy police

The 1974 Commonwealth Games

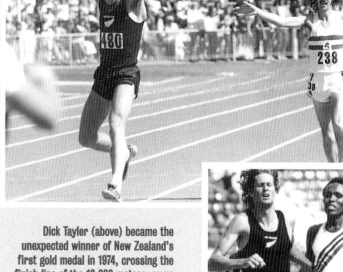

The Duke of Edinburgh opened the 10th Commonweath Games in Christchurch on 22 January 1974. A total of 1,276 athletes and 372 team officials from 38 countries and 40,000 Games tourists attended "The Friendly Games". These were the Games that made weightlifting a nightly television addiction. British competitor Precious McKenzie (below), the smallest lifter, found special favour with the sport's new Kiwi fans and settled here later.

Dick Tayler (above) became the unexpected winner of New Zealand's first gold medal in 1974, crossing the finish line of the 10,000 metres, arms raised in triumph. In 1989, Kiwis voted it the most memorable televised sporting moment in the country's history. On the final day of competition Filbert Bayi of Tanzania beat John Walker in one of the greatest 1,500 metre finals (right). Bayi (3:32.2) and Walker (3:32.5) both broke the old world record. Walker held world records for both the mile and 2,000 metres in the mid-1970s. New Zealand's final medal tally – fourth in the medal tables with 9 gold, 8 silver and 18 bronze.

Poets to the People

Gary McCormick Collection

guards at All Black trial matches. The controversy has divided religious groups, split families, provoked violence and inspired arson. The strains within New Zealand society either created or brought to the surface by the decision to tour South Africa are not of a kind that responsible, intelligent people would ignore, but the tour's promoters and supporters have ignored them without apparent qualms....

This controversy has demonstrated that New Zealanders are too keen on rugby for their own good. It has shown that we either cannot or will not face the unfortunate but inescapable fact that race is now a great issue affecting world politics. [13]

Kirk postponed the 1973 tour by the Springboks after advice from the police and military that even their combined forces might not be able to stop significant civil disorder and violence. As if to underline their point, the grandstand at the Papakura rugby grounds was burnt down. The world outside was taking a harder line on South Africa: the United Nations General Assembly had asked members to stop sporting contacts with the regime. New Zealand was due to host the 1974 Commonwealth Games in Christchurch and a number of African countries said that if the rugby tour went ahead they would boycott the Games. Kirk was not prepared to risk the Games either. The country was rewarded with what one British newspaper called "the happiest Games of all" while another said: "Christchurch has proved that it is still possible to promote a big, international, multi-racial Games."[14]

National was highly critical of Kirk's decision to stop the tour and when they won the Treasury benches they stood by their election promise to keep politics out of sport. An All Black tour of South Africa went ahead, despite large-scale opposition. Many other countries found this separation of sport and politics impossible. As a result of the All Black tour, black African nations boycotted the 1976 Montreal Olympics because New Zealand was participating. In 1977, the Commonwealth countries drew up and signed the Gleneagles agreement which opposed apartheid and supported sporting boycotts of South Africa. Each country was obliged to "discourage" contacts with South Africa. The agreement was expected to end sporting contacts until apartheid was dismantled. But in 1981 the rugby union and Government would have other ideas.

Industrial unrest was a problem neither Kirk nor Muldoon proved able to solve. In this, New Zealand was no different from many other western countries of the era. In 1973, there were nearly 400 strikes, more than twice as many as in 1969. Three years later in 1976 there were 487, four times as many stoppages as the annual average for the 1960s. By the end of the decade, strikes were an accepted part of industrial negotiation for workers in a broad range of occupations – airline crew, seamen, freezing workers, bank staff, shop assistants, timber mill workers, engineers, journalists, shearers, watersiders, boilermakers, and trades such as carpenters. The main causes were dismissals, work hours, work allocation, staffing levels, wage rates and breakdown in union-management negotiations.[15]

In 1973, Labour replaced the increasingly disregarded Arbitration Court with a new three-tier system of industrial relations. Four years later National reintroduced a single Arbitration Court. These rapid changes added to the already destabilised industrial

"Ladism" in verse – Sam Hunt (left) and Gary McCormick.

The country's most widely known poet died in 1972. James K. Baxter, son of writer and First World War conscientious objector Archibald Baxter, was much more than a literary figure. He believed that a poet should be "a cell of good living in a corrupt society, and... by writing and example attempt to change it".[i] His influence was perhaps greatest through his choice of lifestyle, withdrawing from city and consumer society to the small settlement of Jerusalem on the Whanganui River where he was visited by a constant stream of young writers and seekers of a more meaningful and spiritual life.

The mantle of poet as wandering minstrel, reading and reciting in schools, pubs, clubs and on street corners, fell to Sam Hunt and Gary McCormick who traveled the country, together and solo, with poems and themes recognised and understood by "every Kiwi".

[i] James K. Baxter cited in W. H. Oliver, *The Awakening Imagination 1940-1980*, in Rice (ed.), *The Oxford History of New Zealand*, p. 556.

The Murder Case that Lasted a Decade

... I did not help the police and local farmers with the search for Jeanette and Harvey Crewe but by the time I had finished my daily chores by 1 pm I thought it would be too late to go. I thought that unless you could get to the Crewe farm by 9 am you would not be able to assist. I was busy at that time of the year as my cows start calving on 10 June. I do not know how many cows I had in when the search started. I suppose I could of helped for a few hours but I was fairly busy.

I know I have been a suspect all along in this case. I supposed I did use [sic] to chase Jeanette along a bit and used to write to her.

I have read this through and it is true and correct. I have nothing to add.

A. A. Thomas[i]

Harvey and Jeanette Crewe – the file has not been completely closed.

These are the final paragraphs of Arthur Allan Thomas's statement to the police in October 1970. Four months earlier, on 22 June, an 18-month-old baby was found crying in her highchair, alone in a blood-splattered farmhouse in the small North Island settlement of Pukekawa. There was no trace of parents Jeanette and Harvey Crewe. After extensive searches of the vicinity by police and neighbours, the bodies were found in the Waikato River. So began the most celebrated murder inquiry in New Zealand.

Forensic tests on bullets taken from their heads and shotguns taken from farms in the area, wire wrapped round the bodies and an axle used as a weight, together with Thomas's statement to the police, were used by the prosecution to argue that Thomas had killed Jeanette and her husband out of jealousy. Thomas was found guilty of both murders in 1971; an appeal failed. He continued to protest his innocence. A fresh trial in 1973 also convicted him and a second appeal failed.

The court and juries may have been convinced by the prosecution's case but a number of others were not. A leading forensic scientist, Dr Jim Sprott, began his own investigations and suggested it was unlikely a cartridge case found in the garden outside the Crewe house was connected to the bullets in the bodies. A campaign by Sprott and journalist Pat Booth led to another appeal, but this too was unsuccessful.

The tide turned in Thomas's favour when British journalist David Yallop claimed there had been a serious miscarriage of justice and that police actions at the crime scene led to a wrongful conviction. Yallop alleged that the police had planted the cartridge case. A barrister, R. A. Adams-Smith, now carried out yet another investigation and as a result of his reports to Prime Minister Robert Muldoon, Arthur Allan Thomas was finally freed with a full pardon in 1979. He was later paid almost a million dollars' compensation for his wrongful conviction and imprisonment. No one else has been charged with the murders.

The police's credibility took a battering in the 1970s. For the first time the protest movements and use of drugs like marijuana and LSD brought the middle-classes into direct contact and conflict with the police. The further revelation that police were prepared to fake evidence to get a conviction broke a fundamental trust that had existed in the general community up until then. The decade so filled with idealistic passions also brought a loss of innocence.

---

[i] Arthur Allan Thomas, Statement to police, in Bob Brockie (ed.), *I was there! Dramatic First-hand Accounts from New Zealand History*, Penguin Books (NZ) Ltd, Auckland 1988, p. 222.

climate. In 1978 Southland farmers, infuriated by constant strikes at their local freezing works that were pushing up farm costs, staged a graphic and bloody protest. They drove 1,000 ewes into the centre of Invercargill and slaughtered them in the main street.

Personal attacks, bullying and an autocratic Government under Muldoon further curdled the industrial and political scene. Muldoon was a politician who seemed "to regard politics as a version of 'Gunfight at the O.K. Corral'."[16] Political columnist Tom Scott, banned by Muldoon from his press conferences because the Prime Minister disliked his satirical coverage of politics, considered the effects:

> [H]e has made intolerance and prejudice, if not fashionable, then at least permissible. He hasn't changed the New Zealand psyche so much as unleashed a genie that was always present.
>
> Other politicians have got into the act as well. Frank Gill allows his Immigration Department to separate Pacific Island children from their families. If women on the DPB must have sex (and Bert Walker can't see why they should) then Walker's wife retention scheme encourages them to have it with a number of men if they want to retain the benefit. Alan McCready repeatedly makes snide jibes in the House about Mat Rata having to read comics. Warren Cooper from Central Otago would like to see some liberals on a hijacked plane with guns up their backsides to teach them what civil liberties are really about. Bell, the MP for Gisborne, advocates injecting drug pushers with their own products to make them addicts and show them what it is like....[17]

The Seventies also marked the arrival of inflation as a problem that even wage and price freezes could not halt completely. From 1975, inflation was never less than 10 per cent. The sudden economic slump that followed the dramatic rise in oil prices brought the worst drop in our terms of trade – 46 per cent – since the Great Depression. The large surplus in the 1973 balance of payments had become a deficit of $1.3 million by 1975. Bill Rowling as Kirk's Minister of Finance and then his successor as Prime Minister borrowed more heavily overseas than ever before, convinced this recession was a short one that could be ridden out. The alternative was a large increase in unemployment and a Labour Government would not countenance that, as Rowling explained:

> Our borrowing will have a cost. But it is the Government's decision that this will be in the form of serving overseas debt rather than in the form of 50,000 or 100,000 unemployed. It is as simple as that.[18]

The recession did not end; and neither did the borrowing when National swept Labour from Government. Despite this, the numbers of unemployed climbed steadily. By 1979, 25,000 were on the dole and another 31,000 working on job creation schemes. The schemes were a disturbing reminder of the 1930s Depression for all those who had lived through it.

"Sleeping Dogs" was one of two locally made films released in 1977. Based on C. K. Stead's novel "Smith's Dream", the film was very much in keeping with the mood of the time – a violent tale of "Big Brother" government, paranoia and rebellion. Director Roger Donaldson and actor Sam Neill (below) moved on to international movies.

Marti Friedlander

The 1979 United Women's Convention in Hamilton was the fourth and last of the biennial conventions. They were aimed at a wide constituency which by the 1980s was fragmenting into groups of special interest.

Amid all the turmoil of the decade, two political movements rose high above the others – women's liberation and Maori land rights and sovereignty. Both had a major impact on society. Both created splits within their own communities of interest and within the general society. Both began an on-going process of debate and change.

In late 1968, in the first issue of *Thursday*, a new magazine for women, editor Marcia Russell had written:

> *... we can't think of anything less likely to succeed than a magazine that lumps women into one basket and gives it a label. Quite frankly, we wouldn't dare. The sheer impossibility of defining women and womanhood within a few simple and well chosen words....*[19]

This statement became more and more true as the women's liberation movement developed with the Seventies. The contradictions, contrasts and conflict were all there. Those who felt them strongest were working mothers:

> *If ever there was a conversation about someone working or using a nanny, the word "selfish" would be used, and someone would invariably talk about how the child would suffer.... There was terrible conflict. On the one hand you were part of a new generation that was trying to do something new, but at the same time you'd been brought up with this idea that a woman's place was in the home. Then you had all the messages from experts about how children would be damaged if they were put into a childcare centre. Your parents and in-laws,*

September 1st, 1974

Maurice, I dreamed of you last night. You wore
A black track suit, red striped. Saying goodbye

We fought back tears. I woke thinking you dead.
Here in the North manuka is flecked with flowers,

Willows bent in stream-beds are edged with green,
But the tall-striding poplars seem no more

Than ghostly sketches of their summer glory.
Beyond the dunes blue of the sky out-reaches

The blue of ocean where the spirits of our dead
Stream northward to their home. Under flame trees

By Ahipara golf course someone's transistor tells me
The news again, and down on the hard sand

In letters large enough to match the man
The children have scrawled it: BIG NORM IS DEAD.[i]

C. K. Stead

ATL F-217831/4 (Evening Post Collection)

The queue stretches down Parliament Building's front steps and across Parliament grounds as people wait to pay respects while Norman Kirk's body lies in state.

[i] C. K. Stead, "September 1st, 1974", *Quesada*, The Shed, Auckland, 1975, p. 26.

as well as the people around you, thought leaving your child to go to work, or putting it in a childcare centre, was a terrible thing to do too, so there were pressures on all sides. We were in the crossfire, really, trying to cope with all these conflicting ideas.[20]

Groups such as Save Our Homes and Feminists for Life protested that the women's movement was denigrating motherhood and making women feel they had to reject the role of full-time mother. In 1972, the Australian feminist and author Dr Germaine Greer arrived here to promote her book *The Female Eunuch*, and thrust the women's movement onto the front pages. In the same year that an Auckland jury decided the hit rock musical *Hair* was not indecent, Greer was arrested and fined $40 for saying "bullshit" in public. (Round the corner in Auckland's Queen Street, Tim Shadbolt's small alternative publication, *Bullshit and Jellybeans*, had a full window display... with the offending word blacked out on every book cover.) Greer was more gentle about those women who felt threatened by the movement when she spoke to NZ *Woman's Weekly* columnist Cherry Raymond:

I wouldn't dream of trying to tell women what they should do or think. My book really only supports and reinforces women who are already moving towards liberation. So if a woman doesn't want to join the movement, that's her decision. But when she finds she doesn't like things the way they are, when she's taking drugs to make her sleep, drugs to wake her up or sinking a bottle of sherry a day and wondering what she's living for, then I hope she'll turn to us, to the movement, for help. Because we'll be there.[21]

"Mother's little helpers" – father's helper was more likely to be a large daily intake of alcohol – were being dispensed in escalating amounts. The National Society on Alcohol and Drug Dependence recorded in 1972 that 106 million doses of tranquillisers and 52 million anti-depressants were consumed that year.[22]

Throughout the country newly formed women's lib groups were issuing their manifestos. In Wellington, the city's group laid out their philosophy and aims:

WE BELIEVE
– that women are discriminated against and treated as second-class citizens – less than human beings.
– that women must be guaranteed the right and the ability to make real choices about their lives and not be streamed into narrow, subordinate roles which limit their potential.
Therefore WE DEMAND
– the repeal of abortion laws... freely available contraception... free, 24-hour community-controlled childcare centres... equal pay and opportunity NOW....
We also want:
– An end to beauty contests and advertising which exploits women.
– An end to the oppression of lesbian women who are ridiculed for their rejection of the traditional sexual role.
Our goal is the total liberation of womankind, so that we can be free to determine our own futures, and realise our potential.[23]

Student and demonstrator Tim Shadbolt represented those who made protest a way of life, and in the process became one of the country's best-known names and faces.

Art school pop – early Split Enz were part of a new local music scene that abandoned cover versions to write and perform their own songs.

Women march through Wellington in support of abortion. The following year the country's first abortion clinic opened in Auckland.

Fred Dagg, aka John Clark, was New Zealand's first and most successful satirist. Clark's comedy identified local character and humour — laconic, unimpressed by authority, suspicious of "the arts" and gently anarchic.

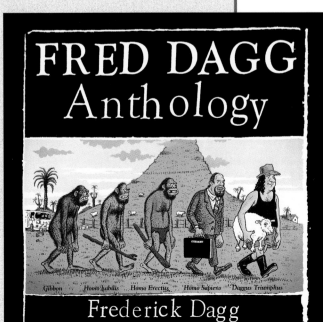

These demands were dismissed by the public and media as ridiculous and extreme. It took a level of courage and commitment to wear the movement's badge of the clenched fist inside the symbol for the female sex, and to admit openly to being a feminist. At Victoria University a group of drunken male students "pulled my hair, kicked my shins and poured beer over me" a woman wrote in the local feminist magazine *Broadsheet*.[24] Ultimately, the three most contentious issues of the women's movement were equal pay, the crackdown on domestic purposes beneficiaries, and abortion.

In 1966, the median income for women was 51 per cent that of men and while 20.9 per cent of men earned more the $3,000 a year, only 1.9 per cent of women did.[25] Giving women pay equal to men would ruin the country, Government and business warned. It was estimated it would cost a "crippling" $85 million.[26] Nevertheless the Equal Pay Act, passed in 1972, came fully into force five years later at the same time the Human Rights Commission Act made it illegal to discriminate in employment on the grounds of sex, religion, marital status or beliefs. In the following decade, the debate entered its second stage — equal pay for work of similar status.

The Domestic Purposes Benefit — 50 per cent of the average wage for men — was introduced in 1973, mainly for solo parents over the age of 16. By 1970 one out of eight babies was born out of wedlock.[27] There was still pressure to give up the children for adoption but attitudes to single mothers were changing, albeit very slowly. A 1971 report on unmarried mothers argued:

Society should put the best face it could on the situation by attempting to ensure that unmarried mothers were given as much help as possible in deciding whether or not to keep their baby.[28]

Nothing breeds success like Hunter

The new Hunter

See it at your Todd dealer today.

Buy one or win one, Kiwis' passion for the car continued. Hunger for motorways was insatiable.

Matron Thelma Smith of the Salvation Army's Bethany Hospital in Auckland agreed: "We have to think about the children and not stand off and morally judge the girl."[29] To receive the benefit, women had to prove the identity of the father in court and get maintenance from him, which was paid to the Department of Social Welfare. The process was adversarial and humiliating. Despite these hurdles, the numbers receiving the DPB increased by 11,000 between 1974 and 1977.[30]

The very existence of the DPB and rising numbers of solo mothers provoked a huge public backlash. The National Government set up a review saying the benefit was putting the family unit at risk, encouraging married women to leave their husbands and single mothers to keep their babies. There was a campaign to stop "benefit abuse". Any relationship with a man could cost the woman her benefit. Social Welfare officers searched houses looking for evidence of male presence; neighbours were encouraged to let the department know of male visitors. In one case, the department tried to get a Hamilton solo mother to sign a declaration that "she would not sleep with her boyfriend more than once a fortnight or have a meal with him more than three times a week".[31] When she refused, they cut off her benefit. It took a 19-month battle and a Supreme Court ruling that her benefit had been wrongly cancelled before it was reinstated. The Government's response to the court's decision was to make legislative changes which meant that solo mothers risked losing their benefit if they had virtually any kind of relationship or affair with a man.

Throughout this period there were constant protests at the

1972 Mini for Mum COMPETITION WINNER... MRS M. ORR

Breaking Down the Barriers

Wednesday, 13 September [1972]. *I'm noticing gradual changes in Parliament's attitude to women. The Speaker has decreed that women may now use the public seating on the floor of the House, and the House Committee has agreed – reluctantly, Warren Freer told me – that women private secretaries may have the use of Bellamy's bars.... Warren had urged that we be given bar privileges in case we had to take official visitors for a drink.*

Rex Willing suggested I accompany him to Bellamy's "to show the flag". Many men wouldn't have accepted me as readily as Rex has done. The general attitude to women private secretaries was once summed up for me by the then Clerk of the House, Mr H. N. Dollimore, who said, "Of course you know we don't like skirts around here." And I am well aware that Rex has an unfair burden in having to do most of the travelling with Mr K, because I usually go only on day trips – it is politically unwise for a woman to travel overnight with her boss. Rex cheerfully bought me a drink in what turned out to be a small, shabby room labelled "Secretaries". It had two chairs, a tin trough for cigarette butts, and a small table set with inch-squares of cheese, and water biscuits.

One result of Mr K's having a woman private secretary is that he is seeing for himself that there definitely is discrimination against women; but the barriers are going down one by one.[i]

Margaret Hayward was Norman Kirk's private secretary from 1971 until his death on 31 August 1974. She was one of only three women private secretaries at that time. Ishbel McTavish was private secretary to Peter Gordon, Minister of Transport, and Jan Burns had recently been appointed private secretary to Doug Carter, Minister of Agriculture.

---

[i] Margaret Hayward, *Diary of the Kirk Years*, Cape Catley Ltd, Queen Charlotte Sound, and A. H. & A. W. Reed, Wellington, 1981, p. 61.

Even before the 1975 general election Rob Muldoon was the target of heated demonstrations. He was reported to have told one of the protesters on this occasion, "Don't be a naughty little girl." Not a comment chosen to cool tempers.

Prime Minister Robert Muldoon poses with Miss New Zealand contestants. The women's movement was much less enthusiastic about beauty contests and made regular attempts to sabotage and disrupt them.

harassment of solo mothers. In the early 1980s a liable parent contribution scheme was introduced to try and get back some of the rapidly growing expenditure on the DPB, but it was easily and overwhelmingly evaded.

In 1985 after a seven-year campaign, the passing of the Adult Adoption Information Act allowed adopted people over 20 and birth mothers to find and contact each other if they wished.

Freely available contraception and contraceptive advice and, more particularly, abortion split the women's movement and popular opinion. Abortion ultimately became *the* issue of the women's movement in the Seventies. At the time, abortion was allowed on "psychiatric grounds" but each hospital interpreted the law differently. On one side of the debate was the Society for the Protection of the Unborn Child and Feminists for Life. On the other, the Women's National Abortion Action Campaign which wanted all abortion laws repealed; and the less radical Abortion Law Reform Association of New Zealand. In 1974, the country's first dedicated abortion clinic opened in Auckland operating under the current law. A bill restricting abortions to hospitals was passed the following year. Staff and women attending the clinics faced constant protests and vigils by anti-abortionists. There were a number of arson attacks against abortion clinics. Further amendments turned the legislation into some of the most restrictive in the world, despite one of the largest parliamentary petitions calling for the repeal of the act. Hundreds of women began flying to Australia to get abortions. At the end of the decade further changes to the law and its interpretation made abortion more accessible to women, although services remained unevenly available.

The large all-inclusive women's organisations had broken up by 1980. They were superseded by single issue groups – access to midwives and home births, equal rights for women in marriage breakdown, gay rights, changes in the treatment of rape victims during trial, rape crisis centres, refuges for battered women and children, self-defence courses, picketing of the annual Miss New Zealand Show, and marches to "reclaim the night". Maori and Pacific Island women had also separated from the main movement, finding tensions of their own in cultural traditions and the growing revival of Maoritanga:

The true revolution for me lies in the harnessing and manifestation of woman power, women being, women spirituality. But in the Maori world the most urgent and desperate sense of political commitment is based on a woman's ethnicity, our Maoriness – which distinguishes and isolates us from the white majority – makes us different, even makes us better.

However, within the racially exclusive confines of the marae, we are seen as WOMEN. We see each other as women – and the men see us as NOA.

Unclean. Profane. Feared. But always secondary.[32]

The American novelist William Faulkner wrote: "The past is never dead. It's not even past." Maori have always known this; in the 1970s Pakeha New Zealanders began to learn its truths:

This stubborn beach, whereon are tossed
white roses from the sea's green bough,
has never sheathed a Norman prow
nor flinched beneath a Roman host;

yet in my bones I feel the stir
of ancient wrongs and vanished woes,
and through my troubled spirit goes
the shadow of an old despair.[33]

TVNZ Publicity

Telethon madness — imported celebrity Lauren Bacall celebrates another dollar milestone reached. New Zealand's first telethon in 1975 to launch TV2 raised about $600,000 for the St John Ambulance. The fundraising totals rose steeply in succeeding 24-hour telethons.

Tim Roberts —
The Rise and Fall of the Manual Worker

Tim Roberts' career parallels the spiralling fortunes of manual labour in the 20th century.

He went to school at Onslow College in Wellington in the 1970s. He wagged a lot, drank at the local pub, and relished basketball, captaining the team. His father was Professor John Roberts of Victoria University, a respected political commentator, but Tim was more interested in motorbikes than books and left school at 14.

Most of my mates did School Cert. But I'd had enough. I wanted a motorbike. I wanted to go to work. Even then people were saying things were getting pretty tough. The Oil Crisis was doing bad things to the economy and jobs were harder to get. But I just thought I should get a labouring job. I was a big strong boy.... I went off looking for construction site jobs and got one.

I was under pressure to continue my education.... Dad valued education really highly and fought like hell to stop me leaving school. I was bone-headed and determined to do it. I didn't see any value in university education at the time. I was much more interested in the working man's romanticism of manual work and hard labour and all of that. I saw uni as... actually it was a strange world to me. It was sort of shut off... an alien place. I never valued institutional learning at that time. And that was part of the reason why I wouldn't listen to them and left.

He laboured here and in Australia working on construction sites and with shearing gangs, among other jobs.

I never looked at going back to school until I was in my thirties and I was in Australia... my body had packed in from all the manual hero labour. That was one reason. And the world had changed. One thing that's changed is the level of respect that a manual labourer gets in society nowadays.... You're essentially seen as a resource that they can drop and pick up at their will.... I started to read the writing on the wall that going into my forties as a manual labourer was not a very nice game to be still doing. So education was partly about getting out of that hole.

He laments the loss of the worker ethic personified in a rural setting by bushman-writer Barry Crump.

There was quite a bit of respect paid to people like that which perhaps still exists in ads for Toyota utes nowadays, but really you're a mug if you're a labourer. That's the way I see society looks at it.... There's so much unemployment there's a surplus of those kinds of workers.... You're not very highly valued.

Source: Edited Ninox transcripts from *Our People, Our Century*, 1999.

The Maori Land March

The march by Maori from Northland to Wellington, to protest not just the failure to return confiscated land but its continued confiscation, signalled a change in Maori relations with the State and the Pakeha majority. For Maori, the 1970s ushered in a "Maori Renaissance" which grew in strength. Donna Awatere was one of its leaders:

> John Rangihau proposed a land march from the northernmost point of the country to Wellington.
>
> When it eventually happened it began as a very lonely affair. No Maori wanted to host us or join us. We had no encouragement. Far from it – we had been warned against provoking a Pakeha backlash, that we would wake the sleeping giant of the state. But a handful of us started out nonetheless with Whina Cooper at the head.
>
> By the time we got to Warkworth the mood was changing; marae started to receive us and support us. And then suddenly they came in their thousands and then their tens of thousands. When we got to the Auckland Harbour Bridge there were so many of us, walking in time, that the bridge began to sway, and I was scared we would bring the whole thing down. As we marched to Wellington no marae was big enough to hold us. We walked for weeks, and the day we walked into Wellington we had a larger crowd than I had ever seen. The country was behind us.[1]

[1] Donna Awatere Huata cited in Bob Brockie (ed.), *I was There! Dramatic First-hand Accounts from New Zealand's History*, Penguin Books (NZ) Ltd, Auckland, 1998, p. 235.

Although three-quarters of the Maori population had joined Pakeha and Pacific Islanders in urban life, and more were attending preschool, completing secondary school and going on to tertiary institutions, a significant gap still remained – in 1966, 70 per cent of Maori men were blue-collar workers. In Auckland and Wellington, together with immigrants from the Islands, they made up a new "under-class".[34] The Government saw in Maori urban migration a renewed chance for integration. Maori saw integration as their old enemy "assimilation" in another guise. Legislative changes to speed government purchase of "uneconomic" Maori land re-awakened fears of its rapid loss. Ancestral land was even more important as a source of identity for those on the new urban marae. Retaining the land became the central issue of the Maori renaissance:

> I never dreamed I would ever march for the land, but we did, of course, in 1975, when we came down all the way from Te Hapua to Wellington. At that time, you know, I had been thinking for a long time, What has happened to the leaders? Our great men are all gone. Apirana is gone; Maui Pomare is gone; Dr Buck is gone; Sir James Carroll is gone... every leader of ours in the Maoritanga is gone. And who is the one to lead? Land is going, land is going. Out of 66 million acres we have less than 2 million acres left.[35]

The speaker, Dame Whina Cooper of Te Roopu o te Matakite, led the Land March from the Far North to Wellington. From small beginnings, it came to number some 50,000 people. In Wellington they handed the Government a Memorial of Rights with 60,000 signatures and requested a guarantee that "not one more acre" of Maori land would be lost. The Government made no firm commitments.

This revival in Maori protest first emerged in 1970 with the Auckland group Nga Tamatoa. The founding members were university and teachers' college students and young urban Maori. They turned old institutional thinking on its head: "There is no Maori problem, what we have is a problem with Pakehas." Nga Tamatoa became the face of protest for Maori grievance using the same tactics as other protesters of the decade and the American civil rights movement – marches, sit-ins, pamphlets, delegations to Parliament, disruption of public meetings. In 1979, engineering students at Auckland University preparing to perform their traditional mock haka became involved in a violent struggle with He Taua, another group of Maori activists, when they tried to stop the students' party and remove their fake Maori clothing. Some older Maori organisations were critical of these tactics, calling them un-Maori.

Nga Tamatoa wanted "ratification of the Treaty of Waitangi, equal Maori representation in Parliament, inclusion of Maori language in schools, return of confiscated Maori land (or compensation for it), correction of the Pakeha bias in history books, and Pakeha respect for Maori culture".[36] In 1971 they demonstrated at the Waitangi Day celebrations and declared a day of mourning for the loss of Maori land. In later years, Waitangi Day increasingly became a focus for protests by the Waitangi Action Committee.

The growing agitation had some effect. By 1976 there were 123 secondary schools teaching Maori to 11,000 students and 100 primary schools had Maori studies programmes.[37] All teachers' colleges had Maori studies on their curricula. In 1975 the Waitangi Tribunal was established. Initially it was only to consider grievances from that date on, but in 1985 the act was made retrospective to 1840.

Within a short time there were 150 claims registered with the tribunal.

There were two significant land protests. The first was a claim by the Tainui Awhiro people, led by Eva Rickard, for the return of the Te Kopua block. The land had been compulsorily taken during the Second World War for an aerodrome and never returned. Instead, it was given to the Raglan County Council which turned it into a golf course with a bunker over a sacred burial site. In 1979, the Government agreed to the return of the land and the golf club had to pay compensation and a "fair rent". The second protest was "one of the most dramatic actions of the radical politics of the Maori land rights movement of the 1970s".[38] For 506 days from the beginning of 1977 the Orakei Maori Action Committee led by Joe Hawke occupied Bastion Point.

The Ngati Whatua of Orakei had been in debate with the Crown since the end of the nineteenth century. After making available thousands of acres on which to establish Auckland, they kept 700 acres at Orakei for their main tribal base. It was not for sale under any circumstances. But as time passed, land was lost. In some instances land given to the Church or Government for special purposes was on sold. Compulsory acquisitions by the Crown took more. In 1952, families still living on the headland were evicted and put in State houses down the hill. For those who had fought to keep the land, the eviction was traumatic. Within a year many of the elders involved were dead.[39] The land was designated for "public purpose" and in 1976 the Crown decided to sell the rest. The occupation by the Orakei Action Committee was the culmination of 100 years of petition and protest by Ngati Whatua.

More than any other event up to that time, Bastion Point made mainstream New Zealand aware of Maori land issues. The occupation ended in the eviction of the

Newsmedia, Auckland (Auckland Star Collection)

Political activist Syd Jackson (above) was one of the founding members of Nga Tamatoa. The actions of Tamatoa, the underground paper "Te Hokioi" and the Maori Organisation on Human Rights (MOOHR) eventually coalesced in the fight for Maori land rights. Below, marchers on the 1975 Land March from Northland to Parliament cross Auckland Harbour Bridge.

Newsmedia, Auckland (Auckland Star Collection)

Early morning at Bastion Point. Police form a circle before moving in on the waiting protesters to begin the evictions.

Newsmedia, Auckland (Auckland Star Collection)

protesters in an early morning police and army action, and the demolition of their buildings. Sharon Hawke was 16 at the time:

Many had spent the nights before speaking till dawn about the procedure for the "arrest" that was to have come weeks ago.

"This is to be a peaceful protest. Remember to remain calm…. Under no circumstances shall you resort to violence…. Bastion Point is Maori land!"

These words became entrenched in my dreams…. The police had already surrounded the camp. There were hundreds of them wearing black coats and white helmets. Some wore black hats with striped bands. They had already arrested my brother, Parata. He had two cops on either side of him escorting him to the processing line. He wiped his eyes. I knew he had been crying but his strength glowed from within and it gave me the courage to meet the two officers who had returned for me…. I… sat on the ground passively resisting their advances. They carted me off with my feet dragging behind. I saw Nanny running out towards me. She had remained staunch in front of the wharenui, Arohanui, where all the waiata and haka were happening. She somehow had broken her resolve to run after and protect her mokopuna. Her sons caught her in time and led her back to the front of the whare to continue the protest. I felt tears fall heavily from my eyes and for the first time since we moved onto the land, I wanted my Mum and Dad.[40]

The debate rumbled on. In 1981, the Government announced that a high-cost housing development was planned for the point. A year later, a 24-hour protest against private housing was broken up when police arrested some of those involved. The Ngati Whatua claim was finally heard by the Waitangi Tribunal. In their 1987 Orakei Report the tribunal recommended that the remaining 700 acres be maintained as a tribal reserve and that reparation was due for the loss of other sections of the Orakei block.[41]

Another sign of unrest in Maoridom was the growth of gangs in the latter part of the Seventies, not just in the cities but in rural areas too. A welter of reasons were given – the large numbers of young Maori in prison, lack of education, high unemployment, and the gang as a new form of tribalism. After two violent incidents at Moerewa and Otara the Minister of Maori Affairs, Ben Couch, invited the main gangs to send representatives to a "gang summit" at Parliament. It was only a partial and temporary success: the Stormtroopers and Black Power agreed to a truce but the Headhunters walked out and the Mongrel Mob never showed.

The winds of change in Maoridom

Shortly after 9pm on 8 August 1979 the residential area of Green Island in Abbotsford collapsed. Seven hectares of historically unstable land slid 50 metres down the hillside. Between 9.10pm and 2.30am the following day 640 people were evacuated. Many others had already left their homes in the preceding days as growing land movement caused houses to crack and buckle. The cost of the disaster was over $4 million.

Otago Daily Times, Allied Press Ltd.

were felt inside Parliament itself when Matiu Rata, PM for Northern Maori, resigned from the Labour Party in 1979. The next year he resigned from Parliament and set up the Mana Motuhake Party. At the by-election caused by his resignation he contested the seat but lost. In the 1981 elections the new party put up a candidate in each of the four Maori seats and although all lost they polled strongly, and pushed National into third place. Labour's special relationship with Maori had been challenged from the inside.

The decade's final years had none of the promise and optimism of its beginning. In keeping with a trend of earlier decades – a sedition trial in the Twenties, a heresy trial in the Sixties – the Seventies not only had an indecency trial, but also the country's only prosecution under the Official Secrets Act. Dr Bill Sutch, the accused, was a retired senior civil servant, noted economist and author who was chairing the Queen Elizabeth Arts Council at the time of the trial. He was accused of obtaining information that might be of use to the enemy – the Soviet Union – and "prejudicial to the safety of the State".[42] After a lengthy trial he was acquitted. He died shortly afterwards.

In 1976, Securitibank collapsed costing investors $13 million. The Mangere Bridge dispute, one of the costliest in the country's history, became a symbol of the decade's industrial troubles. In the year 1978/79, for the first time since the Second

Erebus – Relatives Wait for News

When an Air New Zealand DC-10 with 257 passengers on board on a scheduled sightseeing flight to Antarctica crashed on Mt Erebus on 28 November 1979, it was said that everyone in New Zealand was affected. They knew someone on board, or someone connected with one of those who died.

> At exactly 9.05, when the flight was due, waiting relatives were asked to assemble in the Auckland Regional Authority conference rooms.
>
> Mr Murray [the terminal manager] quietly told about 40 men, women and children that the flight was "not quite normal".
>
> Sobs of horror could be heard as he told them the last radio contact with the plane was at 4 pm when it was 1,500 to 2,000 miles out from Christchurch.
>
> People were distressed, many crying, when Mr Murray announced that the two hours of reserve fuel had just run out.
>
> He said there was no immediate cause for alarm when the aircraft could not be raised after its last check-in call.
>
> There had been a solar flash, a type of sun spot or electrical disturbance.
>
> "They possibly could have gone to have a look at it," he said.
>
> Last night, the relatives huddled together for comfort at the airport.
>
> Some deadened their fears with brandy supplied by airport officials; others picked at food supplied by cafeteria staff who volunteered to work overtime.
>
> In one corner, a couple sobbed uncontrollably into a cardigan and in another a man stared blankly into space.
>
> Hostesses walked sobbing women up and down to calm their fears.
>
> Many of the people who came to meet the aircraft seemed prepared to wait all night.
>
> Police were on duty to drive anyone home or to contact relatives.
>
> A padre arrived about 10.30 to comfort the distressed relatives.
>
> Security guards were helping the best they could, offering cigarettes and words of comfort.[1]

The reasons for the crash, the inquiry that followed, the findings of the judge, Justice Peter Mahon, who said he had been told "an orchestrated litany of lies" by the airline's witnesses, and the overturning of his findings, provoked a controversy which raged for years. The crash brought to an end sightseeing flights to the Antarctic.

[1] New Zealand Herald 29 November 1979, cited in Robin Bromby (ed.), An Eyewitness History of New Zealand, Currey O'Neil Ross Pty Ltd, Victoria, Australia, 1985, pp. 254-55.

World War, New Zealand's population actually decreased. The "brain drain" that had so worried Keith Holyoake in the 1960s had become a torrent:

> *Sir, – If Pat Hanly's mural at Auckland International Airport is indeed situated in the departure corridor, then I don't know why Jeremy Payne is worried that people won't get a chance to see it. Two hundred people a day will be going past it; that's not bad. It's the Hotere in the arrivals lounge that he ought to be worried about.*[43]

Between 1976 and 1980 more than 22,000 working age Kiwis took extended leave overseas.[44] Meanwhile, a second oil price rise in 1979 gave another jolt to the economy. The Government introduced carless days to conserve fuel. The search for alternative energy sources became more pressing.

There were already concerns about the cost and sustainability of the three legs of

Drug syndicate associate Terry Clark, aka Alexander Sinclair.

Newsmedia, Auckland (Auckland Star Collection)

"Mr Asia" – Local Drug Lord

By the end of the Seventies illegal drugs were big business all over the world, including New Zealand. Police estimated in 1978 that New Zealand's biggest drug syndicate had imported $20 million worth of drugs into the country in the previous two years. The head of the drug ring was an Auckland man nicknamed "Mr Asia" by *Auckland Star* journalist Pat Booth and his team because of his drug dealings and connections with that region. He was also wanted in Australia for his involvement with drug shipments there and was under investigation by the American Drug Enforcement Agency. A series of articles were written aimed at unmasking "Mr Asia":

> *A Star investigation into the syndicate's dealings has revealed it to be a major link between drug manufacturers in Asia and local distribution networks.... The ringleader whom we will call "Mr Asia", the most powerful force in New Zealand's growing drug market, continues to live in Asia, a free man.... But after months of investigation, the Star has a dossier of never-before-published facts – profiles of Mr Asia, top drug dealers in the North and South Islands, details of their operations, how they use guns, and threats and money to stay at the top, how much money there is at stake and who gets it....*
>
> *The woman's voice on the other end of the phone was educated, anonymous and pressing. "I am concerned about this Mr Asia drug syndicate story on the front page of the* Auckland Star *tonight. I think I know who you are talking about.... I think you are talking about Martin Johnstone. If you are, I have to tell you, Mr Booth, you have made a serious error of professional and personal judgement. I'm telling you now, Martin will not be pleased."*
>
> *I had never believed, I said calmly, that the person we are writing about would be pleased.*
>
> *And she replied, "Well, I think you should know, Martin is not going to like it."*

A year later, in 1979, Booth received unexpected news about Johnstone:

> *British police retrieved a body from a disused quarry pit. The man, who had been shot in the head, and had his hands chopped off, was identified as a New Zealander called Martin Johnstone, resident in Singapore. Later, his closest associate in the syndicate, the undoubted hit man of the group, Terry Clark, was convicted of murder. Johnstone was the sixth victim to be killed by Clark or on his instructions in the 18 months we had been investigating the syndicate.... In Johnstone's luggage when it was found and searched was a plastic bag of newspaper clippings from the* Auckland Star – *the Mr Asia series.*[i]

Terry Clark died in an English prison while serving out his sentence for murder.

[i] Pat Booth, *Deadline. My Story*. Penguin Books (NZ) Ltd, Auckland, 1997, pp. 195-196.

the welfare system – health, social welfare and the new superannuation system. Muldoon had promised what historian Keith Sinclair called "the most expensive piece of legislation in New Zealand history" before the 1975 election. It countered Labour's newly introduced scheme where a person contributed throughout their working life to a fund from which superannuation was then drawn. Under Muldoon's scheme all benefits were paid from taxation. By 1978, health and social welfare alone accounted for nearly a third of government expenditure.[45]

The Seventies was a time when the country was stirred to life. For every movement or social concern there was an opposing one. The explosion of proponents of change and a more liberal and open society roused to opposition those fiercely committed to the status quo, or even to earlier mores – "bring back the birch" for criminal offenders, "back to basics" in education. Supporters of industrial growth, forestry and mining clashed with the increasingly vocal and organised environmental lobby. But how they conducted the debate often cast more heat than light:

> *Mahatma Gandhi was fond of saying, "Hate the sin and not the sinners." New Zealand needs a mammoth public relations campaign and educational programme to induce people to value ideals and idealists, and to attack the opinions they oppose, and not the opinion-makers. There is a national reflex, sublimated by Rob Muldoon, to knee opposition in the groin rather than challenge its case. We need to tolerate and even respect diversity of viewpoint and dissent as far as we possibly can, and not as an act of patronage, but as a duty to our community.*[46]

In the next two decades, however, whole sectors of society would find that whether they played the man or the ball made no difference – few in Government or the Establishment power bases were listening.

JUST TO PLAY IT SAFE, BETTER GET WILDLIFE TO STICK A COUPLE ON ONE OF THE ISLANDS...

NZ COULD BE EMPTY BY 2096 -MIGRATION FIGURES

Summer roads were regularly slowed by cars towing caravans or boats. In camping grounds some families returned to the same spot each year to set up their holiday home – caravan with canvas extensions – and re-establish relations with their summer-time neighbours.

Nelson Provincial Museum 7819 FR3 (Geoffrey C. Wood/Nelson Evening Mail Collection)

The Grant Family
War and Peace

Donald Grant, 1941.

Donald Grant, the father, would have loathed the description, but he was a Second World War hero, respected – and in some cases revered – by his men. Historian and author David Grant, the son, was also a foot soldier, protesting against the Vietnam War and, later, nuclear ships and the Springbok tour.

At first, the two seem worlds apart, but in fact they decided on their respective actions in almost identical fashion. Newlywed in 1939 when the Second World War began, Donald Grant did not rush to enlist. Instead he made a considered decision, joining in

1941. His son began his protests against the Vietnam War in the late 1960s, after he had examined and weighed up all the issues. Both ended up with strong anti-war feelings although David, who wrote a book about pacifists, does not class himself as one.

Donald Grant returned from the war having been decorated with a Military Cross for "gallant and distinguished service in the field" as well as the American Silver Star. The US citation referred to Colonel D. G. Grant's gallantry near Strada in Italy, on 22 July 1944, where he "deployed his troops with the utmost skill and pressed through enemy resistance to capture his objective capturing 30 prisoners and killing more than 40 of his enemy".

Yet the reserved and undemonstrative Grant was irritated by military recognition of this sort and wrote to his wife:

Darling, I heard not very long ago that I have been recommended for a decoration for the Florence show. I was very annoyed about it as I did nothing to deserve it and sincerely hoped that I would miss, particularly as I have expressed my views on decorations fairly freely around this place....

Donald Grant, a maths graduate, went into teaching, but found it difficult to get a job in the early Depression years when he came out of teachers' college. He eventually got a position at Gore High School. David's mother, Unity, was raised in Waikaia, a Southland hamlet not far from Gore where she met Donald.

They settled in Christchurch after they got married in January 1939. My father was very conscious, as the months rolled by, that he may be needed to participate in this particular war. I know they made a conscious decision not to have children in case he did not return.

He didn't rush off to war as many young people

David Grant, his father Don, aunt Linda and grandfather William (rear) stroll to the third New Zealand-South Africa rugby test, Christchurch, August 1956.

participated in to do with the war. He attended RSA functions when he was invited. He was responsible in Invercargill for organising successful 23rd Battalion reunions and played a key role on ANZAC Day where he would talk to groups of people.

All of it helped his son learn about the war, a subject his father rarely mentioned otherwise, to the disappointment of his young son:

I was very keen to talk to my father about the war. I wanted him to tell me how many Jerries did he kill? I mean this is a typical kid's reaction to his father who was a hero. I wanted to find out these things. He deflected these questions. He wouldn't say. He would smile a slow smile and walk off and change the subject.

did. About 1940 or early 1941 he felt very much that it was his duty to go and fight. He trained at Burnham and quite quickly the military hierarchy realised he had some leadership potential, so he trained as an officer and went to Libya in 1941 as a reinforcement.

I was aware of the war as early as I can remember. I knew that my father had a part to play. There were certain rituals that my father

Donald Grant's only surviving wartime letter to his wife Unity, May 1945. They wrote to each other once a week for 4½ years.

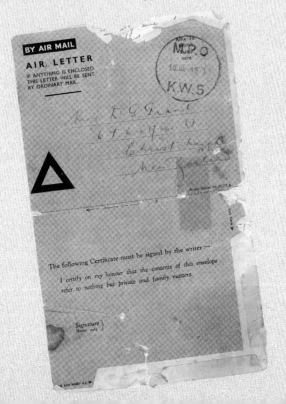

Donald Grant (left) relaxes in Venice after the Allies captured the city in April 1945.

Governor-General Sir Bernard Freyberg invests Lt-Col. Donald Grant with the Military Cross, Wellington 1946.

He certainly did not see himself as a heroic figure, although I did. And he wouldn't participate in the kind of rank and file RSA activities which many of the other men did.

Like many postwar baby boomers, David grew up on a diet of comics and war stories in which there were clear goodies (the Allies) and baddies (Germans and the Japanese). Although his father did not discuss the war, David later discovered more about him as a man with a dry sense of humour, and a commander who put the welfare of his troops first:

… he was a cautious, very thoughtful commander. He tried to minimise the risks in engagement, in contrast to one or two other commanders who would

take risks and probably end up with more glory. But the men respected him for that.

David grew up looking very much like his father, and in his shadow. It was something which he says caused him some angst, as he tried to assert his own self:

When I reached later adolescence there was a kind of questioning where I came up against an attitude where I was told that if I was as good as my father, then I would be a good person, a fine citizen. The rebellion of late adolescence led me to start to reject this scenario and a little voice in me was crying out, "Well that's fine, but let me be me. It's David Grant here. I'm Don Grant's son and proudly so, but I'm David Grant, and in some respects I'm very different to my father...." So that took a while to work through and probably not till the mid-twenties did I work through all that, after his death, and after I'd mourned properly and come to understand about the meaning of the war and my father's role in it. And I think probably now there's that kind of long-lasting respect for his role.

My father died when I was sixteen. It was a tragic time for him to die because at that particular time I was just starting to get to know him as an adult. Before, he'd been my father; sometimes a distant figure, rather gruff, rather preoccupied with other activities, not only at the school where he was overworked, but also his work in the community.

So it was a sad time for me because I was just starting to try and get on even terms with him and communicate with him beyond the child/father relationship which it had been up to then.

The funeral was held in North Invercargill Presbyterian Church and the organisers put loudspeakers outside the building because they knew that they would have a large crowd to mourn the passing of a famous local soldier, educationist and community leader. David remembers hundreds of soldiers, many 23 Battalion veterans and other soldiers, lining up and walking slowly past, placing poppies on the coffin:

My most poignant memory of that particular experience was for the first time in my life seeing grown men with tears in their eyes, which was a very

Donald Grant (third from left) pictured at Jerusalem with other Allied officers in 1942.

On the streets — David Grant, facing, 1972.

time to recover from that. She eventually did remarry, but it wasn't for another 23 years....

Years later the conflict in Vietnam intensified, but initially, at least, held little interest for David:

In the late 1960s... as I understood and read rather more about it, I realised that it didn't seem a war that should be fought. It seemed to me to be a civil war between two countries which had been artificially separated in 1954. There was no doubt that the southern regime was very corrupt.... It seemed very dubious that any Western country should have a presence there. I went to a few lectures. I listened to what the Committee on Vietnam had to say and read some graphic accounts of the war itself. And of course there were other images. It was the first war on television, so you were getting in your living rooms every night details of the atrocities. All these things impacted upon my decision to protest and take part in marches against the Vietnam War.

In Christchurch we also protested against the decision to set up the Omega Station in the foothills of Canterbury... we thought it was going to be a tracking device for American military hardware, notably submarines. And in fact, that particular protest was so strong that the Omega Station was not built there and was later built in Tasmania, I understand. So those were issues of some importance to me at the time.

But he emphasises that at no stage was he a major figure in the protest movements of his time:

I was one of the minions on the streets that was marching, basically. I did march against the war. I did think it was a war which we shouldn't be involved with. I thought it was a war that was immoral, unjust, and subsequent events have proved that. I came to this decision myself that New Zealand shouldn't be involved in this war. We

confusing image for me at the age of sixteen. I grew up very much as a young boy in heartland New Zealand in the Fifties and Sixties. It was a time of black and white. Men and women had particular gender roles. Men didn't cry. They were the leaders. They were the breadwinners. They were expected to be upright and strong, and this was kind of the macho thing of which war was part.

He believes his father should never have gone to war because he had untreated high blood pressure, a condition which David has inherited:

And that experience, four years' hard slog and stress in the desert, then in Italy, followed by a particularly stressful job as Rector of Southland Boys' High School at a time when they couldn't get teachers....

All these stresses impacted upon him in a way that we have a better understanding now than we did then. He had all the conditions – the stress, the overwork, that were ripe for an unwell heart... for what eventually happened to him, in terms of having a heart attack at 55. It was a tragic thing for my mother. They had a genuine, deep and abiding love for each other and my mother took a long, long

shouldn't be seen to be supporting an American regime that was trying to support, trying to win an unwinnable war... I don't think my father would have been at all upset or annoyed at my attitude towards the Vietnam War. He may have shared the same kinds of sentiments.

I objected to the Americans being there... it was an internal conflict between one race of people. But I am not a pacifist in the sense that I don't believe that there shouldn't be war at all times. Having said that, I'm very much a believer in nuclear disarmament as opposed to the other theory of preparedness for war while building up your arsenals.

I believe that's what's happened in places like Bosnia and Angola and so forth in the last ten, 20 years where we've sent a number of troops to keep the peace as part of the United Nations Corps. It's the best way to try and resolve international disputes without heading into some kind of horrendous conflict. And of course the nature of war since the Second World War has changed – the nuclear threat has put a new meaning on the term "war" which my father's generation wouldn't even have conceived of. So that's changed everything....

David was a member of the Peace Squadron in Auckland when Prime Minister Robert Muldoon welcomed nuclear ships – and peace protesters didn't. But long before that, what had made him particularly proud was the stance taken by Labour Prime Minister Norman Kirk, whose Government sent a frigate to the French nuclear testing area in the Pacific as a protest:

They were testing in the open in those days. I felt very proud that we had at last stood up to a great power, a supposedly friendly great power on an issue of international importance. We had defied America and Britain, and Australia by making a physical protest to the Mururoa tests. We were acting alone, we were taking a moral stand on our own and I felt particularly proud at that moment.

And I think that was the beginning of the consideration that New Zealand take a rather more active role in the anti-nuclear sentiment. And it seemed to me just a progression when we had our next Labour Government that the vast majority of New Zealanders were against nuclear power, not

Donald's grandson Cameron (a member of the Wellington City Cadet Corps) with Vietnam War veterans whom he led in parade, Wellington, May 1998.

only in terms of nuclear armaments, but also having any kind of nuclear power in the country.

David's son, Cameron, joined the Wellington City Cadet Corps in 1996. Although he enjoys the uniform and the discipline, he does not believe he will join the Army for a career and believes that, ideally, its role should be for peacekeeping. Both his father and grandfather have influenced him. While a cadet, Cameron is also a budding artist and is particularly proud of one poster he designed – a protest against French nuclear testing.

Sources: Edited Ninox transcripts from *Our People, Our Century*, 1999. All photographs from the Grant Family Collection.

The Kaa Family
Family Matters

Wi Kuki and Keri Kaa grew up in a family of 12 children on the East Coast. Keri says their father Tipi "broke the mould [when he] went and married someone from outside Ngati Porou". Their mother Sophie Whaanga was a "foreigner" from the chiefly line of Ngati Kahungunu and Rongo-mai-wahine. Tipi Kaa also broke a long tradition of arranged marriages. Keri explains:

I think the marriages at that time were all political arrangements. If there were arranged marriages between two chiefly families they were arranged for quite specific reasons to do with whakapapa, with descent, with what some people call impeccable lineage. Also, to do with mana. Occasionally to do with land. Some of the marriages were peace marriages between two warring factions. And the remarkable thing is that people actually liked each other and loved each other dearly. There were long, strong marriages and a lot of the chiefly lines kept the whakapapa quite tightly bound together. I think it made for stable relationships if other members of the whanau were around to provide support. If there wasn't a support system in place, I think it must have been really tough for both parties.

Grandfather Kaa arranged, as best he could, several of his children's marriages. But not his son Tipi's. During my father's ascent from boyhood into manhood arranged marriages and [de facto] relationships were very common practice. In his case, he had a relationship from which there was a son, our half-brother Wallace, who lives in Tolaga Bay. But then came the momentous meeting with our mother who was visiting the village.

Wi Kuki Kaa says of the marriage that had been arranged for his father:

The arranged marriage fell flat because they were second or third cousins and they'd grown up together. She was sort of the girl next door and their relationship as they got older was platonic. She was more interested in some other guy and he was more interested in some other girl. It was never going to work because if he didn't object, she would have.

Tipi and Sophie Kaa had a strong marriage in which each had their roles. Keri says of her mother:

She was the worker in the sense that she toiled morning, noon and night. She sewed. She cooked. She

Sophie Kaa (nee Whaanga), aged 16 years, at Wairoa in 1919, and at Tukaki Marae, Te Kaha in 1983.

Above — Keri Kaa in 1995. Above right — Wi Kuki Kaa.

1958 I think. His first parish was Te Kaha and he was there for four years. Then he came back home. That was his last parish, Waiapu.

Wi Kuki says that while he was still young it dawned on him that for his parents' generation "the holy trinity was the Church of England, the British Empire, and the National Party; that was the meaning of life". The Kaa children grew up in a close community surrounded and supported by an extended family. Most of them spent time at boarding school. When they were home, they helped with the younger children and on the family farm. There was, says Wi Kuki, a routine:

cleaned. She gardened. She scrubbed. She did everything. She used to go to meetings of the Red Cross. She joined the Playcentre movement in the Sixties, got her certificate then for a bit of fun. Nearly fell over when she passed. She didn't relate to too many people but she made some very good friends who were friends right into her old age. But I don't remember her as a mother to whom you would go for a cuddle. She'd demonstrate her love to her loved ones by making us nice food, beautiful clothes, making sure we got scholarships to go to school because she got rent money from all the land she owned or had shares in. Our father was the one who sat people on his knee, who physically cuddled and talked with people. He was quite proper and fairly strict but as he aged and we got older we discovered him to be a wonderful listener. He had a different approach. My parents had two different ways of parenting.

Wi Kuki says of his father:

He was friendly, pretty quiet, and a very steady worker. I found him a lot of fun; and he was always good for sixpence. The old man milked the cows. Mum was the chief gardener after he did his back in. And then as we grew old enough to manage on our own, he became one of those committee collectors. He was on the marae committee, the school committee, the rugby committee. He also became a director of the Ngati Porou Dairy Company and that took up a lot of his time. Eventually, when he was in his fifties, he became a preacher. He was ordained in

On the weekends if you got up first, big brother went to round up the cows. Sometimes you'd light the stove. Once that's going you'd put the kettle on. Then things like feeding the chickens; and every evening you'd gather some kindling wood to start the fire in the morning. Everybody did something. The older girls were the chief babysitters. They did it automatically. When the parents went off somewhere they just took over the kitchen and did the cooking and chased us to bed.

You were part of an extended family. Your aunties and uncles had as much right to tick you off as your own parents did. That was quite normal. You get used to the fact the whole community is keeping an eye on you and you need to perform to their expectations. You would have to perform a bit better than just for Mum and Dad.

Keri remembers that there were real benefits for children growing up in such a community:

We had so many children in our family sometimes the competition for attention and for material things got a bit tough. We had wonderful aunties and uncles around the place. We used to run away to Auntie Huinga and Uncle George Nepia's house. He'd be working in his garden and we would appear at the fence line and not say anything. And he'd walk up the fence line and not say anything and we'd follow behind him. Then he'd come back the other way and we'd come back. That was how we'd signal to him that there'd been an upset at our house. He was fun. He had a sense of humour; he could connect with children. So he would sit down and have a chat with us and make jokes with us and make us laugh, and give us fruit from the orchard. Or I would go round and visit Auntie, have a natter to her, and she'd give me a biscuit or something and cheer us up. Then we'd trot home. I think now they call it "time out".

I think it's very significant because you have a sense of place and a sense of self-worth. You know where you belong. Might not be your first mother or father, but to know that there's a place to call home, and there's a heart to the family in which you dwell when you need it. And you don't get that if you're living in urban or heavily built up areas where there is no granny or auntie, or uncle, or some other parents to take your children to. I think the extended whanau is hugely significant.

In the 1950s and 1960s that support system was beginning to disintegrate as Maori began a period of sustained migration from rural to urban life. Wi Kuki and Keri both headed for the city and further education after they finished school. Wi Kuki began a B.A. at Auckland University and then dropped out to work in forestry. But after a year he went down to Wellington and completed his degree at Victoria University. While he was there he became involved in Victoria's drama club. He considered joining the university faculty as a lecturer, but life in academia wasn't for him. He took a job instead at the Ngauranga freezing works. He intended union work as a career but he became disenchanted with the dog-eat-dog politics he found at its upper levels. He had maintained his drama contacts and he "drifted into acting".

Wi Kuki was in Wellington when Keri first moved there in 1965 from teachers' college in Palmerston North. He was her family support. However, in 1967, Wi left for Sydney; many of his friends were already there, and were sending back stories of a more exciting life and of the good money actors could earn. He was to be away for 15 years. Meanwhile, Keri took advantage of the new freedoms of the late Sixties and Seventies, but within her own strict moral code:

We went to balls and to dances, kind of formally organised things. There was a cabaret in Willis Street where people had balls and you had to make all the ballgowns. People went off in tuxedos and things. And then people went partying, some very wild parties. We'd come out of these strict church boarding schools and these strong tightly guided whanau networks and here we were with all this heady freedom and partying and going out with thoroughly unsuitable people that we knew the old people would have totally disapproved of. Shifting about in relationships and knowing that you could never take this person home, that person would be thoroughly unacceptable. Nothing's changed really. It's just that the moralising in that period was very strong. You learnt to be secretive to protect yourself. And smart people went overseas so that they weren't seen by people in the family.

I joined in the wild times like everyone else but I always knew at the back of my mind, there's all the teaching of the old people. To be careful. Don't come home with a Pakeha. Don't come home with a Catholic. One summer I came home with a failed priest. My mother, who had a wonderful sense of humour, thought this was a great joke. She twigged.

In her late twenties she reached a decision not to marry. She wasn't interested in having children:

I wanted to do other things. I wanted the freedom to choose to write, to join committees. The feminist movement was sweeping through Wellington. I went to that famous hui where Margaret Mead came and spoke. And attitudes were changing: attitudes to men were changing and attitudes to relationships were changing. And one of the things I learnt from my mother was what mattered was who and what you were as an individual. You didn't necessarily have to be part of a relationship to be of worth.

Keri put her energy into her teaching career but when she was 35 she became a whangai to her 15-year-old nephew, Peter Kaa, son of her sister, Mere, who died when he was very young. He and his older brother Brannigan were adopted by their grandparents Sophie and Tipi. Then he lived for a while with an uncle in Hastings and another in Auckland before the family decided he should stay with Keri – "I had the time and at that stage a bit of money to deal with something like that and I was dealing with adolescents anyway." Peter says now of the whangai system:

I don't know how the whangai system is recognised by the courts nowadays but I had to be formally adopted by my grandparents because the courts refused to recognise the whangai system. And they were a bit dubious about a pair of 60-year-olds adopting two boys, one who was three and the other eleven. But it was successful. I think it's a very good system. Who better to look after people in their old age than their grandchildren. And also vice versa. Then the grandchild, or whoever it happens to be, also learns the values of two generations back, and those values are kept alive. As far as I am concerned, that's the way it should be.

Peter was the first of many nieces and nephews who stayed with Keri over the years. There was a small room in her flat put aside for them and it was rarely empty. It was, she says, part of her up-bringing never to turn away a member of the family, and she is known as a surrogate mother. The role she has chosen – to nurture in the Maori sense without being a mother – was a traditional one in earlier Maori families. Keri had her support system too:

I had wonderful flatmates who actually helped with the parenting. I think having to discipline someone and having the support of your mates in the flat was a really big help. And when they thought I was being a bit of a witch, not allowing Peter to go to the disco with all the local kids, they would come and speak on his behalf, say I was being unreasonable. And my friend Julia, when her nieces who ended up living with her would have arguments with her over things,

I would come in as a supporter for the children. So, the networks go on. But if you haven't got a solid emotional base and a bit of strong economic support, it must be tough. If you've got compassion and an understanding and you've worked on the relationship at an emotional level, I think it will work. But it's hard yakka.

In December 1998, Keri retired from teachers' college and returned to the family home in the remote and predominately Maori community of Rangitukia on the East Coast:

I came home because it was time to come home, for spiritual reasons and because I wanted to do something different from what I was doing in Wellington. In terms of my career as a teacher, I felt I'd come to the end of that creative road and now I want to go down another creative road.

I knew this old house needed someone to care for it and look after it and it needed one of us living here. Because it's no use standing in the halls of academia lecturing to hundreds of inner-city students of Maoridom about the principle of your family actually living on the land and keeping the home fires burning, when ours had almost gone out. The flame had almost gone out because the two brothers who had maintained it are both in the family cemetery. So I decided, or the people in the night decided, that that was to be my role. The whanau members in the cemetery made it clear to me that somebody had to come home.

Peter agrees with the importance of her decision:

Auntie Keri returning means a lot of things. The home fires burn brightly again. That warmth of family and having someone in the house again is good. So it's the life force of the house basically. When my grandmother died that power base at home wasn't there for a while. It means going back to Rangitukia is a far happier event than it was in the past few years. Because the house is more than just a house. The house and the people and all the families and relations that live around are all part of it.

Peter Kaa at high school in Wellington during the time he lived with Keri.

Sources: Edited Ninox transcripts from *Our People, Our Century*, 1999. All photographs from the Kaa Family Collection.

1980

1990

Pragmatism versus Ideology

Chapter 9

New Zealand meets the latest member of the royal family and presents Prince William with a piece of kids' Kiwiana – the buzzy bee. The Prince responded by taking his first steps on the lawn at Government House.

W e entered the 1980s, a nation of 3.16 million, with over 2.2 million motor vehicles on the road, in the midst of an economic recession. Unemployment numbers were relatively high – more than 40,000 registered in August 1980 – and inflation was a continuing problem.[1] The Eighties were to be a decade of bitter divisions as well as moments of exuberant unity. We experienced great highs and lows. While seeking an Aotearoa/New Zealand identity in the South Pacific we exchanged some of the elements we had long used to define us in the past for those of a very different ethos.

In Government and business, power passed from the generation moulded by the Great Depression and Second World War to the first of the "baby boomers" who had grown up in the much more prosperous late Forties and the Fifties.

We moved from one of the most regulated economies in the world to one of the least regulated, in less than 10 years. Fortunes were made and lost. Pastoral farming's share of export earnings fell from 84 per cent in 1973 to 50 per cent by 1984. For the first time manufacturing earned significant export dollars – rising from only 8 per cent in the early Seventies to 22 per cent in 1984. Tourism rivalled the wool industry for export receipts.[2] And in trade we finally broke from the security, and tyranny, of Britain as our largest market – to sell to and buy from. In 1980, for the first time, the United States became our single biggest market. During the Eighties it would be replaced in turn by Australia and Japan so that by the decade's end Japan was taking 18 per cent of our exports and Britain had slipped into fourth place, accounting for only 7 per cent. EC countries took only 18 per cent while the Pacific Basin accounted for 75 per cent of our exports.[3] This rearrangement in importance of our trading partners mirrored a reality the majority of Kiwis could no longer ignore:

> *Pakehas have been in New Zealand for more than a hundred and fifty years. In that time the empire that shuffled them to the far corners of the earth declined and in the last decade withdrew into the Common Market. Pakeha New Zealanders are no longer European. They are adrift in the South Pacific and must come to terms with that reality. They have to learn to become Pacific people.*[4]

In ancient cultures, the storms which ushered in the Eighties might have been read as an omen. Twice in 1980, in January and again in June, the southern regions of the South Island experienced their worst floods in decades. The January floods in Southland and Otago were the worst for more than a century. In June, Otago was again inundated by the heaviest rains in more than 50 years. Within 24 hours floodwaters from the Waipori and Taieri Rivers had spilled over their banks to surge across the surrounding plains. The floods caused the region's biggest civil emergency, and hundreds of personal dramas. A Dunedin van driver making bread deliveries reached the bridge over the raging Taieri River in the early hours of the morning:

> *The two centre spans had been washed away by the flood but I didn't realise this because I could see the other end of the bridge. When I got to the middle I ended up in the water. I thought I was trapped inside and the biggest problem was keeping my head. There was only about four inches of air and the water was surging about. I breathed a bit here, got covered with water, and breathed a bit there. All the time I kept saying to myself, "Take it easy, take it easy." I knew I wasn't injured, so it was a question of keeping cool. I got some fairly big surges of water and they filled up the cab. I thought the next time this happens it might be the last, so I thought I'd better get out of there. I grabbed one lantern but it didn't work. Then I found another and that did. Next I found the windscreen was smashed. I swam out and clung to the roof of the cab. Then the water got higher and I got on the van's canopy. All this time*

Newsmedia, Auckland (Auckland Star Collection)

A small idea which completely overwhelmed its instigator. A young Auckland woman, Tania Harris, fed up with the apparent culture of industrial strikes suggested a march in protest to a few of her friends. On the day, in March 1981, an estimated 50,000 to 100,000 people turned up to the "Kiwis Care March".

Radio and Television July 5 - 11 1980

listener 40c

NZM Archive

McPHAIL & GADSBY THIS TIME IT'S SEX, RELIGION, CRIME, MONEY, WAR....

The 1970s comedy show, "A Week of It" developed into "McPhail & Gadsby".

I was flashing the torch as I was floating down the river for somebody – anybody – to see me. We were going at a great pace down the river and I had two problems. I didn't want to fall off and drown, and since it was blooming cold I didn't want to die of exposure, so I kept flapping my arms around.[5]

After more than an hour in the freezing river he was rescued by the Outram Fire Brigade jet boat. Elsewhere, more than 2,000 people were evacuated. Dunedin was cut off from the rest of Otago for several days and its airport was under water for weeks. In both the January and June floods, stock losses were substantial.

Although the 1970s had also been remarkable for the number of floods, the Otago/Southland disaster was the first of nine major floods which devastated parts of the country during the 1980s, causing hundreds of millions of dollars' worth of damage, and culminating in Cyclone Bola early in 1988. In 1982, and again in 1988 and 1989, some of the same regions were scorched by severe drought – the first in Canterbury and north Otago and the second down the east coast of the South Island from Marlborough to Dunedin. And by the end of the decade there was something else for the whole country to worry about – the ozone hole. Climate changes and decades of intensive and often inappropriate land use were proving a devastating combination. Nearly a third of the country's land area was subject to erosion.[6] The Eighties were to confront the farming sector with a series of challenges. Weather was only the first of them.

Cyclone Bola

When Cyclone Bola struck the northern North Island over four days in March 1988, flooding caused huge damage in the East Coast and Hawke's Bay regions. The worst-hit area was around Gisborne. Estimates of the cost of the devastation were put at $75 million.

The government relief package of $50 million for the region's farmers set new records. Farmers and horticulturists were recompensed for 60 per cent of their non-insurable losses. The insurance companies were hard-hit as well. They received nearly 11,500 claims with a total cost of $37,200,000. It was the third largest disaster for insurance companies, topped only by the Southland flood in January 1984 and the 1986 Bay of Plenty earthquake when claims for both disasters exceeded $45 million.

Kiwifruit growers in the East Coast, Taranaki and Northland regions, which bore the brunt of Cyclone Bola, faced losses worth more than $15 million. About 5 per cent of the projected export crop was wiped out. In the East Coast and Hawke's Bay regions, road repairs alone cost more than $34 million, the biggest bill ever faced by the National Roads Board.

A report by the Parliamentary Commissioner for the Environment on the damage caused by the cyclone concluded it was time to change policies and practices to meet "the goal of sustainable land use". The Ministry of Agriculture and Fisheries (MAF Tech) and the Department of Scientific and Industrial Research (DSIR) also recommended returning the land to forest as the only effective way to control much of the erosion in the region. They said that pastoral farming on large areas of the land on the Poverty Bay flats round the Wairoa River was not suitable or sustainable land use as "erosion rates under pasture greatly exceed soil formation rates". The scientists warned that unless farmers moved away from pastoral farming much more of the land would deteriorate until it would be unable to support any kind of vegetation. This was not the first time such warnings had been given. Nor was it the first time the region had been devastated by flooding. In 1938, and again 10 years later in 1948, bad flooding had caused people to leave the Gisborne region. Yet this kind of inundation and the damage it caused had been predicted as early as 1920 after two years of field work. The recommendation then: to stop pastoral farming and put substantial areas back into forest.

Gisborne Herald

Gisborne residents begin the clean-up after Cyclone Bola.

One of the most severe storms to shake the entire nation was of civil and social disorder. The first intimation was no more than a murmured irrelevance: The Tour. And then suddenly those two words were everywhere. For some they were a double-barrelled threat to our international honour; for others, they simply represented a chance to witness a great sporting struggle.

In 1980, the New Zealand Rugby Union chose an inauspicious date to invite the South African Springboks to tour New Zealand – 12 September. Three years earlier on that day, South African Black Consciousness leader Steve Biko had died in police custody. His death was still mourned by the anti-Apartheid movement throughout the world. Those opposed to the tour placed their hope in diplomacy and the terms of the Gleneagles Agreement. The final paragraph of the agreement stated:

> Heads of Government specially welcomed the belief, unanimously expressed at their meeting, that... there were unlikely to be future sporting contacts of any significance between Commonwealth countries or their nationals and South Africa while that country continues to pursue the detestable policy of Apartheid.[7]

Governments were to take every practical step to discourage sporting contact with South Africa. Throughout 1981, tour advocates argued that politics and sport did not mix. But Prime Minister Rob Muldoon refused to intervene to stop the tour. It was, says historian Laurie Barber:

> ... as if Massey had never died but had waited his moment to recreate political issues that would draw the "respectable" and the supporters of "law and order" to support a populist leader.[8]

Muldoon cited as paramount the freedom of sports bodies "to make the final decision on with whom they have contacts as a basic freedom which we will not withdraw".[9] This ignored the Gleneagles Agreement which he had signed.

Rugby stirred strong passions among New Zealanders, especially in rural areas. There, anti-tour dissenters braved the scornful majority to march as part of nation-wide "mobilisations" in May and July:

> They took the turn. Maree Horner, a 30-year-old Eltham housewife, caught her breath. The main street sloped away up a rise, past the Post Office, and just 100 metres distant the crowd began.... She'd never seen the town so full except for the Christmas parade, Eltham's biggest event. The protest group had nowhere to go but up towards it. The crowd from the Eltham Hotel had come up behind. They'd begun a chant: "We want rugby.... We support apartheid. We support racist teams. Give us rugby".[10]

Further on, missiles rained upon the small group which was hurried out of the town centre by the police. It was a hint of what was to come. On 19 July 1981 the 34-man Springbok rugby team stepped from their aircraft in Gisborne – and immediately set Kiwi against Kiwi. Their arrival split families, marriages and workforces and triggered a period of violence and civil unrest unprecedented in our history.

The first real protest at the Poverty Bay-Springbok match on 22 July saw police draw and use traditional truncheons on protesters who had made a determined attack

The Trades Hall Bombing

At 5.19pm on 27 March 1984 a bomb blast ripped through the foyer of the Wellington Trades Hall in Vivian Street killing the caretaker, Ernie Abbott. During that day a number of people had noticed a small green suitcase, abandoned in the foyer. When Abbott picked it up at the end of the day, a mercury switch detonated the bomb.

> Walls nearest the bomb blast were blistered and scorched black while doors in the hallway were shattered or blown off their hinges. Wooden panelling had been smashed and holes punched through walls. The bomb exploded directly behind Mr Abbott's office, where half the glass in the door had been blown out.[1]

Abbott's killing began one of the largest murder inquiries in New Zealand: more than 100 police were on the case at its height and a record $25,000 reward was offered for information leading to an arrest. Abbott, who had been caretaker at the hall for 10 years, was not the target; police believed it was the union movement as a whole. Relations between the unions and Sir Robert Muldoon's National Government were at an all-time low. Opposition leader David Lange and union leaders blamed the Government which they said had run a constant hate campaign against the unions. Muldoon claimed it was the work of a deranged loner.

Messages of condolence were sent by union organisations around the world. On the day of Abbott's funeral a large part of Wellington came to a stop. More than 2,500 people attended the service.

The bomber has not been found.

[1] The New Zealand Herald, 5 April 1984.

Anti-tour protesters and police confront each other at Nelson's Trafalgar Park on 25 August 1981 during the Springbok Tour.

Police with batons confront protesters in Kowhai Street, at the third test in Auckland.

on the fence. They brought down a section of it, but were repelled and tumbled down a bank into a pool of water. For the next hour police and protesters fought in the mud in a vast scrum. It was traditional policing against standard protest, a curtain-raiser for the main event: Hamilton. On 25 July an estimated 4,000 marchers took to the city's streets on their way to Rugby Park. They chanted "Amandla, Amandla Ngaweto" (Power is ours) and "Remember Soweto". At the park they headed for the 2.5-metre fence, weakened it with wire-cutters and invaded the ground. As they poured through the 20-metre breach just before 2 pm, angry rugby fans shouted: "Kill them, kill them."

Once on the field, some 300 protesters linked arms on the halfway line. Helmeted riot police with new long-handled batons surrounded them. Meanwhile, a light Cessna aircraft had been taken from Taupo Airport, and at the rugby ground Police Commissioner Jim Walton, despite reassurances from protest leaders, believed the pilot intended to crash the plane into the crowd. Despite earlier promises that the game would go ahead, it was officially abandoned just after 3 pm. Most spectators left boiling with restrained anger. Others sought indiscriminate revenge among protesters who were escaping from the ground under police protection:

> ... many of them were dropped to the ground by a barrage of fists and kicks. A young girl was kneed in the mouth losing several teeth, and her teenage companion was felled when she was punched in the groin. As the fragile wall of protesters struggled to make it out the gate, they were chased by the crowd and repeatedly hit....[11]

Police could not contain the rage. Ross Meurant, the leader of the elite and controversial Red Squad, had his own views about what had happened:

> What a gutless effort by the police.... A group of 300 had imposed their will on a capacity crowd of 27,000 at the ground and God knows how many more throughout the country. And we had let it happen.... We had failed our oath, we had failed in our duty, we had failed ourselves and most of all we had failed the nation. Had Red Group been deployed in time to meet the mob in the streets we would have stopped them – of that there is no doubt – just as we stopped them so many times subsequent to the Hamilton game.... What a shameful, shameful day.[12]

Hamilton was the turning point in the long, often-violent struggle over the tour. For the protest movement it was the high point, a top story in world news bulletins. It also prompted faraway foreign editors to ask what was happening in sleepy New Zealand:

> I had this wonderful impression of New Zealanders... the ones I've met over here [London] are tall, innocent people; good honest types you'd expect to come from a gentle land that raises woolly sheep and produces lovely butter. And I turn on the old box and what do I see? Brutal faces, police with raised batons, people in crash helmets giving fascist salutes – it's ugly, ugly.[13]

After Hamilton came barbed-wire perimeters, blocked streets and stringent policing which kept protesters hundreds of metres away from the grounds. But still the conflicts between police, protesters and pro-tour elements continued. The worst violence took place outside the final game, the third test at Eden Park. The Auckland Council for Civil Liberties published a report based on the accounts of 20 observers at the park which said in one part:

> We believe that not only protesters and police, but also match-goers and even members of a fourth non-aligned group, engaged in serious excesses.[14]

After the game the Springboks attended a farewell dinner at the South Pacific Hotel. In the midst of this safe haven of Rugby Union hospitality, they were reminded they were not welcome. In their salads some of them found little

Evening Post

ATL D-P314004-A2 (Bob Brockie)

Tempers fray, fists and homemade weapons fly in Wellington as violence between the various factions in the 1981 tour protests becomes more overt.

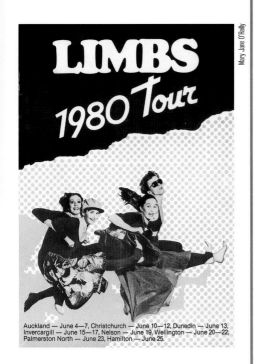

Auckland — June 4—7, Christchurch — June 10—12, Dunedin — June 13, Invercargill — June 15—17, Nelson — June 19, Wellington — June 20—22, Palmerston North — June 23, Hamilton — June 25.

messages on strips of paper saying "Ruck off Boks", "No more tours" and "Don't come back".[15] When they finally flew out of Auckland the following night, New Zealand began to count the cost. The Government had spent $7.2 million on its tour defence; nearly 2,000 arrests had been made, although in court many of these were later struck out, dismissed or withdrawn. A similar pattern followed complaints against police, although the forum was mostly internal. Only a fraction of the cases reached the public courtroom.

Protesters submitted 362 complaints against the police mainly for excessive violence, and police investigated these internally. In 1982 they found 211 of the complaints were unjustified. However, when the complainants turned to the Ombudsman for assistance he investigated 118 cases and sustained 75. His report also specified, however, that the police investigations were, in general, thorough and conscientious.

Protest leader John Minto did not condone the violence around Eden Park. But he thought it was inevitable – "it was a build up of tension on both sides". Minto believed the protests were a "real awakening" for many New Zealanders, and predicted that the country's own racial problems would come more to the fore in the next few years.[16] There were other effects. The Rugby Union may have won the match but they nearly lost the game. Such bitterness and anger would take a long time to dissipate. The 1981 tour and a growing incidence of severe spinal injuries among rugby players contributed to a decline in the game's popularity in the early 1980s. Other sports' popularity increased: one-day cricket, rugby league and the All Whites' unexpected success in getting to the 1982 World Cup. In the mid-1980s there was a resurgence of rugby, leading to the All Blacks' triumph in the 1987 Rugby World Cup and the professionalism and commercialism of the 1990s.

For the Government, the tour's most important outcome came in the

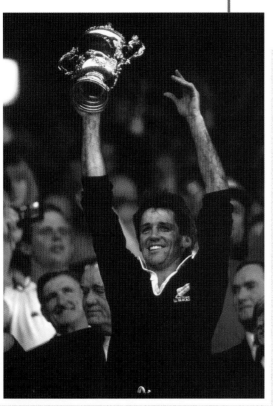

Captain David Kirk raises the first Rugby World Cup: the All Blacks beat France 29 points to 9 in the 1987 final. The team were not expected to win after a poor season the previous year; and in the bitter aftermath of the 1981 tour, "Stand by Me" was chosen as their theme song. The win rehabilitated rugby and for the next two years the 1987 side did not lose a game.

Meanwhile, soccer burst onto the local sporting scene when, against all odds, the All Whites competed for the World Cup in Spain in 1982. To qualify, they had to play more matches than anyone else, travel nearly 160,000 kilometres and score 44 goals (they scored 46). Although the All Whites lost to Scotland, Russia and Brazil in the first round, it was impossible to see New Zealand's World Cup campaign as a failure.

general elections held in November 1981. A close result was predicted and Prime Minister Robert Muldoon was well aware of the tour's influences:

... the impact of the Springbok tour would affect voting differently in different parts of the country and... if, as has always been the case, the provincial areas hold the key to the success or failure of political parties at General Elections, the Government was likely to be ahead in the provincial areas and thus had a good chance of remaining in office.[17]

He was right. National won 47 seats, Labour 43 and Social Credit 2. National had held on to its provincial base, and the Government, at huge social cost.

The 1981 election was not just the post-tour election. It was the election in which Muldoon and his Minister of Energy, Bill Birch, introduced their solution to New Zealand's economic future – "Think Big" – a number of massive energy-based projects. They included an enlargement to the aluminium smelter at Tiwai Point, the construction of a second smelter, the expansion of the steelworks at Glenbrook, a stand-alone methanol plant, a synthetic petrol plant and the expansion of the Marsden Point oil refinery. Before the election Muldoon had promised:

All these are massive building-blocks for the new energy-based dimension to the New Zealand economy that will come on-stream during the 1980s. They will provide, as we go through that decade, the massive external earnings which will not only service the off-shore loans needed to finance them but also provide a substantial surplus to turn around our balance of payments and provide the foundation for yet more jobs, more industries and more activity over the whole economy.[18]

The "Think Big" growth strategy was based on insulating the country against negative impacts from the outside world through the development of recently discovered natural gas and the growing use of hydro-electric power. It would make New Zealand at least 60 per cent self-sufficient in energy, provide a base for expanding heavy manufacturing, and create 400,000 jobs for good keen Kiwis in the process. There was little economic growth at the time, inflation was "a record 15.4 per cent", unemployment figures were above 70,000 and interest rates were climbing.[19] Already in debt, the Government borrowed heavily to finance the projects. They were to fail to provide the bonuses promised, instead saddling the country with enormous debts and crippling interest payments. Muldoon's "Vogelite" policy of heavy borrowing to build a heavy industrial base had only exacerbated the problem.[20]

In his last three years in Government, Muldoon's economic management became more and more authoritarian as he tried to control the local effects of a

Newsmedia, Auckland (Auckland Star Collection)

The $700-million-plus expansion to the Glenbrook steel mill outside Auckland was one of the more troublesome of the "Think Big" projects. Costs escalated, the project fell further and further behind schedule, and there was a downturn in the steel market worldwide. The majority of the mill's increased production was intended for export.

world-wide recession, and to check inflation. As the economy became more and more distorted, old supporters began to criticise him. In cabinet the most constant and vocal dissident, Derek Quigley, was asked for his resignation. Property developer and newspaper columnist Robert Jones, once a true supporter, launched the New Zealand Party with a mix of free market and anti-nuclear policies. Jones used humour to highlight the increasing and sometimes bizarre regulation of life in New Zealand. A week sitting-in for a popular radio announcer provided a perfect opportunity:

> … I sabotaged the ten o'clock news, which caused some distress in the then rather stuffy Radio New Zealand organisation. I announced that Trade and Industry Minister Hugh Templeton would shortly introduce a bill in the House known as the Parrot Compulsory Acquisition Act. Henceforth every household would be required to own one parrot. The economic stimulation provided by the associated economic activities – birdseed growing, cage-making, pet-shop boosting, etc – I quantified at some arbitrary sum of many millions of dollars annually…. I was of the view that [the public was] now so used to being bossed around they would buy into this hook, line and sinker. And so they did. Indignant callers rang in, protesting that they didn't want a bloody parrot. I took the Government's line typical of that period, and accused them of selfishness at the expense of the national interest.[21]

In 1975 Jones had been involved with a number of "stunts" aimed at "laughing the [Labour] Government out of office".[22] That time Muldoon had been the winner. Now times had changed, and so had the leadership of the Opposition. Both Muldoon and Labour's Bill Rowling had survived challenges to their leadership late in 1980. But at the beginning of February 1983 David Lange became leader of the parliamentary Labour Party. A big man with a quick mind and sharp wit, Lange had been an Auckland lawyer before entering Parliament in a by-election in March 1977. He would become as high profile a Prime Minister as Muldoon: both left their mark on the country.

In June 1984, without warning, Muldoon called a snap election for 14 July. The Government's unity was publicly disintegrating. For months now a small group of National MPs had crossed the floor on several occasions to vote with the Opposition in order to defeat the Government. It was only the second early election this century.[23] In the lead-up to it, an increasingly tired Muldoon was in sharp contrast to David Lange's confident, high-energy campaigning. Lange promised an end to the bitter divisiveness that had split New Zealand in the last

In August 1982, Sue Wood became president of the National Party, the first woman to head a major political party in New Zealand.

The "Jones boys" – from left, Norman Jones, Invercargill National MP, property developer Bob Jones and Dail Jones, Auckland National MP, at one of their 1981 fundraisers, billed "The Night of the Jones". Once one of National's generous supporters, by 1984 Bob Jones had established a political party expressly to oppose its leader and his policies.

five or six years under Muldoon, and the chance to work together. He warned constantly that there were major problems and that the next few years would not be easy:

> *Don't expect miracles.... It's going to be a long haul back. You will not wake up on July 15 with a bonanza of riches. I give you very few spending pledges. The challenge to you will be that you stop fighting over a share of the cake and start to turn your mind to those who hope to salvage a few crumbs from it.*[24]

Labour won by a landslide – Labour 56 seats, National 37, Social Credit 2. The New Zealand Party took 12.25 per cent of the votes, much more than Social Credit's 7.6 per cent, but won no seats. However, while voters had clearly rejected National, their support for a Labour Government was not quite as clear cut as it seemed. One in five cast their votes for "a party or candidate other than Labour or National".[25]

1984 was the end of a political era in New Zealand. Sir Robert Muldoon, replaced as leader of the National Party at the end of the year, remained in Parliament until his retirement in 1991, an increasingly isolated and ignored figure, sniping from the Opposition benches. It was a sad end for a man who, a year before becoming Prime Minister, had written:

> *New Zealand is, more than any other country that I know, a land where it is possible to provide for almost everyone the high material standard of living that is made possible by modern technology, while at the same time permitting the enjoyment of the relatively unspoiled natural advantages of our countryside and climate.*
>
> *While independence is a New Zealand characteristic the New Zealander's individualism is leavened typically by a commitment to social justice, and compassion for the less fortunate in the community.*
>
> *Perhaps my strongest motive for becoming involved in politics has been a desire to see this New Zealand way of life preserved even as it evolves in tune with changing times. I am thankful that I was born in this country, and that my children can live in this country, and if Seddon's description "God's Own Country" has become a cliché the reasons for this description remain valid today.*[26]

The year 1984 marked the changing of the guard. The National cabinet was now replaced by a Labour Prime Minister and his Deputy, both aged 41, and a Front Bench with an average age of just over 41 years.[27] There were two women in cabinet and a new Ministry of Women's Affairs. (A total of 12 women MPs were elected in 1984, 14 in 1987.) This was a new-look Labour: far more MPs came from the professions, from universities and the classroom than from more traditional trade union backgrounds. They brought vigour and enthusiasm; and they faced their first challenge within days of winning office. The day after the election the Reserve Bank closed its foreign exchange market. So much money had left the country since the snap election was announced, the bank had been forced to borrow $1.7 billion overseas to protect the value of the New Zealand dollar. A devaluation was expected and recommended. But when David Lange requested the outgoing Prime Minister to order a 20 per cent devaluation, Muldoon initially refused to follow constitutional conventions and act in accordance with the wishes of the in-coming Government.

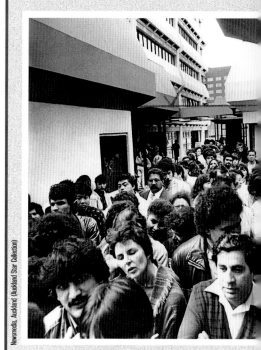

In the late 1980s, for the first time in years, New Zealand began to make major changes in its criteria for accepting immigrants, and to try and improve processes for dealing with applications for residency.

Refugee centres at Mangere in South Auckland gave temporary housing to families fleeing wars and civil unrest in South-east Asia, and a basic introduction to life in New Zealand.

The Queen Street Riot

The thin blue line – police and rioters face off in Queen Street. An official inquiry blamed poor planning by council and police.

On Friday 7 December 1984, an open air concert by DD Smash in Auckland's Aotea Square just off Queen Street in the central city turned without warning and within a short space of time into a full scale riot. It caused almost $1 million in damage. In the shocked aftermath a hastily convened judicial committee met and decided that the cause was easy access to liquor and poor planning by the Auckland City Council and the police. Others were not so sure, citing the high level of youth unemployment, permissiveness, mob fever, lack of family and society values, provocative team policing, and the failure of everyone in society to take responsibility. Julie Roberts was a 16-year-old student caught up in the rampage:

... Suddenly the action intensifies. There's yelling, screaming, more running and throwing missiles. About 2,000 kids burst out of the crowd, charging towards the police.

"We're gonna kill you bastards," someone says. He's joined by a chorus of abuse. "Yeah flatten you f.... Arseholes!"

More kids around me start running to join the mob leaving the square and heading towards Queen Street. I'm forced to go with them, scared of being trampled. I try to run backwards, towards the safety of the footpath. I can't move. Struggling. Fighting. I have to get out. The girl next to me leans down and picks up a broken bottle. All around me people are picking up cans and bottles and hurling them at the police who are standing in a line, about 100m in front of us. Just then they charge. Everyone around me starts running back up Queen Street and that gives me time to get out. There's a gap in the crowd and I dash through to the footpath. Behind me a ghetto blaster plays Duran Duran's Wild Boys.

Hundreds more kids, primarily male Maori and Polynesians, rush forward. The situation is reversed, once again, the line of police is forced to retreat. They're bombarded by bottles and cans as an angry mob chases after them. As the violence heightens people begin to scream and shout....

Next to me is a young Maori girl with her head cut open – she had been clipped by a flying bottle. A little kid of about eight runs past, clutching his right hand, bawling. He has only four fingers. Blood is everywhere. I feel the taste of bile in my mouth and want to be sick. Little kids are crying because they've lost their parents or, like me, are just plain scared. The other half are cheering, roaring, whistling – urging the mob on from the sidelines. A lot of people are actually enjoying themselves – that's evident from the many smiling faces....

The street is a sea of broken glass and empty beer cans. Across the road a car is overturned and set alight. Police immediately set upon the mob, batoning rioters on the backs and arms. I glance at my watch – 9pm. Queen Street is deserted, a wasteland of rubbish, glass, cans and broken bottles. Police and rioters – still clutching batons, still grasping rocks – form ranks on either side of the street. The crowd of onlookers stand motionless and expectant....

Suddenly a young Maori boy tears past me, laden with an armful of fruit. Three cops rush in and grab him. He is struck in the groin and clubbed to the ground....

10pm. Apart from a few sounds of crashing glass the only noises come from the people. Hundreds of footsteps, shouting, laughing voices and in the background the wail of sirens and alarms. The place is a total wreck. Strevens and Warehouse Clothing have had Auckland Star *boxes in their window display areas but their display stands are bare. Sanitarium Health Foods, Woolworths, Horsleys Chemist, Jeffery's Men's Shoes and countless more shops have windows smashed and gaping shelves. On the pavement a poster advertises* International Youth Year '85 – A Year For Action....[i]

The suddenness and scale of the Queen Street riot shocked the city. The question "why?" was never satisfactorily answered.

[i] Julie Roberts, Wild Boys, from After Aotea, *Metro*, Auckland, February 1985, p. 65.

After pressure from some of his own ministers, he announced not only the 20 per cent devaluation but also, under Labour's instructions, the lifting of controls on interest rates and a three-month wage freeze.

The sense of crisis and brinkmanship which existed during those days and that first bold move set the tone for the coming years. Margaret Wilson, who became the Labour Party's first woman president later that year, remembered:

> *It has its own adrenaline.… I think there was a great feeling that this was real, this was somehow big boys' stuff, decision-making stuff. And in many ways it was. These were serious decisions. But if you like, it set the style that was to follow.*[28]

The new Minister of Finance, Roger Douglas, agreed:

> *I guess in a way I was lucky in a sense that I wanted to undertake considerable reform.… And I think we were lucky in that David Lange really got to grips with that and moved that programme forward in a very decisive way. It was undoubtedly a great window of opportunity. It got the ball rolling and in a sense I made every endeavour to make sure the ball didn't stop rolling.*[29]

Roger Douglas was a third-generation Labour MP. In 1980, while in Opposition, he had released an "alternative budget" at odds with both National and Labour policies and was sacked from the "shadow" cabinet. He was influenced by the economic orthodoxy of the time, a mixture of monetarist and supply-side economics, similar to policies already being introduced by Margaret Thatcher in Britain and Ronald Reagan in the United States. Now in a position to implement these theories in New Zealand, Douglas found strong support in Treasury, whose advice had been increasingly ignored by Muldoon. They presented the Labour Government with a 352-page briefing paper in which they laid out their New Right prescription, heavily influenced by the theories of the Chicago School of Economics. In 1984, a confluence of forces, interests and circumstances came together to produce a revolution, nicknamed "Rogernomics".

Over the previous 40 years, government spending on welfare had never reached the levels of countries such as Sweden or Denmark "so that some observers would have placed New Zealand among the 'reluctant welfare states', along with Britain and Australia".[30] In the Seventies and early Eighties social policy continued to be

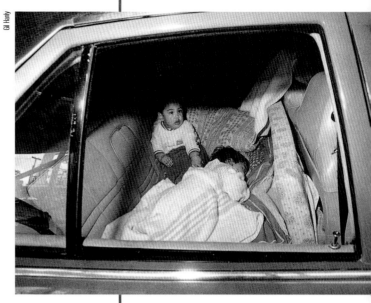

This car became home for a family recently arrived in Auckland. In 1981, there was work but nowhere for them to live. By the decade's end, serious divisions were beginning to appear in New Zealand society.

Substandard housing, over-crowding, poor health, poor nutrition, unemployment and educational under-achievement affected growing numbers of people, Maori and Pacific Island families in particular. There was talk of the creation of a new underclass.

Country came to town, in protest. The changes forced on the farming sector by Labour's new agricultural and financial policies had huge impacts on rural and provincial life. Employment for farm labourers disappeared and many farmers' wives took jobs off the farm.

"pragmatic and ad hoc rather than driven by any single ideology or political agenda".[31] Now Labour promised "to build an even better welfare state on the base of capitalist success".[32] This time pragmatism gave way to theory and ideology. Under Lange and Douglas, the fourth Labour Government was to instigate some of the most significant changes to New Zealand economic, governmental and social structures since the first Labour Government established the welfare state.

During the next three years exchange controls were abolished and the New Zealand dollar floated. A surtax was imposed on superannuitants, so restricting the pension to those who needed it. A Family Care package and later the Guaranteed Minimum Family Income targeted those on low incomes. Universality, until now an integral part of the welfare system, had been breached. Income tax rates were flattened, and a Goods and Services Tax (GST) of 10 per cent was introduced. In 1988 it was raised to 12.5 per cent. Sales taxes were abolished in most areas. Import licensing was phased out and tariffs were reduced. Two of the country's foremost "institutions" were buffeted by the winds of change: state assistance to the agricultural industry was phased out, and business practice was introduced to government departments in the State Owned Enterprises Act.

The Elworthys
The Charge of the "Bullshit" Brigade

Kiwi farmers know that it's not only weather that can make or break them, so they keep an eye on the winds of change from Government. In the Eighties as the Labour Government removed subsidies Chris Elworthy was among the cow-cockie chorus of protest.

... farmers felt that they were getting a very tough deal indeed and farm incomes were dropping rapidly. At that time, interest rates were extremely high and a number of farmers were being forced from the land... there was a great feeling of dissatisfaction.

When we went to Wellington there was a march on Parliament and farmers from all over New Zealand, not just sheep farmers, decided to march... topdressing pilots had gone out in protest as well. Their business had been ruined because farmers weren't spending any money. So there were topdressing aircraft circling pretty close to the Beehive.

Parliamentarians came out to address the assembled crowd of farmers and then about fifty farmers at a time were allowed into the debating chamber to go in and listen to Parliament in process. There were thousands of farmers there, so virtually all day, fifty farmers were going in and fifty were coming out.

The debate would start. Then there would be a roar from the public gallery of "Oh, bullshit!" or "That's not right!" So the Speaker would ask for the public gallery to be cleared and it would let another fifty farmers in and the same thing would happen again. And this went on all day.

So it was very amusing because I can recollect farmers dressed with cows' heads over their own heads and gumboots and black singlets on and it was a good way of letting off steam. I don't think it served any other useful purpose whatsoever.

Source: Edited Ninox transcripts from *Our People, Our Century*, 1999.

Over the years farmers had received a growing number of subsidies from the Government. During 1983/84, $2 billion or 6 per cent of the country's national income went on support to farmers, such as supplementary minimum prices (SMPs), and fertiliser, irrigation and noxious weed control subsidies. SMPs were phased out and other subsidies reduced. Rural Bank interest rates were raised to match general interest rates. The rural communities reeled. In an echo of earlier times, militant farmers took to the streets in protest; some 10,000 marched on Parliament in April 1986. Roger Douglas toured the regions to face hostile and angry audiences in halls all over the country:

> *At the beginning of March [1986] I attended a meeting called by the Rangitikei and Manawatu branches of Federated Farmers in Palmerston North. About a thousand farmers were present. It was the most heated gathering I had been to so far. Once again, over the jeering and booing, I explained what we were setting out to do. I agreed that adjustment hurt to begin with. It did push interest and exchange rates up until, by that means, inflation was brought under control. Labour had attacked government spending as no Government in New Zealand ever had before. "We are taking a hell of a lot of political pain to do that. And you've got to believe we mean it, and you have to respond by adjusting your own actions. So does the rest of the community.... Your council has shown it knows that if we go back to subsidies, the industry will be wrecked permanently. This country can't afford that. If agriculture goes under, we all go under. We will continue to look for ways to help, but they must be ways which do not damage your industry for ever.*[33]

Farmers were also among the first to experience the new concept of business in Government – they started to pay for the advisory services of the Ministry of Agriculture and Fisheries. "User pays", "market forces", "the level playing field", "efficiency and accountability" and "the funder/provider split" became part of a new language to describe a new economic landscape. Citizens became consumers and customers; in hospitals and doctors' waiting rooms patients became clients. State subsidies were removed from State organisations, which now had to pay their own way. Government departments such as Statistics and the Reserve Bank began charging for information. In the drive for greater efficiency, thousands of state service workers were made redundant. They added to a growing number of redundancies from areas of the private sector that were also rationalising, such as the meat industry and harbour boards.

> *I joined the public service deliberately, because, as my parents had often pointed out to me, I had a job for life. I have been through all the training courses, built my home here in Gore and never missed a day's work, except for a fortnight when I had my appendix out. Now I have been told that I am no longer needed. I have really enjoyed my job at the Post Office, and there have never been any complaints, at least not to my face. And now they have wrecked the service by splitting it and sacrificing everything for money. People don't count any more. It is the younger blokes they have kept on. You get punished now in this country for growing old. Loyalty, age and experience mean nothing any more – in fact they are a problem now. What can I do? I'm 47 and have nowhere to go.... I'm stuck.*[34]

Newsmedia, Auckland (Auckland Star Collection)

Local royalty – In 1986, All Black Murray Mexted married the 1983 Miss Universe Lorraine Downes. Downes was the first New Zealander to win an overseas beauty contest.

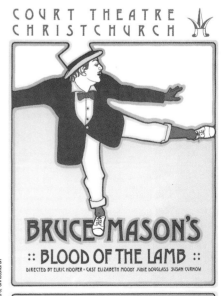

Court Theatre, Christchurch

COURT THEATRE CHRISTCHURCH

BRUCE MASON'S
:: BLOOD OF THE LAMB ::
DIRECTED BY ELRIC HOOPER · CAST ELIZABETH MOODY JUDIE DOUGLASS SUSAN CURNOW

STUDIO THEATRE   September 15th - 27th
                   8.15pm Bookings 66 992

Gil Hanly

However, some areas of the economy were booming, none so spectacularly as the newly freed financial sector. Share markets were bullish here and overseas. We became a nation of speculators. Share clubs sprang up all over the country providing "more fun and excitement than just about any other evening out".[35] The new heroes in these post-Springbok Tour days were the money men, the property speculators, and their companies – Brierley, Chase, Mainzeal, Robert Jones Investments, City Realties, Landmark Properties, Equiticorp, Mace, Renouf, Omnicorp, Goldcorp, Judgecorp, Pacer Pacific, Kupe, Ariadne. Everyone caught the fever: previously staid banks were out trawling for clients to loan money to. Annual general meetings for shareholders were showy theatrical events:

… the huge plush hall, dripping with chandeliers, was crowded to standing room only. The atmosphere was electric. Shareholders, clasping their annual reports, sat on the edges of their chairs to catch every word uttered…. By the time the meeting was half over I was able to announce to the adoring crowd that the shares had hit $1.95, nearly eight times their listing price only a year earlier. To the sounds of cheering, whistling and clapping, the rest of the meeting was buried in an avalanche of raw excitement. We were financial giants. Nothing could stop us now.[36]

Consumption became very conspicuous prior to the stock market crash in 1987. Models cluster on the roof of Auckland's then newest and most exclusive hotel, the Regent.

As Olly Newland of Landmark was to admit later, 1986 saw "greed piled on ambition and heaped on ego". The skylines of downtown Wellington and more particularly Auckland were cluttered with cranes. Fine old buildings, many of them reminders of earlier commercial successes, fell to the demolition ball; mediocre, glassy, mirrored towers rose rapidly in their place. In the midst of this hype and frenzy and sense of invincibility, the country became obsessed with a new (and obscure) sporting event – the America's Cup. Promoted not so much as a yacht race as an international challenge by an increasingly self-aware nation, tens of thousands joined supporters' clubs to help bankroll the challenge and bought a best-selling record *Sailing Away* sung by a "cast of hundreds". Enthusiasm for the America's Cup would long out-last the country's passion for the share market.

Cranes dot the CBD in Auckland during the great property boom of the mid-1980s.

Gil Hanly

On Tuesday 20 October 1987, "Black Tuesday", Kiwis woke to the news that, starting in New York, share prices had collapsed around the world. When the markets opened here, the latest "South Seas bubble" burst. In two months $23 billion dollars was wiped off the stock market boards, nearly 50 per cent of the market.[37] The very rich and ordinary Kiwis, big investors and small, all fell with the market. At the decade's end the local market still had not recovered in the way most overseas markets had, and neither had business confidence. Businessman Alan Gibbs was one of those who lost heavily at the time:

On average New Zealand shares dropped to less than a quarter and many companies' share prices dropped to a tenth or disappeared altogether. Even to this day [1996], the New Zealand share market index is around half of what it was in '87 so it would be very difficult not to be affected by that. Yes, I lost tens if not hundreds of millions.[38]

If you were young, successful and rich, and wanted to let others know about it, then the BMW was for you. In pre-crash days, they filled the car parks of expensive restaurants, bumper to bumper.

Chalkies and brokers work the floor of the stock exchange during the high days of the share boom.

The Stock Market Crash

Property developer Olly Newland was one of the corporate high flyers in the heady days of the stock market boom. On Tuesday, 20 October 1987 he woke to the news that share prices around the world were tumbling. Sick with nerves, he drove in to his office in the centre of Auckland:

The phones remained silent. It was eerie. I could hear the blood rushing in my ears, and my head began to throb. At 9.30 am I walked as nonchalantly as I could up to the Stock Exchange. I wanted to see what the market did when it opened. What did greet me would remain forever in my memory....

The market opened like the roar of a cannon. The steady hum of the operators' voices rapidly rose higher and higher until their shouts became clearly audible to those of us behind the glass looking on.

There was a momentary hesitation. Then the market nosed straight down. "Sell Brierley at $3.60! Sell Brierley at $3.30!" Brierley plunged in the opening moments from $4.20 to $3.10.

The noise became louder, the brokers more frenetic.

The bottom was dropping right out. Giant conglomerate and blue-chip Fletcher Industries crashed 90 cents within five minutes of trading. Now it was selling at $5.20, down from $6.10, and the end wasn't in sight....

The gap between the buy and sell bids yawned wider and wider. Normally only a cent or two separated the bids. Not now. Not in this sort of panic.

"Sell Equiticorp $2.80!"

"Buy Equiticorp $2.50!" 150,000 shares traded.

Brokers were now thrashing about in an ever-increasing swirl of confusion and shouted orders. "Buy!" "Sell!" "Buy!" "Sell!" The sell orders were running ten to one against. With every sell order the market capitalisation slumped lower and lower. There seemed no stopping it.

Looking to the left and right of me, I saw a sea of white faces, mouths clamped tight, brows furrowed. This was even worse than my worst nightmares.

The roar from the trading floor grew even louder. The chalkies were flying up and down the catwalk writing up new quotes and then almost immediately wiping them off again as fresh and lower sale prices were recorded. Smoke from innumerable unfinished cigarettes made the air blue right across the floor of the exchange....

Brokers were jumping and shouting, phones and paper waving in anxious hands. It was bedlam.[1]

¹Olly Newland, *Lost Property: The Crash of '87 – and the Aftershock*, HarperCollins, Auckland, 1994, pp. 84-86.

Labour's anti-nuclear policy was another instrument in redefining our place in the world. Although National was the only political party in the 1984 elections not to campaign on an anti-nuclear platform, when Lange's Government refused entry to the United States ship the USS *Buchanan*, it was an ambivalent public which watched the repercussions. Rapidly we found ourselves off-side with our closest neighbour – Australia – and old allies Britain and the United States. The latter demoted our status from "ally" to "friendly country" and put pressure on the Government as a warning to others considering following our example. America withdrew its security guarantees and ANZUS effectively became inoperative. Britain's Prime Minister, Margaret Thatcher, was reported to be "disappointed" with Labour's anti-nuclear policy.[39] It was a huge change in government attitude from just three years earlier when Muldoon had loaned a frigate to the Royal Navy to patrol in the Indian Ocean and free up one of Britain's ships for the Falklands War.

A public perception that the United States was bullying a much smaller country unnecessarily, and interfering in its right to determine its own internal policies, roused national feeling and began to shift public opinion in support of the Government. But the move to an absolute majority in favour of a nuclear-free New Zealand was provoked by the country's first experience of international terrorism. On the night of 10 July 1985, the Greenpeace protest flagship *Rainbow Warrior* was bombed at its moorings in Auckland harbour by two limpet mines placed by French agents. One crew member was killed. The ship had been preparing to sail to Mururoa atoll to protest against French nuclear tests. David Lange remembered how an outraged public swung in behind Labour's stand, so that by the end of the Eighties even the National Party had followed public sentiment and adopted an anti-nuclear policy:

> The great irony of the last 15 years in foreign policy has been that our foreign policy stance had the seeds of its change in Labour and in my Government. It was nurtured and watered by the American reprisals but it was set in a hanging basket by the French. It was all their own work. The Rainbow Warrior was the defining moment for me because I knew that was the end of any New Zealand commitment to the so-called Western Alliance. It was not when it was sunk that I knew. It was when we knew who'd sunk it that I knew. And then the overwhelming silence from Great Britain. I mean, Margaret Thatcher was prepared to condemn Gaddafi for everything, but the French could go and kill people in our harbour. Hawke never said a word. Ronald Reagan pretended total indifference. We never had a peep out of those people that we were allegedly in a Western Alliance with; those people who fought for democracy.[40]

Labour was voted back to the government benches on 15 August 1987. In an enlarged Parliament of 97 seats Labour held 58 and

ATL D-P331148-A (Peter Bromhead)

FRENCH PRIME MINISTER'S STATEMENT.

New Zealand–French relations reached an all time low during the "Rainbow Warrior" affair. After a mere two week inquiry, France's Bernard Tricot concluded the French Government had not ordered the sinking of the ship, DGSE agents had not been instructed to bomb it and others believed to be involved could not be extradited to stand trial in New Zealand because they were French citizens. "Tricot Washes Whiter" said the French press. New Zealanders were incredulous at the findings and furious at the official French attitude. Prime Minister Laurent Fabius wrote to David Lange (below) reiterating that those responsible were not able to be identified, but that the French Government was determined "no element should remain in the dark". His statements were greeted with national derision.

Gil Hanly

National 39. Social Credit (now called the Democratic Party) and the New Zealand Party failed to win any seats. The programme for the second term was to continue to move the Government's reforms forward and to address social policy. A Royal Commission on Social Policy had spent almost two years consulting widely all over the country before presenting a massive five-volume report in 1988. Simultaneously, other taskforces were reporting on specific areas of social policy. But the Royal Commission's findings did not fit with the Government's chosen direction. "Few governments in any country can have had so much expert advice tendered on social policy in one year, or managed to ignore so much of it."[41] Meanwhile a number of the State Owned Enterprises (SOEs) – Telecom, Air New Zealand, Postbank, the State Insurance Office and Government Print – were sold to private enterprise and the proceeds used to reduce the country's huge overseas debt. Later the Bank of New Zealand and Rural Bank were also sold. As in the Government's first term in office, all of it went ahead with deliberate haste. Finance Minister Roger Douglas explained why:

Gil Hanly

The bombing of the Greenpeace ship "Rainbow Warrior" began New Zealand's first investigation into international terrorism. French agents Alain Mafart and Dominique Prieur pleaded guilty to manslaughter and wilful damage and were sentenced to a total of ten years' imprisonment. In July 1986, the UN Secretary-General ruled that they should be detained for three years on Hao Island, and France was to make an unqualified formal apology to New Zealand and pay $13 million in compensation. For many, it was an unsatisfactory end to the affair.

Newsmedia, Auckland (Auckland Star Collection)

In February 1988, unemployment numbers exceeded 100,000. A march in protest traversed the country culminating at Parliament.

Implement reform in quantum leaps, using large packages. Political Lesson: do not try to advance a step at a time. Define your objectives clearly and move towards them in quantum leaps. Otherwise the interest groups will have time to mobilise and drag you down.[42]

But interest groups also represented democracy in action and many found Labour's rush to reform profoundly anti-democratic.

A hundred years earlier New Zealand had been described as a "social laboratory"; now it was "an economic laboratory engaged in high risk experimentation".[43] Opposition was growing, both within the Labour Party and among the public, to the economic changes, to the continuing cuts in "uneconomic" public services and the hardship experienced by large sections of the community, especially in rural areas. The split was widening again between town and country. Provincial towns and cities were hit twice: first in farming's collapse as subsidies were stripped away, and then as traditionally big employers were "downsized" or closed completely – forestry, railways, freezing works, the post office.

In the major cities, the stock market crash had revealed some very questionable business practices. The heroes of yesterday were found in some cases to be villains. Corporate fraud became another symbol of the period. Along with the company failures were growing reports of white-collar crime – GST fraud, undisclosed loans between companies, accusations of shonky deals and director misconduct, the fraudulent use of shares and criticism of laxness in the stock exchanges. The light and dark of commerce rubbed uncomfortably together. Within three months in 1989 the BNZ recorded the country's worst loss to date and Fletcher Challenge the highest corporate profit to that time. The country had been told that "the market" held the answer. Increasingly, people were questioning the ethics of the market and its ability to provide the great majority of Kiwis with a better life.

But ultimately the Government's second term was poisoned by the bitter split which developed between the Prime Minister and his Minister of Finance over the future direction of economic and social policy. When Lange unilaterally cancelled an economic and tax package at the start of 1988 while Douglas was out of the country, it marked the beginning of the end of one of the closest and most successful relationships in New Zealand's political history. The sixth and ninth floors of the Beehive (where Douglas and Lange had their offices) effectively went to war while

In November 1986 Pope John Paul (above) made a 48-hour visit to New Zealand, complete with his "Popemobile". He received an unprecedented traditional welcome by 10,000 Maori representing most tribes at the start of an open air Mass for 60,000 in the Auckland Domain. The Pope was presented with gifts, including a feather cloak, greenstone cross and carved treasure box. Outdoor services in Wellington and Christchurch also drew large crowds. Open letters from a number of Catholics challenging the Church on the role of Catholic women, the exclusion of divorced and re-married Catholics from the Church, and calling for more authority at local level were published in newspapers before the Pope's arrival.

their ministers communicated almost exclusively by letter and memo. When Douglas sent a letter to Lange in December 1988 saying he could no longer work with him in cabinet if he remained Prime Minister, Lange accepted it as a letter of resignation. However, support for Douglas remained strong among a large group in caucus, out in the business community and with sections of the general public. When caucus voted Douglas back into cabinet in August 1989, Lange resigned as leader. His deputy, Geoffrey Palmer, succeeded him as Prime Minister and Helen Clark became the first woman Deputy Prime Minister.

The public had watched the disintegration of the Government with concern and dismay. Earlier in 1989 Jim Anderton, once Labour Party president and MP for Sydenham since 1984, had resigned in protest at the Government's economic direction. He formed the New Labour Party, which he described as "centre-left", committed to a return to a more managed economy. He said that it would have 100,000 back in work within a year at a cost of $3 billion which would, he said "send Roger Douglas into a faint and lead Don Brash [the new Governor of the Reserve Bank] to slit his throat".[44] At an Auckland regional conference television cameras caught a physical clash between Labour Party factions. Public support and confidence ebbed away with the Government's credibility. There was a growing malaise: disenchantment with politicians and the system, and a sense of impotence among those who did not agree with the absolutes of the new orthodoxy. In a desperate attempt to regain voter support, the Labour caucus replaced Prime Minister Geoffrey Palmer with the populist Mike Moore just weeks before the election. It failed to make a difference. The country had turned its face away. The Government which entered in a landslide was crushed in the worst defeat for an incumbent Administration since the 1935 elections had brought the first Labour Government to power.

Prime Minister David Lange (right) and Finance Minister Roger Douglas (left) were jubilant at the electorate's response in the 1987 election, but within a few months their close working relationship had begun to disintegrate.

The Edgecumbe Earthquake

Bronwyn Joyce was at a cattle sale at the Te Teko saleyards when the 1987 Edgecumbe earthquake started:

The stock stood motionless, like statues, hardly breathing, as if they were waiting for the "starters" gun.

And, as if at a given signal, they all started twitching, pushing, shoving, milling – they were determined to break out of captivity. "What the hell's the matter with them all?" the agent shouted as they pushed against the rails and the gate and rocked the hefty platform he was standing on. The stockmen's dogs took off in all directions with the hair on their backs standing on end. They wouldn't be around if the stock did go berserk and break loose. It was worse than that, all hell broke loose.

The ground at the saleyards lifted at least six feet high in the air, leaving great cavities and fissures that a man could get lost in. It stayed up and shook like shaking a doormat. People were falling around on to the ground trying in vain to clutch at whatever was within their reach. They crawled and rolled and tried to lie flat on the ground but it kept opening up all around them and closing again.

Some men were clinging to the stock pens – they were being shaken like a rag doll in a puppy's mouth, their feet were swinging in the air. Some of the stock agents had been thrown into the midst of the cattle in the enclosures. The concrete slabs under the pens had just about stood on end, the gates burst open. The cattle bolted and clambered through the broken gates stampeding over anything or anyone in their path. Then the ground and concrete slabs dropped back almost to the same position again, leaving only gaping cracks as evidence.[i]

[i] Bronwyn Joyce, The Edgecumbe Earthquake cited in Bob Brockie (ed.), *I was there! Dramatic First-hand Accounts from New Zealand's History*, Penguin Books (NZ) Ltd, Auckland, 1998, p. 251.

NZM Archive

Kohanga Reo (language nest) was first proposed by elders at the Hui Whakatauira in 1981 in response to research which indicated the Maori language was dying out. By 1990, there were 550 around the country and six Kura Kaupapa, total immersion Maori language schools.

People pause to caress Te Mauri, the greenstone boulder that embodied the life force of the "Te Maori" exhibition.

In a decade of increasingly fractious exchanges between Maori and Pakeha in general, and Maori and Government in particular, the Te Maori exhibition provided a momentary truce.

At sunrise one recent morning, two grimacing Maori warriors headed for the steps of the Metropolitan Museum of Art. They wore loin cloths, jabbed the dawn with their spears and stuck their tongues out like lizards. Their faces were tattooed, and the two stood out even in New York.

Crouching and pouncing, the warriors led some 90 Maori men and women (in feathered cloaks, dresses and business suits) past a sizeable crowd of alerted journalists, cameramen, guests, museum employees and joggers winded by the sight. Eventually, the entire assembly entered the museum and proceeded to an exhibition of Maori carvings.[45]

The very foreignness of this newspaper report – the scene and its participants so foreign to American eyes, the writer's description ludicrously foreign to Kiwi readers – comes as a jolt. Just for a moment time shifts, the past comes forward, there is a brief insight into the struggle of the first Europeans to these shores to fit its native inhabitants into more familiar imagery. The Te Maori exhibition, 174 taonga on an

Newsmedia, Auckland (Auckland Star Collection)

Ralph Hotere and Hone Tuwhare

Painter Ralph Hotere, a kaumatua of Maori art and one of New Zealand's leading abstractionists.

Hotere

When you offer only three
vertical lines precisely drawn
and set into a dark pool of lacquer
it is a visual kind of starvation:

and even though my eye-balls
roll up and over to peer inside
myself, when I reach the beginning
of your eternity I say instead : hell
let's have another feed of mussels

LIKE I HAVE TO THINK ABOUT IT, MAN.

When you stack horizontal lines
into vertical columns which appear
to advance, recede, shimmer and wave
like exploding packs of cards
I merely grunt and say : well, if it
is not a famine, it's a feast.

I HAVE TO ROLL ANOTHER SMOKE, MAN.

But when you score a superb orange
Circle on a purple thought base
I shake my head and say : hell, what
Is this thing, called love

LIKE, I'M EUCHERED MAN, I'M ECLIPSED.[i]

Hone Tuwhare – one of the first and leading exponents of Maori literature in English.

Hone Tuwhare's first poems were published in the 1960s. Over the intervening years he has become one of the country's best-known poets, his poems thoughtful and humorous.

Ralph Hotere is among the country's foremost abstractionists and has been referred to as one of the kaumatua of Maori art along with Selwyn Muru, Paratene Matchett and Arnold Wilson. Hotere has works in major public and private collections and has exhibited both in New Zealand and overseas. He said of his work: "I have provided for the spectator a starting point which, upon contemplation, may become a nucleus revealing scores of new possibilities."[ii]

---

[i] Hone Tuwhare, "Hotere", *Come Rail, Hail*, University of Otago, Dunedin, 1970.
[ii] Ralph Hotere, *Waikato Art Gallery Bulletin No. 4*, Waikato Art Gallery on behalf of the Recreation & Cultural Committee, Hamilton City Council.

incredibly successful year-long tour of the United States during 1985 and 1986, was a by-product and the public face of a second Maori cultural renaissance which had begun in the late Sixties. Later, when the exhibition toured New Zealand, local crowds saw it as a celebration of Maori and of New Zealand.

In just one generation, between the end of the Second World War and the early Seventies, "Maori changed from a rural to an urban people, a transition which took Pakeha four generations".[46] In 1945, 88 per cent of Maori had lived in the country; by 1981 over 80 per cent dwelt in towns and cities. By the beginning of the 1980s unemployment figures for Maori youth were up to five times higher than Pakeha's; and there were more young Maori – only 4.4 per cent of Maori were over 60, against 15.6 per cent of non-Maori.[47] "Any Maori," said activist Donna Awatere, "is more likely to be unemployed, will earn a lot less and have to support more people than any white."[48] In a period of rapidly rising crime and prison populations, the percentage of Maori in prison rose even faster, from 18 per cent of the prison population in 1950 to 48 per cent in 1989.[49] Out in the suburbs a new phenomenon became newsworthy: "white flight". In Auckland's Otara 55 per cent of the local schools' population in 1965 was white; by 1980 Pakeha children represented 12 per cent of the school rolls, and in 1981 some schools had less than 3 per cent white children attending.[50] John Minto's prediction in 1981 that local racial issues would become more prominent proved true.

A number of increasingly vocal young Maori radicals challenged white society, its stranglehold on all the institutions of power, its very right to be here. Their polemic was confrontational, challenging everything European society had done since their arrival. They called for the return of Maori land, for a bicultural society, and for sovereignty:

Maori sovereignty is the Maori ability to determine our own destiny and to do so from the basis of our land and fisheries. In essence, Maori sovereignty seeks nothing less than the acknowledgement that New Zealand is Maori land, and further seeks the return of that land. At its most conservative it could be interpreted

KZ-7 represented New Zealand's first attempt to win the America's Cup race for 12-metre yachts off Fremantle during the summer of 1986/87.

Daniel Forster

Gil Hanly

Happy and glorious but not yet victorious... race sponsor Michael Fay (front right) with skipper Chris Dickson parade up Queen Street to a heroes' welcome.

as the desire for a bicultural society, one in which taha Maori receives an equal consideration with, and equally determines the course of this country as taha Pakeha. It certainly demands an end to monoculturalism....

The aim of Maori Sovereignty is not to achieve equality in white terms, but in Maori terms. The aim therefore has nothing to do with getting more "education" or making more money. The aim is to redesign this country's institutions from a Maori point of view. The aim is to reclaim all land and work it from a Maori point of view. The aim is to enter the Pacific arena from a Maori point of view. To forge a distinctive New Zealand identity from a Maori point of view.

Asking questions like "What does that mean for me? Does it mean I have to leave New Zealand?" merely reflect white paranoia and an assumption that we Maori as a race have the same distaste for you as you have had for us all these years.

White people are not superior.

British culture is not superior.

New Zealand is not British.

This country belongs to the Maori. This country is Polynesian. The immigrants who invaded us have always used violence and implied violence against us to impose the white will over the Maori. Nothing has changed. The white line-up has guns, weapons, prisons and a history of domination on its side. Nothing has changed....

The white line-up fingers its weapons. Yet again. Ready to do violence.... There is no sitting on the fence. For the Maori, without sovereignty we are dead as a nation. It is not sovereignty or no sovereignty. It is sovereignty or nothing. We have no choice.[51]

White New Zealand responded often with hostility – there were complaints to the race relations conciliator, accusations that Maori had already received special and preferential treatment over the years to redress inequalities, that what Maori was asking for was separatism, no different from South Africa's much-reviled Apartheid. Once the Waitangi Tribunal was given a mandate to hear claims dating back to 1840, many Pakeha reacted as if their home and hearth were under direct threat of confiscation. At a 1988 New Zealand Planning Council conference on Pakeha perspectives on the Treaty, Sir Ken Keith said that "this is not a time to be comfortable".[52] Many Pakeha were increasingly discomforted. High profile cases, like that of Allan Titford who lost his farm at Maunganui Bluff in a claim by local iwi, represented the anger and incomprehension felt by many whites and the belief that old wrongs were being righted by new wrongs: now they were being treated unfairly.

The Labour Government had adopted a policy of multiculturalism, a word which quickly became part of the debate. Pakeha seized it as a term neatly describing an increasingly racially diverse society. Maori saw this leap from monoculturalism to multiculturalism conveniently vaulting the thorny concept of biculturalism. It was just another way to avoid the issue of their status within the country:

... espousal of multiculturalism is the reactionary Pakeha response to the reality of biculturalism. The ideology of multiculturalism is resorted to as a mask for Pakeha hegemony and to maintain the monocultural dominance in New Zealand....

Biculturalism is predicated on the basis that there are tangata whenua, indigenous people of the land, and non-indigenous colonisers.[53]

Hikoi to Waitangi

Hikoi Hikoi
Walking, running, driving cars
We're all going to Waitangi
Gonna set my people free
Hikoi Hikoi.

Arrive at Waitangi. 4,500 of us. Kaumatua in the front. The Governor-General only wants to see 100 of us. Police blockade the bridge. His demand was designed to create division. We were meant to disembowel each other – "No radicals allowed." Who are the radicals? The old people decide – We hikoi together, we get heard together: it's un-Maori for some to go ahead and the bulk stay behind.

Just as in 1840 when the Treaty was signed on the union jack instead of a korowai as suggested by elders, today in 1984 the intentions of the government are still not honourable. Anything fruitful is not meant to eventuate.

The Governor-General is sad at being kept waiting for two and a half hours. Maoris have been waiting for 144 years on government terms. The press plays up the incident as if to say Maoris missed their chance. We missed an audience with someone who was going to tell us the Treaty is still okay....

Kia ora
a marcher [i]

[i] Waitangi Action Committee, Te Hikoi Ki Waitangi 1984, The Waitangi Action Committee, Auckland, 1984, pp. 54-5.

For nearly a decade Richard Hadlee dominated New Zealand bowling. He was New Zealand's best bowler and later the world's record wicket taker. His amazing consistency, speed and guile helped New Zealand to its success in the "Golden Eighties" of cricket.

Perhaps the most important development of the Eighties was the joining forces of radical protesters and more conservative organisations of Maoridom. In the opening years of the decade, protesters continued to use the ceremonial of Waitangi Day to express their frustration, their anger at lack of progress for Maori and at Governments' failure to act. They did so without the approval of many elders and other groups. In 1984, all that changed. The previous year the New Zealand Maori Council had summarised modern Maori feeling on the issue central to their debate with Government – the land:

Maori land has several cultural connotations for us. It provides us with a sense of identity. It is proof of our continued existence not only as a people, but as the tangata whenua of this country. It is proof of our tribal and kin ties. Maori land represents turangawaewae.

It is proof of our link with ancestors of the past, and of generations yet to

The Underarm Incident

The most infamous ball of the decade – if not of the century. Trevor Chappell delivers the underarm ball to Brian McKechnie. It was the last ball of the day in the third and final one day contest of the Benson & Hedges World Series Cup. The teams were locked at one-all and New Zealand needed six runs to win.

In front of a record crowd of almost 53,000 at the Melbourne Cricket Ground, Australian captain Greg Chappell instructed his brother to deliver a grubber. Australia won the match and the series, but it was a hollow victory tainted by Australia's lack of sportsmanship.

come. It is an assurance that we shall forever exist as a people for as long as the land shall exist. But also land is a resource providing even greater support for our people – to provide employment, to provide us with sites for dwellings, and to provide an income to help support our people and to maintain our marae and tribal assets.[54]

In 1984 for the first time two of the oldest Maori political movements, the Kingitanga which "emerged from behind its isolationist stance in political matters"[55] and Kotahitanga, joined the Waitangi Action Committee for the Hikoi Ki Waitangi, a peaceful march by over 4,000 Maori, representatives of the churches and Pakeha protest groups to stop the celebrations. The Hikoi represented a new Maori solidarity and "a watershed in the Maori struggle for self-determination".[56] One of the activists who had taken part in the occupation of Bastion Point in the late 1970s was among the marchers:

> *For me, I marched because:*
>
> *As a Maori, I know that successive governments have never honoured the Treaty so I'm not going to sit down and pretend everything is okay.*
>
> *The Waitangi celebrations are a slap in the face, it's like being paid wages with a dud cheque.*
>
> *The Treaty has a lot to do with the future of children in this country. I'm not going to sit around and hope someone else will fix it up for me.*
>
> *Maoris have tried all the proper channels, protest might move things faster.*[57]

The final years of the Eighties produced a breakthrough in the Maori struggle to regain some control of resources. A unanimous finding by the Court of Appeal ruled in favour of the Maori Council who had gone to court to stop crown lands being transferred to the newly created SOEs when ownership was under dispute and claims were before the Waitangi Tribunal. The court ruled that "the principles of the Treaty of Waitangi override everything else in the State Owned Enterprises Act... [and that] those principles require that Pakeha and Maori treaty partners [are] to act towards each other reasonably and with the utmost good faith".[58] A similar claim to protect fishing rights was filed by Muriwhenua of the Far North and the Maori Council, first with the Waitangi Tribunal and then in the High Court. It brought a judicial ruling that put an interim stop to the issue of fishing quota under the new Quota Management System until Maori rights to the fisheries were resolved. Attempts by the Government to return 50 per cent of the fisheries to Maori

Television New Zealand

Local content on New Zealand television grew in air time and variety. Comedian Billy T. James (above) earned a huge following and crossed successfully into film in "Came a Hot Friday". There was also "Comedy Playhouse", "Lynn of Tawa" and "Gliding On". Drama series proliferated – "Mortimer's Patch", "Under the Mountain", "Jocko", "Country G.P.", "Inside Straight", "Children of the Dog Star", "Hanlon", "Pioneer Women" and "Gloss" (below). The first telefilms were made, including "Among the Cinders", and three of leading playwright Bruce Mason's plays were successfully adapted for television.

Television New Zealand

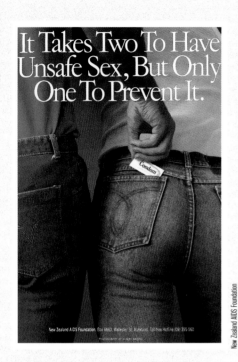

New freedoms had their price and the incidence of sexually transmitted diseases increased in the 1980s. AIDS was the most deadly and had the highest profile, but health workers also warned of the spread of chlamydia, herpes, genital warts and non-specific genital infections. Gonorrhoea and syphilis became less common.

ownership over 20 years brought it under intense pressure from the Opposition in Parliament and the powerful fishing industry. The 1989 Maori Fisheries Act gave back 10 per cent of the fisheries and established a Maori Fisheries Commission with a grant of $10 million.

Twenty years of friction between Maori and Pakeha, of much greater awareness of each other because of closer physical proximity, had produced tensions and conflict. But it had other more benign influences as well. Historian and writer Michael King believed it was responsible in part for the gradual emergence of a "second indigenous culture":

> The existence of the tangata whenua has… put me in touch with symbols that may arise out of the whole of human collective consciousness, but here are Maori and therefore indigenously New Zealand in idiom. It has exposed me to concepts – the mauri of people and places, tapu, mana, whenuatanga, whanaungatanga – that, again, have their roots in this part of the world, but are also universal in occurrence, value and application.
>
> My brush with all these things doesn't make me Maori. But they are an essential part of the experience that makes me Pakeha – experiences I could not have had access to in any other part of the world. For a growing number of people, even those who react negatively to the encounter, Pakeha-ness embraces some experience of Maori history, habits, values and expectations.[59]

The Eighties also saw the flowering of an indigenous culture of another kind. The increasing self-awareness of our place in the world released an outpouring of writing, painting, music, film and theatrical work. New Zealand names appeared in international arenas previously not even approached. In 1985 Keri Hulme's novel *The Bone People* won the British Booker prize. The previous year it had won the fiction prize in the New Zealand Book Awards and the American Pegasus Prize for Literature. Writers such as Janet Frame, Maurice Shadbolt, C. K. Stead, Fleur Adcock, Allen Curnow and Lauris Edmond had audiences overseas as well as locally. Maori writers Hone Tuwhare, Witi Ihimaera, Patricia Grace and Alan Duff described lives and landscapes both familiar and separate.

Vincent Ward's film *Vigil* had an in-competition screening at the 1984 Cannes Film Festival. The late Seventies and early Eighties were the local film industry's most productive period since its inception, until tax changes removed tax shelter aspects in film funding. As finance dried up, many of this new pool of talent moved off-shore to join the industry in Australia, England and America. In the art world painters, print makers, sculptors, photographers and craftspeople brought a stronger and stronger sense of place and exploration of Kiwi lives within it. Conversely, and perhaps because of a growing distance from their forebears' place of origin and increased confidence in their own place here, more and more Pakeha New Zealanders began using the new genealogy sections of public libraries and archives, tracing their family roots, creating their own histories and whakapapa.

Despite all the new freedoms, the century's dark seam of censorship remained. The thought police and the morally righteous who wanted society in their likeness were sometimes savage in their attempts to shut out dissenting voices. And censorship in the 1980s also came from unexpected directions, "the new stormtroopers of the Left"[60] with opinions and beliefs far from conservative. We entered the new territory and terminology of the "politically correct":

> *... among others, the more extreme campaigners against smoking and liquor advertising, those in the Maori community who will not allow the Pakeha voice to be heard, some elements in the campaign against video pornography, and anyone who would deny the right to speak of people who oppose, for example, homosexual law reform or abortion or who favour, for example, the American position on ANZUS.... Those people who howl down arguments with which they disagree, who walk out of conferences when a speaker who cannot be guaranteed to push their line takes the rostrum, who demand that certain points of view should not be published (and who picket publications when they are) betray a fundamental lack of confidence in their own arguments. They seem so threatened by an opposition they must regard as powerfully seductive that they prefer gagging it to defeating it in rational debate.*[61]

At the end of this decade of turbulent change, the outside world broke into Kiwi consciousness and living rooms. Television (now three channels, one of them privately owned by a consortium that included overseas interests) and the newspapers were full of images of the Berlin Wall being broken down by cheering Germans from East and West. In the USSR, President Mikhail Gorbachov with his policy of "glasnost" (openness) took no retaliatory action, unlike his predecessors. The potent and ugly symbol of the Cold War's "Iron Curtain" lay in rubble. Western commentators would soon predict the inevitable demise of communism and capitalism's triumph. Christmas was only days away. The scenes of reunion and joy in Berlin lightened local gloom and seemed an ideal beginning for the century's final decade.

New Zealand Film Archive (NZFC Collection)

Jordan Luck

DANCE EXPONENTS

Prayers be Answered

During the 1980s there was an explosion of local music, drama and dance and an audience with a growing appetite for home grown works.

Bruno Lawrence with Greer Robson in "Smash Palace". The film was successful at home and abroad. The "New York Times" named it one of the 10 best films of the year.

The Win Family
Living with Uncertainty

Michael Win and Nicholas Morgan are from the latest generations of the Win family. In 1842, their forebears emigrated to Nelson with the New Zealand Company from Glamorgan, South Wales. Since then the family's fortunes have waxed and waned, often in tandem with national and agricultural highs and lows. The pattern of Nicholas's and Michael's lives in the 1990s has also echoed the decade's trends.

Michael Win has continued the family connection with agricultural production, albeit beyond the farm gate. From mid-1997 he worked in the meat industry as a sales and marketing manager. In the mid-Eighties, he completed a degree in business studies at Massey University, majoring in marketing. His first jobs were with an insurance company and a brewery, before he and his wife Helen Cameron, a wool buyer, headed overseas. Two years later they returned and settled in Christchurch. It was 1992. Unemployment was running as high as 12 per cent and the local economy in Canterbury was very depressed. Michael's life followed a pattern that became familiar to many during the 1990s:

It took me eight months to secure a job in Christchurch. Since 1992 I have been in four jobs and two were terminated through redundancy. I would say the period of time I've been unemployed is around about two years in total. I don't feel I'm totally hopeless, so I guess for someone like me there's a level of self-confidence the first time where you think, "Yeah, okay. I'm not a slug. I've got a degree. I've got some good solid work experience. I'll find a job. One will come along." And eventually one does.

But the second and the third time, it starts to grind you down a bit: that through no fault of your own, you're again out in the workforce looking for another job. You're competing with people who are of similar ilk, and you are interviewing with people who are just as good as you. So, yes, it starts to sap your confidence. Not in terms of not feeling you are capable. Just the fact that you're having to do the whole thing again and again.

I've always loved New Zealand. I've been overseas and I've seen other countries and I still believe quite honestly that New Zealand is a better place than most of the countries I've seen. You haven't got a huge population. It's got a lot of sound agriculturally based markets. If worst comes to worst, we'll never starve.

I wouldn't wish being unemployed on anyone, and I certainly feel for a lot of people who are out there and are unemployed. It's not pleasant. But you know, you've got to get out there and fight for yourself and look after number one, because no one else is going to hold your hand. If you sit down and do nothing, you're not doing anybody any good. If you get out there and do something, you're being good for yourself and you're still contributing to society. Our family has taken a few knocks; but I don't know that that's isolated. There's a lot of families out there that have taken knocks. I guess it's how you handle those knocks. I think they most

Michael Win – a fervent believer in working to live rather than living to work.

Rebecca and Nicholas Morgan – facing a tougher future than their parents' generation.

likely make you stronger or more philosophical about life. You are dealt a set of cards on a day-to-day basis and you've got to play them effectively. Resenting something is so counter-productive.

I've been working since I left university, and Rogernomics has been a big influence on my working life, as it has been for everybody who's worked since that policy came into place. It has doubtless given a few freedoms that weren't out there before. But it's also taken a few things away – security and things like that, which everybody likes to have. I think the changes since 1984 have been good and bad. In terms of the economy, it has made New Zealand a more mature country, a more globally thinking country, less introspective if you like. But it has also been a bad thing. I still believe there's a large group of middle class people who do all right for themselves. But there's a definite gap out there between those who have a great deal and those who have very little.

Michael's cousin Penny Morgan, Nicholas Morgan's mother, looks at the lives of her children in the 1990s and compares them with her own experience. Penny and Chris Morgan know about the stresses of the current job market – "Chris has been restructured about five times and there's always the threat of redundancy in his job" – but it wasn't like that when they were starting out:

Chris and I were the last of what I would say are the lucky generation – free education, free varsity, picking the job you wanted to when you left school. But for Nicholas and Rebecca I've got grave concerns, the way the country's going. Their future is going to be really tough, tougher than ours, with their student loans and lack of jobs.

Nicholas Morgan is at Lincoln University doing a Bachelor of Resource Studies. He hopes to get a job advising people on the Resource Management Act and environmental monitoring. However, he knows there is no guarantee of suitable work.

When I started out, I thought [the cost] was all right – $1,800 in 1994. Now it's $3,500 and they're talking about next year going up another $700. It'll be over $4,000 for the course. It's one of the most expensive degrees at Lincoln. I don't know if the education is even going to be of value for job prospects. I know people who have done degrees and worked for DoC [Department of Conservation], who have a degree to clean toilets. So what's the use of that! At the end of this year [1998] I'll owe the Government $25,000 for my student loan. I haven't really thought about how I'm going to pay it back yet. There are several options: go out and find a job; go on the dole, I suppose; or, favourite at the moment is to go bankrupt, get rid of it. Don't know if I'll do that.

My generation's been landed with this and I'm a bit pee'd off actually. Everyone else has got a free education and then this generation has been lumped with it. In the future it's going to cost everyone. No one's really thought of that social cost yet.

I've been on a few protests, occupied the Registry, and bashed down the Chamber doors and occupied there two years ago. I'm pretty involved in marches but I haven't been on one this year because assignments and work just came at the wrong time. But there will be a few more marches when the fee-setting round comes up.

The atmosphere among students at the moment is fairly down. People are finding it hard to pass their exams and keep the money going. Lots of people have second jobs. That's hard. Everyone's waiting for a change of Government, waiting for an Alliance Government because hopefully loans will be wiped, and perhaps there'll be lower fees and things like that.

The way things have turned out, perhaps I should have done something else. Perhaps gone to polytechnic and got a smaller loan, or something like that. Because in the end a degree is not worth that much. I know people who are out working now, who've got money. I haven't got any money. I've just got a big debt.

Sources: Edited Ninox transcripts from *Our People, Our Century*, 1999. All photographs from the Win Family Collection.

1990

Chapter 10

Made It, Lost It?

2000

Gil Hanly

Dame Kiri Te Kanawa bringing a love of opera to thousands at open air concerts.

We were the sophisticates of the South Pacific. We had arrived. From the culinary tradition of toad-in-the-hole we now toyed with tabbouleh and tacos, savoured sushi and fell for felafel and feta. On the menus of the cafe society, dishes like hummus and couscous cooed at our curiosity while yum cha challenged it. Along with the best European dishes, all of these were available in the new cosmopolitan New Zealand, together with its fine vintages. From our early wines – which ought to have carried health warnings – we had progressed and now produced some of the world's best.

In other ways too we showed our informal urbanity. At open air opera in Auckland, Kiwis spread their blankets out on the ground of the Domain to hear their own Diva, Kiri Te Kanawa. Beneath a canopy of stars on a warm summer night her voice soared, its purity silencing the 200,000 people before her.

We had other stars too – 1996 Olympic swimming champion Danyon Loader, equestrian Mark Todd, athlete Beatrice Faumuina, yachtsman Sir Peter Blake, our own Academy Award winner Anna Paquin (for *The Piano*), the band Crowded House, and others. For us, arrival also meant departure from old cringes. But among the gains of new-found maturity was also a loss of innocence, as we watched judges, high ranking public officials, businessmen, lawyers, doctors and accountants all go through the courts.

Materially we seemed better off than ever before, but only if we turned our backs on poverty elsewhere. For many homes, two cars were now the standard and not the showy luxury they would have been 30 years earlier. And what cars – new Mercedes and BMWs, and the occasional Ferrari, but mostly Japanese cast-offs with suspect odometers. With more cars came another Nineties term: gridlock. Its chokehold was felt most keenly in the biggest centre, Auckland.

Durable All Black captain Sean Fitzpatrick celebrating the first series win against South Africa in that country.

Winners: Olympic champions Mark Todd and swimmer Danyon Loader. World champion discus thrower Beatrice Faumuina.

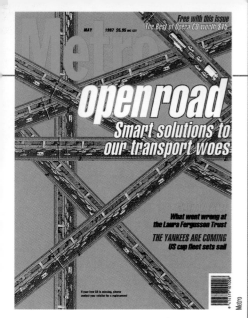

Metro

Gridlock increased. In some parts of the country, journeys of 90 minutes to and from work became not uncommon as an increasing amount of traffic jammed roading infrastructures at peak hours.

We found new distractions in the techno toys of the Internet and email, tolerated infill housing and accepted new inner-city apartments, whose well-heeled occupants prized the new sophistication in dining and nightlife. We witnessed the growth of new crimes like ram-raiding, home invasions and road rage:

> *... very minor incidents... all too often trigger outbursts of what has become known as road rage.... In October* [1996], *a Lower Hutt driver was charged with threatening to kill following an incident where he was tailgated by a truck which he had just overtaken.*[1]

We wondered at another growth – the rise of TB and other conditions from the past, some of them associated with overcrowding and poverty.

There were also plagues of other kinds – a water shortage in Auckland in 1993, fatal flash floods in Northland and droughts in Canterbury. In Auckland in February 1998, retailers, corporates and city apartment dwellers endured the unimaginable – a power blackout which left the heart of the city without reliable power for five weeks. Aucklanders discovered they had no power over electricity supply, or over Mercury Energy, the electricity board they had once owned.

In the South Island High Country the fight against rabbits became ever more urgent as vast hillsides swarmed with the pests first introduced in 1838 to provide shooting sport. Tony Gloag, an Omarama farmer, described the distress rabbits caused as they spread across the land "unrelenting like the tide":

Internet

The Twenties were wired for sound, the Sixties for vision. In the Nineties we were simply wired – and at a rapid rate, as the Internet continued to outstrip expectations. A census of Internet service providers in 1998 showed there were an estimated 215,000 Internet access accounts in New Zealand.

In 1997, Kiwis spent more money on buying PCs than they did on television sets. According to Statistics New Zealand, they spent $156 million on computers and $112 million on TV sets as they found new ways of communicating and entertaining themselves.[i]

Online shopping became more readily accepted as Net users discovered bargains from mostly online stores in the United States. They also became more relaxed about supplying their credit card details as they shopped in cyberspace. But Kiwi net users not only shopped and did business over the Internet – they made friends and even married. Serina Robinson, of Palm Beach Florida, and Darryl Caughey, of Panmure, Auckland, first met in cyberspace. Both were caring for dying loved ones. Both discovered that a computer screen offered more than its television counterpart:

On December 22 last year [1997] *they sent out invitations and celebrated a cyber-wedding in a chat room called Dream Girls with virtual guests, virtual gifts, a virtual celebrant and virtual wedding bands.*[ii]

After a few months they decided to turn the virtual relationship into a physical one and in October 1998 they married – in real time and with real gold.

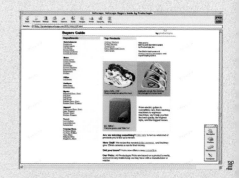

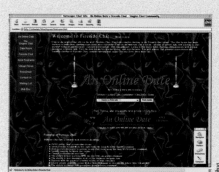

[i] *Management* magazine, February 1998, p. 42.
[ii] *New Zealand Herald*, 1 October 1998.

Years went past with progress made,
Memories of pests began to fade,
Governments came, and governments went,
Policy changed to some extent.
The people said "It's all awry
to kill rabbits with TPI". [Taxpayer input]
Grants and subsidies became passé
Rabbits again came out to play.[2]

In the winter of 1997, the calicivirus was introduced illegally to kill off high country rabbits. Nobody has yet discovered who brought the virus into the country and spread it, but the results for some farmers meant that rabbit control costs dropped from $30,000 to $2,000 a year.

In the Nineties, we sent medical and support teams to two wars – a limited commitment which indicated an important shift in public opinion since the Vietnam conflict nearly 30 years earlier.

We finally grew up not as the Asians some politicians would have had us believe, but as Kiwis living in the Pacific Rim. We looked to Asia for trade and, in the early Nineties, for immigrants. Changes in government policy in the early 1990s resulted in an emphasis on qualifications and financial standing for would-be immigrants. Between 1991 and 1996, there was a 70.8 per cent increase in the number of Asians in New Zealand and they made up 4.6 per cent of the population (160,680). By comparison, the Pacific Island population made up 5 per cent (173,181), their number having increased by 13.2 per cent. Maori comprised 15.1 per cent of the population (523,371), an increase of 20.4 per cent. Europeans were the only group to record a decrease – of 2.1 per cent. Europeans accounted for 74.8 per cent of the population (2,594,688).[3] New Zealand had a new ethnic dynamic, but a nation accustomed to associating the East with the "Yellow Peril" did not adapt easily to the sudden and heavy wave of Asian migration. This increased at such pace that it became a political issue in 1996. The previous year had seen 49,482 residency approvals – more than half of them from North Asia. Britain provided the next biggest source of migrants.[4]

On the election trail in 1996, New Zealand First leader Winston Peters pledged to cut immigration to 10,000 a year. Meanwhile, the new wave of migrants busied themselves and transformed parts of Auckland, where most Asian migrants chose to stay:

How cosmopolitan Otahuhu has become can be seen by strolling along Criterion Lane....
The lane leads to the solid masonry of the Criterion pub, but before pedestrians reach the watering hole they pass the Taro Merchant, Bhula's Foodmarket, the Sun King Tai grocery and the Man Ming barbecue takeaway with rows of basted ducks and spare ribs gleaming brown gold in the window.[5]

NZM Archive

Droughts in Canterbury and elsewhere all hinted at wider climatic change in a warmer New Zealand.

New Zealand First leader Winston Peters, the "People's Treasurer", 1997.

Evening Post

Asians celebrate their culture at a festival in mid-city Auckland in 1999.

Within society there were other dynamics at work, too. The mainstream Christian churches – Anglican, Catholic, Presbyterian and Methodist – all suffered a reduction of membership. Only the Pentecostal churches increased their numbers – and dramatically. Otherwise, New Zealanders were becoming a Godless lot. Those who stated they had "no religion" increased markedly between 1991 and 1996, rising by 33 per cent to make up over a quarter of the population in 1996. By comparison non-Christian faiths – Buddhism, Islam and Hinduism – showed increases of up to 122 per cent, though each of these groups still made up less than 1 per cent of the population.[6]

Throughout the decade Maori consolidated the gains made by their radicalism 20 years earlier. The Crown addressed its obligations under the Treaty of Waitangi with gravity and concern. By 1998 fiscal settlements for claims ranging from land confiscations and other historical injustices amounted to just over $530 million.[7] One of the biggest and most significant settlements was the Tainui claim and the final reading of the Tainui Settlement Bill in Parliament was emotionally charged:

> ... the visitors sang, cried and applauded MPs who stood to support the passing of the Bill.... Speaker of the House Peter Tapsell began the session with a karakia which once again broke with [Parliamentary] tradition. Mr Graham [Minister of Treaty Negotiations] then rose and asked for the Bill to be passed into law. He said the time had arrived to end the struggle for the return of land. During his speech Mr Graham had to pause to regain his composure, as he was overcome by the emotion which was felt throughout the House.[8]

As the delicate process of reaching for an understanding of the Maori-Pakeha past continued, it began to test race relations. When combined with the influx of Asians and other new immigrants from a range of unusual ethnic backgrounds, it forced New Zealanders to confront a diversity of cultural perspectives. But whether they were Maori or migrant, believer or atheist, rich or poor – as Kiwis, they saw dramatic political and constitutional change during the decade. Some of it grew from their own disaffection.

Queen Elizabeth II signing the historic Tainui settlement in Government House Wellington, 1995.

Out of the indecent haste of Labour they came, past the summertime gold of Auckland's 1990 Commonwealth Games, and into the reassuring arms of the Decent Society. In October 1990, New Zealanders dumped the Labour Government. For the past six years Labour, which traditionally stood for working people, had neglected their interests in favour of the market. National, campaigning with a slogan for a "Decent Society", seemed to offer a

return to more consensual policies. And so on October 27, armed with anger and voting papers, Kiwis had their say. National won a majority of 38 seats (67-29). One seat went to traditional Labour stalwart Jim Anderton, who had founded his own breakaway New Labour Party. It was the biggest re-structuring of incumbent politicians since 1935 and, for Labour, the worst result since 1931.[9]

Though the results were flattering it was hardly an endorsement of National's policies for the party increased its share only marginally (by 3.8 per cent).[10] Voters had seen off unpopular Rogernomics, but the long quest for social justice had always collided with another national characteristic – authoritarianism. No sooner were Kiwis out of Labour's experiment than they found themselves thrust into National's social laboratory.

Once again the experiment was guided by economic theory – but theory contradicted the century-old pragmatism of both the populace and its politicians. The cost of their theorising was high and out of the New Right, the New Poor came – and stayed. Foodbanks organised by charities and churches began assisting the families as poverty and unemployment grew. In 1985, 38,419 unemployment benefits were paid out. In 1991, the figure was 146, 812.[11]

For voters, the future seemed to lie with National, but senior Ministers found themselves facing their own financial crises. The first lay with the Bank of New Zealand which needed a $600 million injection of funds. The second lay in Treasury briefing

Polynesians held fast to their cultures in New Zealand and are shown (top) making tapa cloth. Above, a group of Niueans prepare food while below, others are captured celebrating at a multi–cultural festival.

Gil Hanly

Kiwi Ingenuity

Throughout the century, Kiwis continued to tinker and innovate, sometimes in ways which made the rest of the world sit up and take notice. Richard Pearse pioneered flight in this country as the new century began. In Wellington, businessman William Bacon invented a patent lock which he sold to an American company. It is now universally known as the Yale lock. In 1936, Bill Gallagher began experimenting and produced Gallagher Power Fencing (TM) – the electric fence.

Generation after generation used the Thermette, which boiled water rapidly from twigs, leaves or newspapers. It was invented by John A. Hart in the late 1920s and was dubbed the "Benghazi burner" by Kiwi troops who were issued with it during the North African campaign.

In 1973 John A. Hough devised the Tullen snips which can cut anything from cloth to steel. Two years later, Rongotea housewife Norma McCulloch developed the deep freeze pump, a simple cardboard tunnel system of extracting air from plastic bags. In 1992 two Wellington inventors, Graham Collins and Richard Newson, teamed up with Auckland businessman Dennis Tindall to market their now internationally successful chemical-free weed control system. There were countless other inventors and innovations throughout the century. For Kiwis, the challenge of finding solutions, often with meagre materials, has been irresistible.

Sources: Hamish Keith, *New Zealand Yesterdays*, Readers Digest, Sydney, 1984; and Bob Riley, *Kiwi Ingenuity, A Book of New Zealand Ideas and Inventions*, AIT Press, Auckland, 1995.

papers which told the incoming Government that in the absence of changes to government policy, the country faced a deficit of $3.7 billion in 1991/92 and larger deficits in following years. Ruth Richardson later described the dilemma faced by the Government:

> We were caught in a double bind. We had been surprised at the size of the deficits we inherited. At the same time our manifesto contained commitments – particularly on superannuation – that should not have been made. Keeping our promises would make our fiscal task even harder. Failing to keep our promises would cause huge political fallout. The scene was set for the loss of moral authority that would dog the Government for the whole of its first term in office.[12]

Within two months of being elected, National announced a series of benefit cuts which would remove, on average, $25 per week from most beneficiaries.[13] There were tighter eligibility rules and a longer stand-down period (from six to a maximum of 26 weeks) for those who wanted unemployment benefits. National's aim was to remove $1.275 billion from the social welfare budget. Then, in her 1991 Budget, Richardson changed the social landscape and the welfare state. Policy initiatives ranged from new methods of labour bargaining to dramatic increases in State housing rentals and a restructured and untested health system with part charges for hospital services. All of it caused a storm of largely impotent protest and even the august *Oxford History of New Zealand* offered its own condemnation:

> Once again, a major change in social policy had been instituted without any trials or pilot schemes, in quite indecent haste, and almost total absence of consultation with the professionals who actually staffed the health system.[14]

A combination of two policy initiatives had a lasting and damaging impact on New Zealand's emerging underclass: the benefit cuts and the move to put State housing, even with the new accommodation supplement, on a market rental basis. Housing reform showed similar "indecent haste", secrecy and private sector interest, all noted by former Housing Corporation Board member Elizabeth McLeay when she pointed to the absence of consultation with community or housing organisations:

> And because the changes took place as part of successive budgetary packages, the critical scrutinising roles of the Opposition and the mass media were ineffectual....[15]

In South Auckland, poor families voted with their feet, abandoning their State homes to double up with relatives or to sleep in garages, a solution which worried health officials because of overcrowding.[16]

On Budget night 1991, National sacked 14 elected health boards described by Ruth Richardson as "unwieldy institutions". The party's manifesto had promised their retention.[17] The boards were replaced first by appointed commissioners, then by profit-oriented Crown Health Enterprises (CHEs). In 1996 the medicine of reform continued but the conditions of some patients worsened.

Down on the farm with
Prime Minister Jim Bolger (left).

Someone visiting a friend was told that she had to take the bedridden patient home because the hospital needed the bed and could not get hold of the family. The staff nurse said that if the person was not moved, he would be deposited in a motel room at his own expense. How did this patient feel knowing that he was a burden on the crowded hospital that had had a wing close down because of economy? What is happening to us? Why do we make our health professionals into unhappy executioners of a heartless health policy?[18]

The commercialisation of hospital, power and harbour boards prompted alarm from former Labour Cabinet Minister Warren Freer:

Without any electorate approval, it [the Government] has cancelled the public's democratic right to elect people to control our hospitals, harbours and electricity and energy distribution as well as disposing of assets owned by the nation....[19]

By 1992 though, Richardson could point to growth in employment, the continued momentum of the recovery, and 3 per cent growth as well as a substantial reduction in government spending and taxation as percentages of GDP.[20] But, like Douglas before her, she under-estimated what lay outside the balance sheet and in many cases that was outrage. Talkback radio flourished on callers' indignation. At another level, the reforms drew criticism from leading academics who pointed to their secrecy, undemocratic implementation and their lack of mandate.

The Government must now reap the harvest it has sown. It is likely to be a bitter harvest, not merely for the National Party but for the country as a whole.[21]

The widening gap – some drove new BMWs and Japanese models in affluent suburbs while others had their own transport.

Disenchantment with politicians was illustrated by the Heylen Full Trust and Confidence Poll which showed that confidence in them had fallen from 33 per cent in 1975 to 4 per cent in 1992.[22] But that year voters had one last weapon with which to rein in political arrogance. In two referenda held in 1992 and 1993, Kiwis opted to change the electoral system from First Past the Post to proportional representation in the form of Mixed Member Proportional (MMP) representation, and the first election to be held under this system was scheduled for 1996. In the 1993 election National just scraped home, but only after there was a hung Parliament for 10 days. The party won 50 seats, Labour 45 while the Alliance and New Zealand First, led by former Labour MP Jim Anderton and former National minister Winston Peters respectively, each captured two seats.

Theirs were not the only political defections. Almost 200,000 New Zealanders

deserted the National Party during the previous three years, according to final vote tallies for the 1993 election.[23] Ruth Richardson was dropped from the finance portfolio and resigned from Parliament in July 1994. Ironically, by that time the economy had surged ahead providing the highest growth rates of the decade in 1994/95, along with a government surplus. Richardson's legacy largely remained in place, and her successors continued New Right reforms but without her ideological zeal. In 1996 however, they all knew they faced retribution at the ballot box, and from Winston Peters whose populism and attacks on the New Right won him increasing support. In July 1996 Peters said:

> *We believe that the kind of politician depicted by Bolger, Birch and Shipley is not to be promoted into cabinet. As a consequence, we will not have any truck with any of those three people.*[24]

In October he said Labour's policies were "closer to that of New Zealand First than National's".[25] In December he joined National as a coalition partner following election results that showed his party, with its 17 seats, holding the balance of power.

Peters became Treasurer and Deputy Prime Minister and won concessions – including a reversal of the profit-driven motive for public hospitals and free doctor's visits for children under six. In all, Peters secured $5 billion in spending on a variety of social areas, but he had taken a Faustian ride. His credibility vanished along with that of the new Coalition, and a new mood of disenchantment set in among Kiwis over this latest political sleight of hand.

In November 1997, while Prime Minister Jim Bolger was overseas, he was tipped from office in a coup by cabinet colleague Jenny Shipley. After almost a year of tension, the Coalition finally imploded on 12 August 1998, after Peters and New Zealand First colleagues walked out of cabinet over the sale of Wellington airport.

"Electors sold out from day one" read the headline in the *New Zealand Herald*, which singled out Peters and his party for public opprobrium. On 14 August, Prime Minister Shipley sacked Peters and then, as New Zealand First split in half, picked up enough of its dissidents to run a wobbly minority Government. Like many others, former Labour leader David Lange viewed the patchwork quilt of the new Coalition with disdain:

> *There is no moral dignity, or even political purpose, in being propped up by a ragtag crew of bolters, turncoats, illiterates and bounty hunters.*[26]

By the end of 1998, the New Zealand economy was once again officially in recession and the laughing stock of some of the world's press. The influential *Guardian Weekly* compared New Zealand with its northern hemisphere cousin, Norway, which had assiduously avoided New Right policies in favour of consensus and partnership. Since 1993 it had enjoyed growth at double the European average, full employment and price stability. The paper said:

> *Of the three traditional tests of social democracy – jobs for all, reducing inequality and increasing democratic control over the economy – Norway passes them all. New Zealand by contrast has become a laboratory for every*

New Zealand Tourism Board

Going to extremes... white-water rafting, bungi-jumping and snowboarding drew tourists to the country in increasing numbers. Tourism in the 1990s was seen as a growth industry. In 1999 the campaign "100% Pure" was launched to boost New Zealand's image overseas.

New Zealand Tourism Board

New Zealand Tourism Board

Women in Politics

As the Century ended, one woman held the top political office in the land and another sought it. National's Jenny Shipley became the country's first woman Prime Minister in December 1997, after a November coup which deposed leader Jim Bolger. It was an historic moment for both Shipley and the country. Shipley's rival, Labour Leader Helen Clark, could take consolation from the fact that although Shipley was the first female PM, she had not been elected to the office.

Shipley had a rapid rise to her position. Born Jennifer Mary Robson in Gore, Southland in 1952, she was the second child of Presbyterian Minister Len Robson and his wife, Adele. Her father, who helped shape her strong opinions about self-reliance, died when she was 18, and her mother struggled on a widow's benefit.

Shipley scraped through School Certificate but failed University Entrance before joining Teacher's College. She graduated and worked as a school teacher before meeting her husband, Canterbury farmer Burton Shipley, whom she married in 1973 – a year after she joined the National Party. In 1980 she met future Finance Minister Ruth Richardson who was to become her political mentor, and in 1987, after a spell in local body politics, entered Parliament as the MP for Ashburton.

When National took office in 1990 she became Minister of Social Welfare as the Government made its welfare benefit cuts. Between 1993 and 1996, she served as Minister of Health, steering through equally unpopular reforms. Like Richardson, she was often a controversial Minister but she survived and ultimately became not only the country's first female Prime Minister – but also the one who would lead her country for good or for ill, toward the new millennium.

Sources: NZPA, *Evening Post* 4 November 1997, Prime Minister's Office.

Nineties women in power or in search of it. From the top, former Finance Minister Ruth Richardson, Prime Minister Jenny Shipley and Labour Leader Helen Clark.

crackpot laissez-faire notion considered too extreme to be road-tested even in Thatcher's Britain or Reagan's America.[27]

While reformers at the beginning of the century worked to reduce working hours, re-structuring under market reforms led to mass redundancies and longer hours for the corporate survivors, many of whom worked under individualised contracts. According to the 1996 Census, more than one million people worked at least 40 hours a week, 567,807 put in between 45–59 hours, and 180,483 worked for 60 hours or more each working week. There was little doubt that in the Nineties workers were stressed. For Peter Bateman, editor of *Safeguard*, a New Zealand magazine dealing with workplace safety and health, some of the consequences were clear:

Working 60 hour weeks helps weaken the glue that holds families together. People no longer have time to keep up with outside activities. Society slowly unravels, to be replaced by a new way of doing things.[28]

For some, part of the blame lay with the Government's 1991 Employment Contracts Act whose aim was to provide increased workplace flexibility. In *NZ Woman's Weekly* the instability of the measure for some workers was outlined by one angry correspondent, in a Letter of the Week:

I have friends who do not know whether they will have work from one day to the next, and one friend who is on contract work. Every now and then she is put off for a few weeks to be taken on again when there is something for her to do. In the end her job may go because of technology.[29]

Academics researching the effects of the Act discovered profound change, especially in the level of trade unionism which in 1996 was by some estimates, as low as 20 per cent:

The character of trade unionism has changed. Trade unions have yielded the vast majority of workplaces to the unchecked authority of employers.... In unionised workplaces, union membership is high but in only 43 per cent of these workplaces do unions play a significant role in decision making on workplace change.... There has clearly been a progressive downgrading of many employment conditions since 1991, particularly in areas such as penal and overtime rates.... There can be no doubt that a vulnerable underclass has developed.[30]

In 1995, The International Labour Organisation (ILO) found the Act had breached key ILO conventions.

The Wins
Land Connections

In the mid-Nineties Penny Morgan and her husband, Chris, decided that with the uncertainties of the job market they should have more than one source of income. Chris had grown up on a farm, the lifestyle appealed to them, and so they bought a piece of land near Motueka – Glengorm Farm.

We wanted to buy a farm and this was all we could afford. It was very run down, reverting to gorse. Most of our friends thought we were nuts to even contemplate this at our age. Everyone said, "You're going to spend until you go to the retirement home working with a run-down piece of land." Chris's long term aim was to semi-retire and help on this place but he's had to keep working full-time. So all the day-to-day running of this place falls on my shoulders. It's been a real steep learning curve. Most things I can cope with. Some things that are really tricky, I have to give him a buzz at work. We work together well, sort things out.

It's a hard place to farm because it's quite steep, gorsey, hilly terrain. It's not flat and easy country. It's hard on the animals too. Weather can be variable. Cold in winter, we can get snow. And in the summer it's really hot because we are inland and it's very still here. You can get up to forty, forty-five degrees. It's great though. I wouldn't want to be anywhere else.

There was this very derelict old hut standing in the corner of the farm looking forlorn. It needed lots of TLC. So we started doing it up, painting it. On the walls there were quite a few signatures of people who have stayed in the hut over the years, and this name "Win" was there. So I said to my father: "Dad, there are quite a few Wins, and Thornes who are relations of ours too." Then we made the connection. This land was used as a staging post for my ancestors when they came from Dugdale. They used to drive sheep from their farm at Dugdale and summer graze on Mt. Arthur. That hut used to be the stopover for the night. It was really, really odd. They came through here probably from 1900 to 1930-35. Afterwards I sat and thought, "Well, this is really like karma. I've come full circle."

They were hard working people. Unremitting work, long hours, just keep plugging on. Always got somewhere, and had a smile on their face. Real pioneering types. It's quite funny when I look back, because I can see that I have inherited some of those qualities, even though I didn't really realise them until we bought this place. It's brought them out. It's been quite a revelation.

I've done several things in my life. Had kids. Lived in the city. And I've ended up in a place which my ancestors had a bit to do with. It's one of life's oddities, I suppose.

Source: Edited Ninox transcripts from *Our People, Our Century*, 1999.

We had arrived, but where? Were we happier, more secure, more free? As we prepared to enter the new Millennium the answers depended on where New Zealanders found themselves in the new, unequal hierarchy created by the Market Experiment. At the turn of the last century, the country's social experiments promoting the public interest were based on pragmatism aimed at securing greater equality and prosperity. As this century closed, Kiwis witnessed something very different. Government policies, based on economic theory, had enriched the rich and impoverished the poor. Our politicians, who a century ago avoided theory like the plague, now used it to put New Zealand through untested and expensive economic experiments. One result was a corrosive mistrust which steadily ate into the innocence and optimism which had characterised society for much of the century. A restrained anger often showed in letters to the editor:

> *I refer to your front page article "Beneficiaries to have dole docked". I have never been so disgusted in all my life as to where we are headed in God's Own. I used to be proud to be a New Zealander. Now I am not so sure....* [31]

Even the mainstream popular culture of television advertising compared the lost integrity of politicians with the honesty of Kiwi-made Whittaker's chocolate peanut slab. In a 1999 advertisement made by Saatchi and Saatchi, a campaigning politician tries to win votes but, as he eats this honest chocolate bar, reveals the less palatable aspects of his political persona. He tells an elector:

> *Well anyway our party stands for fiscal responsibility and more integrity in Government. But... um... obviously... we'll change our values depending on poll results... and as your MP I'll be abusing the free airfares, as will my wife... and my mistress, um, I'll go joyriding in the government limos. I'll spend a lot of time in bars, massage parlours, that sort of thing. And I'll change parties about three months into my term, refuse to resign, and basically try to hold the country to ransom....*

Elsewhere, there were other signs of breakdown in traditional values among some adults, as this 15-year-old noted:

> *While I was travelling on a bus, a young woman came on board with a baby and a toddler. She looked fairly stressed out, and the toddler seemed restless.... As the young woman walked up the aisle looking for a seat, I was amazed at the number of people who refused to offer her one. People would look at her then quickly turn away.... I stood and offered her my seat. She was so grateful.* [32]

The sense of security once provided for the old, and later for others less fortunate,

Architect Patrick Clifford's own house in Auckland combines new building practice and sophisticated responses to the city's weather with references to earlier New Zealand architectural design, rather than looking abroad for inspiration as earlier local architects had done. Clifford, in describing his house, has written of "boat-like qualities of craft and detail" and a "clear connectedness to a tradition of New Zealand building in attitude, form and materials". [1]

[1] Patrick Clifford cited in Peter Shaw, *A History of New Zealand Architecture*, Second edition, Hodder Moa Beckett, Auckland, 1997, p. 207.

Gil Hanly

Women celebrated the suffrage centenary in 1993.
Pictured third from right is Governor-General
Dame Cath Tizard.

evaporated as political reformers dismantled the welfare state which had assisted them when they were young. Where they had had a free education, they now mortgaged the futures of a generation of students:

Honours graduate Samantha Marks says she is too scared to come back to New Zealand to visit her parents because she fears being detained at the airport for overdue student loans payments. She is one of 29,083 debtors who have defaulted on their payments to the Student Loans Scheme.... [She had a debt of more than $20,000.] "I have just decided that unless I win the Lotto then I am not going to be able to pay this loan off in my lifetime and that terrifies me...."[33]

The rich-poor gap grew, reflected in observations like this:

In Auckland's Parnell it is as if the Crash of '87 never happened. In the bars of the moment, packs of Armani-suited oinkers heft their Motorolas and toss back the chardonnay. Some of these are of the male persuasion. It's six in the evening and they've been at it since three. Outside in the street a homeless person is scuttling for the safety of Ponsonby, being shooed along by a couple of young Bobbies, all hard eyes and ferocious determination....[34]

Women rode into the 20th Century on the first wave of feminist gains. These had given women the vote, and in 1919 the right to stand for Parliament, although the first female MP, Elizabeth Reid McCombs (Labour), was not elected until 1933. However, while women's status had certainly improved, they were still hardly independent individuals, although two world wars had helped change that. While men went to war, women went to work in jobs previously closed to them. At each war's end most were forced out of the workplace. However, the wars provided an occupational tide mark and some women stayed, especially after the Second World War.

Feminism's second wave began in the Seventies. It grew out of the affluent and stable Fifties when a greater percentage of married women were full-time mothers than their mothers and grandmothers before them and their daughters and grand-daughters who followed. The women's movement of the time demanded a total re-think of women's role in society. They sought equality with men in access to jobs, in pay, and in the way they were treated by institutions such as banks. They also marched for the right to control their fertility, and to be free from sexual and physical harassment and assault.

By the end of the Nineties this second wave had ebbed. Women's achievements were mixed. More than 20 years after equal pay became law it remained no more than a legal fiction:

[With] the average female wage still only something like three-quarters of the average male wage. Most chief

"Wearable Art" seemed anything but wearable, but the awards ceremony became a showcase for wondrous creativity.

The Montana New Zealand Wearable Art Awards (The Nelson Mail)

Cave Creek

We continued walking and, as the track became narrower, walked in pairs. I was in approximately the middle of the group as it reached the platform and stepped into a gap on the left hand side of the platform at the front to have a look. I looked over and went to take a step back because I don't like heights. Suddenly, and with no warning except for yells of surprise, the platform was falling under our feet. It began sliding down at approximately 30 degrees and then tipped and fell vertically with everyone falling in front of it.

Carolyn Smith was one of a group of students from the Outdoor Recreation Course at Greymouth's Tai Poutini Polytechnic who visited a viewing platform at a little-known spot which was quickly to become notorious: Cave Creek. On 28 April 1995, 17 of the students crowded

A time to remember and grieve... friends and mourners join in a memorial service for the victims of Cave Creek.

on to a viewing platform which collapsed and fell about 30 metres. 14 students died, and others were seriously injured. In May, District Court Judge G. S. Noble was appointed as the head of a Commission of Inquiry into the causes of the collapse. He found that the dominant cause was that the platform was not constructed in accordance with sound building practice. "This resulted in total and catastrophic failure," he said. His report also examined other causes, finding that substantial "systemic failure was the pre-eminent secondary cause of the collapse". He added:

... it will be seen that no individual or particular collection of individuals was singly or jointly responsible for the Cave Creek tragedy. The root causes of the collapse lie in a combined systemic failure against the background of an under-funded and under-resourced department employing (at least at grassroots level) a band of enthusiasts prepared to turn their hands to any task, but who were subject to pressures not only from the over-zealous anti-conservationist element, but also from altered priorities.... They were doing their best to meet public demand and (in this case) building structures where no proper or appropriate system of control had ever been designed at Head Office level and properly put in place and monitored at regional conservancy and thence at field centre level, to ensure that the procedures were followed.... [A]gainst that background, a tragedy such as Cave Creek was almost bound to happen.

In an epilogue the Judge canvassed what he had heard and seen in the 31 hearing days of the inquiry:

What caused this catastrophe to happen? Standing back and viewing the evidence objectively... I am left with the overwhelming impression that the many people affected... were all let down by faults in the process of government departmental reforms. Society always likes to feel it is progressing, but there are lessons for society in all of this. No Government organisation can do its job without adequate resourcing. In my opinion, it is up to the Government to ensure that departments charged with carrying out statutory functions for the benefit of the community are provided with sufficient resources to enable them to do so....

Source: Department of Internal Affairs, Report of the Commission of Inquiry into the Collapse of a Viewing Platform at Cave Creek, near Punakaiki on the West Coast, 10 November 1995, Department of Internal Affairs, Wellington, 1995.

executive positions in government, commerce and education were still held by men.... [By any measure] New Zealand remained far behind the Scandinavian countries, Holland, Western Germany and the United States.[35]

The debate about pay equity – equal pay for jobs of equal status – had been submerged in the sweeping economic and employment changes. Abortion, one of the pivotal issues of the feminist movement, continued to be a heated subject for debate.

In other ways some women's lives had begun to resemble those of their great-grandmothers. They were marrying later than their mothers, much closer to the age of women in the first decades of the twentieth century. They had fewer children, but like earlier generations were becoming mothers in their thirties and even into their early forties. For quite different reasons – single parent families or households where both parents were in full-time work – a domestic service group re-emerged. Nannies, home cleaners, gardeners and handymen did the chores of the affluent, and for sections of the hard-pressed middle classes.

For Maori, the cultural renaissance gathered pace. The race, which was virtually laid to rest in 1900, confidently affirmed and nourished its culture. But still central to our debates was the land – Maori or Pakeha – and its ownership. Some 2.5 million hectares of scenic landscape in the high country was occupied by only 340 lessees. "[F]riction between run holders, conservationists and high country users has increased."[36] This hinted at a situation which existed before the turn of the century and, combined with other issues, helped generate a pervasive disquiet in an increasingly dysfunctional democracy.

Evening Post

Maori on the march. Maori radicalism took a new turn in the Nineties with land occupations. The most controversial took place at Wanganui's Moutua Gardens, from February to May 1995.

Te Maori, Te Pakeha

Robyn Kahukiwa, "E Hine Ko Koe Te Whare Tangata", 1992, oil and enamel on loose canvas.

Robyn Kahukiwa (Tapu Te Ranga Marae Collection)

The Te Maori exhibition in the mid-1980s gave a great boost to a Maori visual arts movement that was already emerging. The work was both traditional and modern. Robyn Kahukiwa is the best known of a group of Maori women artists which includes Kura Te Waru-Rewiri, Shona Ripira Davies and Emare Karaka. They make "strong use of Western/Pakeha art conventions and models to make strongly Maori visual statements".[i] Kahukiwa has the most accessible imagery of any contemporary Maori artist and her work can be found in a wide range of places, from galleries and private art collections to political posters, book covers and illustrations in a significant number of children's books including some of her own. Her identity as a Maori comes from her roots in the East Coast of the North Island and her tribal affiliations to Ngati Porou, Te Aitanga-a-Hauiti, Ngati Hau, Ngati Konohi and Whanau-a-Ruataupare. Jonathon Mane-Wheoki writing in *Art New Zealand* said of her work:

Over the years the two unambiguous and inter-related questions which her art has constantly addressed have been: what does it mean to be a woman? And, what does it mean to be Maori? Every work, each series, has marked a stage in the process of reclaiming and affirming an identity.[ii]

In her work she provides a visual map of a voyage on which many Maori, especially those who have become dislocated from their tribal and cultural identity, have chosen to embark since the 1970s.

Philippa Blair creates a visual map of another kind, travelling amongst some of the great discoveries of the 20th century, all the time pushing at the boundaries of painting. She is one of a number of local artists who draw inspiration from the Pacific and beyond, not just stylistically but more especially in the content of their work — political issues, history, philosophy, voyages of intellectual and physical discovery. Contained within her work is a conscious search to establish her own whakapapa; to look at the cross pollination of physics and science (her father's work) and music (her mother's talent). Blair has exhibited in the United States and Europe over the past 10 years. In 1991, the Long Beach Museum of Art in California mounted an exhibition titled *Three from New Zealand* showing work from Blair, Ralph Hotere and Christine Hellyar. Art critic Lita Barrie wrote in the catalogue notes of Blair's paintings:

Philippa Blair, "Transverse", August 1998, oil and charcoal on canvas.

Her allegorical journeys reflect the restless spirit of a pioneer who crosses internal and external boundaries to chart out new territories of the mind by exploring different worlds.... Her eclecticism suggests the process through which the New World subject re-inscribes a language borrowed from the old world, with meanings relevant to their own culture.[iii]

In her recent works multiple images refer to music, digital imaging, moving image and screens. There are references to both high-tech and organic imagery, the space programme and astronomy, new inventions and re-invention and the velocity that has come with the acceleration of life in the late 20th century.

[i] Peter Simpson, The Recognition of Difference, in Rice (ed.), *The Oxford History of New Zealand*, p. 581.
[ii] Jonathon Mane-Wheoki reproduced in *Toi Ata – Robyn Kahukiwa: Works from 1985-1995*, Bowen Galleries with assistance from the Arts Council of New Zealand, Wellington, *Art New Zealand*, no. 75, Winter, p. 10.
[iii] Lita Barrie, *Three from New Zealand*, exhibition catalogue, Long Beach Museum of Art and RKS Art, Auckland, 1990, pp. 7-8.

The great outdoors: celebrating wine and fine food at an Auckland wine festival.

Gil Hanly

Pakeha of British stock sought a new identity in "Polynasian" New Zealand, where 25 per cent of the population was Polynesian, Maori and Asian. This was not always easy for a society of Anglophiles cast adrift in the South Pacific. Previous generations often left the country on overseas trips to confirm their roots. By the end of the century this cultural imperative lay closer to home and was defined emphatically by historian and writer Michael King. A quarter of a century earlier he had helped explain Maori culture to Pakeha. In 1999, he affirmed Pakeha culture:

People who live in New Zealand by choice and who are committed to this land and its people are no less "indigenous" than Maori.... [37]

He asked who or what were Pakeha, whether they had comparable rights and whether they were destined forever to be strangers in the country of their birth:

My own people, descendants in the main of displaced Irish, had as much moral and legal right to be here as Maori. Like the ancestors of Maori, they came as immigrants; like Maori too, we became indigenous at the point where our focus of identity and commitment shifted to this country and away from our countries and cultures of origin. [38]

Body surfing at the Big Day Out. However most looked uncomfortably crushed.

Simon Young

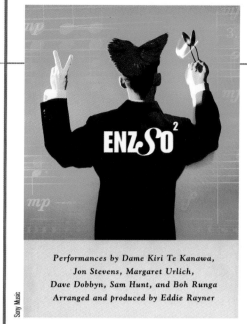

Sony Music

Performances by Dame Kiri Te Kanawa,
Jon Stevens, Margaret Urlich,
Dave Dobbyn, Sam Hunt, and Boh Runga
Arranged and produced by Eddie Rayner

Diva Kiri Te Kanawa, leading Kiwi pop musicians, songwriters and the New Zealand Symphony all joined for these concerts.

Throughout most of the century Pakeha celebrated their roots during royal tours. But by the Nineties, the Queen's visits, which once generated so much excitement, had become the subject of polite and limited curiosity or the target of protest from anti-loyalist and radical Maori. Slowly the Queen and her most loyal and far-flung subjects were moving apart as the first serious debates began about Republicanism.

In other ways it was clear we had arrived at a new cultural maturity. Our outpourings in literature, art and the proliferation of good food and wines proved as much, as our sense of informality grew together with a cosmopolitan cafe culture. Instead of the usual dry descriptions of wines, one restaurant drew its rapture from blokedom, describing one Australian wine on its list:

> *Mate! This wine was produced from grapes grown on the pre-phylloxera ungrafted vines planted on the estate in 1860....*

Our film industry won international acclaim. In 1998, no less than 14 features were under way. "The country is awash with more movies and relatively unknown actors than we've ever seen before" noted *Pavement* magazine in August that year. With the growth of multiplexes and a renaissance in film, Kiwis increasingly swapped the commercialism of television to return to the cinema. And for the young there were events like Big Day Out.

> *If you wanted to single out a defining characteristic of the more than 35,000 fans who attended Big Day Out in Auckland last month, one word perfectly sums everyone up: self-expression. With so many people gathered together to listen to a wide spectrum of modern music, the clothes, the hairstyles, the interactions and the attitudes of everyone attending Big Day Out makes the occasion the remarkable cultural event that it is. From simple T-shirts to elaborate costumes, everyone wore their individuality on their sleeves, so to speak....*[39]

A different musical individuality was also appreciated in the beautiful backdrops of the Bay of Islands townships of Russell and Paihia. In 1985 – the first year of the Bay of Islands Jazz and Blues festival – organisers managed to attract 11 bands who played to an estimated 1,000 people. In the mid-Nineties at six venues, over 40 bands played to an estimated 6,000 jazz devotees.[40]

We took laughter seriously and TVNZ's TV2 organised a successful tonic to winter and other blues in its International Laugh Festival, with 80 different comedy shows, featuring 120 Kiwis. Publicity exhorted people to get out and "have a great, big, healthy, banishing doom and gloom LAUGH!" – and they did, in their thousands. In many ways though, these and other diversions were *fin de siecle* bread and circuses, which helped us escape worrying realities. Linking us together were some common concerns. In that barometer of public sentiment, *NZ Woman's Weekly*, celebrity gossip ruled, but its staple editorial

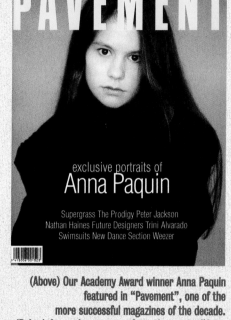

exclusive portraits of
Anna Paquin

Supergrass The Prodigy Peter Jackson
Nathan Haines Future Designers Trini Alvarado
Swimsuits New Dance Section Weezer

(Above) Our Academy Award winner Anna Paquin featured in "Pavement", one of the more successful magazines of the decade. (Below) A rare happy scene from the movie, "Once Were Warriors", based on the book by New Zealand author Alan Duff.

New Zealand Film Archive (NZFC Collection)

New Zealand International Festival of the Arts

Wellington took it upon itself to become not just the political, but also the arts capital of the country and its centrepiece was the New Zealand International Festival of the Arts. The fireworks celebrate its opening.

The Hikoi of Hope marches towards Parliament in an attempt to raise awareness about the issue of poverty.

Evening Post

content remained, casting light on handy hints and disturbing trends alike. In its famous "Over the Teacups" column, readers still shared housekeeping advice the way their grandmothers and mothers had. In some of their letters to the editor, they also revealed their concerns on issues like violent crime:

Another police constable has been shot while on duty. New Zealand is fast becoming a violent country where criminals have no respect for property or people.... Can unemployment be partially to blame for this or is it just a sign of the times?[41]

It was true Kiwis had greater freedoms than ever before in travel, finance, business and in new lifestyles. They adapted and displayed their resourcefulness by adding value to products in rapidly growing industries like the manufacture of electronics and electrical equipment.[42] They now had more purchasing choice, modern and cheap telecommunications and de-regulated television with multiple channels. They no longer controlled their former public institutions, many of which had been sold or commercialised. Instead, ownership in some strategic assets had passed to global multi-nationals in a process welcomed enthusiastically by ruling politicians. However, that process also exposed a small and vulnerable economy, leading to factory closures, widespread redundancies and, in some rural areas, towns which were a ghost of their once vibrant selves. Despite the losses, politicians could still point to gains – a consumer society with seven-day-a-week shopping, lower prices and virtually non-existent inflation.

But overall, the New Society had come at a social cost. By the end of the century, unemployment was entrenched, crime rates high, and a sense of insecurity pervasive. It was all a long way from the optimism of 1899 when the Christmas issue of the *New Zealand Observer and Free Lance* reminded readers that they were privileged:

Peace reigns among us. Smiling prosperity pervades the land. There is no downtrodden class. Dowered with a generous climate. Blest with a fertile soil, and surrounded with the comforts which spring from plenitude of remunerative employment, we are a singularly favoured community.[43]

In fact there was, as there is now, a downtrodden class in 1899; while there was considerable prosperity, its distribution then, as now, was not at all equitable. The difference between the two dates lay in that earlier boundless sense of optimism born of a new country, in a new century. By the end of that century, much of the optimism had been squandered. In 1998, hope was in such short supply in New Zealand that it had to be organised into a Hikoi. As the Anglican Church Hikoi of Hope progressed from the Far North to Wellington to protest poverty, the Experiment continued. After Christmas 1998, the *Sunday Star-Times* railed against its inequalities and the "agonising problem of poverty":

> *After 15 years of the Great Experiment, the poor continue to frustrate the implacable social engineers who rule our lives. It's an infuriating, unsightly nuisance for the political joy-mongers at the official time of celebration. But the beggar at the banquet is not going to go away.*[44]

Every story begins before the beginning. As the millennium neared with all the fanfare over the new Century's first sunrise in New Zealand, we had arrived once more at another beginning.

Gisborne 2000

For Kiwi yachtsmen, the America's Cup was the Holy Grail and when they won it, the team was welcomed home as heroes by crowds which blocked city streets and showered them with tickertape in May 1995. Towards the end of 1999 preparations were well under way to welcome the challengers to the Cup expected from all over the world.

2000 and all that... the dawn of the new century seen first in New Zealand.

References

Chapter One: 1900–1910

1 Malcolm McKinnon, Barry Bradley and Russell Kirkpatrick (eds), *Bateman New Zealand Historical Atlas: Ko Papatuanuku E Takoto Nei*, David Bateman, in association with Historical Branch, Department of Internal Affairs, Auckland, 1997, plate 59.

2 James Drummond, *Life and Works of Richard Seddon*, cited in W. B. Sutch, *Poverty and Progress in New Zealand: A Reassessment*, Second revised edition, A. H. & A. W. Reed, Wellington, 1969, p. 90.

3 Sutch, *Poverty and Progress in New Zealand: A Reassessment*, p. 87.

4 Ibid., p. 140.

5 McKinnon, Bradley and Kirkpatrick (eds), *Bateman New Zealand Historical Atlas*, plate 59; and John McKenzie entry, *Dictionary of New Zealand Biography, 1870–1900*, Bridget Williams Books and Department of Internal Affairs, Wellington, 1993, vol. 2, p. 296.

6 Sutch, *Poverty and Progress in New Zealand: A Reassessment*, p. 144.

7 *The New Zealand Official Yearbook 1900*, Government Printer, Wellington, 1900, p. 317.

8 A. H. McLintock (ed.), *Encyclopaedia of New Zealand*, Government Printer, Wellington, 1966, vol. 2, p. 77.

9 Henry Demarest Lloyd cited in Desmond Stone (ed), *Verdict on New Zealand*, A. H. & A. W. Reed, Wellington, 1959, pp. 65-73.

10 Report on Lunatic Asylums of the Colony [for 1900], *Appendices to the Journals of the House of Representatives 1901*, Session II, vol. 4, H–I, H7, p. 6.

11 McLintock (ed.), *Encyclopaedia of New Zealand*, vol. 2, p. 431.

12 Ray Knox (ed.), *New Zealand's Heritage: The Making of a Nation*, Paul Hamlyn, Wellington, 1971-73, vol. 5, pp. 1837-1839.

13 *The New Zealand Official Yearbook 1901*, pp. 276, 287-88.

14 Paul Gooding cited in Stone (ed.), *Verdict on New Zealand*, p. 101.

15 Adrienne Simpson, *Opera's Farthest Frontier: A History of Professional Opera in New Zealand*, Reed Publishing, Auckland, 1996, p. 164.

16 Florence Harsant, Early Life, Special Collections, Auckland City Library, pp. 3-4, and 12. Also formed part of her book *They Called Me Te Maari*, Whitcoulls, Christchurch, 1979.

17 John McKenzie entry, *Dictionary of New Zealand Biography,1870–1900*, vol. 2, p. 296.

18 Florence Harsant, Early Life, p. 15.

19 I. V. Hughes, *New Zealand Country Annual*, cited in Hamish Keith, *New Zealand Yesterdays: A Look at Our Recent Past*, Reader's Digest Services, Sydney NSW, 1984, pp. 286-87.

20 McKinnon, Bradley and Kirkpatrick (eds), *Bateman New Zealand Historical Atlas*, plate 84.

21 Henry Demarest Lloyd cited in Stone (ed.), *Verdict on New Zealand*, pp. 68-69.

Chapter Two: 1910–1920

1 Judith Binney, Judith Bassett and Erik Olssen, *The People and the Land – Te Tangata Me Te Whenua: An Illustrated History of New Zealand, 1820-1920*, Allen & Unwin, Wellington, 1990, p. 313.

2 Erik Olssen, *The Red Feds: Revolutionary Industrial Unionism and the New Zealand Federation of Labour 1908-14*, Oxford University Press, Auckland, 1988, p. 96.

3 Laurie Barber, *New Zealand, A Short History*, Century Hutchinson New Zealand, Auckland, 1989, pp. 88-89.

4 André Siegfried cited in Stone (ed.), *Verdict on New Zealand*, p. 86.

5 Keith Sinclair, *A History of New Zealand*, revised and enlarged edition, A. Lane, London, 1980, p. 208.

6 Binney, Bassett and Olssen, *The People and the Land*, p. 290.

7 Charles Alexander of the Te Awamutu branch of the Farmers' Union, cited in Barber, *New Zealand, A Short History*, p. 92.

8 Marjorie Lees cited in Peter R. Attwell, 1913 The Rhetoric of the Waterfront Strike and Street Riots in Wellington, research papers, Manuscripts Collection, Alexander Turnbull Library.

9 *Evening Post*, 29 Oct 1913, cited ibid.

10 Otto Roth, Papers on Maori Working Class and Trade Unions, Manuscripts Collection, Alexander Turnbull Library.

11 James Bryce, *Modern Democracies*, Macmillan and Co, London, 1921, vol. 2, pp. 358-59.

12 Charles Plunkett, 2 August 1914, Diaries 1881–1941, Special Collections, Auckland City Library, 1914 vol., pp. 62-63.

13 Barber, *New Zealand, A Short History*, p. 101.

14 The Papal Delegate and the Mayor. An Open Letter to the Citizens of Auckland. Loyal Orange Lodge pamphlet, New Zealand Mission Press, Auckland, c. 1914, p. 6.

15 John A. Lee cited in Michael King, *New Zealanders at War*, Heinemann Publishers, Auckland, 1981, p. 85.

16 Barber, *New Zealand: A Short History*, pp. 101 and 116; P. J. Gibbons, The Climate of Opinion, in Geoffrey W. Rice (ed.), *The Oxford History of New Zealand*, Second revised edition, Oxford University Press, Auckland, 1992, p. 319.

17 King, *New Zealanders at War*, p. 100.

18 Archibald Baxter, ibid., p. 119.

19 Ibid., p. 119.

20 Lieutenant C. Ment, In the Somme Battle. A Record of Five Nights, The Lucretia Grey Scrapbook 1911–1918, Special Collections, Auckland City Library, p. 47.

21 Archibald Baxter cited in King, *New Zealanders at War*, p. 163.

22 Gordon Harper in a letter home, ibid., p. 145.

23 John A. Lee, ibid, p. 167.

24 Florence Harsant, My Everyday Life as Travelling Organiser for Maori Women on Behalf of the Women's Christian Temperance Union, Special Collections, Auckland City Library, pp. 140-41.

25 Plunkett, 10 November 1918, Diaries 1881–1941, 1918 vol., pp. 91-92.

26 M. H. Holcroft, *The Village Transformed: Aspects of Change in New Zealand, 1900–1990*, Victoria University Press, Wellington, 1990, p. 164.

27 Ida Reilly cited in Geoffrey Rice and Linda Bryder, *Black November: The 1918 Influenza Epidemic in New Zealand*, Allen & Unwin and Historical Branch, Dept. of Internal Affairs, Wellington, 1988, pp. 28-29.

28 Ibid., p. 104.

29 R. Goff, W. Moss, J. Terry and J. Upshur, *The Twentieth Century, A Brief Global History*, Third revised edition, McGraw-Hill Inc, New York, 1990, p. 150.

Chapter Three: 1920–1930

1 Alan Bullock, *Hitler: A Study in Tyranny*, revised edition, Penguin Books, Harmondsworth UK, 1962, p. 96.

2 Keith Sinclair, *A History of New Zealand*, revised edition, Penguin Books, Harmondsworth UK, 1969, p. 245.

3 David Thorns and Charles Sedgewick, *Understanding Aotearoa: Historical Statistics*, Dunmore Press, Palmerston North, 1997, p. 75.

4 McLintock (ed.), *Encyclopaedia of New Zealand*, vol. 2, p. 80.

5 Keith, *New Zealand Yesterdays*, p. 101.

6 Carolyn Hall, *The Twenties in Vogue*, Harmony Books, New York, 1983, p. 18.

7 Peter Downes and Peter Harcourt, *Voices in the Air. Radio Broadcasting in New Zealand: a documentary*, Methuen Publications in association with Radio New Zealand, Wellington, 1976, p. 10.

8 Keith, *New Zealand Yesterdays*, p. 156.

9 Downes and Harcourt, *Voices in the Air*, p. 43.

10 Hall, *The Twenties in Vogue*, p. 112.

11 Beryl Ley, Life and Work in a New Zealand Country Store, pp. 33-34.

12 Thomas Woodrooffe cited in Stone (ed.), *Verdict on New Zealand*, p. 117.

13 Alwyn Owen and Jack Perkins, *Speaking for Ourselves, Echoes from New Zealand's Past from the Award-winning 'Spectrum' Radio Series*, Penguin Books, Auckland, 1986, p. 75.

14 Thomas Woodrooffe cited in Stone (ed.), *Verdict on New Zealand*, p. 115.

15 O. T. J. Alpers, *Confident Tomorrows: A Biographical Self-portrait of O. T. J. Alpers 1867–1927*, eds Antony Alpers and Josephine Baker, Godwit Press, Auckland, 1993, pp. 167-68.

16 Owens and Perkins, *Speaking for Ourselves*, pp. 172-73.

17 *New Zealand Illustrated Sporting and Dramatic Review*, 25 December 1924.

18 Downes and Harcourt, *Voices in the Air*, p. 51.

19 Bill Pearson, Note on the banning of The Butcher Shop (endpiece to 1981 edition), in Jean Devanny, *The Butcher Shop*, ed. Heather Roberts, Oxford University Press and Auckland University Press, Auckland, 1981, p. 233.

20 Ibid., p. 226.

21 Rory Sweetman, *Bishop in the Dock: The Sedition Trial of James Liston*, Auckland University Press, Auckland, 1997, p. 11.

22 Ibid., p. 248.

23 Bill Cooke, *Heathen in Godzone: 70 Years of Rationalists in New Zealand*, New Zealand Association of Rationalists and Humanists, Auckland, 1998, p. 50.

24 David Grant, *Out in the Cold: Pacifists and Conscientious Objectors in New Zealand during World War II*, Reed Methuen, Auckland, 1986, p. 25.

25 Sutch, *Poverty and Progress in New Zealand: A Reassessment*, p. 209.
26 Ibid., p. 210.
27 Sinclair, *A History of New Zealand*, 1969, p. 254.
28 Isabel Leighton (ed.), *The Aspirin Age 1919–1941*, Penguin Books, USA, 1949, p. 225.

Chapter Four: 1930–1940

1 Colin J. McKay, The Silver Halfpenny, Manuscripts Collection, Alexander Turnbull Library.
2 Tony Simpson, *The Slump: The 1930s Depression: Its Origins and Aftermath*, Penguin Books, Auckland, 1990, p. 15.
3 *The Herald*, Melbourne, 4 November 1930, cited in Robin Bromby (ed.), *An Eyewitness History of New Zealand*, Currey O'Neil Ross Pty Ltd, Victoria Australia, 1985, p. 158.
4 McLintock (ed.), *An Encyclopaedia of New Zealand*, vol. 2, p. 80.
5 Sinclair, *A History of New Zealand*, 1980, p. 256.
6 Michael King, Between Two Worlds, in Rice (ed.), *The Oxford History of New Zealand*, p. 293.
7 McLintock (ed), *An Encyclopaedia of New Zealand*, vol. 2, p. 80.
8 McKay, The Silver Halfpenny, Alexander Turnbull Library.
9 *The Daily Telegraph, 120 Years: Double Diamond Jubilee 1871–1991*, Daily Telegraph Co., Napier, 1991, p. 17.
10 *The Dominion*, Wellington, 5 February 1931, cited in Bromby (ed), *An Eyewitness History of New Zealand*, p. 162.
11 Stephen Barnett (ed.), *Those Were the Days: A Nostalgic Look at the 1930s from the Pages of The Weekly News*, Moa Publications, Auckland, 1987, p. 15.
12 John Mulgan, *Man Alone*, Second edition, Paul's Book Arcade Limited, Hamilton, 1949, p. 56.
13 Holcroft, *The Village Transformed*, p. 50.
14 John A. Lee, cited in Simpson, *The Slump*, p. 41.
15 Ibid., p. 43.
16 Margaret Tennant, *Paupers and Providers: Charitable Aid in New Zealand*, Allen & Unwin New Zealand Ltd and Historical Branch, Dept. of Internal Affairs, Wellington, 1989, p. 188.
17 James John Mitchell, Papers, interviewed by D. Crosado, H. O. Roth and R. F. Grover, Manuscripts Collection, Alexander Turnbull Library.
18 Sinclair, *A History of New Zealand*, 1980, p. 258.
19 Plunkett, 14–16 April 1932, Diaries 1881–1941, 1932 vol., p. 31.
20 Mitchell, Papers, Alexander Turnbull Library.
21 McKay, The Silver Halfpenny, Alexander Turnbull Library.
22 D'Arcy Cresswell cited in Holcroft, *The Village Transformed*, p. 60.
23 J. N. Findlay cited in Stone (ed.), *Verdict on New Zealand*, p. 146.
24 George Bernard Shaw, ibid., p. 133.
25 Janet Blackwell (ed.), *NZ Woman's Weekly: The First 60 Years, 1932–1992*, Moa Beckett Publishers, Auckland, 1992, pp. 6-7.
26 James Watson, An Independent Working Class?, in John E. Martin and Kerry Taylor (eds), *Culture and the Labour Movement: Essays in New Zealand Labour History*, Dunmore Press, Palmerston North, 1991, p. 184.
27 February 1935, cited in Gil Dymock (ed.), *Good Morning New Zealand: News Stories of the Day from the 1930s*, Moa Publications, Auckland, 1990, pp. 94-95.
28 Mitchell, Papers, Alexander Turnbull Library.
29 Sinclair, *A History of New Zealand*, 1980, p. 267.
30 Barnett (ed.), *Those Were The Days* [1930s], p. 15.
31 Peter Fraser cited in Bryce Fraser (ed.), *The New Zealand Book of Events*, Reed Methuen, Auckland, 1986, p. 337.
32 Erik Olssen, Towards a New Society, in Rice (ed.), *The Oxford History of New Zealand*, p. 283.
33 Alan Grey, *Aotearoa and New Zealand: An Historical Geography*, Canterbury University Press, Christchurch, 1994, p. 361.
34 Eurera Tirikatene's account of the meeting cited in Barber, *New Zealand, A Short History*, p. 138.
35 *The New Zealand Official Year Book 1938*, p. 78.
36 Dymock (ed.), *Good Morning New Zealand: News Stories of the Day from the 1930s*, p. 145.
37 James MacDonald Howden, The Key is under the Whalebone, Manuscripts Collection, Alexander Turnbull Library.
38 Holcroft, *The Village Transformed*, p. 59.

Chapter Five: 1940–1950

1 Nancy M. Taylor, *The New Zealand People at War: The Home Front*, Government Printer, Historical Publications Branch, Department of Internal Affairs, Wellington, 1986, vol. 1, p. 23.
2 Ibid., vol. 1, p. 23.
3 Ormond Burton cited in King, *New Zealanders at War*, p. 168.
4 *The Dominion*, Wellington, 1 April 1940, cited in Bromby (ed.), *An Eyewitness History of New Zealand*, p. 184.
5 Alister McIntosh, cited in Ian McGibbon (ed.), *Undiplomatic Dialogue:*

Letters between Carl Berendsen and Alister McIntosh 1943-1952, Auckland University Press in association with the Ministry of Foreign Affairs and Trade and the Historical Branch, Dept. of Internal Affairs, Auckland 1993, p. 207.
6 Robert Chapman, From Labour to National, in Rice (ed.), *The Oxford History of New Zealand*, p. 367.
7 Taylor, *The New Zealand People at War: The Home Front*, vol. 1, p. 34.
8 McLintock (ed.), *Encyclopaedia of New Zealand*, vol. 3, p. 580.
9 Mary Guthrie, 'The Land Girl', in A. E. Woodhouse (ed.), *New Zealand Farm and Station Verse 1850–1950*, Whitcombe and Tombs, Christchurch, 1950, p. 161.
10 H. L. Thompson, *New Zealanders with the RAF*, vol. 1, p. 74; McLintock (ed.), *Encyclopaedia of New Zealand*, vol. 3, p. 575; and McKinnon, Bradley and Kirkpatrick (eds), *Bateman New Zealand Historical Atlas*, plate 80.
11 Major-General Sir Howard Kippenberger, cited in Ronald Lewin (ed.), *Freedom's Battle III: The War on Land 1939–45*, Pimlico, 1969, p. 78-79.
12 Kevin Ireland cited in Paul Smith, *New Zealand at War*, Hodder Moa Beckett, Auckland, 1995, p. 102.
13 Jack Quinlan, ibid, p. 65.
14 Hugh Price, ibid., p. 100.
15 W. H. Oliver, The Awakening Imagination 1940–1980, in Rice (ed.), *The Oxford History of New Zealand*, p. 539.
16 Peter Price, cited in Smith, *New Zealand at War*, p. 112.
17 Kevin Ireland, ibid., p. 101.
18 J. Phillips and E. Ellis, *Brief Encounter: American Forces and the NZ People, 1942–45*, 1992, p. 9.
19 McKinnon, Bradley and Kirkpatrick (eds), *Bateman New Zealand Historical Atlas*, plate 81.
20 Joy Faulkner, Manuscripts Collection, Alexander Turnbull Library.
21 Mary Crockett, Paul Little and Terry Snow (eds), *The Listener Bedside Book*, Wilson and Horton Publications, Auckland, 1997, p. 21.
22 Mary Hannah, cited in Sue Kedgley, *Mum's the Word: The Untold Story of Motherhood in New Zealand*, Random House New Zealand, Auckland, 1996, p. 117.
23 Mrs Preston Davie of the civilian activities division of Army Emergency Relief, ibid., p. 126.
24 The Very Rev Owen Baragwanath, cited in Smith, *New Zealand at War*, p. 131.
25 John Blacklock, ibid., p. 131.
26 Taylor, *The New Zealand People at War: The Home Front*, vol. 1, pp. 646-7.
27 The Dean of Dunedin in a 1943 address cited in Kedgley, *Mum's the Word*, p. 130.
28 Beatrice Beeby, ibid., p. 139.
29 Ian Middleton, cited in Smith, *New Zealand at War*, p. 96.
30 Kedgley, *Mum's the Word*, p. 142.
31 Ibid., p. 143.
32 Barber, *New Zealand, A Short History*, p. 156.
33 Alister McIntosh cited in McGibbon (ed.), *Undiplomatic Dialogue*, p. 34.
34 George Sutherland cited in King, *New Zealanders at War*, p. 216.
35 Dr Ruth Flashoff cited in Smith, *New Zealand at War*, p. 186.
36 Len Payne, ibid., p. 189.
37 Paul Tasker, ibid., pp. 186-189.
38 Hamish Keith, *A Lovely Day Tomorrow: New Zealand in the 1940s*, Random Century, Auckland, 1991, p. 7.
39 McKinnon, Bradley and Kirkpatrick (eds), *Bateman New Zealand Historical Atlas*, plate 80.
40 Mona Stanton cited in Smith, *New Zealand at War*, p. 189.
41 Squadron Leader Rex Daniell, ibid., p. 145.
42 Wing Commander Bill Simpson, ibid., p. 145.
43 Kedgley, *Mum's the Word*, p. 144.
44 Thelma Hall, ibid., pp. 146-47
45 W. B. Sutch cited in Keith, *A Lovely Day Tomorrow: New Zealand in the 1940s*, p. 72.
46 Ibid., p. 41.
47 *The Auckland Star*, 20 January 1949.
48 Patricia Grace, Two Worlds, Witi Ihimaera (ed.) *Growing up Maori*, Tandem Press, Auckland, 1998, pp. 49-51.
49 Michael King, Between Two Worlds, in Rice (ed.), *The Oxford History of New Zealand*, pp. 287-88.
50 Ibid., p. 301.
51 Michael Rotohiko Jones, secretary to Peter Fraser, ibid., p. 301.
52 Peter Fraser, ibid., p. 301.
53 Te Puea Herangi, ibid., p. 307.
54 Sinclair, *A History of New Zealand*, 1980, p. 281.

Chapter Six: 1950–1960

1 Janet Frame, *Faces in the Water*, The Women's Press Ltd, London, 1980, p. 26.
2 *The New Zealand Official Yearbook 1990*, p. 46.
3 McLintock (ed.), *Encyclopaedia of New Zealand*, vol. 2, p. 82.
4 A. R. D. Fairburn, 'The Bars and Gripes', *Poetry Harbinger*, eds A. R. D. Fairburn and D. J. M. Glover, Pilgrim Press, Auckland, 1958, p. 31.

5. *Realites* November 1956,English translation of the original French version, cited in Stone (ed.), *Verdict on New Zealand*, p. 220.
6. Downes and Harcourt, *Voices in the Air*, p. 153.
7. McLintock (ed.), *Encyclopaedia of New Zealand*, vol. 2, p. 83.
8. *The Weekly News*, 15 February 1950.
9. Ibid.
10. McLintock (ed.), *Encyclopaedia of New Zealand*, vol. 2, p. 807.
11. Barry Crump, *The Life and Times of A Good Keen Man*, Barry Crump Associates, Opotiki, 1992, p. 43.
12. *The People's Voice*, 18 March 1953.
13. Redmer Yska, *All Shook Up: The Flash Bodgie and the Rise of the New Zealand Teenager in the Fifties*, Penguin Books, Auckland, 1993, p. 26.
14. Sutch, *Poverty and Progress in New Zealand: A Reassessment*, p. 275.
15. Sinclair, *A History of New Zealand*, 1969, p. 298.
16. Michael Bassett, *Confrontation '51: The 1951 Waterfront Dispute*, A. H. & A. W. Reed, Wellington 1972, p. 83.
17. Sutch, *Poverty and Progress in New Zealand: A Reassessment*, pp. 281-282.
18. Dick Scott, *151 Days: History of the Great Waterfront Lockout and Supporting Strikes, February 15–July 15 1951*, New Zealand Watersiders Union (Deregistered), Auckland, December 1952, p. 174.
19. Ibid., p. 171.
20. Ibid., p. 115.
21. Bassett, *Confrontation '51*, p. 159.
22. Scott, *151 Days*, p. 177.
23. Gordon Dryden, *Out of the Red*, William Collins Publishers, Auckland, 1978, p. 121.
24. Nash papers, file 2234, cited in Bassett, *Confrontation '51*, p. 185.
25. *Realites*, November 1956, cited in Stone (ed.), *Verdict on New Zealand*, pp. 220, 224.
26. Sinclair, *A History of New Zealand*, 1969, p. 304.
27. *The People's Voice*, 27 February 1952.
28. John Harre, *Maori and Pakeha: A Study of Mixed Marriages in New Zealand*, A. H. & A. W. Reed , Wellington, 1966, p. 127.
29. *NZ Woman's Weekly*, 9 August 1951.
30. Ibid.
31. Leslie Hall, Women and Men in New Zealand, *Landfall*, Caxton Press, Christchurch, 12(1) 1958, pp. 47-57.
32. New Zealand Department of Justice, *Crime in New Zealand*, Government Printer, Wellington, 1968, p. 190.
33. Bob Luman cited in Jim Miller (ed.), *Rolling Stone Illustrated History of Rock and Roll*, Rolling Stone Press, Random House, New York, 1976, p. 30.
34. Author's interview with broadcaster Merv Smith, former 1ZB breakfast host, 18 November 1998.
35. John Dix, *Stranded in Paradise: New Zealand Rock 'n' Roll, 1955–88*, Paradise Publications, Wellington, 1988, p. 22.
36. Sinclair, *A History of New Zealand*, 1969, p. 293.

Chapter Seven: 1960–1970

1. *New Zealand Herald*, 2 January 1960.
2. Barber, *New Zealand, A Short History*, p. 182
3. Barry Gustafson cited in Keith Sinclair (ed.),*Oxford Illustrated History of New Zealand*, Second edition, Oxford University Press, Auckland, 1996, p. 285.
4. Bill Sutch cited in Barber, *New Zealand, A Short History*, p. 182.
5. Ibid, p. 182.
6. Sutch, *Poverty and Progress in New Zealand: A Reassessment*, p. 346.
7. Ibid, p. 348.
8. Author's interview with Sir Keith Holyoake, 1968.
9. John Berry, *Seeing Stars: A Study of Show Folk in New Zealand*, Seven Seas Publishing, Wellington and Sydney, 1964, p. 76.
10. Tom Newnham, *Apartheid is Not a Game: The Inside Story of New Zealand's Struggle against Apartheid Sport*, Graphic Publications, Auckland, 1975, p. 27.
11. Knox (ed.), *New Zealand's Heritage*, vol. 7, p. 2857.
12. Tim Shadbolt, *Bullshit and Jellybeans*, Alister Taylor, Wellington, 1971, pp. 127-128.
13. *Sunday Star-Times*, 29 November 1998.
14. N. E. Evans, J. P. Subritzky, L. Forde and Thomas T. Rangi, *The Vietnam Scrapbook: The Second ANZAC Adventure*, The Three Feathers Publishing Company, Papakura, p. 205.
15. Claire Loftus Nelson, *Long Time Passing: New Zealand Memories of the Vietnam War*, National Radio, Wellington, 1990, p. 52.
16. Eric Linklater cited in Stone (ed.), *Verdict on New Zealand*, p. 215.
17. Austin Mitchell, *The Half-Gallon Quarter-Acre Pavlova Paradise*, Whitcombe and Tombs Ltd, Christchurch, 1972, p. 38.
18. Ibid., p. 95.
19. *Time* magazine, 28 August 1995, p. 46.
20. Margaret Shields cited in Kedgley, *Mum's the Word*, p. 218.
21. Ibid., p. 221.

22. Kathleen MacDonald cited in Charlotte MacDonald, *The Vote, the Pill and the Demon Drink: A History of Feminist Writing in New Zealand, 1869–1993*, Bridget Williams Books, Wellington, 1993, p. 160.
23. Andrea Goodwin, cited in the *New Zealand Listener*, 23 June 1984.
24. Paul Smith, *Twist and Shout, New Zealand in the Sixties*, Random Century Ltd, Auckland, 1991, p. 77.
25. Ibid., p. 72.
26. Hair Raising Problems, *Waikato Times*, 1 September 1969.
27. Gita Mehta, *Karma Cola, Marketing the Mystic East*, Jonathan Cape, London, 1980, p. 6.

Chapter Eight: 1970–1980

1. Keith, *New Zealand Yesterdays*, p. 314.
2. Keith Sinclair cited in Crockett, Little and Snow (eds), *The Listener Bedside Book*, p. 85.
3. Graeme Dunstall, The Social Pattern, in Rice (ed.), *The Oxford History of New Zealand*, p. 456.
4. Fraser (ed.), *The New Zealand Book of Events*, p. 45.
5. Dunstall cited in Rice (ed.), *The Oxford History of New Zealand*, p. 452.
6. Ibid., p. 464.
7. Sinclair, *A History of New Zealand*, 1980, p. 316.
8. Dunstall cited in Rice (ed.), *The Oxford History of New Zealand*, p. 475.
9. *Ohu; Alternative Lifestyle Communities*, Department of Lands and Survey for Committee, New Zealand Ohu Advisory Committee, p. 4.
10. *Mushroom* magazine, November 1974.
11. Sinclair, *A History of New Zealand*, 1980, p. 311.
12. Norman Kirk cited in Margaret Hayward, *Diary of the Kirk Years*, Cape Catley Ltd, Queen Charlotte Sound, and A. H. & A. W. Reed, Wellington, 1981, p. 145.
13. Newnham, *Apartheid Is Not a Game*, p. 52.
14. Donald Saunders of *The Daily Telegraph* cited in Hayward, *Diary of the Kirk Years*, p. 212.
15. Fraser, *The New Zealand Book of Events*, p. 238.
16. Sinclair, *A History of New Zealand*, 1980, p. 315.
17. Tom Scott, *Now Is the Time to Say Goodbye...*, New Zealand Listener, 25 March 1978.
18. Bill Rowling cited in Barber, *New Zealand, A Short History*, p. 184.
19. Marcia Russell's editorial for *Thursday* 3 October 1968 cited in MacDonald, *The Vote, the Pill and the Demon Drink*, p. 154.
20. Jenny Phillips cited in Kedgley, *Mum's The Word*, p. 255.
21. Cherry Raymond, Speaking Frankly, *NZ Woman's Weekly*, 3 April 1972 cited in Blackwell (ed.), *NZ Woman's Weekly: The First 60 Years, 1932–1992*, p. 86.
22. Gordon McLauchlan, *The Passionless People*, Cassell New Zealand, Auckland, 1976, p. 25.
23. Leaflet, An Introduction to the Wellington Women's Liberation Movement, cited in MacDonald, *The Vote, the Pill and the Demon Drink*, pp. 167-8.
24. Therese O'Connell cited in *Broadsheet*, Auckland Women's Liberation, Auckland, July/August 1982, p. 37.
25. Sandra Coney, *Standing in the Sunshine: A History of New Zealand Women since They Won the Vote*, Penguin Books, Auckland, 1993, p. 142.
26. Christine Wren cited in MacDonald, *The Vote, the Pill and the Demon Drink*, p. 170.
27. Kedgley, *Mum's the Word*, p. 272.
28. Ibid., p. 272.
29. Ibid., p. 275.
30. Ibid., p. 276.
31. Ngahuia Te Awekotuku cited in MacDonald, *The Vote, the Pill and the Demon Drink*, p. 190.
32. A. R. D. Fairburn, "In the Younger Land", in J. C. Reid and Peter Cape (eds), *A Book of New Zealand: Revised Edition*, William Collins Publishers, p. 272.
33. Rice (ed.), *The Oxford History of New Zealand*, pp. 462-63.
34. Dame Whina Cooper, broadcast on 28 August 1978 cited in Owen and Perkins, *Speaking for Ourselves*, p. 56.
35. Dr Ranginui Walker, Maori People since 1950, in Rice (ed.), *The Oxford History of New Zealand*, p. 512.
36. Ibid. p. 509.
37. Ibid. p. 513.
38. Waitangi Tribunal, *Report of the Waitangi Tribunal on the Orakei Claim*, Waitangi Tribunal and Department of Justice, Wellington, November 1987, p. 5.
39. Sharon Aroha Hawke (ed.), *Takaparawhau: The People's Story: 1998 Bastion Point 20 Year Commemoration Book*, Moko Productions, Orakei, 1998, p. 19.
40. Waitangi Tribunal, *Report of the Waitangi Tribunal on the Orakei Claim*, pp. 180, 195.
41. Fraser (ed.), *The New Zealand Book of Events*, p. 285.
42. Letter to the Editor, *New Zealand Listener*, 7 January 1978, cited in Crockett, Little and Snow, *The Listener Bedside Book*, p. 157.
43. Roger Douglas and Louise Callan, *Roger Douglas: Toward Prosperity*, David Bateman, Auckland, 1987, p. 14.

44 Sinclair, *A History of New Zealand*, 1980, p. 316.
45 McLauchlan, *The Passionless People*, p. 213.

Chapter Nine: 1980–1990

1 Principle Events, *The New Zealand Official Year Book 1981*.
2 Tom Brooking and Paul Enright, *Milestones: Turning Points in New Zealand History*, Mills Publications, Lower Hutt, 1988, p. 186.
3 W. David McIntyre, From Dual Dependency to Nuclear Free, in Rice (ed.), *The Oxford History of New Zealand*, p. 537.
4 Dr Ranginui Walker, *Nga Tau Tohetohe, Years of Anger*, Penguin Books, Auckland, 1987, p. 228.
5 John Spain in *The Auckland Star*, 5 June 1980.
6 Fraser (ed.), *The New Zealand Book of Events*, p. 368.
7 Barber, *New Zealand, A Short History*, p. 196.
8 Ibid., p. 195.
9 Richard Shears and Isobelle Gidley, *Storm out of Africa: The 1981 Springbok Tour of New Zealand*, MacMillan, Auckland, 1981, p. 37.
10 Geoff Chapple, *The Tour*, A. H. & A. W. Reed, Wellington, 1984, p. 51.
11 *Sunday News*, cited in Tom Newnham, *By Batons and Barbed Wire*, Real Pictures Ltd, Auckland, 1981, p. 32.
12 Ross Meurant, *The Red Squad Story*, Harlen Publishing, Auckland, 1982, p. 34.
13 Shears and Gidley, *Storm out of Africa*, p. 59.
14 Newnham, *By Batons and Barbed Wire*, p. 88.
15 Ibid., p. 89.
16 *New Zealand Herald*, 14 September 1981.
17 Robert Muldoon, *Robert Muldoon Number 38*, Reed Methuen Publishers, Auckland, 1986, p. 53.
18 Robert Muldoon, *My Way*, A. H. & A. W. Reed, Wellington, 1981, p. 159.
19 Alan Robie, The Politics of Volatility, 1972–1991, in Rice (ed.), *The Oxford History of New Zealand*, pp. 395-6.
20 Brooking and Enright, *Milestones: Turning Points in New Zealand History*, p. 186.
21 Bob Jones, *Memories of Muldoon*, Canterbury University Press, Christchurch, 1997, p. 138.
22 Ibid, p. 22.
23 Barber, *New Zealand, A Short History*, p. 203.
24 David Lange cited in Douglas and Callan, *Roger Douglas: Toward Prosperity*, p. 44.
25 Robie, in Rice (ed.), *The Oxford History of New Zealand*, p. 401.
26 Robert Muldoon, *The Rise and Fall of a Young Turk*, A. H. & A. W. Reed, Wellington, 1974, p. 197.
27 Robie, in Rice (ed.), *The Oxford History of New Zealand*, p. 402.
28 Margaret Wilson, cited in Marcia Russell, *Revolution: New Zealand from Fortress to Free Market*, Hodder Moa Beckett, Auckland, 1996, p. 68.
29 Roger Douglas, ibid., p. 69.
30 Geoffrey W. Rice, A Revolution in Social Policy, 1981–1991, in Rice (ed.), *The Oxford History of New Zealand*, p. 484.
31 Ibid., p. 484.
32 Barber, *New Zealand, A Short History*, p. 189.
33 Douglas and Callan, *Roger Douglas: Toward Prosperity*, p. 185.
34 Felix Donnelly, *The World Upside Down*, Penguin Books, Auckland, 1988, p. 111.
35 Olly Newland, *Lost Property: The Crash of '87 – and the Aftershock*, HarperCollins, Auckland, 1994, p. 45.
36 Ibid, pp. 24-5.
37 Russell, *Revolution*, p. 152.
38 Alan Gibbs cited ibid., p. 152.
39 *Dominion*, 19 February 1985.
40 David Lange cited in Russell, *Revolution*, p. 99.
41 Rice (ed.), *The Oxford History of New Zealand*, p. 486.
42 Roger Douglas, *Unfinished Business*, Random House, Auckland, 1993, pp. 220-21.
43 Brooking and Enright, *Milestones: Turning Points in New Zealand History*, p. 188.
44 Jim Anderton, cited in the *New Zealand Herald*, 2 May 1989.
45 Manuela Hoelterhoff, Cult Objects: The Art of the Maoris, *The Wall Street Journal*, 26 September 1984.
46 Brooking and Enright, *Milestones: Turning Points in New Zealand History*, p. 190.
47 Ibid, p. 191.
48 Donna Awatere Huata, *Maori Sovereignty*, Broadsheet, Auckland, 1984, pp. 15-6.
49 Thorns and Sedgwick, *Understanding Aotearoa/New Zealand: Historical Statistics*, p. 131.
50 Awatere Huata, *Maori Sovereignty*, p. 17.
51 Ibid., pp. 10, 32.
52 Sir Ken Keith, *Pakeha Perspectives on the Treaty: Proceedings from a Planning Council Seminar*, New Zealand Planning Council, Wellington, September 1988, p. 79.
53 Walker, *Nga Tau Tohetohe, Years of Anger*, pp. 228, 221.
54 From *Kaupapa: Te Wahanga Tuatahi* cited in Brooking and Enright, *Milestones: Turning Points in New Zealand History*, pp. 192-3.
55 Pat Hohepa and Atareta Poananga cited in *Waitangi Action Committee, Te Hikoi Ki Waitangi 1984*, The Waitangi Action Committee, Auckland, 1984, p. 27.

56 Ibid., p. 31.
57 Hilda Halkyard-Harawira cited in *Waitangi Action Committee, Te Hikoi Ki Waitangi 1984*, p. 57.
58 Brooking and Enright, *Milestones: Turning Points in New Zealand History*, p. 193.
59 Michael King, Being Pakeha from Michael King (ed.), *Pakeha: The Quest for Identity in New Zealand*, Penguin Books, Auckland, 1991, p. 19.
60 Brett Riley, cited in Helen Paske, Editorial: The Lefts and Rights, *New Zealand Listener*, 13 April 1985.
61 Helen Paske, ibid.

Chapter Ten: 1990–1999

1 Road Rage – Your Actions May Trigger It, *AA Directions* magazine, September 1997, p. 12.
2 Tony Gloag, poem, *Rabbit and Land Management News*, June 1995, p. 9.
3 *The New Zealand Official Yearbook 1998*, p. 122.
4 Article on migration, New Zealand Press Association, published in the *New Zealand Herald*, 26 January 1996.
5 Gilbert Wong, Slice of the South, *New Zealand Herald*, 7 July 1992.
6 *The New Zealand Official Yearbook 1998*, p. 121.
7 The Office of the Minister in Charge of Treaty negotiations, 5 January 1996.
8 Final Chapter of Tainui Settlement Bill Closed, *Te Maori News*, vol. 21, November 1995, p. 3.
9 Jack Vowles and Peter Aimer, *Voters' Vengeance: The 1990 Election in New Zealand and the Fate of the Fourth Labour Government*, Auckland University Press, Auckland, 1993, p. 1.
10 Robie cited in Rice (ed.), *The Oxford History of New Zealand*, p. 409.
11 Ian Shirley, Social Services in a Market Economy, *Social Work Review*, July 1992, Table 2, p. 9.
12 Ruth Richardson, *Making a Difference*, Shoal Bay Press, Christchurch, 1995, p. 79.
13 Bob Stephens, Budgeting with the Benefit Cuts, in Jonathan Boston and Paul Dalziel (eds), *The Decent Society? Essays in Response to National's Economic and Social Policies*, Oxford University Press, Auckland, 1992, p. 109.
14 Rice (ed.), *The Oxford History of New Zealand*, pp. 493-494.
15 Elizabeth McLeay, Housing Policy, in Boston and Dalziel (eds), *The Decent Society?*, p. 183.
16 *Sunday Star*, 6 December 1992.
17 National Party Election Manifesto 1990 cited in Toni Ashton, Reform of the Health Services: Weighing up the Costs and Benefits, in Boston and Dalziel (eds), *The Decent Society?*, p. 165.
18 Editorial, *Russell Review*, vol. 17, 1994-95, p. 3.
19 Warren Freer, *New Zealand Herald*, 31 May 1993.
20 Ruth Richardson, *Making a Difference*, p. 174.
21 Jonathan Boston, Redesigning New Zealand's Welfare State, in Boston and Dalziel (eds), *The Decent Society?*, p. 16.
22 Alan McRobie (ed.), *Taking it to the People: The New Zealand Electoral Referendum Debate*, Hazard Press, Christchurch, 1993, p. 17.
23 National's Vote Tally Dips Sharply, *New Zealand Herald*, 20 November 1993.
24 Regarding National... Peters' Words for It, *New Zealand Herald*, December 1996.
25 Ibid.
26 Hanging by a Rat's Tail, *The Dominion*, 21 August 1998.
27 Larry Elliott, Norway Manages to Keep The Faith, *Guardian Weekly*, 12 April 1998.
28 Working Life, *New Zealand Herald*, 20 December 1997.
29 Letter to the Editor from P. E. Keats of Upper Hutt, *Woman's Weekly*, 4 May 1998.
30 Pat Walsh and Peter Brosnan cited in Jonathan Boston, Paul Dalziel and Susan St John (eds), *Redesigning the Welfare State in New Zealand*, Oxford University Press, Auckland, pp. 132-133.
31 Letter to the Editor, *Southland Times*, 3 October 1998.
32 Letter to the Editor from S. M. of Auckland, *Woman's Day*, 28 December 1998, p. 70.
33 Dodging the Debt: Why Students Flee, *New Zealand Herald*, 17 May 1997.
34 The Sir Launchalot Column, *Quote Unquote*, December 1994, p. 39.
35 Brooking and Enright, *Milestones: Turning Points in New Zealand History*, p. 185.
36 Bruce Ansley, Inhospitable Heights, *New Zealand Listener*, 8 August 1998, p. 29.
37 Michael King, *Being Pakeha Now* cited in The Place of Pakeha in Aotearoa, *Sunday Star-Times*, 25 April 1999.
38 Ibid.
39 Big Day Out: The Fans, *Pavement* magazine, February–March 1999, p. 104.
40 Jazz has come to Russell, *Russell Review*, vol. 17, 1994–95, p. 64.
41 Letter to the Editor from Litzi of Otago, *Woman's Weekly*, 11 May 1998.
42 Media release, New Zealand Manufacturers Association, 28 May 1998.
43 Richard Wolfe, Watch Out for Nostalgia, the "Eighth Deadly Sin", *New Zealand Herald*, 21 October 1998.
44 Merry Christmas Mrs Shipley, *Sunday Star-Times*, 27 December 1998.

Index